POWER

AND THE

PALACE

ALSO BY VALENTINE LOW

COURTIERS

POWER
AND THE
PALACE

THE INSIDE STORY OF THE MONARCHY
AND 10 DOWNING STREET

VALENTINE LOW

HEADLINE
PRESS

First published in 2025 by Headline Press
An imprint of Headline Publishing Group Limited

1

Please refer to page 398 for picture credits.

Cataloguing in Publication Data is available from the British Library.

Hardback ISBN 978 1 0354 1881 7
Trade Paperback ISBN 978 1 0354 1882 4

Designed and typeset by EM&EN
Printed and bound in Great Britain by Clays Ltd, Elcograf S.p.A.

Headline's policy is to use papers that are natural, renewable and recyclable
products and made from wood grown in well-managed forests and other
controlled sources. The logging and manufacturing processes are expected
to conform to the environmental regulations of the country of origin.

Headline Publishing Group Limited
An Hachette UK Company
Carmelite House
50 Victoria Embankment
London EC4Y 0DZ

The authorised representative in the EEA is Hachette Ireland,
8 Castlecourt Centre, Dublin 15, D15 XTP3, Ireland (email: info@hbgi.ie)

www.headline.co.uk
www.hachette.co.uk

For Kitty and Orlando

CONTENTS

PROLOGUE

It is the first Privy Council for the new King, who is the oldest sovereign ever to accede to the throne. After delivering a touching tribute to his predecessor, he has to sign the formal declaration of his accession. He is handed a pen, but it does not work very well. 'This is a damned bad pen you have given me,' he grumbles as he signs his name.[1] No, not King Charles III, the beginning of whose reign was also marked by misadventure with a malfunctioning pen; this was William IV, Charles's great-great-great-great-great-uncle, who in 1830 held the record as the oldest monarch on succession until Charles himself became King.

There is no doubt that in pretty much every respect Charles did better at the ceremony than his predecessor, even if he seems to have inherited the family temper. For a start, he was probably able to identify most if not all of the cabinet ministers present, even if some of them had only been in post for a few days, and would not be in a job for much longer, given that this was the short-lived Liz Truss government. In contrast, as the privy counsellors knelt to render him allegiance, William peered at the chancellor of the exchequer and said: 'D'ye know, I am grown so near-sighted that I can't make out who you are . . . You must tell me your name please.'

Apart from pens, and age, William IV and Charles III have one more significant thing in common: William – as Duke of Clarence – commissioned Clarence House, Charles's London home. Like Charles, when he became King he stayed at

Clarence House instead of moving into Buckingham Palace, which he hated. Charles may have moved his office into the palace's Belgian Suite, but he has absolutely no intention of making that vast, inhospitable building his home.

William, who had served in the Royal Navy and was known as the Sailor King, was a rough-hewn, garrulous figure who, while genial, was no great intellect. His reign saw a significant shift in power from the King to the cabinet, and although William did not stand in the way of reform, or at least no longer than was politically wise, he earned a dubious distinction in history as the last monarch to dismiss a prime minister who still had the support of the House of Commons. William had already seen his authority weakened during the stormy passage into law of the 1832 Reform Bill. Two years later the issue which dominated politics was the status of the Church of Ireland. Supporters of disestablishment saw it as invidious that Irish peasants, most of whom were Catholic, had to pay tithes to a Protestant church.

With the Whig government under Lord Melbourne undermined by divisions over the question, and the King increasingly of the opinion that his ministers were no longer up to the job, William decided it was time to put the ministry out of its misery, and informed Melbourne that he would not be acting 'fairly or honourably' if he asked him to continue in office in such circumstances. Melbourne took it all very well, and was replaced by a minority Tory government under Robert Peel. Peel, who thought that the King had miscalculated, lasted just four months, and a humiliated William was forced to crawl back to Melbourne and ask him to form a government once more. The King's ability to make the political weather had been significantly damaged.[2]

The episode illustrates the subtle way that change occurs in the British constitution. Philip Ziegler, the Sailor King's biographer, wrote that when William dismissed Melbourne, 'it was felt by some that [William] had been unprincipled and by many that he had been unwise, but few indeed suggested that his action had been in any way unconstitutional'. After 1834, however, 'he never tried again'.[3] Neither did anyone else. Melbourne's dismissal was a key moment in the ever-shifting balance of power between the monarchy and the government.

In the two hundred years or so since then, the idea of what a constitutional monarchy is has changed fundamentally. In this book we shall survey the extraordinary political life of Queen Victoria, who exerted her will in a way that no monarch has done since, the effect that had on her son Edward VII, and the turbulent and fascinating political times of George V. We shall examine what went on between George VI and Winston Churchill during the Second World War, and discover how Elizabeth II played a crucial role in modernising – and saving – the monarchy. And, finally, we shall see how the sovereign still has a political role to play today. When Sir Keir Starmer visited Donald Trump in the White House and produced from his pocket a letter from King Charles inviting Trump for a second state visit, it was a gesture that spoke volumes about the importance of the monarchy for Britain's international relations. It was also a vivid illustration of the relationship between Buckingham Palace and 10 Downing Street. Whatever Charles's views about Donald Trump, a man with whom he does not share a natural rapport, he knows how much a successful state visit can achieve; and he knows where his duty lies.

My last book, Courtiers, looked at the relationship between the monarchy and the people who advise them. This book is about the relationship between the monarchy and the people who actually run the country: it seeks to understand how, without a single law being passed, Britain has gone from a country where sovereigns assumed the right to appoint the prime minister of their choice to one where they go to almost any length to distance themselves – both metaphorically and literally – from the process. It is a story of how big societal changes and individual personalities have both played their part; from Victoria and Benjamin Disraeli to Elizabeth II and Margaret Thatcher, the personal chemistry between sovereign and prime minister has proved just as important as the constitutional relationship.

As I write, we have a relatively new occupant of the throne, who for all the similarities with his nineteenth-century forebear is a very different sovereign from William IV. Ever since he succeeded his mother, King Charles III has been on his best behaviour, demonstrating to the country that he has put his meddling days behind him and understands how to be a constitutional monarch. At some point in the future, we will have probably another King William, the fifth of that name, who unlike his namesake will not sack his PM or indeed fail to recognise the chancellor of the exchequer. But he will, in his own way, be a political king. Exactly what that means has changed radically over the last two hundred years. And no doubt it will change again, for one very good reason: because the survival of the monarchy depends upon it.

CHAPTER ONE

PARTY QUEEN

AT TWELVE MINUTES PAST TWO in the morning of Tuesday 20 June 1837 King William IV, who had been increasingly ill since the beginning of the year, died at Windsor Castle, aged seventy-one. He timed his death well: the heir to the throne was the only daughter of his late brother the Duke of Kent, and William had long been worried that if he died before Victoria turned eighteen, the princess's mother, the Duchess of Kent – with whom he had a decidedly difficult relationship – would become regent. His antipathy towards the duchess was so vehement that the previous year he had caused a scene at his birthday dinner by making a speech in which he praised his niece and denounced her mother as 'incompetent' and 'surrounded by evil advisers'. It was such an embarrassing tirade that Victoria burst into tears. But William got his way, managing to hang on long enough for his niece to celebrate her coming of age on 24 May. Less than a month later he was dead.

Shortly after the King died – his last words were a muttered 'The Church! The Church!' – a carriage which had been waiting in the castle's Lower Ward set off for Kensington

Palace, where Victoria lived with her mother. Its three passengers were Dr Howley, the Archbishop of Canterbury, Lord Conyngham, the lord chamberlain, and Sir Henry Halford, the late King's doctor. On arriving at Kensington shortly before six in the morning, they had some trouble getting past the porter at the palace gates; having overcome that obstacle, they had further difficulty in persuading the duchess to wake her daughter, until Lord Conyngham told her they had come to see 'the Queen' on state business. That did the trick. 'I was awoke at 6 o'clock by Mamma,' Victoria wrote in her diary,

> who told me that the Archbishop of Canterbury and Lord Conyngham were here, and wished to see me. I got out of bed and went into my sitting-room (only in my dressing-gown), and *alone*, and saw them. Lord Conyngham then acquainted me that my poor Uncle, the King, was no more, and had expired at 12 minutes past two this morning, and consequently that I am *Queen* . . . Since it has pleased Providence to place me in this station, I shall do my utmost to fulfil my duty towards my country; I am very young and perhaps in many, though not in all things, inexperienced, but I am sure, that very few have more real good will and more real desire to do what is fit and right than I have.[1]

Wilful, unafraid to speak her mind, at times even contrary, the young Victoria had a firm sense of right and wrong. She was also determined to break away from the influence of her controlling mother. Instead, she came under the influence of the man who would play a dominating role in the first few years of her reign, Lord Melbourne, her first prime minister. She had her first audience with him at nine o'clock, when she saw him 'of COURSE quite ALONE as I shall *always* do all my Ministers': in other words, without her mother. Significantly, she would hardly see her mother all day. She told Melbourne that she would keep him on as prime minister, and that the government 'could not be in better hands than his'. He in turn gave her the draft declaration which she was to read at the Privy Council meeting that morning, in which she would say that she had been brought up from infancy to 'respect and love the Constitution of her native country'.

Over the coming years her respect for and love of the constitution would become a matter for debate. A set of conventions rather than a single written document, the constitution has transformed over time, with an ability to adapt to changing circumstances that is both its great virtue and also a source of much argument. The young Queen's dutiful expression of respect would be echoed – repeatedly – nearly two hundred years later by the new King Charles III in the days that followed his accession. For the moment, however, Victoria's conduct was beyond reproach: after the Privy Council meeting, the Duke of Wellington declared that 'if She had been his own daughter he could not have desired to see her perform her part better'.[2] She was equally entranced with Lord Melbourne. After her first audience Victoria, who as a result of her suffocating upbringing had had little contact with politicians, decided: 'I like him very much and feel confidence in him. He is a very straightforward, honest, clever and good man.'[3] That day she had no fewer than four conversations with Melbourne, setting a pattern that would continue for the next four years.

When the eighteen-year-old Victoria acceded to the throne Melbourne was fifty-eight years old and had lived quite the life. Born William Lamb into a prominent Whig family, he had married the beautiful but impossible Lady Caroline Ponsonby, who famously had a stormy affair with Lord Byron and later dubbed the poet 'mad, bad and dangerous to know'. His political career, which one writer described as him 'drifting nonchalantly to the top',[4] managed to survive that and two other scandals in which jealous husbands took him to court only to have their cases dismissed. After a spell as Irish secretary he served as home secretary for four years, succeeding Lord Grey as prime minister in 1834. The story goes that when he was offered the post he pronounced the prospect 'a damn bore', but was talked into it by his secretary, Tom Young.

Melbourne was the twenty-seventh prime minister and, later, also the thirtieth. The position had only existed for about a hundred years, and it is hard to pinpoint when exactly it came into existence. The first person to occupy the post was Robert Walpole, who was in office from 1721 to 1742. He hated the title prime minister, which was originally a term of abuse for ministers who had got above themselves: when he was appointed, it was as first lord of the Treasury. Since the Glorious Revolution of 1688 monarchs had been largely dependent on Parliament to raise taxes and pursue policies, and a politician who could deliver control of Parliament for their sovereign was in a powerful position. Walpole's ability to do so ensured he retained the support of George I and later George II (10 Downing Street was a personal gift to Walpole from George II). But it took years for the position to be entrenched in political life, and as late as 1741 Walpole would deny unequivocally that he was prime minister. Exactly one hundred years later Melbourne told Queen Victoria, 'How the power of Prime Ministry grew up into its present form it is difficult to trace precisely.'[5]

By the time Melbourne served as Victoria's first prime minister he was not the man he had once been. Despite his troubled marriage, he had been deeply affected by the death of his wife in 1828, while eight years later their son George, who was epileptic and required significant medical care, also died. But even in his late fifties Melbourne was still strikingly handsome and had lost none of his charm. Victoria could not get enough of him. She loved talking to him, delighting in his stories and his witticisms. 'He has such stores of knowledge,' she wrote, 'such a wonderful memory; he knows about everybody and everything; who they were and what they did.'[6] For his part he was all too aware of the Queen's innocence of statecraft, and took it upon himself to be her political mentor. In effect, for those early years of her reign he acted as her private secretary, sometimes spending as much as six hours a day with her. They would meet in the morning to talk business, and in the afternoon he would go riding with her, often at full gallop. In the evening he would join her for dinner, when he would always be seated next to her.[7] Such was his constant presence that he was given the use of an apartment in Windsor Castle.

Given that Victoria lost her own father when she was just eight months old, it is not difficult to imagine that she saw Melbourne as the father she never had; even Victoria herself understood that. When it looked like he might be forced to resign, she begged him 'ever to be a father to one who never wanted support more than she does now'.[8] Later, after she married Prince Albert, she attributed her affection and admiration for Melbourne to her need for someone to cling to and her natural warmth of feeling. The diarist Charles Greville, who had dealings with Victoria in his role as head of the Privy Council, described her feelings for Melbourne as 'sexual though she does not know it'.[9] The historian Anne Somerset, on the other hand, considers her infatuation with him to have been more girlish and innocent.[10]

But whatever the nature of her devotion to Melbourne – which did not remain unquestioning for ever – it came at a political cost. In May 1839, when his government ran into difficulties over colonial policy, Melbourne told the Queen he would have to resign. This plunged her into 'agony, grief and despair', prompting her to proclaim: 'All, *all* my happiness gone!'[11] Victoria was never one for understatement. She had already decided that she hated the Tories, and to make matters worse had also formed a strong dislike of their leader, Sir Robert Peel, whom she regarded as a 'cold, unfeeling, disagreeable man'. The Tory party was associated with the Church of England, the Crown and the landed gentry. The Whigs, in contrast, were the political descendants of those who had opposed the influence of Charles II's court on Parliament, and had later brought about the Glorious Revolution of 1688. They were more progressive than the Tories and supported the financial interests of the rising middle classes. Melbourne tried to talk her round, saying that Peel was gauche rather than unpleasant, but Victoria was having none of it. On Melbourne's suggestion she sent for Wellington, who when he saw the Queen told her he was too old and too deaf to take the job, and suggested she ask Peel instead.

Reluctantly, and with ill grace, she sent for Peel. Their meeting was a calamity, a combination of awkwardness and miscommunication, sparking the beginning of one of the more damaging and, to modern eyes, odd episodes of Victoria's early reign. Peel, the son of a wealthy Lancashire mill owner, did not have a majority in the House of Commons, and wanted Victoria to demonstrate her confidence in him by making changes in her household. In the nineteenth century the royal household was part of the political arena, and when Victoria came to the throne, Melbourne had insisted that the ladies of her household should be exclusively from Whig families. Peel, understandably, wanted to reverse the resulting political bias surrounding the Queen. His supporters had their eyes on six out of twenty-five ladies whom they regarded as particularly egregious examples of Whig partisanship.

Whatever was said between them, Peel went away from their meeting with the impression that the Queen's ladies related to Whig ministers were going to resign. Victoria, however, told him the next day that she was not going to give up any of them. Meanwhile she had enlisted Melbourne's help, giving him the impression that Peel wanted to deprive her of every lady in her household, which was certainly not the case. Melbourne advised his colleagues on that mistaken basis, with the result that after a highly unusual late-night meeting – at which one minister was very much the worse for wear – they resolved to support the Queen. The obstinate Victoria, who never needed much encouragement to stand her ground, refused to give way to Peel, who duly turned down the invitation to form a government. After that the only option was for Melbourne to resume office.

When Melbourne realised he had advised his colleagues on erroneous grounds, he was distinctly embarrassed, and while many applauded the Queen for standing up to the Tories, the incident damaged the Crown. It was an episode of massive constitutional significance: she had kept Melbourne in office even though he had forfeited the confidence of Parliament, for no better reason than that it had suited her. At Ascot races that June two Tory ladies hissed at the Queen, while Charles Greville wrote: 'It is a high trial of our institutions when the caprice of a girl of nineteen can overturn a great ministerial combination.' In later life Victoria would admit that the so-called Bedchamber Crisis 'was entirely my own foolishness', but she also criticised Melbourne, whom she called an 'excellent man, but too much of a party man and made me a party Queen'.[12]

*

OVER THE NEXT couple of years Melbourne's influence over Victoria slowly began to decline. In contrast to those early days when he could do no wrong, she began to show irritation at his failings, such as not telling her about changes in the Home Office, or not showing up for a state banquet. 'I fear I was sadly cross with Lord Melbourne,' she wrote in her diary. 'It is shameful . . . I cannot think what possessed me for I love the dear, excellent man.'[13] But the truth was that since her marriage in February 1840 to her German cousin Prince Albert, Melbourne no longer occupied quite the same role in her life. After the birth of the couple's first child, Victoria (known within the family as Vicky), Albert began to look after his wife's political affairs, and was given his own keys to the official boxes of government papers that she had to deal with every day. Melbourne was also told that if her ministers could not see Victoria in person, they should communicate with her via Albert.[14] Before long Albert was allowed to be present during discussions between the Queen and Melbourne. The prince thrived in his new-found political role and would steadily increase his involvement, often to the annoyance and resentment of ministers. There was also a downside for Victoria. When the royal couple had time alone together in the evening, she wanted to forget about the business of government while he yearned to discuss it.[15]

In 1841 Melbourne called an election after losing a vote of no confidence, and was defeated by the Tories. This was despite the blatantly partisan efforts of the royal household in the form of Victoria's former governess Baroness Lehzen, a sharp but humourless woman who constantly chewed caraway seeds for indigestion and spent £15,000 of the Queen's money helping the Whigs. Albert was shocked to discover this – he was firmly of the view that the monarchy should be impartial – but Melbourne dismissed his concerns, saying that it was nothing compared to what George III had spent supporting the Tories.[16] Melbourne may have had a point, but the times were changing: Albert recognised that the monarchy could no longer take sides, even if Victoria was slow to see how the tide was turning.

Once again Victoria was greatly saddened at losing Melbourne, albeit not quite as distraught as she had been in 1839; at least this time she had Albert to help her weather the storm. The handover revealed two enduring aspects of Victoria's character – her ability to have radical changes of mind about people, and her propensity to go behind the backs of her ministers, often in ways that seriously undermined the constitution.

Her first 1841 audience with Peel, who was clever and well educated but socially ill at ease, did not go as badly as their previous encounter two years earlier, but was hardly a success. Afterwards she said she was relieved that she would not have to see him again for several days – a contrast to the multiple daily meetings she used to have with Melbourne. Within weeks, however, she started to warm to him, and would later write: 'He is a noble-minded, very fair, very liberal, straightforward & very able man.'[17] In 1843 she told her uncle Leopold, King of the Belgians, that Peel was 'undoubtedly a great statesman, a man who thinks but little of party, and never of himself'.[18]

But that did not mean that she did not miss Melbourne. For some months after his resignation they would write to each other several times a week, with Melbourne even urging her to oppose some of Peel's ministerial appointments. This got back to Prince Albert, who had his private secretary try to warn Melbourne off. Whether Peel himself got to know about this correspondence is not clear, but a few weeks later he told Baron Stockmar, a close adviser to the Queen, that if he ever discovered that the Queen was taking political advice from anyone other than himself he would resign straight away.[19]

One of Peel's initiatives which would have repercussions on the relationship between the monarchy and government for the next century and a half was the reintroduction in 1842 of income tax, which had been abolished at the end of the Napoleonic Wars. With the tax set at a rate of 3 per cent on incomes over £150,[20] Peel asked Victoria if she would pay it voluntarily, so he could announce it in the Commons, 'so that it might appear as [a] gracious act on my part, without any legislation about it. This of course I at once assented to.' She did, however, think it was hard on Albert, who would have to pay £900. Peel's announcement went down well, even though Melbourne wondered whether Victoria was wise 'giving up a principle of the Constitution which has hitherto exempted the Sovereign from all direct taxation'.[21]

The issue that would bring about Peel's downfall in 1846 and split the Tory party for years to come was the repeal of the Corn Laws. Pressure had been mounting for years to remove the tariffs on grain imports, which helped keep food prices high. When the potato crop in Ireland failed, the resulting famine prompted Peel to conclude that the Corn Laws should be repealed as soon as possible. Victoria agreed, telling him, 'the Queen very much hopes that none of his colleagues will prevent him from doing what is right to do'. However, he was unable to persuade his own party to back him. The Tories, who identified with the interests of landowners, were committed to agricultural protectionism and did their best to block the bill, but Peel managed to get it through with opposition support. On the same night that the bill was passed in the Lords, thanks to the persuasive efforts of the Duke of Wellington, Peel lost another vote on a measure to suppress disorder in Ireland, and he resigned as prime minister a month later. Victoria mourned his departure: 'What a terrible loss such a high-minded, honourable & clever man, will be to us and the country.' When Peel died in 1850 following a fall from his horse, she praised his loyalty, courage and patriotism, and called him a 'kind and true friend'. He had one failing: he had been 'kept down to old Tory principles, for which his mind was too enlightened'.[22] By the time Disraeli arrived in Downing Street in 1868, the Queen who had once told Lord Melbourne how she 'hated' the Tories had completely abandoned her once firmly held Whig convictions.

The split in the Tory party that followed the bitter divisions over the Corn Laws saw those who had supported Peel merge with the Whigs and the Radicals in 1859 to form the Liberal party, the precursor to the modern Liberal Democrats. The disruption of the two-party system made politics unpredictable, but it allowed Victoria to play a more significant role in the formation of governments.

IF VICTORIA WAS unrelenting in her efforts to exert political influence, she had to contend with one minister who was equally determined to resist her efforts: Viscount Palmerston. The son of an Anglo-Irish peer, he had been born on the family estate, Broadlands in Hampshire, which would later be the home of Lord Mountbatten of Burma (both Queen Elizabeth II and King Charles spent part of their honeymoons there). Vivacious and self-confident, Palmerston had started off his political career as a Tory before joining the Whigs and later the Liberals. By the time he first met the young Princess Victoria he was foreign secretary, having already spent twenty years as secretary at war. The teenage Victoria found him 'so very agreeable, clever, amusing & gentlemanlike'.[23]

Her early dealings with him as Queen when he was foreign secretary under Melbourne were equally positive. He would tutor her in foreign policy, providing specially drawn maps and a marked-up edition of the *Almanac de Gotha*, the directory of European royalty and higher nobility. He would also give her lessons on how to address her fellow sovereigns, how to end her letters to them – he would write the appropriate wording in pencil, which she could then copy in her own hand before rubbing out Palmerston's original – and what presents to give them.[24] When the Whigs resigned in 1839 (before the return of Melbourne following the Bedchamber Crisis) she told him that his 'valuable services' which had 'so greatly promoted the honour and welfare of this Country in its relations with foreign powers . . . will ever be gratefully remembered'.[25]

However, when Palmerston returned to office in 1846, Victoria's attitude had changed, not least under the influence of Prince Albert. Palmerston had a robust attitude to foreign relations, verging on the arrogant, which Victoria regarded as 'bullying'. She also expected to be deferred to over diplomatic appointments, and to approve all dispatches sent in her name to ministers and ambassadors stationed abroad. Palmerston, who had served under Spencer Perceval ten years before Victoria was born, regarded this as unwarranted interference in the work of the Foreign Office. His solution was simply to ignore her, failing to send dispatches for her approval on the grounds that this would cause unacceptable delay or ignoring her comments, claiming afterwards that it had just been a mistake. Victoria thought his behaviour a 'mockery'.

As well as disliking his conduct, Victoria also had fundamental political differences with Palmerston, whom she and Albert in private called Pilgerstein, a rough German translation of his name. This was a time when attempts were being made to overthrow despotic monarchical regimes, and Palmerston sided with those trying to free themselves from tyranny, while Victoria would take the part of her fellow sovereigns. She and Albert complained that Palmerston seemed to have 'no strong monarchical feelings'. He was, they felt, 'a bad man' with 'not a grain of moral feeling'.[26] In turn, Palmerston regarded Albert with disdain, once telling him that 'he was a German, and did not understand British interests'.[27]

The Queen made repeated attempts to get rid of him. During an early visit to Balmoral, when they were leasing the estate before buying it in 1852, Victoria told the prime minister, Lord John Russell, that Palmerston was making her 'quite ill' and that she could hardly go on with him in office. However, the foreign secretary was a powerful figure – abrasive with his colleagues, but popular with the public (his affectionate nickname was Pam) – and Russell said he did not dare make an enemy of him. Victoria's relations with Palmerston got steadily worse, and she and Albert became so desperate that the prince even resorted to bringing up a tawdry story from the beginning of Victoria's reign.

Palmerston, whose fondness for the opposite sex had earned him the nickname Cupid, had been staying at Windsor in September 1837 when he entered the bedroom of a young woman of the bedchamber, barricaded the door from the inside and tried to force himself upon her. She managed to escape, and the incident was hushed up. Thirteen years later Albert used it as ammunition to try to persuade Russell that Victoria could not possibly take advice from someone guilty of such a 'fiendish scheme'. However, while the prime minister accepted that the episode reflected very badly on

Palmerston, it had happened a long time ago, and he was now a happily married man. To dismiss him for such an offence now, Russell felt, might be seen by the public as unjust and even ridiculous.[28] Those were, indeed, different times.

Palmerston, however, could not ignore Victoria for ever. In December 1851 Louis-Napoleon, who was coming to the end of his term of office as president of France, staged a coup, dissolving the National Assembly and restoring universal suffrage. Victoria gave orders that Britain should remain strictly neutral, but Palmerston had already expressed his approval of the coup to the French ambassador in London. Russell sacked Palmerston for flagrantly disregarding the government line, much to the surprise and delight of the Queen. 'It is a great and unexpected mercy,' she wrote.[29]

This would, however, not be the last that Victoria saw of Lord Palmerston.

A FEW WEEKS after Palmerston's dismissal Russell made a statement to the Commons in which he read out a memorandum Victoria had sent in 1850 warning the foreign secretary that she would 'exercise . . . her constitutional right' of dismissing him if he did not obey her injunctions. It is uncertain whether the sovereign really did enjoy such a right, while for his part Palmerston thought Russell had been wrong to drag her into the affair. The prime minister's behaviour had been 'unconstitutional and ungentlemanlike' and 'very wrong by the Queen', he said. Victoria, on the other hand, was delighted, saying Russell had given a 'lucid definition of the constitutional position of the prime minister & foreign secretary opposite the Crown'.[30]

Russell's statement highlighted the uncomfortable fact that there was no consensus over the nature of the sovereign's constitutional rights. At a time when most European monarchs had a significant role in directing foreign policy, some British ministers thought that the Queen and Prince Albert had overinflated views of their prerogatives. 'They labour,' said one, Lord Clarendon, 'under the curious mistake that the Foreign Office is their peculiar department and that they have a right to control, if not to direct, the foreign policy of England.' Clarendon, a Whig with a sardonic wit, was not overawed by royalty: he made jokes at Victoria's expense and nicknamed her the Missus. When he was foreign secretary she was often annoyed with him, prompting him to write to a friend, 'The Missus and I have had a bit of a tiff.'[31] Victoria's biographer Giles St Aubyn has written that Clarendon's 'jaundiced but recognisable parody of their views' overlooked her 'undoubted right' to be kept fully informed, to be consulted on matters of consequence and to be given an opportunity to influence decisions. 'None of her Ministers challenged these rights in principle, although Palmerston often flouted them in practice.'[32]

Palmerston did not remain out in the cold for long. Within a year he was back serving in a coalition government of Whigs and Peelites, albeit as home secretary, regarded by many as a curious appointment given his expertise in foreign affairs. Three years later, in 1855, the prime minister, Lord Aberdeen, came under heavy criticism over the government's conduct of the Crimean War, in particular the conditions the army were being forced to endure, and lost a vote by the massive margin of 305 votes to 148. In desperate attempts to find anyone other than Palmerston, who was the obvious candidate to replace Aberdeen, Victoria sent for no fewer than three potential prime ministers, none of whom was able to form a government. Reluctantly she turned to her old enemy. Deaf and short-sighted, with dyed hair and false teeth, Palmerston was seventy years old and the oldest person to be appointed prime minister for the first time – a record yet to be broken.

Despite his age, Palmerston seemed rejuvenated by his appointment. Victoria also found herself agreeably surprised by how accommodating he was. When he wanted to send ships to threaten Naples, on discovering that the Queen was against it he dropped the idea, simply to please her. A year later she wrote in her journal: 'Albert & I agreed that of all the prime ministers we have had Lord Palmerston is the one who gives the least trouble, & is most amenable to reason.' Palmerston even came round to Albert. 'I had no idea,' he said, that he possessed 'such eminent qualities'.[33]

Palmerston also pleased her with his written accounts of the day's proceedings in the Commons, at that time a duty that fell to the PM rather than, as is now the case, someone from the whips' office. Like her great-great-granddaughter Elizabeth II, Victoria liked her reports lively and entertaining. In 1860 she thanked him for 'some very amusing reports of the really puerile and absurd conduct of many members of the House of Commons'.[34]

Victoria rewarded him in 1856 with the Order of the Garter. His ministry fell in 1858, but he was back again the following year, serving for another six years as prime minister. However, when war broke out in Italy in 1859 between Austria and the kingdom of Sardinia – backed by France – Victoria and Palmerston found themselves in disagreement once more, with Victoria supporting Austria, and Palmerston and his foreign secretary, Lord John Russell, siding with Sardinia in its efforts to throw off Austrian domination of northern Italy. Their view reflected public opinion, which regarded the Austrians as oppressors.

After a series of Austrian defeats at the hands of Franco-Sardinian forces, an armistice was agreed at Villafranca which was more advantageous to Austria than many had expected. Victoria was delighted, while Palmerston and Russell were furious. Within days France's former president Louis-Napoleon, now the Emperor Napoleon III, began to regret the deal, and Palmerston and Russell nurtured hopes that it would collapse. It was at this point that Victoria began to behave very badly indeed.

Her problem was that Russell had a reputation for proceeding as he saw fit, without necessarily checking with his cabinet colleagues every step of the way, and she suspected that he might try to derail the Villafranca agreement without consulting the cabinet first. Unfortunately for Victoria, in those days – unlike now – the sovereign did not receive the minutes of cabinet meetings, something that Albert called 'a source of great weakness for the Sovereign'. Palmerston would tell her what suited him, and no more. Victoria and Albert got round this difficulty by resorting to espionage, persuading Lord Granville, lord president of the council, to tell them what was going on. Knowing that what he was doing was wholly improper – it was the role of the prime minister and foreign secretary to brief her on foreign matters – he told Albert: 'No one should know that I make any written communications to Your Royal Highness on this subject.'[35]

The Queen grew increasingly exasperated with Palmerston and Russell, whom she thought of as 'dreadful old men', while the prime minister thought Victoria was behaving unconstitutionally by objecting to everything Russell did. On a visit to Osborne, Victoria's home on the Isle of Wight, Palmerston described encountering 'breezy weather'. On his arrival the Queen refused to talk about Italy with him, although he had a long talk with Albert; it was only after dinner that she agreed to discuss the matter.

However, Palmerston and Russell were isolated within

the cabinet, where their colleagues sided with the Queen, and by the beginning of 1860 Palmerston was forced to abandon his pro-French stance and come round to her view that Napoleon was essentially untrustworthy. This delighted Victoria, who in turn changed her mind about Palmerston and Russell, declaring that she was 'very much pleased' with the 'two old boys'.[36]

Palmerston was even able to help Victoria with a tricky personal matter. Her eldest son, Bertie, the future Edward VII, led a hedonistic lifestyle which was a constant worry to his mother. When Palmerston was informed about his unseemly behaviour, he told the Queen, who asked the prime minister to write to Bertie 'very strongly warning the Prince of Wales of the precipice upon which he stands'. Sovereigns asking their ministers to assist with controlling the more unruly members of their family is a theme that would crop up repeatedly over the next century or so. Palmerston died in office in 1865, two days short of his eighty-first birthday. Victoria said he had always behaved well towards her, although she added: 'I never liked him . . . He was very vindictive, and personal feelings influenced his political acts very much. Still, he is a loss.'[37]

IF VICTORIA never really warmed to Palmerston, that cannot be said to have been the case with Benjamin Disraeli. He set out to woo her, and succeeded like no other prime minister had done before. But he did not get off to a good start. The son of a well-to-do Jewish man of letters who had converted to Anglicanism, Disraeli had a reputation in his twenties as a ruthless adventurer, turning to novel writing in order to pay off debts incurred as a result of some unwise investments. He made three unsuccessful attempts to win a seat at Westminster, first as a Radical and then a Tory: as a young backbencher who opposed the repeal of the Corn Laws he clashed repeatedly with Robert Peel in the House of Commons, much to Victoria's disapproval. She called him 'the obnoxious Mr Disraeli' and described him as 'detestable, unprincipled, reckless, & not respectable'.[38]

In early 1851, as Lord Stanley was trying – unsuccessfully – to form a government, the suggestion was made that Disraeli might become home secretary, a prospect that Victoria found unsettling. She told Stanley that 'she had not a very good opinion of Mr Disraeli on account of his conduct to poor Sir Robert Peel'.[39] But, not for the first time, she was to change her mind. When Stanley – who by then had succeeded to the title of Earl of Derby – eventually became prime minister in early 1852, he made Disraeli chancellor and leader of the House of Commons, in which capacity Disraeli was invited to dinner at Buckingham Palace. Victoria described him as 'most singular, – thoroughly Jewish looking, a livid complexion, dark eyes, & eyebrows, & black ringlets. The expression is disagreeable, but I do not find him so, to talk to.' She also enjoyed the accounts of Commons debates that he sent to her, saying that she liked their 'very flowery' language. They were, she said, 'much in the style of his books'. Albert was less impressed and spoke disapprovingly of Disraeli's 'democratic tendencies' (in the days before universal suffrage, this was in many eyes a bad thing) and said that if he indulged them he had the potential 'to become one of the most dangerous men in Europe'.[40]

In 1868, after Lord Derby resigned on grounds of ill health, on his recommendation Victoria appointed Disraeli prime minister. In his letter thanking her, Disraeli hoped she would give him the benefit of her guidance, saying that her extensive experience 'must give your Majesty an advantage in judgement, which few living persons, and probably no living prince, can rival'.[41] That set the tone for their relationship: no compliment was so overblown that it could not be wielded with shameless abandon by Disraeli, or gratefully received by Victoria. She sent a copy of the letter to her daughter Vicky, telling her: 'He is full of poetry, romance and chivalry. When he knelt down to kiss my hand which he took in both of his, he said "in loving loyalty and faith".'[42]

Disraeli once explained his technique for dealing with Victoria. 'I never contradict,' he said. 'I never deny; but sometimes I forget.' His other maxim was: 'Everyone likes flattery; and when you come to royalty you should lay it on with a trowel.' He also understood Victoria's appetite for political gossip, a trait she shared with Elizabeth II and which Harold Wilson, arguably Elizabeth's favourite prime minister, understood. Victoria's lady-in-waiting Lady Augusta Stanley told Lord Clarendon: 'Dizzy writes daily letters to the Queen in his best novel style, telling her every scrap of political news dressed up to serve his own purpose, and every scrap of social gossip cooked to amuse her. She declares that she has never had such letters in her life . . . and that she never before knew everything.'[43]

Despite Disraeli's skill at managing his Queen, there were limits to what he was able to achieve. After the death of Prince Albert in December 1861, Victoria had largely withdrawn from public duties. Disraeli had some success in getting her to do more, but even he was unable to stop her from going to Balmoral for an extended period in May 1868. The government was in a precarious position and her ministers needed her to be available, but Victoria, who complained of extreme fatigue, was insistent. She was, she said, ready to return from Balmoral at short notice if necessary, but that did not prevent widespread criticism, including in the columns of The Times. Disraeli had to join her at Balmoral for a ten-day visit which he dreaded, saying it 'would quite finish me', but was unable to get out of it. She did at least go out of her way to make it bearable for her prime minister, insisting that on a visit to Braemar all the ladies of the household should accompany her, 'to make it amusing to Mr Disraeli'.[44] Victoria's insistence on putting her own convenience before constitutional duties would be a recurring theme for the remainder of her reign.

Disraeli's first term as PM lasted less than a year, but in 1874 he was back in Downing Street after he defeated Gladstone's Liberals, winning the first Conservative majority since 1841. From 1868 until Disraeli's death thirteen years later he and Gladstone would alternate as prime minister. When Disraeli arrived to kiss hands, he declared to Victoria: 'I plight my troth to the kindest of *Mistresses*.' The combination of poetry and flattery continued as before – when he wrote thanking her for some primroses, he described them as 'an offering from the fauns and dryads of the woods of Osborne' – but some of those close to Victoria were sceptical. Sir Henry Ponsonby, her private secretary, thought he was 'humbugging' the Queen. Behind her back Disraeli, who had a habit of alluding to *A Midsummer Night's Dream*, called her the Faery, a nickname that managed to combine affection with a hint of gentle mockery. In private he was prepared to speak more frankly. He once told Lord Derby, who was a receptive audience for such talk: 'She was very troublesome, very wilful and whimsical, like a spoilt child.' On another occasion he described her as 'very mad'.[45]

Disraeli's efforts to please his mistress caused him some political discomfort in 1876 when she told him of her ambition to have the title of Empress of India – one already used informally – officially conferred upon her. Disraeli, who knew that a law would have to be passed, tried to get it through Parliament on the quiet, but made the mistake of failing to square it with the opposition beforehand. (A century later,

John Major's defence secretary, Michael Portillo, would make a similar mistake over the proposed replacement of the royal yacht, Britannia; a decade after that George Osborne, in his overhaul of royal finances, did not.) The bill immediately ran into opposition, with many feeling that the title of empress was un-British; one republican MP called it an 'obnoxious' measure that only 'toadies, snobs and sycophants' could support. In the end the bill passed, but Victoria was deeply angered by the objections, which she regarded as personally offensive. When two parliamentarians who had spoken against it made an appearance at a royal garden party, they were warned by the Princess of Wales to keep out of the Queen's sight: 'You are not forgiven and never will be.'[46]

When Victoria made Disraeli Earl of Beaconsfield later that year, it was widely seen – not least in a cartoon in Punch – as a reward for his efforts in securing her own title. As the historian Richard Aldous has observed, Victoria and Disraeli exploited their closeness 'for mutual advantage'.[47] However, Disraeli was badly damaged by the episode: according to Aldous, the bill 'shattered Disraeli's authority in the House of Commons'.[48]

During Disraeli's second ministry both the prime minister and the Queen were arguably guilty of bending the constitutional conventions of the time. When war broke out between Russia and Turkey in 1877, partly because of Russia's ambition to win back territory lost in the Crimean War, Victoria was strongly anti-Russian, and threatened to abdicate if Britain did not take a stronger line. That she would use the threat of abdication as a tool of political coercion seems extraordinary now. She also wrote memoranda for the cabinet pushing her view, which was a breach of the convention that she was meant to accept the advice of ministers rather than try to influence policy. When one cabinet minister,

Lord Carnarvon – who was critical of the Turkish treatment of Christians living under the Ottoman empire – visited Windsor, she made a robust attempt to change his mind, complaining that he 'did not take the proper view'.[49]

Meanwhile Gladstone suspected Disraeli of passing on to her details of cabinet discussions, including which ministers were against taking a firm position against Russia. If Disraeli was really betraying his fellow cabinet members, said Gladstone, he 'was guilty of a great perfidy'. Even when Victoria went to Balmoral for her spring break she continued to be heavily involved. 'The Faery writes every day and telegraphs every hour,' said Disraeli. 'This is almost literally the case.'[50]

Their mutual disregard for constitutional niceties continued even after Disraeli lost the 1880 general election. Victoria wrote to him telling of her 'grief' that they had to part, only to decide a short time later that they did not have to have 'a real parting' after all. Instead she suggested she could write to him 'on many a *private* subject and without anyone being astonished or offended, and even more without anyone knowing about it'. But their correspondence, she said, could also cover 'great public questions', which was going against the rules given that he was in opposition. It was not, of course, the first time she had written to an opposition politician in such a way: she had done the same with Lord Melbourne after he left office in 1841. She hatched a plan to communicate with Disraeli using intermediaries, but when it was suggested to her private secretary that he might help, Ponsonby wanted nothing to do with it. 'Most decidedly not,' he said. Despite that, Victoria managed to write to Disraeli without Ponsonby's help, and also saw him in person from time to time.

The following year Victoria had a sharp disagreement with the government over the decision to evacuate Kandahar following the British victory in the Second Afghan War. So strongly did she object to the handing of Kandahar back to Afghanistan that she refused to announce it as part of the government's programme in her speech at the opening of Parliament. She was often difficult about the state opening. For several years after Albert's death she refused to attend the ceremony, only returning in 1866 when Parliament was about to vote on an allowance for her daughter Princess Helena. She still made a frightful fuss, comparing it to an 'execution', despite the fact that she did not even read out her own speech, insisting instead that it was read by the lord chancellor on her behalf.[51] Only after the cabinet threatened to resign did she give way, with characteristic ill grace. When ministers next visited her at Osborne she was still sulking and refused to speak to them, although the home secretary did manage to tell her that the speech was not meant to contain her views, but those of the government. After she complained about this to Disraeli, he assured her that such a doctrine was 'a principle not known to the British constitution.'[52] This of course was complete nonsense: since 1841 the speech had been accepted as a statement of government policy for which the sovereign accepted no personal responsibility.

Disraeli had been in ill health for some time, and when it became clear that the end was near she asked if she could visit him. 'No, it is better not,' he said. 'She will only ask me to take a message to Albert.' Instead she sent her doctors, and enough flowers to fill the house.[53] When he died, she told Lord Salisbury that she was 'overwhelmed with this dreadful loss', adding (referring to herself in the third person, as she often did): 'His devotion, unselfishness and kindness she can never, never forget; her gratitude is everlasting.'[54]

*

WHEN SHE FIRST knew William Gladstone, whom Prince Albert had held in high regard, Victoria was equally impressed. 'He is very agreeable,' she wrote, 'so quiet & intellectual, with such a knowledge of all subjects, & is such a good man.'[55] Even when he first became prime minister in 1868 there was little to suggest that she would come to regard the eloquent, high-minded Gladstone with visceral loathing. Quite what led to their falling-out is a matter for argument: historians have suggested that it was differences over church patronage or the importance of army reforms. She also strongly disagreed with his desire to achieve home rule for Ireland. But perhaps of equal if not greater importance was the simple fact that Gladstone had no idea how to handle her. Disraeli once told a colleague who asked how to deal with the Queen: 'First of all, remember she is a woman.' If Gladstone was aware of that advice, he certainly paid it no heed. Victoria is said to have complained, 'Mr Gladstone addresses me as if I were a public meeting,' and she was not the only one to find his conversational manner overbearing. Henry Ponsonby told how Gladstone 'forces you into his groove' with 'a terrible earnestness' and 'an intensity which scarcely allows him to suppose there can be any truth on the other side'.[56] The writer Emily Eden, a friend of Lord Melbourne and prime minister Anthony Eden's great-great-great-aunt, described how he 'does not converse – he harangues – and the more he says the more I don't understand . . . if he were soaked in boiling water and rinsed until he was twisted into a rope, I do not suppose a drop of fun would ooze out'.[57]

Gladstone was slow to pick up on how much Victoria disliked him, but it is clear that long before the end of his first term as prime minister she had turned against him. She described him to her eldest daughter, Vicky, as 'a very danger-ous minister – and so wonderfully unsympathetic', and when he lost office in 1874 a much-relieved Queen told Vicky that she had found him 'so very arrogant, tyrannical and obstinate, with no knowledge of the world or human nature'.

Throughout Gladstone's time in Downing Street – he served as PM four times between 1868 and 1894 – Victoria was repeatedly difficult and obstructive. In 1869 she refused to open Parliament, claiming she was suffering from a 'severe headache' but also admitting that her refusal was connected with her disapproval of Gladstone's plan for the disestablishment of the Church of Ireland.[58] They crossed swords over her insistence on going to Osborne or Balmoral during times of political crisis when Gladstone wanted her to be on hand to exercise 'her great and just influence and mediating power',[59] and she worked against Gladstone by writing to cabinet ministers urging them to defy the prime minister.[60]

Visits to Balmoral were, however, not as bad as might be expected. Gladstone and Victoria often got on better in person than their fractious relationship might suggest – what she could not bear was his interminably long letters to her – although after his visit in September 1869 she told Vicky: 'I cannot find him agreeable and he talks so very much.' John Brown, her Highland servant with whom Victoria had a close and devoted relationship, clearly felt the same: once, when Gladstone was in full flow, Brown cut him short by curtly announcing: 'Ye've said enuf!' Unlike Disraeli, however, Gladstone found much to enjoy in the Highlands, and would go for long walks and rides – up to forty miles a day – long after he was seventy. He was rare in that respect: Lord Salisbury loathed the place, and Henry Campbell-Bannerman found it cold and dull, with the household bored to death. 'It is the funniest life conceivable,' he told his wife, 'like that of a convent. We meet at meals . . . and when we have finished each is off to his own cell.'[61]

Loath as she would be to admit it, Victoria had cause to be grateful to Gladstone. In November 1871 the Prince of Wales was taken ill with what turned out to be typhoid, the disease that was thought – possibly erroneously – to have claimed the life of Prince Albert. Bertie came close to death, but after he recovered a relieved Victoria wondered whether there might be some kind of thanksgiving service. At a time when the royal family was quite unpopular because of Victoria's neglect of public duties, and republicanism was on the increase, Gladstone saw this as an opportunity to rehabilitate the monarchy. However, the prime minister and Queen were at cross purposes: Victoria had been talking about a form of service to be distributed to churches around the country, and was dead set against any kind of national service that she would attend. She dismissed the idea as 'a display' which in terms of religion would be 'false and hollow'. Gladstone managed to talk her round, and the thanksgiving service, which was held at St Paul's the following February, was a triumph. Crowds cheered the Queen as she was driven through the streets with the prince by her side, and when she 'took dear Bertie's hand and pressed it – people cried', a delighted Victoria wrote afterwards. It was, she said, 'a most affecting day'.

However, whatever capital he gained with that success, Gladstone managed to lose it all with his proposal to send Bertie to Ireland as viceroy. Victoria was against the idea, arguing that he would merely be undertaking ceremonial duties, which would not do the wayward prince any good at all. Bertie was also strongly opposed. But Gladstone, who was set on finding useful employment for the prince, would not let it go, and sent the Queen letter after letter trying to overcome her objections, much to her annoyance. In the end he had to accept defeat, but the episode again set back Gladstone's relations with the Queen.

After losing to Disraeli in 1874, the Liberals won again in 1880 following a series of storming foreign policy speeches by Gladstone in his Scottish constituency in what became known as the Midlothian Campaign. However, Victoria was determined not to have Gladstone – who was no longer party leader – as prime minister. Appalled by his attacks on Disraeli, she said she would 'sooner *abdicate*' than 'send for or have any *communication* with *that half-mad* firebrand' who wished to become a 'Dictator'. Nevertheless, after forty-eight hours of consultations it became clear that Gladstone was the only one who would be able to form an administration. Although their first audience went relatively smoothly, it soon became apparent that the intervening years had not mellowed either of them. Victoria and the GOM (an acronym of Grand Old Man; he was also known as the People's William) clashed over Irish home rule, empire policy and military estimates. An exhausted Gladstone complained that 'the Queen alone is enough to kill any man' and would never be satisfied until she had 'hounded him out of office'.[62]

Their relationship took a turn for the worse in 1885 when Britain suffered a setback in Sudan, then a dependency of Egypt, which was itself indirectly ruled by the British. Forces under a religious leader known as the Mahdi were attempting to expel the Egyptians, and after defeats at the hands of the rebels a force was sent under General Gordon to evacuate British and Egyptian personnel stationed in Sudan. When Gordon became besieged in Khartoum, Gladstone ignored warnings – including from Victoria – that a relief force should be sent to rescue him until it was too late. By the time the delayed rescue mission arrived, 7,000 British and Egyptian soldiers and 4,000 civilians had been massacred. With Gladstone out of London, Victoria sent him a scathing telegram: 'These news from Khartoum are frightful, and to think that all this might have been prevented and many precious lives saved by earlier action is too frightful.' Such a message was strong meat in itself, but Victoria deliberately sent the telegraph *en clair* instead of using a cypher, which meant that it could be read by anyone. Gladstone was shocked at his public dressing-down and considered resignation. Henry Ponsonby had to step in to smooth his ruffled feathers. A few months later Gladstone confessed to a colleague: 'My relations with the Queen have lately become so unpleasant that I shall not be sorry when they are terminated.' He resigned the following month.

After a brief third term in office in 1886, lasting less than a year, Gladstone spent six years in opposition while the Marquess of Salisbury, a member of the Cecil family and a direct descendant of Elizabeth I's adviser Lord Burghley, was prime minister. Salisbury had a much better psychological appreciation of Victoria: he understood her ways, could adapt to her moods, and appreciated the importance of not overburdening her. Her admiration for him was summed up in the memorandum she wrote after he lost to Gladstone in the general election of 1892: 'It seems to me a defect in our much famed constitution to have to part with an admirable government like Lord Salisbury's for no question of any importance or *any reason*, merely on account of the number of votes.'[63] For a supposedly constitutional monarch, that is an interesting use of 'merely'. She also sent Gladstone a note saying she had received Salisbury's resignation 'with much regret', which the new prime minister took as the insult it was no doubt intended to be.

Gladstone was so old by then – eighty-two when he took office – that Victoria did not expect him to last long, but he managed to stick it out for eighteen months, during which they indulged in their usual disagreements. These culminated in an argument over naval spending – he thought that the Admiralty's proposed budget was madness, while Victoria believed that the Royal Navy should get everything it asked for. When it became clear that Gladstone was isolated in the cabinet, he resigned, to Victoria's great joy. After their final audience she sent him a brief letter which contained, he said, 'not a word of regret or gratitude'. Later he would complain that his departure from public life after more than half a century of service was handled with 'the same brevity [that] perhaps prevails in settling a tradesman's bill'.[64]

There is a farcical footnote to the long, sad saga of Victoria and Gladstone. In her Diamond Jubilee year of 1897 she held a garden party at Buckingham Palace which was attended by her former prime minister. He was determined to speak to her; she was equally determined to avoid him. After an absurd game of hide-and-seek he finally cornered her, and she gave him her hand: Victoria, as graceless as ever.[65] He died on 19 May 1898, and was accorded the honour of a lying-in-state at Westminster Hall, although his death was not mentioned in the Court Circular, which Victoria claimed was an oversight. At his funeral in Westminster Abbey the Prince of Wales acted as one of the pall-bearers. An annoyed Victoria asked him what precedent he had acted on and what advice he had taken. The reply was short: there was no precedent, and there had been no advice.[66]

IN MAY 1865, a few days before the birth of the Prince of Wales's second son, the future George V, the first of a series of articles on the English constitution appeared in the Fortnightly Review, a magazine founded by Anthony Trollope among others. They were written by a former barrister from the West Country who had later turned to banking and then journalism; at the time of their publication he was editor-in-chief of *The Economist* following the death of its founding editor, James Wilson, who happened to be his father-in-law. The articles were published as a book in 1867, and the author would become one of the most celebrated names in British constitutional writing: Walter Bagehot.

Bagehot was nothing if not ambitious. The British constitution is the set of laws, rules and conventions that determine how the country is run. It includes how laws are made, how elections are held, how Parliament works and what powers the monarchy has. People often maintain that Britain does not have a written constitution, but that is misleading: much of it is written down, including important laws such as the Bill of Rights of 1689, which established Parliament's rights over the Crown and recognised that Parliament is sovereign. 'Uncodified' is a better description. Unlike most other countries, Britain does not have a single document setting out its constitution, and many important parts of it, including the principles that govern what powers the sovereign has in relation to the government that rules in their name, including the royal prerogative to appoint prime ministers and dissolve Parliament, are indeed not written down, but are based on convention and precedent. And whenever there is convention and precedent, there is scope for interpretation – and argument.

Bagehot set out his arguments more memorably than anyone else. His work on the English constitution, which appeared at the same time as the 1867 Reform Act expanded the electorate to 2.5 million, meaning that he had to bring out a revised edition in 1872, is best known for its exploration of the relationship between Parliament and the monarchy. Some of it is familiar to those who have never opened a copy of the book: his distinction between the 'dignified' and the 'efficient' parts of the constitution, his injunction that 'we must not let in daylight upon magic',[67] and his observation on royal weddings, that 'a princely marriage is the brilliant edition of a universal fact'.[68] Most famous of all is his assertion that in a constitutional monarchy the sovereign has three rights: to be consulted, to encourage and to warn. A wise monarch could use these rights with 'singular effect', according to Bagehot: they could say, 'I do not oppose, it is not my duty to oppose; but I observe that I warn.' And a minister would have no choice but to listen to them.[69]

Less widely appreciated is that Bagehot had some pretty robust opinions. He was no unquestioning admirer of royalty. Due to the 'early acquired feebleness of hereditary dynasties' and the poor education typically received by princes, he said that a constitutional sovereign was likely to be 'a man of inferior ability'. He was equally scathing about the House of Lords: 'The cure for admiring the House of Lords was to go and look at it,' he wrote. But he was also an unashamed elitist, describing the 'lower orders' variously as 'the coarse, dull, contracted multitude', 'the poor and stupid' and 'the clownish mass'. With contemptuous disdain for universal suffrage, he declared: 'The masses are infinitely too ignorant to make much of governing themselves.' For her part, Victoria did not approve of Bagehot. She reacted with concern when she heard that her grandson the Duke of York was reading his economic essays, describing him as a 'radical' writer.[70]

Part of the reason his writings still command our attention today is that his book, unlike most constitutional textbooks, is commendably short. And Bagehot's journalistic skill with words ensures that The English Constitution is infinitely more readable than other worthier, weightier tomes. In the words of the historian Peter Hennessy, 'it's poetry, not plumbing'.[71] If you want a pithy summary of Queen Victoria's lack of legislative power, it is hard to improve on this: 'She must sign her own death warrant if the two Houses unanimously send it up to her.'[72]

The problem with Bagehot is not his anti-democratic tendencies, but the fact that he was writing about what he thought ought to happen, not what was actually going on. In his review of Anne Somerset's book on Victoria and her prime ministers, historian Lord Lexden recalled Bagehot's description of a monarch's rights before declaring: 'Victoria accepted no such limitations on her constitutional role. She was for ever pouring out her opinions and wishes, often accompanied by sharp reprimands, in letters and memoranda to her prime ministers.'[73] When she berated the government over its failures in a letter to the foreign secretary Lord Granville in 1881, ordering him to show the letter to Gladstone, the PM's secretary Edward Hamilton was shocked. 'This from a constitutional monarch!' he said.

The question is, just how much of a constitutional monarch was she? And indeed, what is a constitutional monarchy? Essentially, it is a system in which the head of state is a monarch, but that person does not rule the country: the ability to pass laws lies with an elected parliament. So a king or queen is a constitutional monarch to the extent that they recognise that it is not they who are in charge, but the elected representatives of the people. For all that Victoria behaved in a blatantly partisan manner, the constitutional historian Sir Vernon Bogdanor has argued that during her reign the growing importance of the political parties and the increase in the size of the electorate through the Reform Acts of 1832 and 1867 meant that the power of the sovereign became increasingly circumscribed. 'The expansion of the franchise meant that what happened outside parliament was coming to determine what happened inside the Palace of Westminster and that the political centre of gravity was coming to be moved away from parliament to the platform. The growth of party was coming to deprive the sovereign of the power to choose the prime minister.'[74] But that did not stop her from harassing or obstructing her government, or intriguing behind its back.

Victoria's reign also saw the end of the sovereign's supposed special responsibility for foreign affairs, says Bogdanor,[75] giving rise to what Anthony Seldon has called 'the golden age of the foreign secretary'. But no foreign secretary could stop her influencing her daughter the Empress of Germany, or her granddaughter the Tsarina of Russia. Victoria's biographer Giles St Aubyn wrote: 'Given the unrivalled awe in which the Queen was held, particularly in the later years of her reign, Ministers had little alternative but to concede her the status her fellow Sovereigns accorded her.'[76] This notion would have an intriguing echo a century or so later during the latter years of the reign of Queen Elizabeth II.

In Victoria's defence Anne Somerset quotes a number of her prime ministers who said that she behaved entirely correctly as a constitutional monarch, including – not surprisingly – Disraeli ('There never was a more constitutional monarch than our present Queen') and – much more surprisingly – Gladstone. At a Golden Jubilee party at his country home, he said: 'All the principles of the constitution have been observed by the Queen . . . in a manner more perfect than has ever been known in the time of any former sovereign.' Lord Shaftesbury, on the other hand, called her 'our most unconstitutional Queen'.[77] Victoria herself declared that she 'cannot and will not be the Queen of a democratic monarchy',[78] which is exactly what she was meant to be. But while Somerset argues that it is hard to pinpoint any political event where Victoria dictated the outcome, 'none of this detracts from the fact that Victoria was extraordinarily politically active, and her political presence was considerable'.[79] As late as 1894 she was still able to exercise her prerogative when she chose the Liberal Lord Rosebery as prime minister, who protested that he was reluctant to take the job. 'I am very fond of Lord Rosebery,' she told her daughter Vicky, 'he is so much attached to me personally.'[80]

Victoria's reign saw another fundamental change, according to Bogdanor. As the role of the Crown was transformed from one of power to one of influence, its authority was actually strengthened, not weakened. The effect was to give the monarchy 'a massive emotional significance in the new age of popular government'. Instead of there being a politically active monarchy, 'the sovereign could prove a beneficent influence only in so far as he or she abstained entirely from seeking to rule. Only then could the head of state become the head of the nation.'[81] But while that radical reshaping of the purpose of the monarchy would clearly be accepted by the royal family today, it would not have been accepted or even understood by Victoria herself.

No subsequent monarch has meddled quite like Victoria. She constantly interfered in political matters – trying to promote her own agenda, particularly in foreign affairs, attempting to influence the appointment of ministers and acting in a shamelessly partisan manner. The tragedy, at least in terms of her reputation as a constitutional monarch, is that Albert died when he did. Under his influence Victoria acted in a much less partisan manner than she had done in the early years of her reign, occupying a position of broad neutrality between the parties. After his death she returned to her old partisan anti-Liberal ways. In the latter years of her reign she exerted her influence as vigorously as she had ever done, but with the growth of democracy and the burgeoning strength of the political parties, she had become a relic of the past, a sovereign at odds with the times in which she lived.

The days of meddlesome sovereigns were over. But the monarchy did not give up without a fight. As we shall see, Victoria's successors would continue to play an active political role for many years to come.

CHAPTER TWO

MARCHING WITH
THE TIMES

DINNERS WITH QUEEN VICTORIA could be a dull business,
with the conversation rarely straying beyond the resolutely
trivial while the guests prayed silently for the sweet release of
bedtime. But the royals could also do family rows on an epic
scale. One such row took place at Windsor, shortly after the
death in 1863 of King Frederick VII of Denmark prompted
a dispute between Denmark and Prussia over the duchies
of Schleswig and Holstein. There is no need to be unduly
bothered by the details of this famously complicated quarrel: Lord Palmerston is said to have remarked later, possibly
apocryphally: 'Only three people have ever really understood the Schleswig-Holstein business: the Prince Consort,
who is dead, a German professor, who has gone mad, and I,
who have forgotten all about it.' Suffice it to say that among
those gathered at the dining table were Fritz, the future
Frederick III of Prussia, who was married to Victoria's eldest
daughter, Vicky, and Bertie's wife, Alexandra, known in the

family as Alix, whose father, Christian, had just acceded to the Danish throne.

The evening did not go well. Alix declared that 'the Duchies belong to Papa', which prompted Victoria – who was firmly on the side of Prussia – to complain that she came 'from the enemy's camp' and 'was not worth the price we have paid for her'. Fritz, meanwhile, valiantly pressed the claims of Prussia. The whole thing became so heated, and Victoria so upset, that eventually she had to ban the company from discussing the subject at all.

For the twenty-two-year-old Prince of Wales, who had taken his wife's side, the row had an important legacy: it helped his mother form the view that her eldest son lacked discretion and judgement. As Giles St Aubyn put it, 'How could she trust him with confidential documents when he was known to betray state secrets over the dinner table?'[1] Victoria was not necessarily wrong: for a time the Foreign Office used to send him papers, but Disraeli complained that the prince spoke indiscreetly to his friends about government secrets, and Victoria put a stop to the practice. Her mistrust – bolstered by Bertie's warm relations with Gladstone, whom he used to entertain at Sandringham – would continue for the rest of her life, which meant that Bertie was consistently denied access to state papers that would have helped him prepare for his role as King.

Some twenty years later, when the resentful prince used a roundabout approach via Gladstone in an attempt to get access to papers, Victoria wrote on a note from her private secretary: 'The Queen thinks he should be told things when things are no longer secrets . . . for he is not discreet.' When Gladstone asked for clarification about what cabinet reports he could show Bertie, Victoria wrote in her familiar purple pencil that it would be 'quite irregular and improper' to show him anything on a regular basis; the only things that could be shared with him before they were made public were the most major policy decisions.[2] The Prince of Wales was forty-three years old at the time.

During Gladstone's last term of office, however, Bertie did manage to get foreign secretary Lord Rosebery to send him confidential dispatches once more. They were conveyed in a red leather box, to which there were supposed to be only three gold keys, held by the sovereign, the prime minister and the head of the Foreign Office. The good news for Bertie was that Rosebery found another key, which had belonged to Prince Albert; the bad news was that it didn't work. Or so the prince thought. It turned out that there was a knack to it – you had to push it in, turn it a bit, then push it in again – but even when Bertie had mastered the key he was still disappointed. The dispatches were of no interest, he complained, and to supply him with nothing would be 'preferable to the rubbish they send!'[3]

WHEN BERTIE became King Edward VII in January 1901, everything changed. He made Buckingham Palace the centre of royal life in a way it had not been for years under Victoria, and restored to the monarchy a glamour that had been sorely lacking. The big ceremonial occasions, including the State Opening of Parliament, were lavishly reshaped to be as grand as possible. Unlike his mother, the King also made a conscious effort not to meddle in domestic politics. In foreign affairs, however, it was a different matter. His great coup was a masterstroke so audacious that it seems hard to fathom how he pulled it off.

Britain had spent most of the nineteenth century pursuing a policy of 'splendid isolation', avoiding any permanent alliances in continental Europe, but the growing strength of Germany meant that the country had to make a choice between aligning with the Franco-Russian camp or the Germans. The Balfour government favoured the idea of an alliance with France, but that was easier said than done because of the strength of anti-British feeling there. Someone had to break the political impasse, and that someone was the King.

In the early spring of 1903 Edward set off in the royal yacht for a visit to Europe which was meant to take in Portugal and Rome. He had with him seventy pieces of luggage, and was accompanied by his assistant private secretary, a Portuguese minister and, instead of the usual cabinet minister, an undersecretary from the Foreign Office. What almost no one knew – not the foreign secretary, not the British ambassador to France, not even his wife, Alix – was that the real purpose of the trip was to see the French president in Paris on his way home. The British government only learned of his plans when the King was at Gibraltar on his way to Italy.

The King arrived in Paris on a special train, and as he was driven in the president's state carriage to the embassy he was jeered by crowds shouting anti-British slogans such as 'Vivent les Boers!' and 'Vive Jeanne d'Arc!' One of his party remarked that the French did not seem to like them. 'Why should they?' replied the King. But from that point on the visit was a triumph as Edward, with his faultless French and charming manners, completely won over the locals. A speech in which he spoke of feeling as if he were at home – he had sampled the delights of Paris many times over the years – helped turn the tide, but it was just one moment among many. A gesture that went down particularly well came during a visit to the theatre when – despite the concerns of the Paris police – he was mingling with the crowd in the foyer and spotted a well-known actress. Going up to her, he kissed her hand and said: 'Oh, Mademoiselle, I remember how I applauded you in London. You personified there all the grace, all the *esprit* of France.' The French could not resist such gallantry, and before long the taunts of his first day were replaced by shouts of 'Vive le Roi!'

Edward was not directly responsible for the series of agreements between Britain and France – mainly settling colonial disputes – which were signed the following year and came to be known as the Entente Cordiale. But there is no doubt that he created the favourable conditions that enabled the two governments to come to such an understanding. And he did it on his own initiative. As the historian Jane Ridley has written, 'Acting without official support, he upstaged the politicians; but he was not opposing government policy, he was facilitating it – or at least facilitating what he thought government policy ought to be.' Politicians would later play down his role, including Arthur Balfour, who said that he had 'nothing to do with the entente'. However, Ridley quotes the eminent diplomat Eyre Crowe, who argued that Edward was responsible for dissipating French suspicion of the British: 'The French nation having come to look upon the King as personally attached to their country, saw in HM's words and actions a guarantee that the adjustment of political differences might well prepare the way for bringing about a genuine and lasting friendship.'[4]

FOR ALL THE attention he paid to foreign affairs, Edward was scrupulous – on the surface at least – about not being seen to interfere with the machinery of Westminster politics. In 1905 Arthur Balfour, whose Tory government had run out of steam, resigned, and Edward invited the Liberal leader, Henry Campbell-Bannerman, a shrewd and often underestimated Scot, to form a government. At their first audience the sixty-nine-year-old Campbell-Bannerman – the oldest first-time prime minister of the twentieth century – was greeted with a warm handshake by the King, who told him: 'We are not as young as we were, Sir Henry!' A moment of awkward comedy followed when the PM stepped forward, expecting to kneel and kiss hands, only to be interrupted by the King. When Edward had finished speaking, Campbell-Bannerman tried stepping forward again, only to have his hand shaken by the King once more, which he took as an indication that the audience was over.

Shortly afterwards Edward set off for a house party in Dorset, which has since been interpreted as a deliberate attempt by him to steer well clear of the process of cabinet appointments. A few weeks earlier, however, there had been a concerted secret bid by a cabal of Liberal grandees – when the downfall of the Balfour government seemed inevitable – to get Edward very much involved. The plotters, who included the future prime minister H. H. Asquith, wanted to have Campbell-Bannerman kicked upstairs to the House of Lords so that Asquith could effectively run the show from the House of Commons. The King's private secretary Francis Knollys – Lord Knollys – gave the plotters some tentative support, but Edward himself, whose supposed role was to get the Liberal leader to accept a peerage, refused to have anything to do with it: having met Campbell-Bannerman over lunch in August, he had discovered to his surprise that he rather liked him. On taking office, Campbell-Bannerman, who had no interest in going to the Lords, roundly outmanoeuvred the plotters by offering them all top jobs in his government, which they of course accepted.[5]

Asquith, who was appointed chancellor, became prime minister two years later when Campbell-Bannerman resigned because of ill health, dying three weeks later. David Lloyd

George succeeded Asquith as chancellor, a promotion that would set off a chain of events resulting in one of the greatest political crises of Edward's reign – and that of his successor, George V.

In April 1909 Lloyd George – a crafty, charismatic Welsh-man, remembered as much by history for his philandering as his political brilliance – introduced his so-called People's Budget, which funded new social welfare programmes including an increased old age pension by raising taxes on the lands and incomes of the wealthy. Lloyd George, who was supported by his young ally Winston Churchill – initially a Conservative MP, at the time a Liberal, although he would later return to the Conservatives – called it a 'war budget', saying: 'It is for raising money to wage implacable warfare against poverty and squalidness.' The government struggled to get it through the Commons, and did not get it passed until November, when they faced another battle in the Lords, where it was obvious that the bill would be rejected by the Tory majority.

Lloyd George made inflammatory speeches attacking the Lords, egged on by Churchill, and the King and others feared that a constitutional crisis was imminent. In an attempt to avert disaster Edward obtained the prime minister's permission to summon the opposition leaders Balfour and Lord Lansdowne to Buckingham Palace to persuade them not to block the bill in the Lords. The meeting was not a success: Balfour and Lansdowne did not respect the King, and did not trust his private secretary Knollys.[6] (The feeling was mutual. The King told Asquith that while he liked Lansdowne he was 'not a clever man'; as for Balfour, Edward heartily disliked him, describing him as 'the greatest political shuffler of our day' with 'no sense of honour or truth'.[7]) The bill was rejected by the Lords in less than a week.

An affronted Asquith asked for and obtained a dissolution of Parliament, and in the ensuing election one of the main battlegrounds was 'The Peers Against the People'. Asquith wanted a mandate for a new measure to limit the powers of the upper chamber, and if the bill did not pass he wanted the King to flood the Lords with new Liberal peers to ensure that he got his way. Here history was repeating itself: the Whigs had wanted William IV to create new peers to get the 1832 Reform Bill through the Lords, something he repeatedly resisted doing until the pressure finally became overwhelming. Some eighty years later, Edward was similarly reluctant.

Unfortunately, the general election of January 1910 solved nothing. The Liberals were returned with a vastly reduced number of seats, only just beating the Conservatives, and the government was no closer to getting the Budget through. The Liberals were now dependent on Labour and the Irish nationalists for their parliamentary majority, and the Irish had a price for their support: home rule. To achieve that, they demanded measures to remove the Lords' veto over legislation, because the Tories in the upper house were as opposed to home rule as they were to Lloyd George's Budget. The government proposed to do this by means of the Parliament Bill, which would remove the right of the Lords to amend or reject finance bills, and also laid down that any law passed by the Commons but rejected by the Lords would automatically become law after two years. To counter the increased power this gave to the Commons, the parliamentary term was reduced from seven years to five.

Now the pressure on the King began to mount. Asquith made it clear, without actually saying so, that if the Parliament Bill did not pass he would ask the King to flood the Lords with Liberal peers. Edward, who was in Biarritz in an increasingly poor state of health, was furious with Asquith, not to mention Lloyd George, Winston Churchill and the Irish nationalists, and was quite depressed about the whole business. 'It is simply disgusting,' he wrote. 'Thank God I am not in London.'[8] When he returned home he was still so cross with them that he asked Knollys to stop Asquith, Lloyd George and Churchill from meeting him at Victoria Station. They turned up anyway, which no doubt did not improve his mood. He died nine days later, with the political crisis still unresolved. His last words were 'I am so glad' after hearing that his horse Witch of the Air had won the 4.15 at Kempton Park.

Edward has been called the first truly constitutional monarch. It is a claim that is also made for Queen Victoria, but Edward's claim is far more convincing: Victoria's constant political meddling would surely rule her out. Edward was scrupulously impartial between the political parties, and made no attempt to exert his will upon his ministers. Not only did he not scheme against ministers he disagreed with, when he became aware of plots he went out of his way to avoid involvement. But he showed how the Crown could exert significant influence on Britain's foreign relations, and when he did act it was to promote the national interest rather than pursue his own political aims. And by restoring pageantry as a principal means of royal self-expression he bolstered both the standing of the monarchy at home and Britain's image abroad.

Edward did, however, have one thing in common with his mother: he did not do enough to prepare his son for the challenges that lay ahead. And in George V's case, that meant inheriting a constitutional crisis the moment he acceded to the throne in May 1910. The political temperature had cooled somewhat for a few months as the party leaders tried to sort out their differences over home rule and the Parliament Bill at a constitutional conference. But the talks failed, and in November 1910 Asquith went to see the King at York Cottage – his home on the Sandringham estate, relatively modest by royal standards, which George once described as resembling 'three merrie England pubs joined together' – to say that the cabinet was demanding an immediate election.

George had an uneasy relationship with Asquith, who was nicknamed Squiffy on account of his fondness for drink. The prime minister's first assessment of the new King, whose main recreational interests were stamp collecting and game shooting, was not flattering: he was struck by 'the contrast between the worldly experience of King Edward and the unsophisticated mind and tastes of his son'.[9] For his part George had made his views plain when he was Prince of Wales. After dinner at Windsor one night in 1908, he told Churchill that he trusted Asquith but thought him 'not quite a gentleman'. Churchill of course repeated this, and at lunch a short while later George admitted he might have 'put his foot in it'. His wife, May, later Queen Mary, was unsympathetic: 'You said it, George, at the top of your voice. Everyone heard you.'[10] Looking back on his indiscretion a few years later, he said: 'I ought not to have said it, and it was a damned stupid thing to say; but Winston repeated it to Asquith, which was a monstrous thing to do, and made great mischief.'[11]

At their meeting at York Cottage, Asquith made no mention of demanding guarantees that the King should create Liberal peers if the Lords rejected the Parliament Bill, but three days later he did come out with it, which put George in a fix. He did not want to create the peers, because it would make him look as if he was on the Liberals' side; but he thought that if he did not, the government would resign, there would be an election and he would be blamed for it. What made matters more complicated was that George had

46

two private secretaries: Lord Knollys, who had worked for his father, and had the job of liaising with the government, and Arthur Bigge – later Lord Stamfordham – who had worked for Victoria and then George when he was Prince of Wales. Knollys had originally been against the creation of more Liberal peers – he called it 'the greatest outrage' – but for some reason by the time Asquith told the King of his plans he had changed his mind. Not only that, but he was also guilty of deceiving the King. George thought that if he refused, an election would inevitably follow, but this was not true, and Knollys – a strong Liberal – knew it. He had been present at an earlier meeting at which the Tory leader, Arthur Balfour, had said that if Asquith resigned he would be prepared to take office. However, Knollys never passed on this crucial piece of information to the King, which would have given George the means to call Asquith's bluff: when the King found out about Knollys's failure years later, he was outraged and never forgave him.[12]

Cornered, George felt obliged to give the prime minister a secret guarantee that if the Liberals were returned after the election, he would give Asquith the peers he required. The election of December 1910 was an almost exact repeat of January, with the Liberals taking office once more with the support of Labour and the Irish nationalists. However, the agreement to flood the Lords with peers did not emerge until July 1911, when the Parliament Bill once more faced deadlock and the cabinet decided it was time to cash in the King's undertaking.

Balfour was accordingly informed of the secret deal to create peers if necessary, and many of the bill's opponents in the Lords realised that the game was up: they decided it was better to accept a diminution of the powers of the upper chamber than to face the creation of more than 350 new peers. The King helped swing the vote, secretly using his influence behind the scenes to get the Unionists – as the Conservatives were known in the early twentieth century – to vote in favour, and while there were still some diehards willing to fight it all the way, the bill was passed on 10 August by 131 votes to 114. The King, whose relief was said to be 'immense', wrote in his diary that night: 'I am spared any further humiliation by a creation of peers.'[13]

Having got the Parliament Bill through, the government then set about repaying its promise to the Irish nationalists by pressing on with a bill to establish home rule for Ireland. It was hardly full-blown independence: while an Irish parliament was planned for Dublin, the British government would still retain responsibility for tax, defence and foreign policy. This was enough, however, to excite extremely strong feelings among the Protestants of Ulster and prompt fears that it would ignite civil war in Ireland. It also put the King in a pickle, as became starkly apparent at an excruciating dinner at Buckingham Palace attended by Andrew Bonar Law, the Glasgow industrialist who had succeeded Balfour as leader of the Unionists at the end of 1911. Bonar Law told the King in blunt terms that he would either have to accept the Home Rule Bill, in which case one half of the country would think he had acted against them, or dismiss his ministers and appoint another government, in which case supporters of the bill would think he had acted against them.

The King flushed and Bonar Law asked: 'Have you never considered that, sir?' The King replied: 'No, it is the first time it has been suggested to me.' Bonar Law said of the conversation later: 'I think I have given the King the worst five minutes that he has had for a long time.'[14]

Genuinely fearful of the prospect of civil war in Ireland, George was in a quandary. He even wondered whether he should use his theoretical right to refuse to give assent to legislation, something that had not happened since the reign of Queen Anne. 'Whatever I do I shall offend half the population,' he told Asquith in a handwritten memo. 'No sovereign has ever been placed in such a position.' Privately, Asquith was dismissive of the King. He told his daughter Violet that George was 'in an awful state' about home rule. 'He is just in a blue funk,' he said. 'Poor little man he isn't up to his position.'[15] However, the supercilious Asquith may have underestimated the King. Vernon Bogdanor has written that on this question 'the king's judgement was superior to that of his prime minister'. The dangers were all too real. As Bogdanor said, 'There was no chance whatever of Ulster agreeing to send representatives to an Irish parliament, and sooner than accept Home Rule, Ulster would resist by force.'[16]

In an attempt to broker a solution, George suggested holding a conference at Buckingham Palace. Asquith was not keen on the idea at first, but with no agreement in sight he finally agreed. July 1914 saw the main party leaders, together with one supporter each, meet for four days in the 1844 Room at Buckingham Palace, one of the palace's grandest reception rooms. The principle that Ulster should be excluded from home rule had already been conceded: the problem was how to draw the map. Not surprisingly, they failed to come to an agreement.

A week later Britain was at war with Germany, and a bill to postpone home rule until the end of the war was rushed through Parliament. This was regarded as a betrayal by Irish nationalists, and it was not until November 1920 that a new Home Rule Bill, which partitioned Ireland into north and south, was finally passed.

No one claims that the Buckingham Palace conference was anything other than a failure. George's biographer Kenneth

Rose called it 'ill-advised', saying: 'It offered little hope of success, yet involved a constitutional sovereign in the most contentious of all political issues.'[17] Yet Jane Ridley has argued that it showed the emergence of a new type of monarchy, 'politically neutral but intervening to promote the public good and broker agreement'. George, she said, 'had reinvented the public role of the sovereign'.[18]

DESPITE THEIR differences, the King eventually came round to Asquith, and spoke warmly of him. The same could not be said of his relationship with Lloyd George, who became prime minister in December 1916 after Asquith lost the confidence of the cabinet over his conduct of the war. The King and the Welsh firebrand had not got off to a good start: at a dinner party some years earlier, when George was Prince of Wales and Lloyd George was chancellor, the prince leaned across the table to the permanent secretary to the Treasury, Sir George Murray, and said in a loud voice: 'I can't think, Sir George, how you can go on serving that damned fellow Lloyd George.'[19]

Despite this indiscretion, there were moments when things were not too bad between them. When George first became King, Lloyd George did his best to be helpful, and after his visit to Balmoral in 1910 he described George as 'a very jolly chap but thank God there's not much in his head'.[20] The following year his Balmoral visit did not go so well. 'The whole atmosphere reeks with Toryism,' he wrote. 'The King is hostile to the bone to all who are working to lift the workmen out of the mire. So is the Queen.'[21] Not all their differences were on matters of political philosophy: when Lloyd George attacked landowners by claiming – absurdly – that their pheasants devoured whole fields of mangold-wurzels (a variety of beet), his howler provoked 'terrific denunciations' from the King, who as a Norfolk countryman knew all about pheasants and, indeed, mangold-wurzels.[22]

After ousting Asquith from Number 10 – essentially by threatening to resign himself, a move that prompted the King to denounce him as 'a blackmailer' – Lloyd George proved surprisingly anxious to please during the early days of his premiership. Responding to some advice from the King about how to deal with a parliamentary question, Lloyd George said: 'I am profoundly impressed by the wisdom of the course suggested by Your Majesty.'[23] Cordial relations did not last for long, however. Until Lloyd George, the prime minister had always written for the sovereign – by hand – a summary of that day's cabinet business, but Lloyd George decided that for the sake of efficiency the cabinet should have its own secretariat and appointed Maurice Hankey as the first cabinet secretary. As a result, instead of receiving a handwritten account from the prime minister, the King was sent printed minutes of each cabinet meeting in the same way as its members. George was deeply distressed at the loss of the personal touch.

Lloyd George's casual way of dealing with the King extended to other areas, such as leaving letters unanswered and failing to turn up to Privy Council meetings without explanation or apology – a far cry from Disraeli's emollient dealings with Queen Victoria. Lloyd George was happy to admit that he treated the King 'abominably'. Frances Stevenson, his mistress, secretary and later his second wife, ticked him off for not paying the King enough attention. She wrote in her diary: 'He gets out of going to the Palace if he can, and has constantly refused invitations to Windsor. He cannot be surprised if the King is a little hurt.' As Kenneth Rose put it, 'Whereas Asquith recognized the need to humour a monarch who could be needlessly loquacious and interfering, Lloyd

George displayed a nonchalance not far removed from contempt.'[24]

The King did not always take this treatment lying down. In February 1917 Lloyd George, who saw Douglas Haig's conduct of the war as unnecessarily wasteful of troops' lives, made a half-baked attempt to place the British forces in France under the command of the new French commander-in-chief, Robert Nivelle. The coup collapsed after Lloyd George failed to win the backing of the cabinet. The King, who was after all the head of the British Army, was not informed of the prime minister's plan in advance – he only found out two days after it was unveiled at a conference in Calais – and later tore a strip off him for being kept in ignorance. The army, he said, would strongly resent being placed 'under the command of a foreign general', and the country would agree.[25] As he berated his prime minister, George, who as a young man had been tasked with writing a digest of Bagehot's *The English Constitution*, was no doubt mindful of the monarch's right to be consulted; if Lloyd George had ever read Bagehot, he managed to put it to the back of his mind.

The business with drink did not help, either. In the spring of 1915, when Lloyd George as chancellor was concerned about the impact of heavy drinking on workers, especially in munitions factories and shipyards, he persuaded the King to set an example by giving up alcohol for the duration of the war and banning it in the royal household. George, who drank only modestly, agreed, but found that his sacrifice was not the national inspiration that he had hoped for. He remained stoical, but in private would allow himself a small moan. 'It is a great bore,' he told his uncle the Duke of Connaught. How strictly he kept to his pledge is an interesting question: according to the Prince of Wales, the future Edward VIII, his father would slope off after dinner 'to attend to a small matter of business'– assumed to be a small glass of port. Queen Mary, who was fond of sparkling Moselle with her dinner, revealed her own feelings to Asquith in one of the colloquialisms she occasionally indulged in: 'We have been carted.'[26] Or, as a more contemporary royal might put it, 'We have been stitched up good and proper.'

IN MARCH 1917 George received bad news from Russia. Revolution had broken out in St Petersburg (at the time known as Petrograd), and Tsar Nicholas II was forced to abdicate. The Tsar was the King's first cousin on his mother's side, and although they only met occasionally, they were fond of each other. 'I am in despair,' the King wrote in his diary. He sent his cousin a telegram saying how distressed he was at what had happened, and assured Nicholas, 'I shall always remain your true and devoted friend.' The telegram never reached him, however; the provisional Russian government, which at the time was trying to protect the ex-Tsar's life, thought it might provoke violence against him. Foreign minister Pavel Milyukov then suggested via the British ambassador that the imperial family be given asylum in England. The Foreign Office stalled, but when the Russian request became more urgent a message was sent from London that the King and the government were prepared to offer the Romanovs asylum.

Unfortunately for the Tsar and his family, the provisional government delayed doing anything about the offer. As Kenneth Rose, who revealed the story in his 1983 biography of George, wrote: 'The delay proved fatal. It allowed those Russians who sought revenge on the fallen Tsar to consolidate their strength; and it prompted the King to have second thoughts about his cousin's future.'

A few days later Stamfordham wrote to foreign secretary Arthur Balfour saying that the King was wondering whether the offer of asylum was wise after all. Balfour showed no interest in backtracking, so some days later Stamfordham wrote another letter in which he said that the King thought the Romanovs' presence in Britain 'would raise all sorts of difficulties'. Just in case that was not enough, that letter was followed by another the same day in which he said their presence 'would be strongly resented by the public, and would undoubtedly compromise the position of the King and the Queen'. Stamfordham finished off by going to see Lloyd George in Downing Street, where he persuaded the prime minister of the merits of his argument. While the King feared for his popularity – there was plenty of evidence that the arrival of the Tsar and Tsarina in England would not go down well – Lloyd George had his own reasons for keeping them out: he wanted to keep on the right side of the new Russian government in order to keep them in the war, and the extremists holding the imperial family under house arrest showed no signs of wanting to let them go.

It is perhaps doubtful that any of this made any difference: even if Britain had sent a warship to the Baltic, it is far from certain that they could have got the imperial family out. But as Rose concluded: 'What does remain certain is that the King, by persuading his government to withdraw their original offer of asylum, deprived the Imperial family of their best, perhaps their only, means of escape.'[27] The family were shot and bayoneted to death by Bolshevik revolutionaries in a basement in Yekaterinburg in July 1918.

DURING THE LATTER years of Lloyd George's term in office his relationship with the King, rarely harmonious at the best of times, was marred by scandal over the sale of honours – which in theory were in the name of the sovereign, but in practice were on the advice of ministers – to boost party funds. The bestowal of honours in return for money or political support was nothing new, but Lloyd George was more systematic and more brazen than his predecessors, charging – via a tout called Maundy Gregory – £10,000 for a knighthood and £40,000 or more for a peerage. Matters came to a head after the notorious 1922 birthday honours list, which included five peerages, four of them for known criminals or tax evaders. The King, who was never happy with the practice, described the ennoblement of Sir Joseph Robinson, a South African gold and diamond magnate who had been convicted of fraud, as 'an insult to the Crown'.[28] Robinson was pressured into turning down his peerage, and the sale of honours was subsequently made illegal.

The coalition government led by Lloyd George had been under strain for some time, and finally collapsed when the Conservatives withdrew in October 1922 after disagreements over the possibility of going to war with Turkey. Lloyd George resigned, and was succeeded by the Conservative Bonar Law, who was in office for just 209 days before retiring the following May with terminal throat cancer.

There then followed two days of intense political melodrama as the King faced a choice between the chancellor, the pipe-smoking, middle-class Stanley Baldwin, and the foreign secretary, the experienced but high-handed and bombastic Lord Curzon. Bonar Law, who was too ill to travel, would not say whom he preferred, so the King's private secretary Lord Stamfordham, who was in London while the King was in Aldershot, asked the former prime minister Arthur Balfour for his advice. Balfour was in Sheringham, where he was meant to be on a golfing holiday but was suffering from phlebitis and unable to walk or stand. Despite his doctor's advice not to travel, such was the urgency suggested by Stamfordham's telegram that he got into his car to make the journey from Norfolk to London.

Stamfordham also asked J. C. C. Davidson, Bonar Law's parliamentary private secretary, for his view. Davidson told Stamfordham that it should be Baldwin, who had honesty, simplicity and balance on his side, while Curzon was unable to inspire confidence in his colleagues. Historians have argued about whether this was also Bonar Law's view or, more importantly, whether the King was given to believe that was the case, but the fact was the King agreed: he thought it was inappropriate to have a prime minister from the House of Lords. This was not yet a constitutional convention, but it was on the way to becoming one. (In an illustration of the nebulous way the constitution changes over time, the Cabinet Office's 1954 precedent book, which laid down rules about the workings of government, said that the passing over of Lord Curzon 'may possibly' represent a new constitutional convention banning peers from being prime minister.[29])

In 1923 perhaps the overwhelming argument in favour of Baldwin was that Labour, by then the official opposition, had no representatives in the Lords. However, the King was aware that his decision would be hurtful to Curzon, who assumed that the job was his – The Times backed him, at least initially, as did Lord Salisbury. George got Stamfordham to summon the foreign secretary to London so he could be told in person before it was made public. Curzon made his way from Somerset to London by train, so confident that his time had come that he spent the journey drawing up plans for his government. When Stamfordham – obviously embarrassed, according to Curzon's account – broke the bad news to him at the foreign secretary's official residence in Carlton House Terrace, Curzon was furious, questioning the principle that no member of the House of Lords could be prime minister and announcing that he would retire from public life in protest. 'We shall see,' a sceptical King wrote in his diary. 'I much regret having hurt his feelings.' Twenty-four hours later Curzon changed his mind and said he would stay at the Foreign Office.[30]

Although George probably made the right choice, the crisis did not show the process by which the Crown appointed a prime minister in a good light. The idea that the decision should be taken after a series of secret conversations between the sovereign's private secretary and a select group of political insiders did not accord with the newly democratic spirit of the times. It would, however, not be the last time that the sovereign made a decision about the appointment of a prime minister after taking confidential soundings.

IN NOVEMBER 1923 Stanley Baldwin committed a massive political blunder which paved the way for the outcome that George dreaded most: a Labour government. But the way in which events unfolded would surprise many, including the King himself. Baldwin, who wanted to combat unemployment by introducing protectionist trade tariffs, felt that he should call a general election to give himself the mandate he needed. Many of his colleagues were unenthusiastic, and the Tory leader in the Lords, Lord Salisbury, called it 'a profound mistake'. He was not the only one who was worried. 'The King is really afraid of a Labour government,' wrote the Conservative politician and diarist Lord Crawford, 'probably more so than circumstances justify.'

Salisbury was right. The election in early December saw the Tories lose 86 seats, leaving them with 258 against 191 for Labour and 158 for the Liberals. It was not exactly a triumph for Labour, let alone for the Liberals, but it was a disaster for the Tories. Baldwin initially wanted to resign, but was persuaded by the King and others to hold on until Parliament reopened in the new year to see how negotiations played out. This was not to keep Labour out, but the exact opposite: Baldwin thought it was politically unwise for the Conservatives and Liberals to unite with the sole purpose of keeping Labour out. Surprisingly, the King had come to the same conclusion. He told Davidson that 'a Socialist Government would have an opportunity of learning their administrative duties and responsibilities under favourable conditions and that it was essential that their rights under the Constitution should in no way be impaired'.[31] But that did not mean that there was no nervousness at the palace.

There had been a lot of excitable speculation in the newspapers about what a Labour government would do, fuelled by some inflammatory talk from the Clydeside group of left-wing MPs, and the Labour leader Ramsay MacDonald got his colleague Jimmy Thomas – of whom more later – to calm nerves at the palace. Thomas telephoned Stamfordham to tell him that a Labour government would conduct policy 'on sound lines', adding: 'In spite of all the evil prognostications of the Press, no extreme legislation will be introduced or violent administrative changes carried out.' In reply the relieved Stamfordham told Thomas that the King felt no uneasiness because 'he never doubted their loyalty or patriotism and felt sure the best interests of the Country would be the primary aim of their policy'.[32] Reassured by his conversation with Thomas, Stamfordham decided that 'the sooner the Labour Party comes into power the better'. 'Personally I am not alarmed,' he wrote to a friend, 'and, unless they are upset by their own extremists, it would not surprise me were they to remain in office for some time, during which they may do considerable good.'[33]

The King opened Parliament on 15 January, and Stanley Baldwin was defeated and resigned a week later. Later that day MacDonald was sworn in as a member of the Privy Council, and was then asked by the King to form a government. Their first conversation went better than anyone could have expected. George talked so much that MacDonald could hardly get a word in edgeways to thank him. 'Most friendly' was the new prime minister's verdict. At their second meeting, when MacDonald was actually appointed PM, the King brought up what he called an 'unfortunate incident' at the party's victory rally at the Albert Hall, at which 'The Red Flag' was sung. MacDonald said he hoped the King would understand the difficult position he was in regarding the extremists in his party, and said that if he had tried to stop the singing of the socialist anthem there would have been 'a riot'.

Both sides went away pleased with their first encounter. 'He impressed me very much,' the King wrote in his diary, 'he wishes to do the right thing. Today 23 years ago dear Grandmama died, I wonder what she would have thought of a Labour Govt.' MacDonald wrote in his diary: 'King plays the game straight, though I feel he is apprehensive. It wd. be a miracle were he not.'[34]

Despite his nervousness, and despite his Tory instincts, which were so deep-seated that they used to drive Lloyd George into paroxysms of rage, George managed to have good relations with his new Labour ministers. Davidson, chancellor of the Duchy of Lancaster in the previous Conservative government, described George as a 'marvellous' man who managed to persuade the Labour party that he was entirely neutral. 'It was remarkable how he hid from the world that he was an absolutely dyed-in-the-wool conservative.'[35] After the new cabinet had collected their seals of office the King was asked what he thought about the change of government. He was said to have replied: 'My grandfather would have hated it; my father could hardly have tolerated it; but I march with the times.'[36] George even had positive things to say about the sort of out-and-out left-wingers who wanted to abolish the monarchy. After receiving health minister John Wheatley, a former miner and publican and leading member of the Clydeside group of MPs, the King wrote in his diary: 'He is an extreme socialist & comes from Glasgow. I had a very interesting conversation with him.'[37]

One obstacle to smooth relations between the government and the palace was the question of dress. George was a stickler for correct attire – he once told off the Conservative lord chancellor Lord Birkenhead for failing to wear a silk top hat at a Downing Street conference, a rebuke that prompted a decidedly snippy response from Birkenhead[38] – but the new Labour ministers were not of a class to own court dress. It soon became a political issue. For a levee, or formal reception, at the palace, guests were supposed to wear court uniform of white breeches and white stockings, and some ministers flatly refused. The King tried to be conciliatory, conceding that full dress was too expensive – it cost the equivalent of more than £4,000 in today's money – and saying that they could wear black evening dress and knee breeches. Whatever happened, he pleaded, everyone should do the same. His words fell on deaf ears. At the first levee three ministers, including MacDonald and Thomas, came in court uniform, while the others wore black evening dress.[39]

Other, more substantial changes were also introduced. Some of the grander positions in the royal household such as lord chamberlain and lord steward were traditionally political appointments, but as Kenneth Rose observed, 'Labour simply could not produce the men of aristocratic lineage and private means who traditionally occupied these great offices of State.'

Stamfordham had long been trying to make the lord chamberlain a non-political, permanent post; now that Labour was in office, both sides were only too happy to make the change.[40]

Harold Nicolson, George's official biographer, described the relations between MacDonald and the King as being of 'unhesitating' mutual confidence. He wrote: 'The King was attracted by Mr MacDonald's quiet moderation, by his unfailing considerateness, by the deliberate blend in his manner and voice of silk and tweed, of cosmopolitan distinction and common sense.' For his part, MacDonald was flattered and even 'dazzled' by the King: by his friendliness, his eagerness to help the government, and his candour.[41] Their relationship was made easier by the fact that MacDonald went out of his way to keep his sovereign informed, a distinct contrast with predecessors such as Campbell-Bannerman, who had been 'almost insultingly casual' in keeping the King up to date with government decision-making.[42] Michael Adeane, Stamfordham's grandson, who served as Queen Elizabeth II's private secretary for nineteen years, said: 'One reason King George V got on so well with Labour ministers was that he found them so much more agreeable than Lloyd George to deal with.'[43] Jane Ridley, however, believes that there was rather more calculation to the King's warmth and support. The King, she wrote, 'needed MacDonald in order to contain the deferential, respectable working class within a moderate Labour Party and split them off from the Bolsheviks and Red Clydesiders'.[44] Whatever the reasons for the warmth of their relationship, it served both sides well, and shows the importance of the personal chemistry between monarch and prime minister.

MacDonald was not the only minister to enjoy a cordial relationship with the King. Jimmy Thomas was a Welsh former railwayman who as a union official had been a key player in the first national rail strike in the summer of 1911. As an MP, he had been used by Ramsay MacDonald to liaise with Buckingham Palace because he already knew the King: when the 1911 strike was settled just after midnight, Thomas was given a message that George wanted to know how the railwaymen viewed the settlement, and he was to ring the palace at once. As his biography noted, it was a contact that was 'to prosper and endure'.[45] Eight years later, during negotiations over another strike, Thomas – by now general secretary of the National Union of Railwaymen – was received in audience at Buckingham Palace. 'He is a good and loyal man,' the King wrote in his diary.[46]

Given the job of colonial secretary in 1924, Thomas threw himself into his work with enthusiasm. It was said that when he turned up at the Colonial Office for the first time he said he was there to make sure there was 'no mucking about with the British Empire'.[47] Indeed, he was loyal to a fault. He was also not one of those Labour ministers who baulked at embracing palace rigmarole. The diarist Chips Channon recounts how at a state ball Thomas was asked 'by a white-wanded equerry' if he would escort the Duchess of Atholl into the ball. 'Rather,' replied Thomas in a loud voice, before leaving his 'house-keepery little wife to fend for herself'.[48] Davidson was referring to Jimmy Thomas in particular when he said that the King managed his relations with MacDonald 'and the rest of them' so well that they became 'more royalist than the King'.[49] The idea that working-class ministers are susceptible to sentimentality about the monarchy would crop up again in the Labour governments of the 1960s and 70s.

In his biography of George V, Kenneth Rose, an outstanding snob, described Thomas as 'a man of coarse speech and coarser wit'.[50] That may well have been the case, but his manners – and his wit – went down well with the King. George particularly liked a quip Thomas made on the subject of knee breeches at the expense of his fellow minister Sidney Webb and his wife, Beatrice, the sociologist and social reformer. 'Of course Sidney Webb can't put 'em on,' he said. 'His wife wears 'em.'[51] One story, recounted by Harold Nicolson, goes that when the King was suffering from septicaemia in 1929 he was visited by Thomas, 'who was always apt to regale His Majesty with ribald jokes'. Nicolson wrote: 'The King laughed so uproariously at one of Mr Thomas's stories that he had a further relapse.'[52] That story may be apocryphal, but the two men were undoubtedly close: on one occasion later in George's reign Thomas was seen walking across the lawn at a Buckingham Palace garden party with his arm around the King's shoulder, both 'laughing their heads off'.[53] George also never held back in advancing his friend's cause. When Labour was re-elected in 1929, he suggested him as foreign secretary, although MacDonald had other plans.

There was also a suggestion – not from the King – that Thomas might become Viceroy of India, although that came to nothing. Kenneth Rose suggested that he might not have had the diplomatic skills required, recalling Thomas's reply to the Prince of Wales – David, the future Edward VIII – who asked him about a trip to west Africa, where children were dying of dysentery and malaria: 'Gawd, it's a bugger of a country.' Rose also quoted Queen Mary's assessment of him: 'He is such a very straightforward man.'[54] If that sounds reminiscent of one of the acid putdowns uttered by Maggie Smith as *Downton Abbey*'s Dowager Duchess of Grantham, then it is as well to note that Mary appeared to hold Thomas in some esteem. During a stay at Balmoral in 1933 he and the King took long walks together during which George poured out his family troubles – presumably focusing mainly on the errant

Prince of Wales. When he said goodbye to the Queen, Mary exclaimed: 'I can't tell you what a lot of good you've done the King and how you've cheered him up.'[55]

There was another facet to their relationship, one that crops up from time to time in the history of the modern royal family: how royals get politicians they trust to help them in moments of family strife. We have seen this before, when Queen Victoria got Lord Palmerston to write to the miscreant Prince of Wales in an attempt to get him to mend his ways. This instance involved another Prince of Wales, David, whose affair with Wallis Simpson was causing his parents much anguish. The story comes from Lord Lee of Fareham, a snobbish figure who was no friend of Thomas (he declared that 'his inexhaustible vein of vulgar humour and consistent dropping of aitches had misled the King and Queen into believing that he was an authentic spokesman of the "common people" and a rugged patriot as well'). Lee wrote in his memoirs that Thomas had boasted of having been 'consulted by the Queen', who, he alleged, had begged him to use his influence with the prince, saying, 'You must 'elp us, Jim; this 'ere bloody thing 'as got to stop.'[56]

George also recruited prime ministers in his efforts to solve thorny family problems. When he was having trouble with his younger son Prince George, who wanted to marry a rather fast young lady called Poppy Baring, who was, in the King's eyes, wholly unsuitable, he asked Stanley Baldwin to write to the young man. 'I only hope it may have the desired effect & stop this infernal thing going on,' George wrote.[57] When Ramsay MacDonald was in Number 10 and the King was having difficulty in persuading David to give up the dangerous practice of riding in point-to-points, he got the prime minister to write to his son. 'Pray do not put me down as an interfering person who having no zest in life himself wishes to knock it out of others,' MacDonald wrote. But if the prince were to have an accident, he said, 'who could take your place?' David carried on regardless.[58]

George died before Jimmy Thomas left public life in disgrace. Found responsible for leaking Budget details to stock market speculators, he resigned from the government and the Commons. When he went to return his seals of office to the new King, he slumped on a chair in tears as Edward VIII tried in vain to comfort him. As he left the room he paused to say, 'Thank God your old dad is not alive to see this.'[59]

The bond between Thomas and the King is ambiguous in its implications. Was it mutual admiration or political calculation? Did George entertain Thomas because he thought it was good for his image, or because he liked him? The evidence seems to point overwhelmingly to the latter, and this was not the first time that a member of the royal family has formed a strong bond with a member of the working classes; Queen Victoria and John Brown, her Highland servant, is an obvious example. And it would happen again a quarter of a century later when Ernest Bevin, who started his working life as a labourer and lorry driver, became a palace favourite. Decades later Tony Blair would write in his memoirs of the royal preference for '"authentic" Labour people ... who spoke with an accent and who fitted their view of how such people should be'.[60]

I believe that the King was genuinely fond of Jimmy Thomas. But there is one piece of evidence that, although hardly conclusive, offers a contrary view, and it would be wrong not to mention it. Sir Frederick Ponsonby (known as Fritz), keeper of the privy purse, passed on to his brother Arthur Ponsonby, a Labour MP, the King's opinions of his first Labour ministers. George liked MacDonald, he said, but 'quite saw through Thomas – thought him a poseur and not genuine'.[61]

THE 1924 LABOUR government lasted little more than nine months before it was brought down in a general election dominated by talk of the communist threat. Stanley Baldwin returned to Downing Street, but just under five years later made another of his political miscalculations by calling a general election which he expected to win. He didn't. The result was a hung Parliament, with Labour gaining 287 seats, the Tories 260 and the Liberals 59. When MacDonald arrived at Windsor for his audience on 5 June 1929 he found the King, who was convalescing from a long illness, in his bedroom wearing a brightly coloured Chinese dressing-gown. He kissed hands while George remained seated on a sofa and actually forgot to ask MacDonald to form a government. The constitution survived this oversight. 'Nothing,' the King said, 'could have been nicer than [MacDonald's] manner and all that he said about my illness and the attitude of his party towards me during the long and anxious time.'[62]

One issue that caused some difficulty between the palace and the government at this time was the Soviet Union. When MacDonald first took office in 1924 Stamfordham warned him against restoring diplomatic relations with Russia because the King would find it personally abhorrent to shake hands with any representative of the regime that had murdered his cousins. When MacDonald returned to power Stamfordham renewed his plea, but with the government insistent on recognising the Soviet ambassador, international diplomacy trumped the King's personal feelings. A compromise was reached by which the King received the Soviet envoy, but only shook hands in private.[63]

Two years later Britain was in the grip of an economic crisis following the stock market crash of 1929. Unemployment was approaching three million, exports had halved and the government was under pressure to introduce severe cuts in spending, in particular a reduction in unemployment benefit. The cabinet was split on the issue, and on the morning of 23 August 1931 a downhearted MacDonald went to tell the King that with the threat of ministerial resignations hanging over him he was not sure he would be able to carry on.

The King refused to accept MacDonald's resignation and suggested the formation of a national government – an idea that had been floating around for some months – under MacDonald, made up of Liberals and Conservatives and whatever Labour people MacDonald could get to follow him. A cabinet meeting later that day saw MacDonald fail to persuade his colleagues to agree to cuts, and eight ministers resigned. He returned to the palace intending to resign himself, but once more the King talked him out of it, telling him he was 'the only man to lead the country through this crisis'. MacDonald was torn: forming a national government would mean breaking with the political party he had helped found in 1900. But he also could not ignore the entreaties of his King: as Jane Ridley caustically puts it, 'he was a snob and sensitive to royalty'. Even if she overstates her case, it is clear that the strong bond between this monarch and prime minister had a significant impact on the political history of the country. The following day the three party leaders met at Buckingham Palace, where they were all but instructed to form a national government. The King, MacDonald wrote in his diary, was 'not merely the facilitator of the National Government, but the instigator of it'. As for George, he said that MacDonald had 'burnt his boats' with Labour but had done the right thing for the good of the country.[64]

MacDonald and the tiny coterie of ministers who followed him – including Jimmy Thomas – were swiftly expelled from the Labour Party, and he has been vilified for what was seen as his betrayal ever since. In the election that ensued three months later the National Government won by a landslide, while Labour was reduced to a rump of fifty-two MPs. Worn down by age and ill health, MacDonald increasingly became a figurehead while others did the work of running the country, and in 1935 he stood down in favour of Stanley Baldwin.

As the King lay dying in January 1936 MacDonald attended his last Privy Council meeting at Sandringham. George was barely able to sign the order paper, and as the counsellors left the room he dismissed them with a nod and a smile. 'I was the last out,' MacDonald wrote, 'and I shall never forget the look illuminated by attention . . . my final farewell to a gracious and kingly friend and a master whom I have served with all my heart.'[65] The King died later that night; MacDonald died the following year, aged seventy-one.

There is no doubting that George was a constitutional monarch, but not in the way we understand that today. He played the role of mediator when he thought it was necessary to avoid civil war in Ireland, and he took an active role in the appointment of prime ministers when it was called for, neither of which would be acceptable in the twenty-first century. But he managed to adapt to the increasingly democratic Britain of the early twentieth century, which had seen women given the vote in 1918 and then ten years later the same voting rights as men: as he put it himself, he marched with the times. His reign was also marked by relatively harmonious relations between Buckingham Palace and Downing Street. The same could not be said for the reign that followed.

CHAPTER THREE

LUNCH ON TUESDAYS

WHEN EDWARD VIII acceded to the throne in January 1936 Winston Churchill gave a characteristically florid tribute to the new King, expressing his 'heartfelt wishes that a reign which has been so nobly begun may be blessed with peace and true glory; and that in the long swing of events Your Majesty's name will shine in history as the bravest and best beloved of all the sovereigns who have ever worn the island Crown'.[1] Edward did not, however, shine in history: his short, calamitous reign ended in abdication after less than a year, his name for ever tarnished. During the crisis over Edward's relationship with Wallis Simpson, Churchill remained a loyal and supportive friend, albeit at the cost of considerable damage to his own political career, but Edward's subsequent behaviour meant that they did not remain good friends. While the former King languished in exile, Churchill staged a remarkable political recovery, and as Britain's wartime prime minister became a trusted friend and confidant of George VI.

Churchill, however, was not always a friend of kings. Edward VII thought he was a cad, and George V regarded him as impossible. But to truly understand the turbulent nature of Churchill's relationship with the royal family, and indeed how close those ties were, one has to wind back the clock to before Winston was even born, to his father, Lord Randolph Churchill, the third son of the future 7th Duke of Marlborough. Randolph was a precociously influential figure in the Conservative party, a radical with a talent for invective who might have gone far had it not been for a tactically misjudged resignation when he was chancellor. He was ambitious and energetic, but suffered from mood swings and could be phenomenally rude.

A friend of the then Prince of Wales — Bertie, the future Edward VII — Randolph met an American beauty, Jennie Jerome, at a reception at Cowes given by the prince in 1873, the year before Randolph became an MP. Three days later they were engaged. Randolph's father disapproved of the match — Jennie's father had just lost all his money in the financial crash of that year — as did his older brother the Marquess of Blandford, and Jennie's parents would not let the marriage take place unless the Marlboroughs approved. In desperation Randolph appealed to his friend Francis Knollys, the prince's private secretary, for help. After Bertie wrote to Blandford arguing in favour of the match, the family relented and Randolph and Jennie were married in Paris in April of that year. Among their wedding presents was a silver cigarette box from the Prince of Wales. Their son Winston was born at the end of November. Decades later Bertie — by then Edward VII — would say of him, 'If it had not been for me and the Queen, that young man would never have been in existence.' As he explained, 'The Duke and Duchess [of Marlborough] both objected to Randolph's marriage, and it was entirely owing to us that they gave way.'[2]

A couple of years later Bertie and Randolph had a massive falling-out which would lead to Randolph being forced to leave the country. Randolph's older brother Blandford was having an affair with Edith, the wife of the Earl of Aylesford. Aylesford – nicknamed Sporting Joe – wanted to divorce his wife, which would have caused a massive scandal, not least because everything came to a head when he was in India with Bertie. An added complication was that the prince was suspected – although it is impossible to be certain – of also having had an affair with Edith. Randolph got his hands on some flirtatious letters that Bertie had written to Edith, and showed them to Bertie's wife, Alix, who until then had managed to pretend that the prince was the faithful husband he so clearly was not. Randolph also threatened to publish them unless Bertie talked Aylesford out of divorce.

In the end the Aylesfords did not divorce but agreed to a legal separation. However, Randolph had behaved so outrageously – for a long time he refused to apologise to the prince, and when he did so it was in as ungracious a manner as he could manage – he was forced into exile. He went first to America, a decision that Jennie described as the result of having had 'serious differences of opinion with various influential people'.[3]

Eight years later Randolph's banishment was over, and by 1886 the two old friends were reconciled. Randolph was extremely grateful for Bertie's kindness; however, he did not have long to live, dying in the December of that year from what was thought at the time to be syphilis but may have been a brain tumour. Meanwhile Jennie had become a good friend of the prince, although quite how good a friend is open to question. Given Bertie's reputation, and indeed Jennie's – she had a string of lovers during her marriage and afterwards

– some assume that they had an affair, but there is no proof. They saw each other often, and in his letters Bertie would call her *ma chère amie*.[4] They remained close for several decades.

FOR A WHILE at least Bertie seemed to approve of young Winston. As Prince of Wales he always took an interest in him, and when Churchill wrote a book in 1898 about the British campaign on the North West Frontier, the prince – not generally a great reader – wrote him a letter praising it as 'excellent'.[5] As King he had him to stay at Balmoral in 1902 – which, as Roy Jenkins pointed out in his biography of Churchill, was a rare honour for a twenty-seven-year-old backbencher. 'I have been vy kindly treated here by the King, who has gone out of his way to be nice to me,' Churchill wrote to his mother. 'It has been most pleasant & easy going & today the stalking was excellent, tho I missed my stags.' He also gave his mother, who was due to see the King a few days later, strict instructions to 'gush to him about my having written to you saying how much etc etc I had enjoyed myself here'.[6]

However, after a few years on the throne Edward became increasingly exasperated with Churchill, who had become a Conservative MP in 1900 only to defect to the Liberals four years later. They disagreed on a whole range of issues, but more than anything the King just did not like his style. Churchill was pugnacious, ebullient and not afraid of making enemies, of which he had a considerable number; the King found it all horribly grating. When in 1905 Arthur Balfour's government was in trouble and the prime minister was being regularly pummelled in the Commons, the King let Balfour know that he was 'disgusted' by Churchill's 'crude and vulgar attacks'.[7] After the change of government at the end of 1905, Churchill became a junior minister, but the King remained unimpressed. He wrote to the Prince of Wales (later George V): 'As for Mr Churchill, he is *almost more* of [a] cad in office than he was in opposition.'[8] He did, however, occasionally feel more positively about Churchill, once sending him a decidedly pointed letter commending him for becoming 'a reliable Minister and above all a serious politician which can only be obtained by putting country above party'. He stopped short of adding, 'and not a moment too soon', but that was no doubt understood.

The rest of Edward's reign, however, was punctuated by differences with Churchill: over naval rearmament in the face of the threat from Germany, over the Parliament Bill and over Ireland. During the 1909–10 political crisis sparked off by the People's Budget, Churchill made a speech that annoyed the palace so much (on a technical point over whether the sovereign or the prime minister granted peerages) that Francis Knollys – who detested Churchill – wrote a letter to *The Times* dissociating the palace from the views expressed. 'He [Knollys] and the King must really have gone mad,' Churchill wrote to his wife.[9]

Despite this, Churchill was underneath it all a devoted monarchist, and he wanted to please his King. When he became home secretary in February 1910 he inherited the task of writing a daily letter to the King on proceedings in Parliament, a job that had previously been the responsibility of the prime minister, but since Campbell-Bannerman's premiership had been delegated to the home secretary. Churchill would write his daily 400–500 words as he sat on the front bench. As Roy Jenkins observed, for a less fluent minister this would have been a real burden, but Churchill approached the task with gusto. 'What he did was pour out a stream of uninhibited consciousness interspersed with whatever aphorisms came into his mind as he went along . . . The whole exercise encapsulated his attitude to the monarchy: a great respect for the institution . . . combined with a total confidence and freedom in the expression of his own views.'[10]

Edward VII died in May 1910. In his final hours Winston Churchill arrived at Buckingham Palace, claiming that it was his right as home secretary to witness the demise of the monarch. He was obliged to stay downstairs, however, and did not even make it as far as the antechamber to the King's bedroom. Afterwards Queen Alexandra blamed Edward's death on Asquith and Churchill and all the pressure they had put on the King during the constitutional crisis over the Parliament Bill. 'They have killed him, they have killed him,' she cried. In fact he died of emphysema and heart failure, and as Jane Ridley wrote, it was not Asquith and Churchill who did for him, but his cigars.[11]

Edward lay in state in Westminster Hall, the first time that the ceremony had ever been held there for a sovereign; the last lying-in-state for a king had been for George III, at Windsor. An estimated half a million people filed past over three days. After the doors closed for the last time, four cars drove into Palace Yard and the Churchill family got out, led by Winston and including his mother, Jennie. When they tried to enter, Sir Schomberg McDonnell, the keeper of Westminster Hall, refused to let them in. A heated argument ensued, with Churchill insisting it was his right, but McDonnell stood his ground. Eventually they left. Afterwards McDonnell described it as 'an amazing instance of vulgarity and indecency, of which I should not have thought that even Churchill was capable'.[12] Fifty-five years later Churchill had his own lying-in-state at Westminster Hall: for three days the hall was kept open for twenty-three hours, and some 320,000 people paid their respects.

*

AS WE HAVE SEEN, George V learned an early lesson about Winston Churchill when as Prince of Wales he told him that he regarded Asquith as 'not quite a gentleman', a remark that Churchill promptly repeated back to Asquith. Their relationship did not improve when George became King. A few days after his accession, Churchill had a formal audience with the new King during which he told him that he thought a great change was necessary in the constitution. Given that his father had not even been buried at this point, this was a remarkably tactless and insensitive thing to say. Smarting from Churchill's lack of sympathy, George said merely that he was against all violent change.

Fortunately for Churchill, the King also had cause to be grateful to him. A rumour had been floating around for many years that George was a bigamist. This had first reached him in 1893 when he was about to become engaged to Princess May of Teck, and for a while he had done his best to laugh it off. 'I say, May,' he told her, 'we can't get married after all. I hear I've got a wife and three children.' After he became King a republican newspaper, published in Paris but sent free to every MP, claimed that while serving in the Royal Navy he had secretly but legally married one of the daughters of the admiral commanding the Mediterranean fleet based at Malta. This would, of course, have made his children by May, including the future Kings Edward VIII and George VI, illegitimate.

His advisers were in two minds about what to do: if they sued, it would draw attention to an article most people were unaware of, and there was also the danger of George being called as a witness, although his lawyers would argue that the King could not himself give evidence. However, Churchill, who had taken personal charge of the case in his capacity as home secretary, was bullishly in favour of going ahead in order to clear the King's name, whatever the risks. His determination paid off: the author of the article, Edward Mylius, was prosecuted for criminal libel, found guilty and sentenced to twelve months' imprisonment. Within hours of the verdict being delivered a relieved George wrote to Churchill in his own hand to thank him for his role in proving 'to the world at large the baseness of this cruel and abominable libel'.[13]

Churchill was sufficiently in favour to be invited to Balmoral, where he greatly enjoyed the stalking. 'Quite the best day's sport I have had in this country,' he told his wife. 'Four good stags and home early . . . I hope they won't think I shot too many.'[14] He had also resumed writing the parliamentary letters that he had first written for Edward VII. If George V was a less sophisticated man than his father, Churchill did not temper his style to suit his new audience, although possibly there were fewer jokes. One letter, however, produced an extraordinary reaction from the King, prompting a row that lasted a whole week and even involved the prime minister. This concerned the debate on the right to work, and included a reference to 'tramps and wastrels' and what to do about them. Churchill – the same Churchill who had been so rude about the House of Lords – added a provocative final line: 'It must not however be forgotten that there are idlers and wastrels at both ends of the social scale.'

This kind of impertinence went down very badly at the palace. Knollys wrote to the prime minister's private secretary complaining that Churchill's views were 'very socialistic' and that his remark about idlers and wastrels was 'superfluous'. Downing Street passed on the letter to Churchill, whose reply – sent directly to the King – showed a quite remarkable refusal to back down. While expressing 'deep regret' at incurring the King's displeasure, he said he had just been doing what he had done when Edward VII was on the throne, that is to say, writing 'freely and frankly' on the debates in the House of Commons, while also adding 'expressions of personal opinion'. Given that there were excellent accounts of the proceedings at Westminster in the daily newspapers, Churchill said he would have 'serious difficulty' in writing the parliamentary letter if what the King wanted was just a narrative of the debate, as he feared that 'in a moment of inadvertence or fatigue some phrase or expression may escape him' that might produce 'an unfavourable impression' on the King. As he was very busy, he concluded, perhaps it would be best if some other minister did the job.

This response – a masterpiece, Roy Jenkins suggested, of dumb insolence – went down equally badly. 'I don't think the tone of the letter is quite a proper one,' wrote Knollys, 'nor has he taken the matter in the right way.' He told Churchill that the King just wished that he had suppressed the remark about idlers and wastrels, and added: 'The King directs me to add that your letters are always instructive and interesting and he would be sorry if he were to receive no further ones from you in the future.' A stand-off ensued, and more letters were fired back and forth between Churchill, Buckingham Palace and Downing Street. Churchill remained as combative as ever, but in the end agreed to continue writing the parliamentary letters. They were perhaps a little shorter and duller at first, but Churchill could not restrain himself for long, and was soon back to his old form.[15] History seems to be on Churchill's side here: Kenneth Rose concluded that the episode was an error of judgement on the King's part – he certainly should not have felt obliged to defend society wastrels from Churchill's contempt – but one provoked by Winston's character more than anything else. George just did not like the cut of his jib. His father thought Churchill was a cad, and so did he.[16]

*

WINSTON CHURCHILL was made first lord of the Admiralty by Asquith in 1911, and remained in this post for the first year of the First World War. It was a role that gave him plenty of scope for more disagreements with the King. When he was first appointed, the King liked the way Churchill was all in favour of naval rearmament (which had not always been the case), but was less keen on the plan to withdraw battle-ships from the Mediterranean to protect British waters. The King thought the Mediterranean was important, and said so. Churchill did not appreciate his contribution. 'The King talked more stupidly about the Navy than I have ever heard him before,' he wrote to his wife in May 1912. 'Really it is disheartening to hear this cheap and silly drivel with which he lets himself be filled up.'

Churchill's tactlessness and obstinacy got the better of him when he suggested that one of the battleships being built in 1911–12 should commemorate Oliver Cromwell. When the name was submitted to the King, George replied that His Majesty's Ship *Oliver Cromwell* could have no place in the Royal Navy. Churchill tried submitting the name again a year later, with the same result. Stubbornly undefeated, he wrote to the King's private secretary, Lord Stamfordham: 'Oliver Cromwell was one of the founders of the Navy, and scarcely any man did so much for it.' Cromwell, he maintained, had also been part of the forces 'which, through a long succes-sion of Princes, have brought His Majesty to the Throne of a Constitutional and a Protestant Country'. He concluded: 'The bitterness of the rebellions and tyrannies of the past has long ceased to stir men's minds; but the achievements of the country and of its greatest men endure.'

Stamfordham remained unconvinced, not least given that the turmoil in Ireland showed that 'the bitterness of the rebellions and tyrannies of the past' had by no means 'ceased to stir men's minds'. It was a good point well made, but the clincher was a note from Prince Louis of Battenberg (father of the 1st Earl Mountbatten of Burma), who was about to become first sea lord, telling Churchill that when it came to naming ships the sovereign's decision was final. Prince Louis also warned: 'I am inclined to think that the Service as a whole would go against you in this choice.' For once Churchill knew he was beaten, and dropped the matter.[17]

The King and Churchill had a later significant difference of opinion over Admiral John Fisher – known to all as Jacky – who had been first sea lord between 1904 and 1910. Fisher was an innovator and brilliant strategist who had modernised the navy, but was also autocratic and imperious. He and the King had known each other since they were in the navy together in 1882, but their initial friendship soon soured and was replaced by a lingering feud as George became more disillusioned with Fisher's ruthless methods. (Despite rarely showing sensitivity to the feelings of others, Fisher was a wonderful dancer. Grand Duchess Olga, sister of Tsar Nicholas II, once wrote to him: 'I believe, dear Admiral, that I would walk to England to have another waltz with you.') In 1914, when Churchill needed to appoint a new first sea lord and decided to bring the seventy-three-year-old Fisher out of retirement, the King was fiercely opposed. He could do nothing to stop Churchill but made sure that his disapproval was noted by writing to Asquith that he only signed the appointment 'with some reluctance and misgivings'.

For all that Churchill had championed Fisher, having two such powerful and incendiary characters working in close proximity was a recipe for disaster; and so it proved. In the winter of 1914–15 Churchill became an ardent supporter of a plan to relieve pressure on Britain's Russian ally in the Caucasus by forcing a passage through the Dardanelles and capturing Constantinople. Fisher was against it from the start, arguing that the North Sea was where the naval war should be fought. The Gallipoli campaign, as it became known, was one of the great disasters of the war. It should have been an integrated naval and military operation, but Churchill had pressed for a solely naval attack, and it was only six days before the naval bombardment began that the decision was taken to send troops. 'The detachment was too little and too late,' wrote Jenkins, 'and one of the First World War's human catastrophes resulted.'[18] In the nine-month campaign 46,000 Allied and 65,000 Turkish troops died.

Although he had been proved right, Fisher behaved appallingly, resigning at the height of the Gallipoli fighting. Persuaded by Asquith to return, he then made such outrageous demands as a condition of his reinstatement that Asquith thought he had gone mad and accepted his resignation after all. In the crisis that followed the campaign Asquith formed a coalition government with the Conservatives, and Churchill, who was regarded by the Commons as being most to blame for the catastrophe, was demoted to chancellor of the Duchy of Lancaster, a sinecure. The King could not have been more relieved. 'I am glad the Prime Minister is going to have a National Government,' he told the Queen. 'Only by that means can we get rid of Churchill from Admiralty . . . He is the real danger.' Churchill, he wrote in his diary, 'has become impossible'.[19]

Even with Churchill sidelined, the animosity continued: George did not like it when Winston criticised the appalling human cost of the Somme campaign, and when Lloyd George ousted Asquith in 1916, one of the Conservatives' conditions was that Churchill should be denied office, which suited the King well. Churchill had put up with his non-job for five months before resigning to command an infantry battalion in France. It was only in 1917 that Lloyd George felt it was safe to bring him back as minister of munitions.

Time, however, is a great healer, and when Stanley Baldwin formed a new government after the collapse of the first Labour administration in 1924, to the King's astonishment he brought back Churchill as chancellor of the exchequer. Churchill had begun the process of returning to the Conservative fold, and the King's mistrust had softened, but it would be a long time before he fully gained the trust of the royal family.

IN THE EARLY 1920s, despite being a government minister – he was made colonial secretary in 1921 – Churchill led quite a surprisingly convivial social life ('rackety' was the word used by Roy Jenkins); and that involved seeing a fair amount of the Prince of Wales, the future Edward VIII. He wrote of one party he attended: 'Unhappily in dancing I trod with my heel upon the P. of W. toe & made him yelp. But he bore it vy well – & no malice.'[20] Indeed, the prince would later come to owe Churchill a considerable debt of gratitude for his support during the abdication crisis – not that it did either of them any good. In the meantime, they kept up their acquaintance, even friendship: Churchill would have him to lunch at Buck's Club, to talk 'polo and politics'.[21] Later, during the years when Churchill was politically out of favour as well as financially down on his luck, the prince was among a group of wealthy friends who clubbed together to buy him a car, an expensive Daimler.[22]

When Edward VIII acceded to the throne in January 1936 some of those closest to him were concerned that trouble lay ahead in the form of his lover, the American divorcee Wallis Simpson. At that point she had only been divorced once, being still married to Ernest Simpson; that marriage was fated not to last the year, however. Churchill was firmly on the King's side, and could not see what the fuss was about. Meanwhile the ageing Baldwin, a prime minister on his way out, found himself having to grapple with a growing crisis. When Honest Stan, as he was known, was first told that the King wanted to marry Mrs Simpson he refused to believe it. He knew what was going on, but was slow to get involved, a reluctance for which he has since been criticised. Not that he approved: as he told war secretary Duff Cooper, 'If she were what I call a respectable whore, I wouldn't mind.'[23]

Over the summer Edward's obsession with Mrs Simpson became ever more glaringly obvious – her appearances with the King were even included in the Court Circular – and the problem became harder to ignore. 'I have grown to hate that woman,' Baldwin told a senior civil servant that autumn. 'She has done more to damage the monarchy in nine months than Victoria and George the Fifth did to repair it in half a century.'[24] In October Edward's private secretary Alec Hardinge, who was increasingly worried about what was going on, learned that Mrs Simpson's divorce case was impending and begged Baldwin to talk to the King. His hope was to stop the divorce and to get Edward to be more discreet in his dealings with Mrs Simpson.

The mild-mannered Baldwin called on the King at Fort Belvedere, his Windsor home, where he surprised Edward by asking for a whisky when it was still mid-morning. As they sat in front of the fire in the octagonal drawing room, each smoking his pipe, Baldwin set out his stall, telling the King that he couldn't 'go on like this and get away with it' because the public would not stand for it. When he finally asked the King if he could not have the Simpson divorce put off, Edward brushed him off. 'I have no right to interfere with the affairs of an individual,' he said disingenuously. 'It would be wrong were I to attempt to influence Mrs Simpson just because she happens to be a friend of the King's.'

Afterwards the two men had very different recollections of their conversation. Baldwin thought his warnings had hit home, but Edward told associates that instead of opposing his wishes the prime minister 'had shown every sympathy with his personal difficulties'. Edward later wrote that, as he left, Baldwin said he was glad the ice had been broken. 'It was on the tip of my tongue to say that so far as I could see, the only ice that had been broken had long since melted in his drink . . . but Mr Baldwin's sense of humour being intermittent and unpredictable, I thought better of it.' They parted on good terms: as he left, Baldwin gave the King 'an excellent suggestion for replanting the herbaceous border in the coming spring'.[25] It did not, however, take long for Baldwin to realise that his cosy fireside chat with Edward had been a complete waste of time.

As the autumn progressed, rumours began to grow that MPs sympathetic to Edward would form a so-called King's Party, led by Churchill, although he never confirmed this. Concerns that it could happen – which seemed a distinct possibility at the time – were exacerbated by the fact that such a party would have the vocal backing of the Beaverbrook and Rothermere press. One fear was that if there was an election, there might therefore be a pro-King side and an anti-King side, thus destroying the sacred constitutional principle that the sovereign is above politics.

Meanwhile, with Edward determined to marry Mrs Simpson even though it was quite clear that the British public would not accept an American divorcee as their queen, a potential compromise solution was suggested: that Edward and Mrs Simpson should contract a morganatic marriage – one in which two people of unequal social rank wed under the condition that the lower-status partner and any children of the union have no right to the position or privileges of the higher-status spouse. Under this arrangement Wallis Simpson would not become Queen, and any children the couple might have would be excluded from succeeding to the throne. Edward liked the idea, but the prime minister did not. 'He wanted Mrs Simpson to be a Duchess,' Baldwin complained, 'not to be royal, but less than royal, but rather better than the ordinary Duchess.'[26]

The idea of a morganatic marriage never got off the ground. When Baldwin presented it to the cabinet he also said that the King had been encouraged to believe that Churchill was prepared to form an alternative government, with all the risks that entailed. Given that the morganatic marriage idea probably came from Churchill in the first place, and would have looked like a humiliation for Baldwin had it gone through, that was enough to scare the cabinet into blocking the plan. The Dominions followed suit, and most of those involved started coming round to the conclusion that the King's abdication was inevitable. However, Baldwin then made an error by allowing the King to see 'an old friend with whom I can talk freely'. That turned out to be Churchill, who Edward had been forbidden from seeing up to that point because of the government's fear that they would plot together. As the historian Alexander Larman wrote, 'Now, there was nothing stopping the principal members of the "King's Party" from assembling and scheming openly.'[27]

Churchill, loyal to the last, spoke out on the King's behalf in the Commons, and was later to be found 'ranting' in the corridors: 'I am for the King, and I will not have him strangled in the dark by ministers, and bumped off without the chance of saying a word to Parliament or the country in his defence.' When he went to see Edward at Fort Belvedere,

Churchill found him 'gay and debonair' for the first quarter of an hour, although it soon became obvious that the strain he had been under 'had exhausted him to a most painful degree'. There was in any case little Churchill could do. The only advice he could offer was to play for time, but in reality time was running out. Another avenue for the King had been closed off earlier that day when his proposal to address the nation via the BBC in order to put his case was blocked by Baldwin. There was no alternative to abdication.

The next evening Baldwin visited the King. It was an emotional encounter, and after they had walked the grounds together Baldwin was so overcome that he asked for a whisky and soda. When it arrived he toasted the King with the words, 'Well, Your Majesty, whatever happens my Mrs and I wish you the most complete happiness.' At that Edward broke down in tears, which in turn prompted Baldwin to start crying. The King and prime minister sat on the sofa together, united in their tears, until Baldwin finished his drink and returned to London.[28]

Edward signed his abdication papers on 10 December, and broadcast to the nation the next day. In his address he spoke of being unable to carry out his duties as he would have wished without the support of 'the woman I love'. His speech was, like others he had made before, partly written by Churchill.

The abdication was a pivotal point in the relationship between the government and the monarchy. For all Edward's patronising of his prime minister, there was no doubt where the power lay. The crisis firmly established the convention that the sovereign cannot marry against the wishes of his or her ministers. As Vernon Bogdanor has explained, as the wife of the King, 'The queen becomes, like the king, a representative of the people. If the sovereign seeks to marry someone who might not suitably fill the position of queen, that would damage the monarchy. Therefore, in the choice of a wife, the view of the nation, through its elected ministers, must be heard.'[29]

That the crisis had weakened the monarchy was all too apparent. During the last weeks of the drama Edward's younger brother, the Duke of York, who would shortly replace him as King George VI, told his private secretary of his fears that the whole fabric of the monarchy could 'crumble under the shock and strain of it all'.[30] But the crisis also demonstrated the weakness of the monarch relative to the government in other ways that were not apparent at the time. In 2013 Cabinet Office files were published which showed that the home secretary of the time, Sir John Simon, had ordered the bugging of the phone lines between Fort Belvedere and Buckingham Palace, and also Fort Belvedere and continental Europe.[31] The aim, according to Alexander Larman, was to gather information about 'the monarch's mental and political state', and may have been motivated in part by Edward's rumoured sympathy towards the Nazi regime in Germany.[32]

The crisis also had a dramatic effect on the reputation of two of its main political protagonists. On the day of the abdication Baldwin gave a speech in the Commons in which, speaking informally and without notes, he told of everything that had passed between him and the King. The intensity of the crisis had left him little time to prepare a speech, he said, 'so I must tell what I have to tell truthfully, sincerely and plainly, with no attempt to dress up or adorn'. It was a brilliant performance, and afterwards Harold Nicolson described it as 'the best speech that we shall ever hear in our lives'. Since then history has not been kind to Baldwin, who is regarded by many as a second-rank prime minister who was responsible for Britain's failure to rearm against the growing threat from Nazi Germany. But right then, as the abdication played out, he was the man of the hour.

For Churchill, the abdication represented a major setback. It was not so much the fact that he nailed his colours to the King's mast, but the way he did it. A couple of days before the abdication he made a speech in the Commons which so misjudged the mood of his fellow MPs that it was little short of a major disaster. One MP said he was 'absolutely howled down', while Harold Nicolson wrote: 'Winston collapsed utterly in the House yesterday . . . He has undone in five minutes the patient reconstruction works of two years.'[33] Roy Jenkins wrote that the abdication saw him 'diverted down one of the most foolish and least rewarding branch lines of his life'.[34] Yet for all his support for the King, his relationship with Edward – thereafter the Duke of Windsor – did not survive.

During the negotiations with his brother, now George VI, over his future, Edward pleaded poverty, saying he had very little money of his own and arguing that he should be allowed to keep Sandringham and Balmoral, which he had been left in his father's will. George was not having that, but agreed to give him a generous tax-free allowance as long as he behaved himself. It later emerged that Edward had much more money than he let on. George was very put out at being lied to; so too was Churchill, who had been similarly deceived. Churchill did not at first believe that Edward had pulled the wool over his eyes, but later told Ulick Alexander, keeper of the privy purse, that he was sure of it. 'And that,' wrote Alexander, 'occasioned the rift between Winston and the Duke – when Winston discovered that the latter had double-crossed him.'[35]

Relations between the two cooled after that, and the duke discovered that he could no longer rely on Churchill as he had in the past. When Churchill was prime minister during the Second World War he dealt quite firmly with Edward, packing him off to be governor of the Bahamas to keep him out of harm's way. In later life, however – after he had resigned as PM in 1955 – he had lunch with the Windsors on at least one occasion while holidaying in the south of France. But when he was a guest on Aristotle Onassis's yacht, and was asked if the Windsors could also be invited, he gave a firm no. He had not revised his opinion of the duke, whom he regarded as an 'empty man', and thought that the Windsors' presence would involve a lot of 'jumping up and down'.[36]

NEVILLE CHAMBERLAIN, who became prime minister shortly after King George VI's coronation in May 1937, was a very different proposition from his predecessor. While Baldwin was the reassuring embodiment of Middle England, Chamberlain was a more austere figure: severe in appearance, with his dark eyebrows and beaked nose he looked like a cross between a crow and an old-fashioned schoolmaster. He was confident in argument, wielded sarcasm like a deadly weapon and had a reputation for being cold and aloof. Churchill's faithful disciple Brendan Bracken nicknamed him the Coroner.

George was wary at first, telling anyone who would listen that he did not really know his new PM yet, while Chamberlain set out on a deliberate campaign to woo his sovereign: 'I want him to realise as soon as possible that I am not really an alarming person.'[37] After one conversation of more than an hour he said: '[The King] is a bit tired but pleased with the way things are going and is evidently gaining in confidence all the time.' It was no surprise that he lacked confidence: George was a shy man with a stammer who had never expected, or wanted, to be King. The events of 1936 had been a terrible shock to him.

What did not help was Chamberlain's habit of failing to keep the King properly informed. When Anthony Eden, the foreign secretary, resigned in February 1938 because he was opposed to Chamberlain's policy of appeasement towards Hitler and Mussolini, the first George knew of it was when he read about it in the newspapers. He was understandably angry that the prime minister had not briefed him that Eden was threatening resignation, and demanded that steps be taken to ensure that such an oversight never occurred again. (The King's reaction reminded me of what I was told by a former senior adviser to the late Queen, who said that one of the reasons nowadays there is such a close relationship between the sovereign's private secretary and the principal private secretary at 10 Downing Street is to avoid unpleasant surprises for the monarch. 'There should never be an occasion – it would be a failure on my part if there were – where the boss switches on the evening news and there is a reshuffle taking place and she doesn't know about it.'[38] There is a long institutional memory at Buckingham Palace.)

However, relations between Chamberlain and the King soon warmed up. One of the things they had in common was their fervent desire to avoid war, and when Chamberlain returned from Munich in September 1938, having sold Czechoslovakia down the river to buy peace by handing over part of its territory to Hitler in exchange for Germany making no further demands for land in Europe, the King was so relieved that he wanted to congratulate him in person. When the prime minister arrived at Buckingham Palace a large crowd had gathered outside, and the King suggested they go out on the balcony to acknowledge the people's enthusiasm for what Chamberlain called 'peace for our time'.

However, what George had conceived as an innocent gesture turned out to be highly controversial. The Munich agreement was highly unpopular with a number of high-profile Conservatives, including Winston Churchill, as well as Labour MPs. Even the foreign secretary, Lord Halifax, who had embraced the policy of appeasement, was beginning to have doubts about the wisdom of it all. By seeming to endorse Chamberlain's actions, the King had laid himself open to criticism. For the moment, he was sure Chamberlain had done the right thing, but it would not be long before he changed his mind. By the time Germany annexed the rest of Czechoslovakia in March 1939 the King had realised that war was inevitable.[39]

When Britain declared war on Germany, Churchill, who had been calling for a national coalition, and Eden were both brought back into the government – Churchill as first lord of the Admiralty and Eden into the Dominions Office. 'Winston is difficult to talk to,' the King wrote, 'but in time I shall get the right technique I hope.'[40] They were getting on better now, not least because Churchill had supported him when George refused to allow the Duchess of Windsor be styled Her Royal Highness, a controversial decision that to many smacked of vindictiveness. But that did not mean that their early meetings always went well. In October the King wrote in his diary of seeing Churchill to tell him of his visit to the fleet. 'He seemed very sleepy, stifling yawns or trying to, or perhaps it was boredom!'[41]

In the early days of the conflict – before Dunkirk, before the Battle of Britain, when it was still what became known as the phoney war – the war secretary was Leslie Hore-Belisha, who is usually remembered now only as the man who gave his name to the yellow beacons at pedestrian crossings. At the time he was a bright, ambitious politician who was brimful of ideas about how to modernise the army. He was also a self-publicist and an abrasive figure with a remarkable capacity for rubbing people up the wrong way. On top of all that he was Jewish, which in an age when antisemitism was rife did not help his career. The generals did not like him, not least because he had sacked a number of them. The commander-in-chief of the British Expeditionary Force (BEF) in northern France, General the Viscount Gort, could not stand him, while his chief of staff Lieutenant-General Sir Henry Pownall referred to him in his diary as Ikey, a nasty slang term for a Jew.

When during a trip to France in November 1939 Hore-Belisha criticised the BEF for its slowness in constructing concrete defences, a furious row ensued. Visiting London, Pownall went to the palace, where he bent the ear of the King's private secretary, Alec Hardinge, about Hore-Belisha's failings. Another general spoke to the King himself. The anti-Hore-Belisha briefings continued when the King visited France, after which Pownall noted: 'Both the King and Hardinge are under no illusions about Hore-Belisha and realise he must go . . . There's no doubt we have the Palace on our side against him.'[42] On his return from France the King spoke to Chamberlain about the visit, and also discussed a change at the War Office.

Although there were others who thought Hore-Belisha should go, including senior Whitehall figures, when he suddenly resigned many assumed that George was behind it. Chips Channon, a friend of Hore-Belisha's, wrote: 'The Crown decided to intervene dramatically and sent for the PM, told him to get rid of Leslie . . . The PM, startled by the King's complaint, gave in.'[43] After Chamberlain dismissed him, the prime minister asked the King to try to soothe Hore-Belisha's hurt feelings when he came to the palace to return his seals of office, but also to warn him not to make any public fuss. The King ignored the request to warn him off, but did a good job of being nice to the sacked minister. He told him how much he regretted his departure, and said that he hoped – and indeed expected – that he would be back in office before long.[44] Hore-Belisha went away about as happy as he could be in the circumstances.

The question is, did the King overstep the mark constitutionally? Andrew Roberts, in his iconoclastic book *Eminent Churchillians*, says that he 'actively conspired' to bring down the war secretary.[45] However, Sarah Bradford in her biography of George VI says he did no more than alert the PM to the rift between Hore-Belisha and the generals, 'something which he was not only constitutionally entitled but also bound to do'.[46] Either way, it showed that George was a sovereign who did not shy away from involvement in the appointment of ministers. He was less blatant than Queen Victoria, and lacked her party-political motives, but his intervention was no less real for all that. It would happen again after the end of the war.

AFTER THE GERMAN invasion of Norway in April 1940 and the subsequent debate in the Commons over Britain's conduct of the Norway campaign, Chamberlain realised he could no longer continue as prime minister. The King thought his successor should be Lord Halifax, who believed that a negotiated peace with Hitler might still be reached, and he was the obvious, reliable choice. But as he sat in the House of Lords and did not see himself as a war leader, he had ruled himself out of contention, so Chamberlain's unhesitating advice was that George should send for Churchill. According to Harold Nicolson, the King's official biographer, John Wheeler-Bennett, believed that George – who remained loyal to Chamberlain – was 'bitterly opposed' to Churchill. Alan Lascelles, the King's assistant private secretary, said later: 'When Chamberlain fell the King felt that he ought to send for Halifax. Alec Hardinge [the King's private secretary] knew that Winston was the man, but had a hard job of selling him to the King as the Queen was very anti-Winston.'[47] Disappointed – 'I thought that H. was the obvious man' – George summoned Churchill to the palace.[48] According to Churchill's account, the King greeted him in an almost playful mood. 'He looked at me searchingly and quizzically for some moments, and then said, "I suppose you don't know why I have sent for you?" Adopting his mood, I replied, "Sir, I simply couldn't imagine why." He laughed and said, "I want to ask you to form a Government." I said I would certainly do so.'[49]

Five months later Chamberlain was dead. The King wrote to his mother, Queen Mary, saying he had lost a trusted friend. 'When he was PM he really did tell me what was in his mind, & what he hoped to do. I was able to confide in him . . .'[50]

In time George was also able to confide in Churchill; in fact, they developed one of the closest relationships between a sovereign and prime minister in British history. It did not, however, start off like that. The King did not like Churchill's unpunctuality or the way he treated him. Halifax recorded in his diary how George 'was funny about Winston, and told me that he did not find him very easy to talk to. Nor was Winston willing to give him as much time, or information, as he would like.'[51] One of the Queen's ladies-in-waiting, Lady Hyde, said that the King and Queen were 'a little miffed' at Churchill's approach to meetings. 'They much preferred Chamberlain's habit of going to the Palace regularly, once a week, and explaining the situation in a careful and unhurried way. Winston says he will come at 6.00pm, puts this off by telephone to 6.30 and is inclined to turn up for ten hectic minutes at 7.00.' Churchill's reaction was that he had a war to run.

When the prime minister made the surprising decision to appoint the newspaper baron Lord Beaverbrook minister of aircraft production, the King dashed off an immediate objection. 'I wonder if you would not reconsider your intention of selecting Lord Beaverbrook for this post,' he wrote. 'I am sending this round to you at once, as I fear this appointment might be misconstrued.'[52] Here was the King getting involved once more in ministerial appointments, but also staying within the Bagehot guidelines of encouraging and warning. Although Churchill ignored him over Beaverbrook, on other occasions he listened to the King's advice. During one cabinet reshuffle the King suggested that Lord Cranborne – a friend as well as someone he admired greatly – should become lord president of the council. Churchill was making plans on that basis when George's private secretary Sir Alan Lascelles – known to all as Tommy – told the King that he would be wasted there and much more use as Dominions secretary. Lascelles was sent to Downing Street to pass this on to the PM, who was ensconced with Anthony Eden, both smoking large cigars as they grappled with the reshuffle. Eden agreed with Lascelles, and Cranborne duly became Dominions secretary.

With time mistrust turned to warmth and friendship, and Churchill began to take the King into his confidence. In September 1940, at the height of the Battle of Britain, the King suggested that instead of having their regular audiences (once a week at that point, but twice a week at the beginning of the war, and only about once a month before the war) they should have lunch together every Tuesday. At first they had well-trusted servants to wait on them, but as their relationship strengthened and they began to discuss more secret matters, they got rid of the servants and just helped themselves from a sideboard. Churchill would fetch things for the King, and the King would fetch things for Churchill.

As the historian Robert Rhodes James recorded, Churchill gave the King the most secret information in the government's possession. 'He also always told the King more frankly than any of his ministers, let alone parliament or the press, the grim realities of the war situation.'[53] For most of the war the King was sent regular intelligence reports, which would be burnt after he had read them, and after 1942 Churchill ordered that the King should be told everything about future operations, no matter how secret.[54] The warmth of their relationship was evident at one of their lunches in 1943 when the King produced a bottle of French wine from the 1941 vintage. Churchill wanted to know how on earth he had got it, but the King, enjoying his little advantage over the prime minister, refused to tell him. (It turned out it had been brought back by the former captain of the King's Flight, who was then flying secret missions to France.[55])

An intriguing entry from Alan Lascelles's diary on 3 March 1944 reveals two things: how the King was privy to more war secrets than people assumed, and how he was also part of the war effort in ways few could have imagined. 'Two MI [military intelligence] men called on me yesterday and explained how the King's visits in the next few months could assist the elaborate cover scheme whereby we are endeavouring to bamboozle the German intelligence regarding the time and place for "Overlord".'[56] As Dr Rory Cormac, an intelligence expert behind a Channel 4 documentary of 2019, said: 'It gives us a little hint that the King not only knew about one of the biggest secrets of the war, but had an active and personal role in it himself.'

British intelligence was trying to deceive the Germans as to the intended location of the Allied invasion of Europe. Cormac revealed that George's visits to troops in southern England were part of an elaborate disinformation campaign to persuade the Germans that Calais would be the site of the landings rather than Normandy. Newspaper coverage of the

King's visits did not reveal the exact location of the troops he saw, but small clues backed up by reports from German spies who were actually working as double agents for the British encouraged the Germans to think they had worked it out for themselves.[57] George's participation in this exercise made a positive contribution to the war effort, and highlights the importance of the strong rapport that had built up between the King and the prime minister: it is worth considering whether there could have been such fruitful cooperation in a top-secret venture during the First World War when George V was on the throne and Lloyd George in Number 10. Perhaps not.

On their last lunch before the landings, the King asked Churchill what his plans were for D-Day. The prime minister said he would be on one of the ships bombarding the German coastal defences, at which point George – who had been mulling over a similar idea himself – said he would like to join him, which seemed to go down well with the prime minister. 'He reacted well,' the King wrote in his diary. 'It is a big decision to take on one's own responsibility. W. cannot say no if he goes himself, & I don't want to have to tell him he cannot.' George told the Queen, who was 'wonderful as always' and encouraged him to do it.[58] Lascelles, however, thought it was madness. 'This will never do,' he wrote and, adept in the wiles of the experienced courtier, managed to talk the King out of it. 'I think I shook the King by asking him whether he was prepared to face the possibility of having to advise the Princess Elizabeth on the choice of her first Prime Minister, in the event of her father and Winston being sent to the bottom of the English Channel.'[59]

Talking the King out of this foolish idea was relatively easy; persuading Churchill was another matter entirely. The King made repeated attempts to get Churchill to change his mind, without success: Churchill was determined to be there. At one point George wrote to him: 'There is nothing I would like better than to go to sea but I have agreed to stop at home; is it fair that you should then do exactly what I should have liked to do myself?' By this time Churchill – who was on his way to Portsmouth to join Eisenhower's headquarters – was simply not replying, and the King got so angry that he threatened to drive to Portsmouth himself to stop the PM from boarding the cruiser HMS *Belfast*. It was a phone call from Lascelles to Churchill that finally got the prime minister – 'very grudgingly, and rather ungraciously', according to Rhodes James – to back down.[60]

Despite such moments their bond was real and strong, and showed once more the importance of the personal relationship between monarch and prime minister. The King would write to Churchill as 'your very sincere and grateful friend', and Churchill trusted him with some of the closest-kept secrets of the war. George knew about the atomic bomb research in New Mexico being carried out under the code name TUBE ALLOY and the first bomb test, at a time when even the deputy prime minister, Clement Attlee, did not.[61] When the King met President Truman and the US chiefs of staff a few days before the first bomb was dropped on Japan, naval chief of staff Admiral William Leahy was impressed by how much the King knew about the programme. Leahy, however, did not think the bomb had much future as a weapon. 'It sounds like a professor's dream,' he said. 'Would you like to lay a little bet on that, Admiral?' the King replied.[62]

The end of the war in Europe was followed by the break-up of the National Government and an immediate general election. The King, along with many others, not least the Labour party leadership, was surprised by the result – a Labour landslide. George was profoundly sad when Churchill came to the palace to tender his resignation and advise him to ask Labour leader Clement Attlee to form a new government, and told him that he thought the people were very ungrateful 'after the way they had been led in the War'. Five days later, concerned he had failed to express his feelings properly when they met in person, George sent two handwritten letters to his former prime minister, saying how sad he was and how he would 'always remember our talks with pleasure'. He added: 'For myself personally, I regret what has happened more than perhaps anyone else. I shall miss your counsel to me more than I can say.'[63]

TACITURN AND blunt, Clement Attlee was a very different character from Winston Churchill. While Churchill was loquacious tending to poetic, the pipe-smoking Labour leader – with his clipped moustache and clipped speech – verged on the monosyllabic. Although the King had seen much of Attlee during the war, and liked and respected him, he really had not got to know him. George would sometimes struggle to hear what he was saying, and used to call him 'Clam' Attlee.[64]

Neither the King nor Attlee had much small talk, which meant that their first audience was a particularly awkward affair. Laurence Helsby, the prime minister's private secretary from 1947, told historian Peter Hennessy how his predecessor Leslie Rowan had said that it was so excruciating that after that first occasion their respective aides gave them speaking notes before every audience to make sure they had something to talk about. 'They're terribly shy, and they're both staring at their shoes,' said Hennessy. 'And finally Attlee can bear it no more and says, "I won the election!" And the King goes, "I know, I heard it on the six o'clock news!"'[65]

That first audience was also notable for the way the King – not for the first time – tried to influence the appointment of a cabinet minister; on this occasion he was successful. There was a pressing need to appoint a foreign secretary to go with the prime minister to the Potsdam conference to negotiate the terms of the post-war settlement. However, the election result had been such a surprise that Attlee had not had time to discuss with his colleagues who should have the top jobs. Attlee said he was thinking of appointing Hugh Dalton, but the King disagreed and said that with foreign affairs being such a crucial area Ernest Bevin – who had been pencilled in for chancellor – would be a better choice.[66] This is confirmed by Lascelles, who wrote in his diary that the King 'begged' him to choose Bevin.[67] Attlee acquiesced: Bevin was appointed foreign secretary, and Dalton became chancellor. It was a decision in which the personal and the political were inextricably entwined, but as events unfolded it was also one that would prove to be undoubtedly correct.

First, the personal. George VI could not stand Hugh Dalton, and was not the only person to feel that way. He had known him for a long time, as Hugh's father, Canon John Dalton, had been chaplain to Queen Victoria and tutor to the future George V and his older brother Eddy, who died aged twenty-eight. The royal family seems to have taken an early dislike to the young Hugh. One story has it that Queen Victoria had him to tea, and after watching him stuff his face remarked: 'What a horrid little boy!' The story may be apocryphal, but as Dalton's biographer Ben Pimlott observed, the point was that it was widely retold, and believed.[68]

Dalton was educated at Eton and Cambridge, where he became active in left-wing student politics and was known as Comrade Hugh; George V once told Canon Dalton never to bring 'your anarchist son' into his presence again.[69] Towards the end of his life George VI told Hugh Gaitskell that there was 'only one of your people that I really cannot abide', and that was Dalton. Gaitskell gathered that the dislike went back to when Dalton's father was tutor to George's father. Dalton senior was apparently very like his son 'in having a loud voice and bullying manner'.[70] Pimlott also said that the King had been angered shortly before the end of the war by Dalton selling off royal gifts to his parents. In 1947 Dalton had to resign as chancellor after being held responsible for a Budget leak, a development that no doubt delighted the King as Dalton had been in the middle of some very tetchy negotiations with the palace over the allowance that Princess Elizabeth would get after her wedding. Dalton's successor was the supposedly austere Stafford Cripps, who agreed a far more generous settlement than Dalton had been prepared to offer.[71]

Bevin, on the other hand, was a palace favourite. Former general secretary of the Transport and General Workers' Union, he was minister of labour under Churchill. When he was sworn in as a privy counsellor the King noted in his diary that 'he looks a strong man & a leader'. Like Jimmy Thomas, he never suffered from nervousness in the presence of royalty, although he was always courteous, but in a way that did not preclude him speaking his mind. According to one tale, as he was being sworn in the King asked him how he had acquired so wide a knowledge of public affairs. 'Sir,' he replied, 'it was gathered in the 'edgerows of experience.'[72] He smoked and drank with dedication, much to the frustration of his doctor, Alec McCall, who liked to joke that he was unable to find a sound organ in Bevin's entire body apart from his feet. Introducing McCall to the King, Bevin said: 'This is Alec. 'E treats my be'ind like a dartboard.' The King laughed uproariously.[73] When a new equerry – Group Captain

Peter Townsend of Princess Margaret fame – complained that
Bevin kept his other hand in his pocket when shaking hands
with the King, George told him the important thing was not
his manners but the fact that he was 'a real Englishman. I
like him.'[74]

Attlee later played down the importance of the King's
advice in deciding on Bevin as foreign secretary, saying it
was not 'a decisive factor'. But perhaps he would say that. In
any case, regardless of whether he did swing it for Bevin, the
point is that George thought it was his role – and his right –
to do so. In Attlee's account, what changed his mind was the
realisation that Bevin would be better than Dalton at standing up to Stalin. 'I thought affairs were going to be pretty
difficult and a heavy tank was what was going to be required
rather than a sniper.'[75] But why did the King want Bevin and
not Dalton at the Foreign Office? Was it just personal dislike?
After all, Dalton would still get one of the great offices of
state, although it is true that George would have seen more
of him as foreign secretary than he would as chancellor.

This brings us to George's political motives. He too saw
Bevin's suitability for the job, and it was indeed an inspired
appointment. Bevin is regarded as one of the great foreign
secretaries of the twentieth century, carving out a clear role
for Britain as a staunch ally of the US in the Cold War against
the Soviet Union and becoming a central figure in the creation of NATO. One Foreign Office private secretary recalled
that Bevin got on 'particularly well' with George: 'He was
most punctilious about keeping the King informed about
what was going on in the field of foreign affairs. On various
occasions when I saw them together Ernie would put a large
hand on the King's back and lead him into a corner where
he would tell him some story which usually evoked roars of
laughter.'[76] In 1949, when Bevin got a new private secretary,

the man was told by Lascelles that his main job was to make sure his boss did not work himself to death, 'since it was in the country's interest that he should carry on as Foreign Secretary for as long as possible'.[77]

MANY OF ATTLEE'S colleagues regarded the King as a reactionary, and it is true that, although he was meticulous in observing the constitutional proprieties, George did not always refrain from criticising aspects of the government's programme.[78] But Attlee himself got on with him, and liked the King's informality. While Victoria had made her ministers stand for audiences, George liked to sit down for a cigarette and a gossip.[79] When George died, Attlee was genuinely saddened. As he walked into a Labour party meeting after hearing about his death – looking, it was said, as if he had had a stroke – he said: 'The King is dead; he was always very nice to me.'[80]

Attlee's respect for the monarchy grew while he was in office, so much so that when his ministry was on its last legs in 1951 – the economy was faltering, the government had run out of ideas and there had been a spate of ministerial resignations – he called an election for October when he should have waited for the economy to recover. He did so because the King was about to go on tour to Australia and New Zealand and Attlee thought it irresponsible not to have a more secure government in place before he left As his biographer Michael Jago wrote: 'It is ironic that Attlee, a socialist Prime Minister with a deep belief in the value of the monarchy, had acted out of respect for George VI and called an election at a highly unpropitious time.'[81] In the event, the tour was postponed because of the King's health; the Conservatives won by a small majority, and Winston Churchill returned to Number 10.

CHAPTER FOUR

SECRET CONCLAVE

WHEN WINSTON CHURCHILL was returned to power in October 1951 neither he nor George VI were the men they had been at the time of their great partnership during the war. At seventy-six years old Churchill was rather deaf and suffering from the frailties of old age, while the King had severe circulation problems as a result of years of heavy smoking. He also had lung cancer, although he was not told this, even when he had his left lung removed a month before the election. Despite his failing health, George still took an active interest in political affairs: when Churchill submitted his list of ministerial appointments, the King objected to the designation of Anthony Eden as deputy prime minister as well as foreign secretary. Deputy prime minister may have been Attlee's title in the coalition government during the war, but the King was against it becoming a permanent position, on the grounds that it infringed on his constitutional prerogative to choose Churchill's successor should he die in office or become incapacitated. Churchill backed down. Eighteen years later that constitutional prerogative would be a cause of contention during the reign of Queen Elizabeth when Harold Macmillan resigned on grounds of ill health.[1]

George VI died in his sleep of a coronary thrombosis at Sandringham on 6 February 1952. He was fifty-six years old. The death was discovered by his valet at 7.30am, and an hour later assistant private secretary Edward Ford was sent by Lascelles to tell the prime minister. At Downing Street, Ford was directed to Churchill's bedroom, where he found him writing in bed, surrounded by paperwork. 'I've got bad news,' Ford recalled, 'the King died this morning.' Churchill was taken aback. 'Bad news?' he said. 'The worst!' His joint private secretary Jock Colville later found him in tears. When he tried to reassure Churchill by saying how well he would get on with the new Queen, 'all he could say was that he did not know her and that she was only a child'.[2]

In the Commons the prime minister gave a moving tribute in which he revealed for the first time how the King and Queen had narrowly escaped serious injury when Buckingham Palace was bombed in September 1940. Talking of those dark days, when Britain's fate seemed to be on a knife edge, he said that George had 'lived through every minute of this struggle with a heart that never quavered and a spirit undaunted'.[3] On the card accompanying the government's funeral wreath he wrote, 'For Valour', the inscription on the Victoria Cross. Attlee's tribute as leader of the opposition was couched in less florid and emotional terms, but was in its own way equally moving, praising the King for his 'good judgement and . . . sure instinct'. (It is worth noting here historian Ben Pimlott's assessment of George. Describing his 'nervous courage and mule-like conservatism' and 'lack of imagination', Pimlott wrote that these were seen by many as an advantage, as they put him more in touch with 'the bewildered common man'. Pimlott also wrote: 'In private, prime ministers found him almost intolerably slow, yet they respected his honesty and decency, and his desire to do his best, and they felt protective towards him.'[4])

Princess Elizabeth became Queen while at the Treetops Hotel in Kenya, on the first leg of a tour on which she and Philip, Duke of Edinburgh, were standing in for her parents after the King had been forced to cancel because of his ill health. She was just twenty-five. When she arrived at London Airport, emerging from the aircraft in her mourning black, she was greeted by a line of politicians including Churchill and Attlee. Churchill, who had served in government under her father, grandfather and great-grandfather, and been in the army under her great-great-grandmother, seemed so overcome with emotion that he was lost for words.

While Churchill was swept up in his romantic vision of the new Elizabethan age, perhaps seizing on it as an excuse to put off any thoughts of retirement until after the coronation, it did not prevent differences of opinion arising between the new monarch and her government. There was also the question of the royal family's name, which was an uncomfortable issue for the new Queen, and saw the cabinet asserting its authority over her in a manner that brooked no argument.

Word had reached Queen Mary – Elizabeth's grandmother – that Lord Mountbatten, Philip's uncle, had been boasting that 'the house of Mountbatten now reigned'. Mary summoned the prime minister's private secretary to register her displeasure. Churchill – no friend of Mountbatten – 'went through the roof', and had no difficulty in getting the cabinet to agree that he should advise the Queen that the name of the royal house remain Windsor.[5] This put the Queen in a difficult position, caught as she was between her husband and her government, not to mention her mother and grandmother. She did not have much option other than to give in and agree that the royal family should continue to be known as Windsor, although one of Philip's sympathisers said that Churchill 'steamrollered' her into the decision, pleading the national interest. Philip was very unhappy and did not hold back from saying so. 'I am the only man in the country not allowed to give his name to his children,' he complained.[6]

Lascelles, who had not always been an admirer of Churchill (the coolness was mutual: for years Churchill had insisted on calling him Alan, when everyone else knew him as Tommy), was a steadfast ally of the prime minister on this one. When the Queen gave her formal approval to the proclamation, Lascelles stood over her, in his words like 'one of the Barons of Runnymede'. Years later she would speak frankly to a government minister at dinner about the relationship both she and her father had with Lascelles. 'We just had to do what he said, the whole time,' she told him. The minister said: 'She had seen her father do what he was told, and she and her mother assumed that they had to do the same.'[7]

The coronation was a political issue from the start. While the natural thing might have been for it to take place as soon as possible – King Charles III was crowned eight months after his mother died – Churchill was adamant that the coronation should not be held until the following year. That Westminster Abbey was in the process of being restored was one factor, but Churchill made it clear that the economic situation was the main reason. It was, he said, 'vital that not a single working day should be unnecessarily lost in this year of crisis'. As he put it to Lascelles, 'Can't have Coronations with the bailiffs in the house.'[8]

The next big question was whether it should be televised. The coronation committee – which had the forward-looking Philip as chairman, counterbalanced by the earl marshal, the Duke of Norfolk, as vice-chairman – decided against, and their decision was endorsed by the cabinet. Churchill thought that having television cameras in the abbey would put too much pressure on the Queen, who initially at least agreed with him. However, public opinion was overwhelmingly in favour of televising the ceremony, and there was massive pressure from the press and MPs for ministers to change their mind. The Queen had a change of heart, and dispatched Lascelles to sort out a compromise whereby television cameras would be allowed into the abbey to film the service but not the communion. Churchill was said to be taken aback at her decision but went along with it, saying, 'After all, it was the Queen who was to be crowned and not the cabinet. She alone must decide.' The prime minister's private secretary was impressed. 'Thus it was,' wrote Colville, 'that the new 26-year-old sovereign personally routed the Earl Marshal, the Archbishop of Canterbury, Sir Winston Churchill and the Cabinet, all of whom submitted to her decision with astonishment, but with a good grace.'[9]

The Queen, however, did not win all her battles. When she acceded to the throne she and Philip were living at Clarence House, which they had decorated according to their tastes and suited them very well. They suggested that they should carry on living there, and just use Buckingham Palace – a daunting, unfriendly place, and not like a home at all – for entertaining and ceremonial duties. But Churchill insisted that it had been the official London residence of the sovereign since Queen Victoria, and should remain so. 'Prince Philip didn't want to go to Buckingham Palace,' one of the Queen's household said, 'but all the old codgers like Lascelles said "you must go".' With Churchill on his side, Lascelles won the argument with ease. (At the time of writing, King Charles and Queen Camilla are still using Clarence House as their London home, as it has been for years. Their original excuse was that Buckingham Palace was being refurbished, but as the works drew to a close it became increasingly obvious that the couple had no intention of moving. The palace remains 'monarchy HQ', however.)

Such moments of tension between the Queen and Churchill were, however, the exception rather than the rule. Their relationship, according to her biographer Sarah Bradford, was 'tender and romantic': by the time Churchill neared retirement Colville would describe him as being 'madly in love' with her. The aged prime minister was dazzled by the radiant young Queen, and she in turn had a deep reverence for this towering figure of the twentieth century. Bradford wrote: 'His huge grasp of world affairs, his fierce patriotism and his rolling periods of speech spiced with puckish humour fascinated her, and they shared a passion for racing.' Churchill was a keen racehorse owner, and cabled her when one of her horses won a race; she in turn wrote to him when his horse Pol Roger won at Kempton Park.

Their audiences – which were held once a week, following the tradition of Churchill's lunches with George VI – had an almost 'jaunty air', according to Ben Pimlott. 'The premier would arrive wearing a frock coat and top hat, with a gleam in his eye, and disappear happily into secret conclave.' One of his private secretaries said he used to come away from his audiences 'purring' – a word that half a century later would be used by David Cameron about another conversation between sovereign and prime minister, much to his subsequent embarrassment. Over time the meetings got longer and longer, prompting Jock Colville to ask Churchill what they talked about. 'Oh, mostly racing,' he replied.[10] On another occasion he emerged from the audience saying, 'She was asking me about my pig-sticking days on the North West Frontier.'[11] A couple of decades later she was asked with which of her prime ministers she had enjoyed her audiences the most. 'Winston, of course, because it was always such fun,' she replied. Asked then whether it had been like Melbourne with the young Victoria, she replied: 'Not at all . . . He could be very stubborn . . .'

But she took her work seriously, and was always diligent in reading her red boxes of government papers. She was by then used to reading such material; Attlee started sending Princess Elizabeth cabinet minutes and memoranda shortly after she turned twenty-four.[12] Once a telegram arrived from the British ambassador in Baghdad which Jock Colville thought was important. He accordingly put it at the top of the prime minister's box with a note suggesting he should read it. But as it was a long telegram Churchill put it aside and told Colville to bring it up at the weekend. The weekend came and went and he still had not read it. When he went to see the Queen for his audience on Tuesday she asked him what he thought about the Baghdad telegram. He had to admit he had not read it. Colville recalled: 'He came back in a frightful fury and asked, "Why wasn't I shown it?" So I said, "This is going too far. I've been trying to get you to read it for the last four days." "Well, let me see it at once." He read it and found it interesting – but the Queen had caught him out.'[13] Catching out ministers was a game that her father also liked to play; and it was not the last time that one of Elizabeth's prime ministers would discover to their cost that it paid to go into audiences well prepared.

With Churchill's physical energy and mental agility on the decline, some thought was given to how he might be persuaded to retire. One suggestion was that the Queen might bring it up, on the grounds that his monarch might be the one person he would listen to. Churchill's doctor Lord Moran mentioned it to Lascelles, but he dismissed the idea because he thought that Churchill would not listen even to her. Then, at the end of an official dinner at Number 10 for the Italian prime minister on 23 June 1953, Churchill was leading the men to join the ladies in the drawing room when he staggered and slumped into a chair. He had had a massive stroke. He was determined, however, to carry on, and the next day told Colville not to let anyone know that he was temporarily incapacitated. Instead the story was that everything was carrying on as normal.

What happened next was an extraordinary constitutional conspiracy. By the Friday, three days after his stroke, Churchill was almost completely paralysed, and Moran thought he might not last the weekend. However, his intended successor, Anthony Eden, was in Boston in the USA, about to have an operation. Colville realised that if Churchill died that weekend it would cause a serious constitutional problem, and therefore decided to ignore his boss's orders by ringing Lascelles to tell him that the Queen might have to appoint a new prime minister on Monday morning. With Eden also incapacitated, the other obvious candidate was the chancellor, R. A. Butler (always known as Rab), but Eden had been waiting for so long to lead the country that they felt it would be wrong to deny him his chance. The two private secretaries therefore put their heads together and drew up a scheme whereby, in the event of Churchill's demise, the Queen would be advised that a caretaker administration would be formed under Lord Salisbury. He would not be called prime minister, but would head the government until Eden was well enough to take over, and Rab Butler would be kept out of Number 10 – not for the last time, as it turned out. Nothing of Churchill's condition, let alone the conspiracy about his replacement, leaked out; all the press was told was that the prime minister was tired and 'in need of a complete rest'.[14]

Amazingly, Churchill survived, and by August was well enough to drive to Windsor to see the Queen. Two weeks later she invited him to the races at Doncaster to watch her horse Aureole run in the St Leger, and then travel with her in the royal train to Balmoral. At Doncaster the crowd gave him a huge cheer. Elizabeth thought his improvement since she had seen him some six weeks earlier was 'astonishing'. On everyone's mind, of course, was the thought: when would he retire? It was a question that had been lurking in the background for some time, and had even been on George VI's mind. The King – according to Harold Macmillan, who got it from Anthony Eden, who was told by the Queen – had made up his mind a short while before he died to have a talk with Churchill about his plans. His death, however, meant that the conversation never took place.[15]

After recovering from his stroke Churchill gave a good enough performance at the Conservative party conference in Margate to avoid calls for him to go, and by the end of November had the excuse that the Queen was away on a five-month tour of the Commonwealth. When she got back in May 1954 he still showed no sign of stepping down, much to the frustration of his cabinet colleagues. Harold Macmillan, then chancellor, wrote in his diary that summer about a rumour that the Queen was 'considering some intervention to get Churchill to resign'. He also mentioned 'the possibility of four or five of us' going to the Queen to ask her to step in. 'Churchill is now quite incapable – mentally as well as physically – of remaining Prime Minister.'[16]

Churchill finally agreed to retire in April 1955. Colville thought that as his service as prime minister had been so exceptional, the Queen might offer him a dukedom in the same way that his ancestor Sir John Churchill was made Duke of Marlborough after his victories in the War of the Spanish

Succession. The message from the palace was that the only dukedoms that were going to be created were royal ones, but the Queen was prepared to offer him one – the Duke of London was the suggested title – as long as Downing Street could guarantee that he would turn it down. Churchill was wholly opposed to becoming a duke, so everything seemed fine.

Or so Colville thought. As he recalled, after his final audience he asked Churchill how it had gone. 'Do you know, the most remarkable thing – she offered to make me a Duke,' he replied. Anxiously, Colville asked him what he had said. 'Well, you know, I very nearly accepted, I was so moved by her beauty and charm and the kindness with which she made this offer, that for a moment I thought of accepting. But finally I remembered that I must die as I have always been – Winston Churchill. And so I asked her to forgive my not accepting it. And do you know, it's an odd thing, but she seemed almost relieved.'[17]

During this audience Churchill did not tell the Queen who his successor should be, which may in part have been because it was entirely obvious. Eden had for some time been effectively deputy prime minister, even if the constitution – as George VI had made plain – did not recognise such a position. But it was also because Churchill was insistent that once he had resigned he had no right to advise the sovereign. Although Churchill had told colleagues that Eden would succeed him, he wrote after his final audience: 'She asked me whether I would recommend a successor, and I said I preferred to leave it to her.'[18]

Under the constitution, she had the right to ask whoever she liked to form an administration, as long as they had the confidence of the House of Commons. That was the royal prerogative, and no one was yet about to challenge it. Given that at the time the Conservative party did not elect its leaders, she had a free hand. And with that free hand she chose Eden. If she ever took any soundings, no outsiders ever knew about them. As Ben Pimlott observed, the first prime ministerial changeover of her reign went totally smoothly. This may have hinted – however subtly – at the fact that Queen Elizabeth had no desire to seek a more active role, something that would become a lot clearer a little less than two years later.

ON 26 JULY 1956, just over a month after he became president of Egypt, Colonel Gamal Abdel Nasser nationalised the Suez Canal – which until then had been owned by an Anglo-French company – in order to fund his great infrastructure project, the Aswan Dam, which the Americans had refused to back. Tolls from ships passing through the canal would pay for the construction of the dam, a key element in Egypt's planned industrialisation. With half of the UK's oil passing through the canal, the move was greeted in Britain with inevitable indignation. Anthony Eden said that 'Nasser had his thumb on Britain's windpipe', while the Labour leader Hugh Gaitskell likened his actions to the aggression of Hitler and Mussolini in the years before the Second World War.

In response, the British, Israeli and French governments drew up a secret plan for Israel to attack Egypt, which would provide the pretext for France and Britain to demand a cease-fire and launch a temporary occupation of the Canal Zone by their own forces. Israel launched its attack on 29 October, followed two days later by assaults from airborne French and British troops, while the RAF bombed Egyptian airfields, destroying Nasser's air force. Opposition MPs were outraged that Britain had attacked a country with which it was not actually at war, and there was an open breach between Britain and the US, which had proposed a UN resolution calling on the Israelis to withdraw, only to have it vetoed by Britain. Commonwealth prime ministers all joined with the US in siding against Britain.

The whole exercise, which caused Britain to be seen as both duplicitous and inept, and highlighted its decline as a world power, was a woeful mixture of incompetent military planning and diplomatic blundering. By the time the main British and French forces landed at Port Said on 6 November the Israelis and Egyptians had agreed to a UN ceasefire, which the British government was forced reluctantly to accept.[19] Eden was humiliated, and the Soviet Union, which had threatened to intervene by sending troops to help Egypt, increased its influence in the Middle East.

The question that has been asked many times since is, how much did the Queen know? And what could she have done anyway? Eden, who resigned in 1957 and was made Lord Avon, told the writer Robert Lacey twenty years later that the Queen 'understood what we were doing very well'. But, as Lacey admits, this assertion is open to many interpretations. Eden insisted that she did not disapprove of the operation, but 'nor would I claim that she was pro-Suez'. Pimlott said she was in the frustrating position of knowing everything but being unable to do anything about it. He quotes one former adviser as saying that she received all the Foreign Office telegrams and papers, and was in some ways better informed in advance than many members of the cabinet. Another said: 'She knew the inside story . . . Nothing was kept from her. She knew about the secret deals beforehand.' On the other hand, her assistant private secretary Edward Ford believed it was unlikely that the Queen knew of Britain's secret deal with Israel. He told the historian Andrew Roberts: 'I don't think Eden was totally frank with her. You see, she was under

30 and had only been on the throne four years, and so was hardly in a position to make her opposition – if, indeed, she felt any – count. The prime minister certainly ought to have told her of the secret collusion.'[20]

British public opinion was divided over the operation, and this was reflected in the royal household. Sir Michael Adeane, who had taken over from Lascelles as private secretary to the Queen, was personally pro-Eden but concerned that Elizabeth should observe the constitutional proprieties, while her assistant private secretaries, Edward Ford and Martin Charteris, were both strongly anti-Suez. As the Queen said, 'I have three Private Secretaries and all of them give me different advice.'[21] As for the Queen's own view, that is hard to discern, but one former aide said: 'I think the Queen believed Eden was mad.' Not that the Queen would have expressed it like that, of course. But she had her own way of putting things. As one former courtier suggested, 'She may have said to Eden something like, "Are you sure you are being wise?"'[22] Nearly forty years later Charteris told the historian Peter Hennessy: 'Suez was a matter which gave the Queen a great deal of concern . . . I think the basic dishonesty of the whole thing was a trouble.'[23]

Eden did not survive long. He had been in poor health anyway, the legacy of a bungled bile duct operation, and gave a defiantly ill-judged performance in the Commons in which he not only defended his actions but lied to MPs, saying 'there were no plans to get together to attack Egypt . . . there was no foreknowledge that Israel would attack Egypt'.[24] At the beginning of January 1957 he drove with his wife to Sandringham, where the Queen was having her extended Christmas break, to discuss his resignation. The couple had dinner with the Queen and spent the night, and the next day he saw her again at Buckingham Palace and formally resigned. (In order to stave off any awkward questions about why the Queen was cutting short her holiday, the palace put out a holding story that she was returning to London to see her dressmaker.[25]) Eden, who had a warm relationship with Elizabeth – in his retirement they would enjoy a friendly correspondence – was deeply touched by the Queen's kindness after he stepped down: she wrote him a handwritten letter in which she made no mention of Suez but said how deeply she felt about his resignation. 'I am only anxious that you should realize that [your] record, which has indeed been written in tempestuous times, is highly valued and will never be forgotten by your Sovereign.'[26]

The events that ensued marked one of the first significant constitutional challenges of the Queen's reign. There was no clear-cut successor to Eden, which meant that for the first time since George V had chosen Stanley Baldwin over Lord Curzon, the sovereign was faced with a real choice. Like Churchill before him, Eden was a strong believer in the royal prerogative – the legal power invested in the monarch – and did not formally advise the Queen on whom she should choose. He did, however, suggest that elder statesman Lord Salisbury – Bobbety, as he was known to friends, the former Lord Cranborne on whose behalf George VI had intervened in a cabinet reshuffle – should take soundings from the cabinet. Critically, Salisbury discussed this idea with Adeane, so the Queen was fully aware of how the Tory party was choosing its new leader.[27]

There were two obvious candidates: Harold Macmillan and Rab Butler. Accordingly, Salisbury, who had difficulty pronouncing his Rs, stationed himself in the Privy Council office with lord chancellor Lord Kilmuir and asked as a succession of cabinet ministers filed in, 'Is it Wab, or Hawold?'

The expectation in the nation was that it would be the former chancellor, Butler, one of the more creative thinkers in the party, who had been responsible for the 1944 Education Act which made secondary education universal and free for the first time. He was also Eden's choice, according to the former prime minister's official biographer. In a note dictated by Eden at the time, he made it clear that although he had given her no formal advice he had left the Queen in no doubt that his preference was for Butler.[28] Not a single newspaper other than the London *Evening Standard* expected that it would be Macmillan, a complex figure described by Sarah Bradford as 'a curious mixture of idealism, histrionics, Machiavellian guile and ruthlessness'.[29] His wife, who conducted a notorious long-running affair with the Tory MP Bob Boothby, was a daughter of the Duke of Devonshire, but Macmillan's own antecedents were more humble: his grandfather was a poor Scottish crofter. However, Butler was seen as indecisive, and had managed to earn the enmity of both sides of the Tory party for his behaviour over Suez. The cabinet overwhelmingly went for Macmillan, as did Winston Churchill, who had been persuaded to go to the palace to offer his opinion. Macmillan was also the choice of the backbenches.

Having ascertained the wishes of the Conservative party, Salisbury informed the Queen; the Queen summoned Macmillan (who had spent the morning reading *Pride and Prejudice* – 'very soothing,' he recalled) and the whole changeover seemed to have been conducted as smoothly as anyone could have wished for. But to the outside world, which was expecting Butler, it was a surprise, and there was criticism of the murky and clandestine way the succession had been arranged. It was not so much that it was a fix, or that the wrong person had been chosen, but how it all looked. In the aftermath of Suez, which had raised uncomfortable questions about Britain's place in the world, the idea that a whiskery old cabal should connive in the appointment of a new prime minister seemed inappropriate.

As Robert Lacey wrote, 'It was a miscalculation for Elizabeth II to let it appear that she had selected a prime minister to run her country solely on the say-so of two elderly men with no clearly defined constitutional function.'[30] The more conspiratorially minded wondered whether the Queen had been manipulated by her parents' old friend Bobbety. She had not, but the Queen had not really exercised her prerogative either; instead she had willingly surrendered it to a coterie of aristocratic Conservative party insiders. It was the first clear indication – much more so than when Eden took over in 1955 – that she had no desire to enter the political arena. As the journalist Malcolm Muggeridge wrote, 'Nothing in her temperament would have induced her to exercise her own judgement, even assuming – which is unlikely – that she herself had any particular preference or opinion.'[31] For the Labour party, the controversy helped clarify its own ideas about how such changeovers should be conducted when it was in power: it announced that in future it would have a vote of the parliamentary party before accepting a new prime minister. For the Queen, however, it would be several more years before she was able to fully extricate herself from political decision-making.

ALTHOUGH HE NEVER became PM, Butler, who became home secretary in Macmillan's administration, had extensive personal contact with the Queen. He often saw her when Macmillan was away on foreign business, and had previously had a number of audiences when Eden was recovering from illness at the end of 1956. According to Robert Lacey, who interviewed him, Butler had been struck by the 'refined variety of gossip' that she enjoyed. 'She seemed fascinated by parliament – who was rising, who falling,' wrote Lacey. 'And, apart from the national interest, she enjoyed evaluating to what degree the government had suffered a setback or had scored points in political terms. She appeared totally to appreciate the personal ambition inspiring the political animal, and was fascinated by the length one would go to to secure his own advantage at the expense of another.' Butler also noticed how she tended to keep her views to herself. 'She would never give away an opinion early in the conversation, but would always ask first for his opinion and listen to it right through.'[32]

For his part Macmillan was impressed with her diligence and her attention to detail. He had noticed it when he became foreign secretary in 1955, writing in his diary: 'She shewed [sic] extraordinary knowledge of all that is going on, and obviously reads the F.O. telegrams very carefully.'[33] Later the same year she wanted to hear about what had gone on at a Cold War summit in Geneva. 'I did my best in half an hour to explain the posn [sic] to her, without boring her. She showed (as her father used to) an uncanny knowledge of details and personalities.'[34] She could also be tough with him. When he proposed making Butler deputy prime minister in 1962, she told him firmly that, like her father, George VI, she did not approve of the title. 'The Queen has in the past rightly pointed out that there is no such official post,' Macmillan wrote in his diary. 'I must not be accused of trying to appoint my successor, and thus injure the prerogative.'[35]

As well as their weekly audiences, he would send her long reports when he was away at meetings and conferences, and she would write back in what he called 'a very informed and informal style', writing in her own hand and even addressing the envelope herself. Macmillan, it was clear, greatly enjoyed his relationship with the Queen, even if as Sarah Bradford suggested he might have exaggerated their closeness. But their meetings always made for a good story, which he would enjoy telling afterwards. Once he was talking to the Queen in her sitting room at Windsor when Princess Margaret walked in in her dressing-gown, saw him and said huffily to her sister, 'No one would talk to you if you weren't the Queen,' before storming out and slamming the door.[36]

The reference in Macmillan's diary to his fear of boring her was nearer the mark than perhaps he realised: according to his biographer Charles Williams, he did bore her. Although he revered the Queen and respected her prerogative, he was not the first Balliol man to struggle to suppress his sense of intellectual superiority. And although he approached his audiences with a formal gallantry that echoed Disraeli's relationship with Queen Victoria, he also – like Gladstone – had a tendency to submit his Queen to 'long and stultifying lectures'.[37] Williams wrote: 'When Macmillan visited Balmoral a junior secretary was detailed to take him for very long walks to get him out of the Queen's way. She was, in short, bored at being lectured to and not being listened to.'[38]

For all his respect for the Crown, the Machiavellian Macmillan was not above using the Queen for his own political purposes. In 1959 the prime minister, who was still considering when to call a general election, was trying to persuade US president Dwight Eisenhower to visit Britain as a way of boosting his election chances. He wanted Britain to be seen as a big player on the world stage, and closeness to the US was a way to achieve that. The trouble was, Eisenhower was not interested. Macmillan suggested it would somehow be an insult to the Queen which would never be forgiven if he did not come, which – among other factors – helped Eisenhower change his mind. Williams wrote: 'His mention of the Queen had been decisive. Eisenhower, ever courteous and respectful, could not ignore it.' A UK visit was announced for August, and when it emerged that the Queen would remain in Balmoral because she was pregnant (with Prince Andrew), that was even better: Eisenhower would have to go to Scotland to see her.

The visit included a television broadcast showing president and prime minister having a friendly chat in Downing Street – blatant electioneering, even though no election had been called. A few days later Macmillan flew to Balmoral, where he gave the Queen what Williams called 'a pedantic lecture' on her right to refuse a request for a dissolution of Parliament. Which, of course, she was never going to do.[39] The election, which was held in October, saw a third successive victory by the Conservatives, who increased their majority to one hundred.

Macmillan's awareness of the political and diplomatic value of the Queen was manifest again a couple of years later following her visit to newly independent Ghana. She had originally been slated to go in 1960, but that had to be postponed because of her pregnancy. The country's founding president, Kwame Nkrumah, was an unpredictable character who was also being wooed by the Soviet Union. Such was Ghana's strategic importance as an emerging African nation that the Queen had sent her assistant private secretary Martin Charteris to Accra to break the news to him in person. The visit went ahead the following year, despite a spate of political violence and Nkrumah's increasingly despotic behaviour. It was a great success. A picture of the Queen dancing with Nkrumah went round the world, and Ghana's *Evening News* famously called her 'the world's greatest Socialist monarch'. Afterwards Macmillan, who had been keen to persuade the

US to join Britain in investing in the construction of the massive Volta Dam despite misgivings about Ghana being a vocal proponent of African nationalism, called up President John F. Kennedy to say: 'I have risked my Queen; you must risk your money.' Financial backing for the project from the US came through shortly afterwards.

IN AUGUST 1963 the Queen's private secretary, Sir Michael Adeane, turned down an invitation to a shooting party in Scotland on the grounds that Harold Macmillan would be among the guests. His reason, which seems excessively punctilious now, was that there had for some time been much talk in political circles about when the prime minister would call a general election, and for Adeane to be seen with him might give rise to speculation that would embarrass the Queen. What he did not foresee was that events that were shortly to unfold because of Macmillan's actions would prove to be far more embarrassing, and damaging, to the Queen than any gossip about election dates.

By 1963 Macmillan was losing his political lustre. His reputation had been dented by the conviction of Admiralty clerk John Vassall for passing secrets to the Soviet Union, followed a few months later by the Profumo scandal. He was also having health problems, and had made up his mind to retire before the general election. On 8 October, just as he was having second thoughts about not fighting the election, he was taken ill and admitted to hospital for an immediate prostate operation. The next day he wrote to the Queen to say he had to resign immediately.

His favoured successor was the foreign secretary, Lord Home, who had the disadvantage of sitting in the House of Lords. Second choice was the lord president, Lord Hailsham, who would shortly renounce his peerage to become Quintin

Hogg. The one person Macmillan did not want was Rab Butler, who had lost out on becoming prime minister six years earlier and was again seen as a front runner. A few other potential candidates were also floating around, including the chancellor, Reginald Maudling, and the leader of the house, Iain Macleod. The problem was that there was no accepted mechanism for choosing the new prime minister. At this point it started to get messy. According to Macmillan, who was still technically prime minister, the palace let it be known that the Queen would be asking for advice. As he had not yet resigned, he was still in a position to give it. 'It therefore became necessary for me to do what I would have preferred to avoid,' he said later – to get involved in the choice of his successor.

From his bed in the King Edward VII Hospital, where he was still recovering from a general anaesthetic, Macmillan started getting busy. He issued instructions to the cabinet as to how consultations should proceed and less than a week after his operation saw all the candidates. It was clear that the party was deeply divided. Home had the support of most MPs, but the constituency parties backed Hailsham followed by Butler, with Home a complete non-runner. However, Home seemed to have the most support within the cabinet, which was enough for Macmillan to advise the Queen, if and when he was asked, that it should be him. Meanwhile the palace was coming under pressure, with backbench MPs ringing up to say that this candidate or that would be a complete disaster and a couple of senior figures telling Adeane that they would not serve under Home. Sir Edward Ford recalled: 'Our response was "You're the party, choose your undoubted leader and we will inform the Queen."'

Finally Macmillan sent his letter of resignation to the Queen. Three-quarters of an hour after his departure was announced, the Queen arrived at the hospital for her final audience with Macmillan, who at that point was an ex-prime minister, and therefore had no constitutional authority whatsoever. When she got there she asked for his advice, and he handed her a memorandum he had prepared recommending Home. He also advised her to get back to the palace and send for Home immediately in order to prevent a revolt by the defeated candidates.

The Queen was more than happy with the choice. Butler was not 'her cup of tea', according to an aide, but Home – who would renounce his peerage and serve as Sir Alec Douglas-Home – certainly was. The aide told Pimlott: 'When she got the advice to call Alec she thought "Thank God." She loved Alec – he was an old friend. They talked about dogs and shooting together. They were both Scottish landowners, the same sort of people, like old school friends.'[40] That made him among the last of the dwindling breed of prime ministers who moved in similar social circles to the Queen; the next PM who came anywhere close was David Cameron, nearly fifty years later.

Choosing Macmillan's successor did not mean that the saga was quite over, however. When the Queen summoned Home and asked him to form a government, he said he would have to go away to see if he could put an administration together, knowing he would not be able to do so without Butler agreeing to serve. However, as it soon became clear that he had the Queen behind him, many of the potential rebels melted away, and he was able to form a government. He returned to the palace to kiss hands the following day.

After Home had accepted, his mother, the dowager countess, said: 'So good of Alec to do prime minister.' The sense of *noblesse oblige* encapsulated in that remark offers a clue as to why the changeover was one of the most criticised episodes of the Queen's reign. The criticism was aimed not so much at the Queen as the Tory party and the 'magic circle' of Old Etonian grandees which had supposedly fixed the succession on behalf of a candidate who was one of their own, and whom many saw as inferior to Butler. But it did not look good for the Queen either: by summoning the 14th Earl of Home, a man who belonged more on the grouse moor than he did in modern Britain, the palace seemed equally out of touch. Ben Pimlott's verdict on the Queen was that her decision to opt for passivity and in effect collude with Macmillan's plan to block Butler 'must be counted the biggest political misjudgement of her reign'.[41]

That is not everyone's view. Vernon Bogdanor has argued that by carrying out a much more thorough canvass of the Conservative party than had happened in 1957, Macmillan could not be accused of misrepresenting Tory opinion. He also said that with the Conservatives so obviously divided, it would have been a mistake for the Queen to get involved in the party's internal politics; the straightforward course was for her to follow Macmillan's advice. It was up to the Conservative party, if it so wished, to make it clear that it could not accept Home as prime minister.[42] The historian Peter Hennessy said: 'I think she did the only thing she could have done, [which was to] listen to her outgoing prime minister.'[43] The soundings ordered by Macmillan may have left a lot to be desired, Hennessy wrote in his book on prime ministers, 'but not to have accepted his resultant advice, once given, would have been tantamount to saying her premier of six years was misleading his Monarch'.[44]

I would offer another opinion: that what went wrong was that the Queen was ahead of her time. Because of her temperament and the age at which she acceded to the throne, she was reluctant to interfere in the political process. Malcolm Muggeridge was right: she did not want to exercise her own judgement. But it was more than that. She saw that in the post-war world the growing power of democracy and the decline of deference meant that it was no longer appropriate for an unelected sovereign to wield the sort of political power that had been exercised by her grandfather George V and even her own father. She recognised that, but the political establishment – and in particular the Conservative party – had not caught up by evolving a viable and plausible alternative method of selecting a prime minister.

Almost exactly a year later Douglas-Home was replaced as prime minister by Harold Wilson. Some four months after that, the Conservative party published its new procedure for selecting the leader of the party, which would involve a ballot of MPs and be run not by the party leadership but by the backbench 1922 Committee. As Robert Lacey summed it up: 'This left the royal prerogative strictly for the occasions when the mechanisms of democracy got into a genuine deadlock they could not resolve without the help of a presiding agency seen to be fair, strong-willed and independent.'[45] That did indeed sound like a perfect arrangement. But it wouldn't last.

CHAPTER FIVE

FRIENDLINESS NOT FRIENDSHIP

WHEN HAROLD WILSON won the general election of October 1964 with a wafer-thin majority, it took a little while for the new PM and his sovereign to get used to each other. Wilson was not like the Queen's other prime ministers. After three Etonians and a Harrovian, he was the first premier of her reign not to have been to public school, although the grammar school-educated Labour leader was solidly middle class – he had been an academic at Oxford before going into politics. Wilson smoked a pipe and had a strong Yorkshire accent, and was not, unlike his predecessors, a habitué of grouse moors and the grander country houses. Even his arrival at Buckingham Palace to be asked to form a government gave notice that he was going to be a different kind of PM: two cars drove into the palace forecourt, containing not just Wilson and his wife, Mary, but also his father, his two sons and his political secretary, Marcia Williams. Normally it was just the prime minister who turned up, possibly with his wife.

The group sat on a sofa in the equerry's room and were given sherry while Wilson went in to kiss hands (as he pointed out in his memoirs, by this time prime ministers no longer actually had to kiss hands, although the expression survives to this day). Marcia Williams was not impressed: 'A number of anonymous Palace individuals were there. To me they all looked exactly alike. As I recall it, the conversation centred on horses. Perhaps it was assumed that everybody was interested in horses, though my knowledge of them was minimal and the Wilson family's less.'[1]

There was also an interesting exchange of telegrams with Prince Philip, which revealed that Wilson felt relaxed in his dealings with the royal family rather than tongue-tied by deference. Philip sent Wilson a congratulatory message in which he referred to the fact that the prime minister had a bungalow on the Scilly Isles, on what is Duchy of Cornwall land. 'Delighted to see that resident of the Duchy of Cornwall is new tenant at Downing Street,' wrote Philip. Wilson replied: 'Thanks to the generous attitude of the Duchy, my residence within the Duchy of Cornwall is a freehold as against the tied cottage status of my tenure at Downing Street.'[2]

At his first weekly audience with the Queen, Wilson made the mistake of underestimating how seriously she took such meetings. She asked him a question about something that had come up in the cabinet minutes, which she was always sent, only to find that Wilson was unprepared and unbriefed. Unhappy at being caught out, Wilson made sure after that he always did his homework.

They soon found that they both enjoyed their time together. The former Oxford don took pleasure in explaining what his government was doing, and the Queen – who had been bored by Macmillan's lectures – was flattered by his willingness to take her into his confidence. His private secretary and the Queen's would discuss in advance the points that each of them would like to bring up, and the Queen would have a small piece of paper with notes on it on a side table which she occasionally referred to. Sometimes they had a cup of tea or coffee, but not always. In general, he said, they 'just used to sit and chat'. It wasn't about racing, either. He wrote in his memoirs how the Queen 'was fascinated at the account I was able to give of what life was like in the "back-to-back" houses she had seen in Leeds and in the industrial villages of the North'.[3]

Commentators have occasionally suggested that the claim that Wilson was the Queen's favourite prime minister was a line pushed by Wilson himself, but that they got on well does seem to have been the case. Richard Crossman, a member of Wilson's cabinet, wrote in his diary: 'He's devoted to the Queen and is very proud that she likes his visits to her.'[4]

'Harold did get on very well with the Queen and she was very fond of him,' an aide recalled. 'His audiences got longer and longer. Once he stayed for two hours, and was asked to stay for drinks.'[5] That was not normal royal behaviour. If prime ministers have drinks after their audience, it is downstairs in the private secretary's office, where their own private secretary has spent the last hour or so catching up with their opposite number. One royal servant recalled that 'a great respect' grew up between the Queen and Wilson. 'The old guard who made up some of the Household were very suspicious.'[6]

Bernard Donoughue (now Lord Donoughue), head of the Downing Street policy research unit from 1974, said that the key to their relationship was that Wilson was 'not stuffy like some of those boring Tory prime ministers'. But Wilson definitely enjoyed his audiences too, he said. 'Harold got excited before going to see the Queen. He really enjoyed it. He said to me, "The reason we get on is that we have one important thing in common. We both love political gossip."[7] It was the same trait that Rab Butler had spotted in the 1950s.

That love of gossip was to the fore in 1974 when Wilson spoke to the Queen about a 'scurrilous' story that had appeared in the London *Evening Standard* claiming that the French president, Valéry Giscard d'Estaing, had a habit of cruising the streets of Paris at night looking for what Wilson called 'lighter ladies of the town'. The following week Wilson told her he had to go to Paris for talks with Giscard, at which the Queen said 'ho ho', as if Wilson was only going there to engage in similar 'extra-mural activities'. When he got back he told her about the talks, only for the Queen to ask: 'And what about ho ho?' 'Ma'am,' he replied, 'there was no ho ho.' Unfortunately something he ate at the official dinner in Paris had disagreed with him, and he spent the rest of the night feeling 'as sick as a dog'. The Queen, he said, 'was terribly disappointed'. Wilson's admiration for the Queen did not extend to all things royal. At the state banquet at Windsor Castle for the German president, a troop of pipers entered the hall at the end of dinner. 'Here comes the deterrent,' muttered Wilson.[8]

Despite the best efforts of his personal staff, Wilson never revealed what he discussed with the Queen. The only exception was when he told Marcia Williams that the Queen had just had a new style of riding habit made for Trooping the Colour. What was noticeable, however, was that he would come back from the palace in a euphoric mood, and would sometimes seem to have adjusted his opinions on some matter of the day. 'When he resigned,' wrote his authorised biographer, 'she sent him a photograph of them in the rain at Balmoral, which he thereafter carried in his wallet.'[9]

As inevitably happens when there is a real flesh-and-blood family at the heart of the constitution, there was an occasional blurring between the official and personal roles of the prime minister. In 1967 Australian prime minister Harold Holt disappeared while swimming off a beach near his holiday home in Victoria. Wilson was preparing to fly to Australia for the memorial service when the Queen asked if he thought it was a good idea for Prince Charles to join him. He agreed, and the Queen called her eldest son in. 'Charles,' she said, 'the Prime Minister has very generously said that he will take you to Australia. Now you will do exactly what he tells you. If he says go to bed, you just go to bed even if you have to break off in the middle of a sentence.'[10] Prince Charles was nineteen years old at the time.

When it came to her son and heir, however, the Queen did not always take Wilson's advice. In December 1965 – a year before Charles was due to leave school – the Queen and Prince Philip invited Wilson and a number of others, including Lord Mountbatten, the Archbishop of Canterbury and the Dean of Windsor, to dinner at Buckingham Palace to discuss the next stage of his education. The next day Wilson told Richard Crossman that the discussion 'had gone on for a couple of hours because it was so interesting'.[11] Wilson thought that Charles, who did not shine academically at Gordonstoun, should go to a provincial university rather than Oxbridge, which would fit in with the idea that the heir to the throne should have the experience of getting to know people from other backgrounds.[12] Instead Charles went to Trinity College, Cambridge, where the master was none other than Rab Butler, who had been given the job by Harold Wilson. The man who had been so perceptive about the Queen would play a significant role in shaping the education of her son.

WHILE WILSON revelled in his dealings with the Queen, other Labour politicians were more sceptical about the whole royal rigmarole. Richard Crossman, a left-wing former Oxford don who, like Rishi Sunak much later, had been head boy at Winchester, was particularly scathing. In his posthumously published diaries he described in spikily dismissive terms the rehearsal that he and other new ministers had to go through before being sworn in as privy counsellors. 'I don't suppose anything more dull, pretentious, or plain silly has ever been invented.' Ministers ('sixteen grown men') were taught how to kneel on one knee on a stool, raise their right hand while holding the Bible, advance three paces towards the Queen, kiss her hand and then walk backwards without falling over their stool.

When it came to the real thing, he said that both ministers and the Queen were uneasy. 'Then at the end informality broke out and she said, "You all moved backwards very nicely," and we all laughed.'[13] What he missed out, however, was that despite the rehearsal he still struggled. 'Dick Crossman of Winchester was the clumsiest,' wrote his fellow minister Barbara Castle.[14] At a later meeting she said: 'No stools today. Dick always disgraces us by falling over them. These Winchester men have no breeding.' The Queen, however, did not seem to mind when things went wrong. The clerk of the council told Castle about one swearing-in where the counsellors knelt on the floor instead of their stools, and then when their mistake was pointed out shuffled forward on their knees to get to them. One particularly inept individual missed his stool entirely and only stopped himself from falling over by grabbing the Queen's hand. Throughout the farce the Queen stood there with a face like thunder. Afterwards, when the clerk thought he was going to get a roasting from the Queen, she merely giggled and said, 'Wasn't it funny!' 'I thought you looked very displeased, ma'am.' 'If I hadn't looked like that I should have burst out laughing,' she replied.[15]

Crossman also described having drinks with the Queen at Buckingham Palace, where they were served 'quite ordinary gin and tonics'. When it was his turn with the Queen she talked about her corgis, 'as I am told she always does'. He wrote: 'I asked what good they were and she said they were Welsh dogs used for rounding up cattle by biting their legs.' When they had exhausted that topic they talked about cows, and how one of the Queen's Jerseys had just won a show. Afterwards Crossman complained that he had drunk plenty but had very little to eat, and 'felt terrible' the next morning.[16] If there is a strong thread of Crossman's Winchester-and-Oxford intellectual superiority in all of this, at least he was honest enough to know what he was doing. Describing Privy Council meetings as 'the most idiotic flummery', he said: 'I must admit that I feel morally superior to my colleagues in despising it.' He turned down so many invitations to grand occasions that they stopped asking him, he said. 'I know my attitude is partly a piece of conscious arrogance – I want to prove to myself that I don't like these things, although I sometimes find myself mildly enjoying them and I even slightly resent myself for refusing ever to attend them.'[17]

Crossman might be forgiven his dismissive view of Privy Council meetings. Despite its history and seeming grandeur, this formal body of advisers to the sovereign is less the beating heart of the constitution and more of a harmless relic. Once powerful, as political authority shifted to the cabinet its role became more formal. The Privy Council advises the sovereign on the issuing of royal charters and appointing members to certain professional bodies. Its other roles include issuing royal proclamations, such as declaring bank holidays or announcing new coinage, and recommending the approval of Channel Islands legislation. Membership is for life, and there are now some 750 members, including members of the royal family and the royal household, all cabinet ministers, senior opposition politicians including party leaders, senior members of the judiciary and the Archbishops of Canterbury and York. Despite its lack of political relevance, MPs place great store on being made privy counsellors, which allows them to style themselves 'the Right Honourable'. Michael Portillo once said that it was a title much coveted, 'partly because no one outside Parliament knows what it means'.[18]

As his views on the Privy Council perhaps illustrate, tact and diplomacy were not Richard Crossman's strong suits. Once over dinner with Lord Porchester, a racehorse breeder who would become the Queen's racing manager, Crossman – then housing minister – got into a furious row with his host about the monarchy, in which he railed against the 'snobbery of the people who love the monarch and the dreary role both of the monarchy and of the court'. At that point Porchester declared: 'The Queen is one of my greatest personal friends, and I am a tremendous admirer.' Crossman knew that perfectly well, but it had not stopped him. 'In a way that put me in my place,' he wrote, 'but I said, "Well, maybe! But she finds me boring and I find her boring and I think it is a great relief that I don't have to see her."' A couple of weeks later Crossman happened to meet the Queen. 'Ah,' she said, 'Lord Porchester was telling me about you.'[19]

He did, however, occasionally find something to admire. He was spending the day at Sandringham when he found her doing 'an enormous, incredibly difficult jigsaw'. He wrote: 'Her lady-in-waiting had told me she was jolly good at jigsaws and sure enough while she was standing there talking to the company at large, her fingers were straying and she was quietly fitting in the pieces while apparently not looking round.' He also enjoyed some of his encounters with the Queen. Over drinks after a Privy Council meeting, she described –

miming every grapple and hold herself – an all-in wrestling match she had watched on television. 'She said what tremendous fun that kind of all-in wrestling was. "Do you want a Royal Charter for them?" I asked, and she said, "No, not yet." . . . It was quite an eye-opener to see how she enjoyed it.'[20]

Crossman's chippiness about the monarchy blinded him to one of the obvious truths about the Queen and her forebears: that they have no inbuilt prejudice against Labour politicians on a personal level, even if they do not always agree with their policies. He once asked Godfrey Agnew, clerk of the Privy Council, 'whether she preferred the Tories to us because they were our social superiors'. Agnew replied: 'I don't think so. The Queen doesn't make fine distinctions between politicians of different parties. They all roughly belong to the same social category in her view.'[21] Even if they did go to Winchester. The former Conservative cabinet minister Sir Malcolm Rifkind tells of a conversation with the Queen which backs up this view. 'She said, "The Shah [of Iran] once asked me whether I had had more years with Conservative or Labour prime ministers since I became Queen. I had to say to him that I hadn't the faintest idea." I remember thinking – although I didn't say it – "Of course you haven't the faintest idea. You couldn't care less what their parties are." What she did care about was their personalities – how she would get on with them.'[22]

Although on the left of the party, Barbara Castle had more of an open mind about the absurdities of all the palace folderol. Her first state banquet was 'pure Ruritania' but the food was excellent and included 'the best green pea soup I have ever tasted'. In the drawing room afterwards she was brought over to talk to the Queen ('giving my usual half-bow because I won't curtsey') but found the Queen spoke to her 'very sensibly' about Africa. Their conversation came to a premature end when a flunkey came and whispered in the Queen's ear and she excused herself, 'saying laughingly that "poor Charles" was doing his O-levels the next day and just wanted a bit of reassurance'. When she came back Castle was talking to Princess Margaret, and the Queen said to her sister: 'You and I would never have got into university.' In the state room afterwards Castle's husband told her: 'You've been monopolizing the Queen.' To her surprise, she had 'enjoyed myself far more than I thought I would'.[23] She had sporadic contact with the royals over the years, occasionally finding herself sitting next to Prince Philip at a lunch, when they would always 'argue like mad'. But she enjoyed that too. 'I like his utter lack of stuffiness.'[24]

CROSSMAN WAS NOT the only public-school left-winger to have astringent opinions about the monarchy. Anthony Wedgwood Benn (Westminster and Oxford), who became Viscount Stansgate on his father's death and fought a campaign for the right to renounce his peerage so he could continue sitting as an MP (he later became known as simply Tony Benn), was postmaster general in Wilson's first government. Benn was made a privy counsellor at the same time as Crossman, and had similar views. He chatted throughout the rehearsal, and did his best to look as if he was not taking it seriously. 'I'm afraid the officials were profoundly shocked,' he wrote. At the actual ceremony he affirmed rather than swearing on the Bible, even though he was a Christian, because he disapproved of religious oaths for anything other than religious purposes. 'I left the Palace boiling with indignation and feeling that this was an attempt to impose tribal magic and personal loyalty on people whose real duty was only to their electors.'[25]

Nevertheless, tribal magic, as Benn was to discover, can exert its influence in surprising ways, and the story of Tony Benn and the stamps is a cautionary tale of naivety, hubris and learning where power lies. As postmaster general, one of the things Benn wanted to do was to issue postage stamps without the Queen's head on them, something that at the time was considered almost unthinkable. Benn, however, thought he was on a bit of a roll with this: when he mentioned it in a speech to the Oxford Labour Club in 1963 as an example of what a Labour government should do, he said it was the most popular thing in his talk. 'Republicanism is on the increase,' he wrote in his diary.[26] Possibly a little prematurely.

No sooner had he been put in charge of the Post Office after the election the following year than he invited designers to submit designs for new commemorative stamps. The Queen agreed to give him an audience to discuss stamps, at which he explained that designs for commemorative issues that did not have the Queen's head on them were never submitted because it was understood that she refused to consider them. 'The Queen was clearly embarrassed and indicated that she had no personal feeling about it at all,' he wrote. When she said she would be interested in seeing some new designs, he casually said that he happened to have some in his bag, spread out on the floor a series of designs by the artist David Gentleman (father of the journalist Amelia Gentleman), and knelt down to pass them up one by one for the Queen to examine. It had, he said, been a 'hilarious' scene as he 'tried as hard as I could to do a little Disraeli on her with all the charm I could muster'. He obviously thought it had worked, because she agreed that he could submit stamps for her consideration including ones without her head. A fifteen-minute audience had ended up lasting forty, and he left the palace 'feeling absolutely on top of the world'.[27]

Four months later she rejected the designs he had submitted without her head. In case Benn did not get the point, three months after that Downing Street let him know that he was not going to get his way with the stamps. Wilson had no intention of upsetting the monarch, and the Queen's head was staying. Benn was furious. He had got some way with the Queen, who had seemed amenable to his suggestions, but he had failed to reckon with the power of her private secretary. Sir Michael Adeane had, he believed, gone behind his back to Harold Wilson and threatened to make a fuss. The Queen might not care about the stamps, wrote Benn, but 'Adeane and all the flunkies at Buckingham Palace certainly do. Their whole position depends on maintaining this type of claptrap . . . This is exactly how the Palace works. It doesn't want to appear unpopular, yet at the same time it does not want certain things to happen and it uses the threat of controversy to stop any changes going too far.'[28] He concluded: 'The plain fact is that I shan't get the Queen's head off the stamps and it's probably rather foolish of me to go on knocking my head against a brick wall.'[29]

Wilson told him later that the Queen did not want her head removed: 'She is a nice woman, and you absolutely charmed her into saying yes when she didn't really mean it.'[30] Benn, meanwhile, reckoned that the prime minister was set on making the Labour government 'more royal than the Tory Party'. He wrote: 'This may give him a certain short-term advantage and he is exploiting it as hard as he can.' But in the end, said Benn, all it did was strengthen 'the reactionary elements in our society'.[31]

In July 1966 Benn was promoted to technology minister. When he went to the palace to be affirmed the Queen said:

'I'm sure you will miss your stamps.' He wrote in his diary: 'I replied, "Yes indeed I shall. I shall never forget your kindness and encouragement in helping me to tackle them." She gave me a rather puzzled smile.'[32]

ONE OF THE issues that bedevilled the Wilson government, and also involved the Queen, was the rebellious self-governing British colony of Southern Rhodesia (now Zimbabwe), whose ruling white minority wanted independence but to retain control of its government. However, Britain would only agree to independence on condition of majority rule. The country's prime minister, Ian Smith, responded in 1965 with a unilateral declaration of independence (UDI). Harold Wilson imposed sanctions, but disagreed with those in the Commonwealth – and the Labour party – who favoured military action. The Queen found herself pulled in two directions: while African members of the Commonwealth were bitterly hostile to white rule in Rhodesia, many settlers there felt an old-fashioned loyalty to the Crown.

During the build-up to UDI, Smith – a former RAF Spitfire pilot – came over to Britain for the funeral of Winston Churchill in 1965. Wilson asked the Queen to invite Smith to a reception at Buckingham Palace; because Rhodesia was not at the time independent, he had not originally been on the guest list. However, after an hour the Queen noticed he was not there. An equerry was dispatched to look for him, and he was eventually tracked down eating a steak in a nearby hotel. He claimed he had never received the invitation, but allegedly it was in his pocket all the time. 'He stammered out his excuses to the Queen,' wrote Wilson, 'I thought unconvincingly.'[33]

Just before Smith declared UDI, Wilson enlisted the help of the Queen by getting her to agree to an announcement that there could be no question of her accepting the role of head of state of a rebel regime. He also got her to write a personal letter to Smith saying: 'I have followed the recent discussions between the British government and your government with the closest concern and I am very glad to know that Mr Wilson will be paying you a visit.'[34] However, her handwritten letter to Smith had the opposite effect to that intended. Smith read it out at a banquet held for the British prime minister, describing it as 'a wonderful message from this gracious lady',[35] making it sound as if the Queen was on his side. On the eve of UDI Smith made a final appeal to the Queen, declaring that Rhodesians would never swerve in their loyalty. The Queen sent what Barbara Castle described as 'a beautifully formal reply', saying she was confident that 'all her Rhodesian people will demonstrate their loyalty by continuing to act in a constitutional manner'. Castle noted: 'Harold has certainly got her superbly organized.'[36] It seems likely that the strength of the personal relationship between the Queen and her prime minister allowed him to persuade her to take such an active role in the crisis.

One scheme to get the royal family's help came to nothing, however. In Rhodesia the governor, Sir Humphrey Gibbs – whose family knew the Queen Mother – had refused to recognise UDI but had nevertheless remained in the country. When his wife went to Northern Ireland to stay with the province's prime minister, Terence O'Neill, a plot was hatched to bring down the Smith regime by flying the Queen Mother to Salisbury, where her 'fantastic natural charm would win the day'. O'Neill told Wilson: 'Vast crowds would gather outside Government House to express their loyalty . . . All those in the regime of British stock would fall over themselves to meet her . . . She might just bring it off.' Instead of dismissing it out of hand, Wilson referred the madcap plot to Herbert

Bowden, the Commonwealth secretary, who warned that it might backfire and embarrass the Queen Mother.[37] Predictably, it came to nothing.

The Rhodesian rebellion rumbled on until 1979, when years of guerrilla war came to an end with the signing of the Lancaster House Agreement, which paved the way for free elections and the introduction of black majority rule.

WHETHER IT WAS because he admired the Queen, or simply saw her as useful and therefore not worth antagonising, Harold Wilson's efforts to accommodate her extended to not causing trouble over money. Royal finances have been a cause of strife between monarchy and government throughout history, and the issue became particularly sensitive in the late 1960s. Inflation meant that the palace wage bill had grown disproportionately, causing significant cash-flow problems in the Queen's official accounts, but at the same time the booming economy and her immunity from tax meant that her personal fortune had increased considerably. The Queen had to make staff cuts, and faced having to use her private income to cover the growing deficit.

The matter became headline news in 1969 when Prince Philip said in a US television interview that the royal family would go into the red in 1970. 'We may have to move into smaller premises, who knows?' he said. In remarks almost designed to alienate public opinion, he said that he had already sold a small yacht and might have to give up polo. Philip's remarks put an issue that was usually the subject of confidential negotiations into the public domain in a way that embarrassed both the royal family and the government. Wilson had to act, but when he brought the royal finances up in a meeting with key ministers he got a cool response from left-wingers including Castle and Crossman, who pointed out that the Queen did not pay any estate or death duties. Castle asked why the Civil List should be increased 'to enable Philip to play polo, when his wife was one of the richest women in the world?'[38] Wilson's solution was to defer the problem, by agreeing to set up a new select committee on the Civil List, but delaying it until after the election. Everyone was relieved, including Crossman. 'If Harold had mishandled it,' he wrote, 'we should now be in a long unpopular row in which we would lose votes by seeming to be mean to royalty.'[39] Politicians, almost without exception, will go a long way to avoid unnecessary rows with the royal family.

Labour expected to win the election in June 1970, but to their surprise it was Edward Heath who secured a majority. The Queen, said Wilson, 'was very warm and gracious' after his defeat. 'Obviously she could not say that she was sorry,' but she asked after his wife, Mary, and said she hoped he would be able to have a rest.[40] That 'obviously' is interesting: Victoria had no compunction in making her views about election results quite plain, and even George VI told both Neville Chamberlain and Winston Churchill how sorry he was to see them go. But times had changed.

That, however, was not how Tony Benn saw things. When he went to the palace for his farewell audience with the Queen, he said the courtiers – including Adeane – 'could scarcely conceal their delight' at Labour's defeat. When he saw the Queen they talked about stamps, and Concorde, the Anglo-French project for which Benn had been a driving force. She thanked him for all his work, prompting this strange conclusion by Benn: 'It was very courteous of her but I am sure that the idea that the Queen's Ministers are simply advisers, and that she is really the Government, in a position to thank them before they go, is deeply entrenched at the Palace.'[41]

EDWARD HEATH was cut from a different cloth to his Tory predecessors. His father ran a small building firm in Kent, and his mother was a lady's maid. But while Wilson's provincial roots had proved no obstacle to forming an easy relationship with the Queen, Heath's social awkwardness meant that they never bonded in the same way. He had no small talk, and was hardly one for jokes: he was stiff, inhibited and had little time for women.

As a junior whip in the 1950s he had been invited to lunch at Buckingham Palace. He was placed next to Princess Margaret, and as he had been told not to initiate conversation with a member of the royal family, he remained silent. So did she. Eventually he cracked and said, 'Have you been busy lately, ma'am?'

'That,' she replied, 'is the sort of question Lord Mayors ask when I visit cities.'[42]

Heath said he always used to look forward to his audiences with the Queen. 'It was always a relief to be able to discuss everything with someone, knowing full well that there was not the slightest danger of any information leaking.'[43]

However, their meetings do not sound like fun. 'Harold was fine, because he loved her and treated her marvellously,' an ex-courtier told Ben Pimlott. 'But Ted was tricky – she was never comfortable with him.'[44] His biographer John Campbell described his relations with the Queen as 'correct but cool'. As Campbell said, 'In part it was simply that Heath's normal reserve was increased by the formality with which he naturally approached his weekly audiences.' Heath's description of his audiences to Elizabeth Longford does nothing to dispel that notion. 'I believed in telling the Queen everything. There was always an agenda drawn up in agreement with the private secretary. She had it on a card on the table beside her to make sure that the items were covered, but I believed in telling her a good deal else of what was going on, which I hadn't mentioned to the private secretary, because I knew she would be interested.'[45] There wasn't much 'ho ho'.

The Queen's weekly audiences with Heath were not her only means of keeping in touch with what was going on politically. She also had her daily dispatches describing the day's proceedings in Parliament, which, as we have seen, used to be written by the prime minister and, memorably, were once written by Winston Churchill, but were now the responsibility of a member of the government whips' office with the title of vice-chamberlain of the royal household. During Heath's premiership they were written by Bernard Weatherill (always known as Jack), who would later become speaker of the House of Commons. The Queen seems to have liked them. In October 1972 her assistant private secretary William Heseltine wrote to Weatherill, saying: 'The Queen has told me that I am to write to thank you for the last in your series of very readable accounts of Parliamentary proceedings, and to assure you that she has read all the reports which you have sent with the greatest interest and instruction.'

Weatherill was not shy about expressing his opinions, variously describing MPs' questions as 'fatuous', 'irrelevant', 'silly' and 'frequently rude'. 'The trouble with Welsh Questions is that to an Englishman they are largely unintelligible,' he wrote. 'To a student of language however they are a joy.' Nicholas Ridley, he said, 'does tend to upset the opposition'. When the shadow housing minister Anthony Crosland made an ill-judged admission it was, Weatherill wrote, 'a very unfortunate start and the laughter it caused was not entirely confined to the government benches. It was perhaps fortunate that he could not see the expression on some of the faces behind him.' During one particularly dull debate on unemployment, 'the benches quickly emptied and those who remained evidently found it easier to concentrate with their eyes shut'. The next day was no better, and Weatherill was clearly determined not to bore the Queen with an account of the white paper on expenditure 1975–6. 'This is a matter for the experts of whom, happily, we have quite a number. It is however too complicated to simplify and I hope Your Majesty will forgive me if I do not try.'[46]

Some of the dispatches written for the Queen may have been even more spicy than Weatherill's. Sir Sydney Chapman, the Conservative MP who had the job under John Major, was once asked about what he thought about his letters becoming public. 'Given what I wrote about some of my colleagues,' he replied, 'I would be very happy to be six foot under before they were published.'[47]

The Queen and Heath had sharply differing views about the Commonwealth, to which Elizabeth was devoted. Campbell wrote: 'She was deeply unhappy with Heath's undisguised disrespect for the institution in general and most African leaders in particular.'[48] In 1971, when the first Commonwealth Heads of Government Meeting (CHOGM) was held in Singapore, the Queen was expecting to attend – she had arranged with Wilson when he was still in power that she would arrive in the royal yacht – but Heath told her not to. He was about to unveil a controversial new policy resuming arms sales to apartheid South Africa, and there was a danger that she could be dragged into an embarrassing dispute. Heath wrote in his memoirs: 'The Queen rightly pointed out that, if the conference had been in London, she would certainly have had to be there, and the situation would have been no less explosive. Therefore, the possibility of it being explosive in Singapore did not seem to her a conclusive reason for not going.'[49] But he stuck to his guns, and sent her his formal advice not to go. The meeting was indeed explosive, which 'greatly upset' the Queen, but those who went to Singapore agreed that Heath had made a mistake by not allowing her to go. Emeka Anyaoku, a future Commonwealth secretary general, told the writer Robert Hardman: 'I believe had the Queen been there, the atmosphere and the tone of the discussion would have been a lot more even-tempered.'[50]

A couple of years later the next CHOGM was in Ottawa. Once more Heath did not want the Queen to go, but she insisted. The way this was fixed, according to Hardman, was that once it was decided the meeting would be in Canada, the country's prime minister invited Elizabeth. Because she was going as Queen of Canada she did not have to consult her British prime minister. And once she was going, he had to go too, somewhat to Heath's annoyance. It was the 'Queen's firmness' in sticking to her decision to go that ended his 'sulky attitude', according to the secretary general, Arnold Smith. 'He could hardly stay away if she were there. So he came.'[51]

Meanwhile the palace had had a bruising time during the select committee hearings into the Civil List. The committee had a Tory majority, and was chaired by the chancellor, Anthony Barber, but its members included a number of Labour MPs prone to asking awkward questions, including the veteran anti-monarchist Willie Hamilton. The committee put the Crown on the defensive on a range of subjects, including how hard the Queen worked, her immunity from taxation and the size of her private wealth. As Ben Pimlott wrote, 'The emphasis, more than ever before, was on justifying, not merely expenditure, but also the need to incur it . . . The Queen, through her close advisers, had to present a convincing case that she gave value for money.'[52]

However, as well as the obviously loyal Tory members such as William Whitelaw and Norman St John Stevas, the Queen had a significant ally in the form of the leader of the opposition, Harold Wilson. As *The Times* put it, he went out of his way 'to be protective towards the Queen and her interests'. The palace was nothing if not grateful. 'When it came to re-doing the Civil List,' a former courtier said, 'Wilson was frightfully helpful. He used all his political skills and knowledge to get her what she wanted.'[53] One of the more radical proposals came from a Labour member of the committee, Douglas Houghton, who wanted to turn the royal household into a government department. This had the advantage that if inflation meant more money was needed, it would be clear that the increased funding was going into official expenditure rather than – as some critics might suggest – the Queen's pocket. The palace voiced strong objections, and after talking to the lord chamberlain, Lord Cobbold, the Treasury got the impression that the Queen might threaten to move out of Buckingham Palace if the idea went ahead. In the end the committee decided the scheme was too costly, and it was voted down in the Commons.[54]

Although the committee made some radical recommendations, including putting the Queen on an annual salary of £100,000 and reducing the annuities paid to the Queen Mother and Duke of Edinburgh, they were also voted down in the Commons. The Queen got her Civil List increased from £475,000 to £980,000, and royal trustees were appointed – including the prime minister and the chancellor – who would keep it under annual review and report to Parliament every ten years. As Pimlott wrote, 'Now, the List was to be continually scrutinized, and future additions to it were likely to depend on the reputation of the Royal Family, the mood of the nation, and the political colour of the House.'[55]

DISMISSIVE OF the Commonwealth, Edward Heath was a passionate European. On 1 January 1973 he took Britain into what was then known as the European Economic Community (EEC) or Common Market, later the European Union (EU). One week before, the Queen had broadcast the monarch's traditional Christmas message, which customarily is a homily free of politics or controversy or anything else that might upset viewers across the Commonwealth on Christmas Day. It is one of the very few addresses by the Queen that is not written on advice from the government, although as a courtesy Downing Street does get to see it before broadcast. A glimpse of the level and tone of the discussions between the palace and Number 10 can be seen in a letter from William Heseltine – then the Queen's press secretary – to Heath's principal private secretary, Robert Armstrong, shortly before the 1971 broadcast: 'As we said yesterday, the text is most decorously apolitical.' Armstrong wrote to Heath: 'It is customary for the Queen's Christmas broadcast to be submitted to 10 Downing Street for clearance. This text seems unexceptionable.'

A year later, however, politics made a rare but unmistakable appearance. Not everyone in the Commonwealth welcomed Britain joining the EEC – farmers in New Zealand and Australia would see their exports hit – but the Queen was happy to speak up in favour of entry. 'Britain is about to join her neighbours in the European Community and you may well ask how this will affect the Commonwealth,' she said in her message. 'The new links with Europe will not replace those with the Commonwealth. Old friends will not be lost; Britain will take her Commonwealth links into Europe with her.' These words were the result of extensive negotiations between the palace and Number 10, starting at the beginning of November. A letter from the Queen's private secretary Sir Martin Charteris reveals that there had been significant Downing Street input into the Christmas 1972 address. 'Many

thanks . . . for your thoughts on how the Europe/Common-
wealth passage of The Queen's Christmas broadcast might be
phrased,' he wrote. 'These are most useful and it is, of course,
also most valuable to have an indication of the Prime Minister's thinking in this matter.'

This was highly unusual. Armstrong wrote:

> This broadcast is a broadcast to the whole of the Com-
> monwealth, not just to The Queen's subjects in this
> country and . . . the text of the broadcast is not therefore
> a matter on which The Queen expects to receive formal
> advice from the Prime Minister. The Queen is, however,
> proposing on this occasion, with the Prime Minister's
> warm approval, to refer both to Northern Ireland and
> to our forthcoming entry into the European Commu-
> nity; and on these questions we agreed it was right that
> the Prime Minister should be given the opportunity of
> seeing the text of the broadcast, and giving such advice
> as he thought fit.

Number 10 did have tweaks to suggest, on both Europe
and Northern Ireland, which was then three years into the
Troubles: Downing Street asked for a sentence to be inserted
saying that people in Northern Ireland were 'steadfastly carrying on with their ordinary business of life'. It all needed a
sensitive touch. As Armstrong wrote, 'I think that the broadcast deals with Northern Ireland and the Commonwealth
and Europe in a balanced way which should not expose
the Queen to criticism on the grounds of taking sides in
controversial issues.' A reply from Charteris made clear that
he regarded Number 10's involvement as a one-off: 'In the
normal run of events, the text of The Queen's Christmas
Broadcast is not a matter in which Her Majesty expects to
receive formal advice.'

The following year, however, politics intruded yet again, and the Queen was not quite so happy about the result. At the end of 1973, industrial action by coal miners and railway workers meant dwindling coal stocks were affecting electricity production. On 13 December, Heath announced the temporary reduction of the working week to three days, to come into effect in the new year. Four days later the Queen wondered whether she should include a few sentences at the end of her Christmas broadcast, which she had already recorded, in the light of the deteriorating situation. Charteris drew up a form of words, which the Queen planned to bring up at Heath's weekly audience. As Robert Armstrong wrote in an official note:

> The argument for saying something was that The Queen should be seen to be aware of and concerned by the problems which the British people were undergoing; the argument against was that it was very difficult to think of anything which She could say which might not be interpreted as an attempt to intervene in or affect industrial disputes. Since She would be addressing Herself specifically to the situation in Britain, She would have to speak on the advice of Her Ministers; and there was a danger that anything that She might say might be misconstrued as an attempt by politicians to use or involve the Queen in matters of political controversy.

The Queen's proposed words seem pretty harmless now. She planned to say:

> Because my Christmas broadcast goes to all the Commonwealth, it had to be recorded some time ago, before special difficulties which Britain is now facing came upon us. I cannot let Christmas pass without speaking

to you directly of these difficulties because they are of deep concern to all of us as individuals and as a nation. Different people have different views, deeply and sincerely felt, about our problems and how they should be solved. Let us remember, however, that what we have in common is more important than what divides us. I want you all to know that my thoughts are with you today.

Heath, however, thought it was too much, and told the Queen not to add it to her broadcast. Armstrong wrote that what had already been recorded 'could be taken as covering the situation sufficiently', which is an interesting assertion, given that her original broadcast did not cover the situation at all. The Queen, of course, had to accept this, and she did. However, Charteris wrote to Armstrong that she wanted to keep the option of saying something open until the last moment. 'The trouble is that whatever The Queen says in her broadcast will be heard and judged in the climate that exists on the day,' he said. If the industrial situation improved, all would be well. But if it got worse, or if there were growing questions about what the Queen was going to say on the subject, then perhaps it would be hard for her to remain silent.

Charteris came up with another form of words, to be used as an introduction rather than a postscript: 'I cannot let Christmas pass without speaking to you directly of the hardship and difficulties with which so many are faced because they are of deep concern to all of us as individuals and as a nation. But I have felt that Christmas is so much a family occasion that you would wish me not to harp on these difficulties but to let you hear and see something which was recorded some time ago about events both in the Commonwealth family and in my own family.'

However, Heath was not wearing that, either. Armstrong agreed that the option of making an addition should always be kept open, but only if something exceptional like a major bomb outrage occurred. The problem with Charteris's proposed introduction, he said, was that it had the Queen saying she wanted to talk about the difficulties, and then proceeding 'to sheer smartly away from them'.[56] So the Queen remained silent. However, it is clear from the correspondence that she desperately wanted to say something about Britain's calamitous situation, however bland and inoffensive, but was banned from doing so by Heath.

Faced with continuing unrest, Heath called a snap general election two months later, using the slogan 'Who governs Britain?' The answer, when it came, was not the one he had been looking for.

THE DATE OF the election coincided with a royal tour of the Pacific islands and Australia. Times had moved on since Victoria, who had expected politicians to accommodate their plans to her convenience, or even George VI, around whose travel arrangements Clement Attlee had fitted the 1951 general election. Heath expected his Queen to be on hand, and so Elizabeth flew back from Canberra in time to hear the result. Labour was the biggest party, with 301 seats, against the Conservatives' 297, with the 14 Liberals and the 9 Scottish and Welsh nationalists holding the balance of power. Under normal practice, Heath would have tendered his resignation and advised the Queen to send for Harold Wilson as the leader of the largest party in the House of Commons. That, however, was not how the Conservative leader saw it, not least because the Tories had won more votes – but fewer seats – than Labour. He felt justified in trying to form a centre–right coalition with the Liberals, who had secured nearly six million votes,[57] so spent the next four days negotiating with their party leader, Jeremy Thorpe. Meanwhile Labour was content to sit and watch. Heath was under no obligation to resign. As Charteris wrote, 'The Prime Minister remains Prime Minister until he resigns . . . So there was this rather agonizing weekend when we weren't quite sure what was going to happen.'[58]

Despite two face-to-face meetings, Heath and Thorpe could not agree, with the sticking point being the Liberals' demands for electoral reform, and the negotiations were going nowhere. On the Monday Heath bowed to the inevitable and went to the palace to resign, accompanied by Robert Armstrong. After Charteris had taken Heath to see the Queen, he came back down to the equerry's room to pick up Armstrong and escort him to his own office. 'When we arrived there,' Armstrong wrote in an official account of events, 'he made some expression of sympathy: I do not remember exactly what he said, but I remember that I nearly broke into tears when he said it.' It was a moment that serves as a reminder that the relationship between the sovereign's private secretary and the prime minister's principal private secretary is an extremely close one. That relationship is often characterised as a dimension of the Golden Triangle, a term coined by the writer Philip Ziegler to describe the connection between the private secretary at the palace, his counterpart at Number 10 and the cabinet secretary. The monarch and the PM might see each other once a week, but their private secretaries often speak every day. Sometimes they become good friends. Armstrong no doubt swiftly composed himself, and then it was back to business: the two men agreed the announcement that would be put out by the palace, and discussed what the Queen would do next. They agreed that after opening Parliament she would resume her tour by flying to Indonesia, 'as evidence of a return to more normal conditions'.[59]

The Queen then called Wilson to ask him to form a government. 'Our relaxed intimacy was immediately renewed,' he wrote.[60]

Subsequently, the Queen became fond of Heath. 'She found him entertaining,' said Michael McManus, his private secretary in later life. In 1996 she went to a party thrown by John Major at Downing Street to mark Heath's eightieth birthday. 'He had this affliction of his thyroid gland,' said McManus. 'He just could not stay awake.' At the dinner he was seated next to the Queen. 'After finishing with the dignitary on her right she turned to Heath,' wrote Ziegler, 'only to find that his eyes were closed and he was snoring peacefully.'[61] The Queen gave him a gentle nudge to wake him up. 'That showed a certain affection,' said McManus.[62] She could also tease him. In 1992 she was talking to Heath and US secretary of state James Baker at a palace reception about how Heath had gone to Iraq the previous year to negotiate the release of British hostages. Why, Heath wondered, had Baker not gone to Iraq when he wanted to speak to the regime? 'But he couldn't!' said the Queen. 'He couldn't go to Baghdad like you could.' Why not, asked Heath. 'You're expendable!' said the Queen.

DURING WILSON'S second term his closest confidante was Marcia Williams, his former private secretary who had risen to become his political secretary and then head of his political office. Clever and sharp-witted, she had more power than most cabinet ministers, but her tirades caused tensions within Number 10 and meant she was a deeply divisive figure. There was also speculation that Wilson had an affair with her, but if that did happen it was over long before he came to power: in 2024 The Times revealed that while in Downing Street he had an affair with his deputy press secretary Janet Hewlett-Davies.

Williams, who was made Baroness Falkender in July 1974, was deeply suspicious of the palace, but not for the usual Labour reasons. Bernard Donoughue, head of the policy research unit at Number 10, who was often at odds with Williams, described in his diary how she blamed him for the Queen getting a favourable financial deal. Joe Haines, Wilson's press secretary, told Donoughue how Williams was 'furious and jealous' that Donoughue had been to the palace and not her. 'She is also blaming me for the way in which the Civil List increase was slipped through Cabinet and thinks it is linked to my going to the Palace. A plot whereby I act as the Queen's agent to persuade the PM to agree to her increase in grant: totally bonkers.'[63] A short while later Haines revealed to Donoughue that the reason Williams was so furious he had been invited to the palace was that she claimed her mother was the illegitimate daughter of Edward VII. 'One of the king's officials, named Falkender, took the blame,' wrote Donoughue. 'But really she is in direct line to the throne – and that is why the Queen is afraid to invite her to the Palace!'[64]

It was, however, even more complicated than that. When she got a CBE in 1970, Williams was not prepared to go to Buckingham Palace for the investiture on the grounds that the Queen 'is a Tory'. When the palace sent the insignia to her, she complained that it arrived 'in a brown paper parcel'. Her feelings did not abate with time: when she sat next to Charteris at a dinner in 1975, her opening gambit to the Queen's private secretary was said to have been 'I suppose you realise I loathe all you stand for?'[65]

MARTIN CHARTERIS also played a role in one of the most constitutionally controversial episodes of the Queen's reign, one that continues to have political reverberations to this day: the sacking in 1975 of the Australian Labor prime minister, Gough Whitlam, by governor general Sir John Kerr, the Queen's representative. It raised questions about what the Queen knew, and whether Australia can ever be a truly independent nation while the British sovereign remains its head of state.

Whitlam had been elected in 1972 with a small majority in the House of Representatives, while the opposition – under Malcolm Fraser – had control of the Senate. Rocked by scandals and a worsening economic crisis, by 1975 Whitlam's government was in serious trouble as Fraser used his Senate majority to block the passage of bills needed to finance government expenditure. To break the deadlock Kerr used his reserve powers to sack Whitlam in mid-November and install Fraser as acting premier pending an election. Whitlam lost the subsequent election by a landslide.

In 2020 letters were released on the orders of Australia's highest court which showed that Kerr did not tell the Queen of his intention to remove Whitlam. On the day of the sacking he wrote to Charteris saying, 'I decided to take the step I took without informing the Palace in advance . . . it was better for Her Majesty NOT to know.' The Queen was duly grateful. However, the letters also revealed that the governor general had written to the Queen on the subject of his reserve powers, including the power to dismiss the prime minister, as early as two months before the dismissal. In a letter to Kerr, Charteris wrote that to use his reserve powers of dismissal was 'a heavy responsibility and it is only at the very end when there is demonstrably no other course that they should be used'. This wasn't the palace trying to talk him out of it.

While the Queen managed to stay above the fray, twenty-seven-year-old Prince Charles – showing, perhaps, his naivety – did voice an opinion. Four months after Whitlam was dismissed, the prince wrote to Kerr to express his support. 'What you did last year was right and the courageous thing to do – and most Australians seemed to endorse your decision when it came to the point.'

Ever since 1975 Australia's gravest constitutional crisis has provided fuel for the country's republican movement, even if voters remain divided over whether Kerr acted correctly. And although Jenny Hocking, the academic who campaigned for the release of the palace letters, has argued that the correspondence shows that the Queen was 'intensely' involved in what happened, the general verdict is that Elizabeth emerged with her reputation intact. Regardless of whether she knew that Kerr was set on sacking Whitlam, she certainly did not order his dismissal. As for Charles, it is surprising that republicans have not made more of his unwise letter to Kerr.

Kerr resigned as governor general in 1977, cutting short his five-year term. In 2015 it emerged that the Queen had been glad to see him go. The palace had apparently been worried about Kerr's behaviour, reliability and apparent pursuit of his own interests: they thought he and his wife were greedy. Paul Hasluck, Kerr's predecessor as governor general, who had stayed in contact with Charteris, gained the impression after speaking to the private secretary that 'the palace had brought pressure to bear on Kerr to retire'.[66]

*

ONE OF THE MORE tangled sagas of Harold Wilson's second term as prime minister is the story of how he came to resign in 1976. There has been often wild speculation about why he stood down after just two years, including paranoia about the security services and suggestions that he was suffering from the early symptoms of dementia. His resignation plan, which he announced on 16 March, five days before his sixtieth birthday, was a closely guarded secret within Number 10, but there was one person with whom he was prepared to share his strategy: the Queen.

In September the previous year Wilson had made his traditional annual visit to Balmoral together with his wife, Mary. Without any detectives to cramp their style, the Queen drove the Wilsons to a small lodge on the estate, where she filled the kettle and they had tea, and the prime minister told her of his intention to resign in six months' time. Afterwards Elizabeth and Mary donned aprons and washed the dishes.[67] He confirmed his intention at an audience in December, when he told her he would be going around 11 March. Donoughue wrote in his diary the next day: 'HW told the Queen about his retirement last night. She was sympathetic. But apparently her secretary Martin Charteris is flapping and saying it will be a disaster.'[68]

According to Barbara Castle, Wilson actually told the Queen even earlier than that – nearly two years previously, when he was elected. She wrote in her diary that he told her: 'When I became PM this time I told the Queen the date on which I would retire from this job. She's got the record of it, so no one will be able to say afterwards that I was pushed out.'[69] However, as Ben Pimlott wrote, his attempt to prove that he went of his own volition, at a time of his own choosing, did not work: 'So complete, by this time, was the assumption by the press both of Wilson's ambition and of his deviousness, that the obvious explanation – that he had had enough – was the hardest to accept.'[70]

The Queen, however, did not want Wilson to go. Wilson's private secretary, Kenneth Stowe, told Donoughue that she was 'very concerned'. Donoughue wrote: 'She doesn't want him to do it and there has been discussion of trying to get him to change his mind.' Charteris discussed it with the cabinet secretary, John Hunt, but was talked out of doing anything about it – partly because it would have been constitutionally inappropriate, but also because Wilson had made up his mind to go. He was not the man he had been during his first term: he was tired and drinking more. When his usual whisky failed to arrive during preparations for prime minister's questions, he said: 'If they don't hurry up, I shall answer Questions cold sober, which will create a record.'

When he left office, the Queen made him a knight of the Garter, which she had done for all her retiring prime ministers, including Heath, but not Macmillan, who refused it. She also attended a Downing Street dinner in his honour, the first time she had been in Number 10 since Churchill's retirement dinner twenty-one years earlier. There was a bit of a fuss about the guest list, however: Wilson wanted Kenneth Stowe to ask if the Queen was willing to be at the same occasion as Falkender, what with her being the illegitimate descendant of the Queen's great-grandfather (allegedly). If she was not, then Wilson would just have family at the dinner. If she was, he would invite members of the cabinet and people like Haines and Donoughue. 'Ken was absolutely bewildered by this bizarre request,' wrote Donoughue. 'God knows what the Queen will make of it. I imagine she would be quite intrigued and perhaps a little jealous to meet someone as powerful as Marcia – especially being a close relative.'[71]

Marcia, it turned out, was welcome at the dinner, and it was a very enjoyable occasion: there was some 1945 claret and 1931 port, and the Queen stayed much later than expected. Some of the guests, recalled Donoughue, were not entirely sober – including himself. 'I became conscious that I was unable to walk straight.' As people mingled in the reception rooms after dinner, some of the more distinguished guests were ushered over to talk to the Queen – left-winger Michael Foot, interestingly, had at least fifteen minutes with her – but not Lady Falkender.[72]

Wilson's departure from Number 10 was marred by the controversy over his resignation honours list, which recognised a number of wealthy businessmen including Lord Kagan, who was later convicted of fraud. Martin Charteris said that the Queen – who had to approve all honours – felt strongly about the list, but thought that she could not remonstrate with him, much less turn it down. Journalist and biographer of George V Kenneth Rose wrote in his diary after lunch with Charteris at Claridge's: 'Wilson was merely asked whether he really wanted to recommend so many more names than his predecessors had done; and whether they were the names which on reflection he would still wish to put forward. To both questions he replied yes, and there the Queen felt that her right to interfere had ended.'[73] Decades later eyebrows would be raised at the palace over the first draft of Boris Johnson's controversial resignation honours list. 'OK, prime ministers want to hand out honours,' said a Whitehall source. 'But the palace would want reassurance that proper process had been followed, that all the due diligence checks had been done.'[74]

There is a touching coda to the Queen's relationship with Harold Wilson and his wife, Mary. In her later years, after her husband died, Lady Wilson lived in Westminster near former cabinet secretary Robin Butler – Lord Butler – and his wife, Gillian. The Butlers were friendly with Lady Wilson, and Lady Butler would occasionally help her with errands. As Lady Wilson's hundredth birthday approached, Lord Butler rang up Number 10 to let them know and to suggest that it might be nice if the Queen sent her a special message. The next thing he knew he got a phone call saying the Queen would like to give an audience to Lady Wilson, if she was up to it. So the Butlers ended up driving Lady Wilson to the palace and going up with her to the audience room, and then sitting in as the ninety-year-old Queen chatted to the hundred-year-old Lady Wilson. 'It didn't appear in the Court Circular,' said Butler. 'There was no attempt by Buckingham Palace to give any publicity to it. It was just a delightful gesture. And we felt tremendously privileged to be witness to it.'[75]

IN 1976 ONE question that needed to be resolved was how to handle the changeover from Wilson to his successor. Labour had agreed with the palace on what to do if a prime minister died in office – basically, an extremely swift leadership election by Labour MPs – but not if a prime minister simply wanted to stand down. After talks between the palace and Number 10, Charteris suggested that Wilson should resign as party leader, but stay on as prime minister until a successor was chosen.

Foreign secretary James Callaghan won the vote. Wilson then engaged in some adroit constitutional footwork: he let the palace know the result of the leadership election, but when he had his final audience was careful not to advise the Queen who to call. All he did, he said later, was tell her that 'she was already aware of the voting figures I had sent her'. It was another step in the erosion of the sovereign's prerogative to choose the prime minister – a welcome one in the Queen's view, as had been made apparent earlier and would become even clearer later on, but one that raised one or two eyebrows among those wishing to cling to the old ways. The right-wing National Association for Freedom described the way the succession was handled as a 'constitutional impertinence'.[76]

The avuncular but tough Callaghan was, like Wilson, a devoted monarchist, but less starry-eyed about the Queen than his predecessor. He was not one to talk of 'relaxed intimacy', but instead offered a more nuanced assessment of the relationship between prime minister and sovereign. He told Elizabeth Longford that his audiences used to last between an hour and an hour and a half ('no drink'), which was the norm for previous prime ministers. They were all, he said, treated the same. 'But each thinks he is treated in a much more friendly way than the one before! Though I'm sure that's not true. The Queen is more even-handed. What one gets is friendliness but not friendship.' Above all, she offered understanding of her prime ministers' problems, only rarely offering advice. 'Of course she may have hinted at things, but only on the rarest of occasions do I remember her ever saying, "Why don't you do this, that or the other?"' Speaking to another biographer, he revealed the Queen's reply to his question about what to do about a certain problem: 'That's for you to decide,' she told him. 'That is what you are paid for.'[77] She was, Callaghan told Longford, very interested in the political side – 'who's going up and who's going down'. But not so passionate, he said, about the minimum lending rate.[78] Callaghan's assessment was almost word-for-word that offered by Rab Butler a generation earlier.

In his memoirs Callaghan gave an example of how the Queen could use her Bagehotian right to encourage her prime minister. In early 1976, amid extensive guerrilla activity in Rhodesia, Callaghan was mulling over whether to make an approach to Ian Smith offering a way forward. After a chance encounter with the Queen at a dinner, she let him know the next day that she thought his initiative was worth the effort, despite the risk of failure. Encouraged by her he went ahead. Although the attempt failed because of Smith's intransigence,

Callaghan concluded: 'I have always thought that the Queen's initiative on Rhodesia was a perfect illustration of how and when the Monarch could effectively intervene and encourage her Ministers from her own wide experience and with complete constitutional propriety.'[79]

The Queen once offered her own perspective on prime ministers and audiences, saying in the 1992 television film *Elizabeth R*: 'They unburden themselves – tell one what's going on – sometimes one can help – one's a sort of sponge – Occasionally you can put your point of view which they hadn't seen from that angle . . .'[80]

As in Wilson's day, the Queen and Callaghan would both have little cards on which the subjects for discussion that week had been typed. But the conversation could also stray to family or farming (Callaghan had a farm in Sussex). Sometimes, if it was a nice evening, they would spend some time walking round the gardens at Buckingham Palace. It may not have been quite the same as in Wilson's time, but they clearly connected on a significant level. Callaghan's daughter Baroness Jay said he had 'a pretty positive' relationship with the Queen. 'He was socially conservative – he was quite a fan of the concept of the monarchy. That started from a good place as far as she was concerned – this wasn't some awful kind of hard-nosed lefty.' When Callaghan – who was brought up a Baptist – went to Balmoral and the Queen drove him to picnics in the Land Rover, she very much enjoyed 'heartily singing nonconformist hymns together to pass the time'. The Queen, he said, was so easy to get on with, because she knew all the words.[81]

Pimlott reckoned there was a 'flirtatious frisson' to their relationship – Callaghan would compliment her on her clothes, and she would 'respond with banter'.[82] Once as they walked round the palace gardens she picked some lily of the valley for his buttonhole. 'He was obviously vastly impressed and very pleased,' one of his officials recalled.[83] 'She really is professional in her approach,' said Callaghan, 'and I admire her, and am very fond of her.'

If Wilson was discreet about his conversations with the Queen, Callaghan was even more so. While the prime minister and sovereign spoke in the audience room upstairs, their private secretaries would be downstairs in the private secretary's office having a parallel chat of their own. After the audience the prime minister would sometimes join the secretaries for a debrief – but not always; David Cameron used to do it about half the time, depending on how busy he was. After a conversation with the former assistant private secretary Edward Ford, Kenneth Rose wrote in his diary: 'The Private Secretary would get hold of the PM on his way out, give him a drink and listen to what he had discussed with the Sovereign. This worked well with Winston (who would drink anything) and with Wilson (who liked a glass of brandy), but Charteris would complain that he could get nothing out of the teetotal Callaghan.'[84]

Callaghan, who gave up drink during his premiership, later told Rose: 'It was not that I don't drink whisky. I deliberately refused to talk to Martin about our audiences, which I regard as confidential between the Queen and her PM. Sometimes the Queen would talk to me of her family matters, for which she has so few people to confide in.'[85] The Queen's discretion was appreciated by other ministers too. In 1988, when chancellor Nigel Lawson was having a difficult time with Margaret Thatcher, he used his Budget audience with the Queen to tell her – because she was 'the one person to whom I could unburden myself in complete confidence' – that the prime minister was 'making the conduct of policy impossible'. The Queen was 'clearly sympathetic but appropriately non-committal'.[86]

While Callaghan was at Number 10 Prince Charles asked him for opportunities to educate himself in what he called 'statecraft'. Callaghan arranged a dinner with ministers at Chequers, at which the prince put his foot in it with Denis Healey by asking whether his youthful membership of the communist party had reduced his effectiveness as chancellor. Healey was irritated, and explained about his generation's fears about the rise of fascism in the 1930s. Later in the meal he got his revenge. Charles told a story about a Qantas stewardess asking if being Prince of Wales meant he would later be King. When he said yes, she replied: 'Gee! That's pretty scary, isn't it?' At that point Charles said solemnly: 'When you think of it, it is pretty scary.' Healey leant across the table and, in a gesture echoing the comedian Eric Morecambe, patted him on both cheeks and said: 'Well, you shouldn't have joined.'[87]

IN 1977 THE QUEEN marked her Silver Jubilee. Nowadays, after a string of successful jubilees – the Queen went on to celebrate her Gold, Diamond and Platinum Jubilees – it seems axiomatic that such milestones should be marked with great national celebrations. But in 1977 it was far from obvious. Martin Charteris was enthusiastically pushing the idea, but the government needed some convincing. Callaghan and home secretary Roy Jenkins were 'dubious at first', according to one ex-courtier.[88] However, Callaghan soon warmed to the concept, and when civil servants wanted to put restrictions on the floodlighting of buildings in the capital during the celebrations, he scribbled on a memo on the subject: 'I think this is pernickety bureaucracy. Let them light up for a bit during the warm summer weeks.'[89]

In May that year the Queen gave an address to both Houses of Parliament that was possibly the closest she has ever come to political controversy in one of her speeches. At a time when Scottish nationalism was gathering strength, she said: 'I cannot forget that I was crowned Queen of the United Kingdom of Great Britain and Northern Ireland. Perhaps this jubilee is a time to remind ourselves of the benefits which union has conferred, at home and in our international dealings, on the inhabitants of all parts of this United Kingdom.' The Scottish nationalists did not like that one bit. One MP called her remarks 'unprecedented and ill-advised'. The question was, however: was this a case of the government inserting its own agenda into her speech, and thus using her in a politically inappropriate way, or was the Queen just expressing her own opinion? Government memos make it clear that the speech was written by the palace, but with the full approval of the government. The passage on devolution was specifically tweaked in accordance with the wishes of the Scottish secretary, Bruce Millan. The prime minister's private secretary, Kenneth Stowe, wrote: 'There has been no constitutional impropriety in the preparation of the speech and the substance of it on devolution is wholly in accordance with Government policy.' A draft response for Callaghan to give if required said: 'It was a personal response by the Queen . . . I saw it myself before it was delivered and saw no reason to alter it in any way.'[90]

However, later Callaghan seemed to have had a different memory of events. According to the writer William Shawcross, when Callaghan heard the speech he was alarmed by her apparent hostility to devolution, and asked his office if it had approved the speech beforehand.[91] Which, of course, it had, as well he knew. In the light of that, it comes as less of a surprise that Charteris should feel that the Queen was badly let down by her prime minister. 'Martin's distrust of Jim Callaghan springs from the occasion when the Queen was to address both Houses of Parliament,' Kenneth Rose wrote in his diary. The speech was cleared with Callaghan, said Rose: 'Then Callaghan disowned the speech.'[92]

Two years later Britain would have its first woman prime minister. Margaret Thatcher's relationship with the Queen would be very different from that enjoyed by her predecessors. There would be no more flirtatious frissons or relaxed intimacy.

CHAPTER SIX

SHALL WE JOIN
THE LADIES?

TWO SNAPSHOTS OF Margaret Thatcher with the Queen. The first comes from shortly after she was elected leader of the Conservative party in 1975. Thatcher, a woman who always wanted to observe the proprieties, had to write to the Queen, but had got herself in 'a tizz' about how to sign off the letter. She asked her diary secretary, Caroline Stephens (now Lady Ryder), who suggested that she simply write 'Yours sincerely'. That, unfortunately, was the wrong answer; the correct form was 'I remain, Madam, Your Majesty's obedient servant' or some variation of that, as Stephens was informed later ('very sweetly') by the Queen's private secretary, Sir Martin Charteris.[1] Stephens was asked to let her boss know, and while history does not relate how Thatcher took this, one can only assume that she was absolutely mortified. The grocer's daughter from Grantham was a monarchist to her very core, and wanted more than anything else to make sure her interactions with the Queen were correct in every way. The fact that they turned out to be anything but was a source of great distress to her.

Snapshot two. It is the spring of 1979, and the Shah of Iran, the autocratic Mohammad Reza Pahlavi, has just been overthrown in the Islamic revolution. He got out of Iran in time, and is travelling from country to country trying to find a safe haven. He has not made a formal approach to Britain, but has used intermediaries to put out feelers to see if he might be given asylum. Prime minister James Callaghan thinks it would be a mistake to take him in, as does the foreign secretary, David Owen, who had earlier given the Shah his public support, saying 'real friends are those who stand by you when you are under attack'. But two significant people are on his side. One is the opposition leader, Margaret Thatcher, who has told a go-between, 'I would be ashamed to be British if we could not give the Shah refuge.' The other is the Queen, who although she is of course in no position to tell the government what to do, is said to have expressed the view that Britain should show loyalty to the Shah for the way he had long supported British interests in the Middle East.

After her victory in the May general election, however, Thatcher's resolve wavered. The Foreign Office put forward various arguments as to why it would be unwise to welcome the Shah including economic ones, but the clincher was that British citizens in Iran including embassy staff would be at risk. Thatcher was persuaded, and the Shah was no longer welcome. The episode had echoes of how George V was persuaded to backtrack on the offer of asylum to Tsar Nicholas II.

According to the author of a book on their relationship, Dean Palmer, the Queen was angered by the way Thatcher reneged on her promise. 'Once you give your word,' she allegedly said at a dinner party, 'that's it.'[2] The provenance of that quote is not entirely clear, and William Shawcross, author of a book on the Shah's exile, was more circumspect in how he put it. 'It was said,' he wrote, 'she believed that states must recognize personal as well as national obligations.' But when it became clear that the Shah needed asylum, 'the queen's views, expressed only privately, were discounted'.[3] It would be a gross exaggeration to say that the Queen's anger, if that is what it was, was the start of a feud between her and Margaret Thatcher, but it was the first indication that they had somewhat divergent world views. The tensions between them would be a recurrent theme throughout Thatcher's eleven years in Number 10.

Rumours of an uneasy relationship between the two women were bubbling away before Thatcher became prime minister. Harold Wilson was told a story by the Queen about the Tory leader fainting during a palace function, but the important point was not so much the fainting as the way the story was told – with some glee, apparently. 'She doesn't like her,' Wilson said. It was not the only time Thatcher felt faint, and when it happened another time the Queen said: 'She's keeled over again.'[4] Lord Powell, who as Charles Powell was Thatcher's foreign policy adviser, tells the story of how she fainted at the annual diplomatic reception at Buckingham Palace. 'I got down on my knees to try to help revive her, and said to [her husband] Denis, "What do we do?" Denis said, "Pay no attention! She's always doing this."' A woman from the Vietnamese embassy came over, said she was a doctor and asked if there was anything she could do to help. 'Yes,' said Powell. 'Keep her alive!' They decided to take her back to Downing Street, but unfortunately Thatcher's security detail had gone for dinner and her car was nowhere to be seen. Powell spotted another government car, waved the driver over and got him to return Thatcher to Number 10. It turned out to be Geoffrey Howe's car, and the foreign secretary was 'mortally offended' that his transport had been commandeered in that way.[5]

NO ONE, other than the prime minister and sovereign themselves, ever knows what goes on during the weekly prime ministerial audiences. They take place in the audience room of Buckingham Palace, a large room painted duck-egg blue with a gilt mirror over the marble fireplace and a Canaletto on one wall; no one else is present. But all the indications are that with Margaret Thatcher – the first prime minister to be a contemporary of the Queen: Thatcher was just six months older – they were not relaxed, convivial occasions in the way that they were with Harold Wilson or Jim Callaghan. The fact that they were both women did not lead to a bond of sisterhood; on the contrary, for years Thatcher's awkwardness in the royal presence hampered the development of any warmth or familiarity.

The Tory leader's former private secretary Robin Butler said that the Queen 'was held in awe by Margaret Thatcher', whose middle-class provincial background meant that the palace was an environment in which she 'never felt comfortable'. He said: 'The court slightly looked down on her. But in the way they do: they would go out of their way with showing good manners to make her feel as comfortable as possible, but in such an obvious way that it had the reverse effect.'[6] Thatcher's discomfort and desire not to put a foot wrong manifested itself in different ways. She would curtsey lower than anyone else, much to the amusement of some at the palace, and was so worried about being late that she would turn up fifteen or even thirty minutes early instead of the usual five. When asked about this, she would say she worried about traffic, even though Downing Street is only five minutes away from Buckingham Palace. After her audience she would join Butler and the Queen's private secretary (at that point Sir Philip Moore) in his office, where she would be given a drink. 'Margaret Thatcher was notoriously quite tense with the Queen,' said Butler. 'She needed a whisky afterwards.'

But if she was not fully at ease in the royal presence, that did not stop her talking. Richard Luce (now Lord Luce), who served as a minister under Thatcher and later became lord chamberlain, head of the Queen's household, recalled: 'I did once say to Margaret Thatcher, "Did you, when you talked to the Queen at your weekly meetings, ever allow the Queen to get a word in?" I knew her well enough to say that. Denis was sitting there. "Oh yes," she said, "I had very good conversations with her, very broad-ranging." Denis said: "Margaret!"' Her husband, it seems, knew who would have done most of the talking. The Queen's private secretary Sir William Heseltine once asked if her audiences with Thatcher were like Victoria's with Gladstone, who she complained addressed her as if she were a public meeting. 'No,' said the Queen, 'it wasn't at all like that . . . but I wasn't given much encouragement to comment on what was said.'[7]

For all the respect that Thatcher had for the Queen, it would seem that she did not always regard her audiences as the most productive use of her time. On a number of occasions she ruled out her weekly audience because it clashed with other commitments, including a meeting over drinks with top-level French bankers. She was reluctant to commit to dates when Parliament was in recess, and sometimes wanted to change the time of an audience to suit her diary. This seemed to cause some irritation at the palace. When Number 10 wanted to change the time of an audience yet again, her private secretary Clive Whitmore wrote: 'I really think this will be pushing our luck with the Palace.' Correspondence published by the

Mail on Sunday in 2013 after a Freedom of Information request also revealed the notes that Thatcher took into the audience with her on the topics to be discussed: in February 1981 they included Irish matters, funding for British Leyland and British Steel, and Rupert Murdoch's takeover of *The Times*, which had just been given the go-ahead.[8]

Lord Powell said it was never a question of Thatcher dreading her audiences with the Queen. 'But there were a couple of times when it was not wildly convenient. She would say, "Oh gosh, do I have to go? We've got this debate tomorrow morning, and I have to finish my speech for that." But I think she found them on a woman-to-woman basis quite helpful sometimes.'[9]

Their relationship was, according to one description, 'more business-like than warm', and the truth is that they were very different characters. In the words of the Queen's biographer Sarah Bradford, 'Thatcher was revolutionary and missionary where Elizabeth was conservative and distrustful of change.' Lord Charteris (as the Queen's private secretary became) told Peter Hennessy he thought that 'the Queen prefers a sort of consensus politics rather than a polarized one . . . If you are in the Queen's position you are the titular, the symbolic head of the country, and the less squabbling that goes on in that country, obviously the more convenient and the more comfortable you feel.'[10] Margaret Thatcher was no consensus politician. She was also no countrywoman, which made the annual visit to Balmoral awkward. When she first went, as education minister, a lady-in-waiting was delegated to take her for a walk, but Thatcher did not have any country shoes and had to be forced to borrow a pair of Hush Puppies and multiple pairs of socks.[11] For Thatcher, Balmoral was 'purgatory', according to Ben Pimlott. On the day she was due to leave, she would be up and ready to go at six in the morning, recalled a former adviser. 'She couldn't get away fast enough.'[12] Famously, Thatcher was so shocked at seeing the Queen doing the washing-up without gloves that when she got back to London she sent her a pair of Marigolds in the post.

THATCHER'S REVERENCE for the royal family meant that calibrating risk could pose challenging questions. In 1982, after Argentina invaded the Falkland Islands and Britain sent a task force to recover them, the question was raised as to whether Prince Andrew, then a twenty-two-year-old helicopter pilot with the Royal Navy, should be allowed to go. 'Prince Andrew is a serving officer,' the palace said in a statement in response to questions about the Queen's attitude, 'and there is no question in her mind that he should go.' What was not revealed at the time was that Thatcher was dead set against it, because of the political implications and the risk of hostage-taking. The palace, however, 'dug their toes in in a big way', according to the then chief whip Michael Jopling.[13] The Queen also had other ministers on her side. Lord Carrington and Richard Luce, foreign secretary and minister of state respectively, who both resigned over the invasion, also advised Number 10 that he should go – the last thing they did before resigning.[14] Andrew went with the task force, and returned not only unscathed but with his reputation greatly enhanced – for a while, at least.

Lord Owen believes that the Queen's view of Margaret Thatcher was transformed by the Falklands War. 'I think the whole of the royal family's view of her changed. At long last they had a prime minister who made them feel proud to be the royal family and her proud to be queen . . . The queen had lived through the humiliation of Suez and now it could be argued that shame had been put to rest.'[15]

After British forces retook the islands there was a victory parade in the City of London at which Margaret Thatcher took the salute rather than the Queen. The contrast with the parade to mark the end of the Second World War, when the King took the salute and Churchill and Attlee remained at a discreet distance, was noted. It was, in the view of some, a mistake, and smacked of hubris. But it also reflected the way that the prime minister had led, directed and been identified with the war, while the Queen had remained quietly in the background. As part of the celebrations, Thatcher gave a dinner at Downing Street for those most closely involved in the victory. Space was so tight that there was no room for spouses at the table: instead they were invited for drinks in the drawing rooms afterwards. At the end of the dinner the prime minister, who was the only woman at the meal, rose to her feet and said, 'Gentlemen, shall we join the ladies?'[16]

There is a suggestion that the Queen did not agree with Thatcher over every aspect of the Falklands War. The journalist and former Labour MP Woodrow Wyatt, who was close to Thatcher, recounts in his diary an incident at Balmoral in which everyone was 'being beastly' to the prime minister. The Queen's cousin Lady Mary Colman told him that the Queen was 'horrid' to Thatcher. He wrote: 'They were talking about the Falklands and the Queen sharply in a loud voice said, "I don't agree with you at all," and Mrs Thatcher went red and looked very uncomfortable.' Colman felt that the Queen was 'trying to put Mrs Thatcher down all the time', knowing that she was unaccustomed to upper-class society.[17]

Richard Luce returned to the Foreign Office in 1983, where his responsibilities included the Middle East. When he visited Jordan that year King Hussein made it clear to him that he would welcome a visit by the Queen. Luce recommended it to Thatcher, arguing that close relations with a strong, stable leader like Hussein made strategic sense. A state visit was organised for March 1984, with Luce accompanying the Queen because foreign secretary Geoffrey Howe was otherwise engaged. However, at the last minute it faced being cancelled because of the threat of terrorist violence. Two days before the visit a bomb exploded in a hotel used by the media, and there were fears that the group believed to be responsible – Black June – would carry out more attacks during the Queen's visit in an attempt to embarrass the Jordanians.[18] The day before the Queen was due to leave Luce had a meeting with Thatcher at Chequers, together with Howe and Michael Heseltine, the defence secretary.

'Both Heseltine and Howe said, "No, she should not go,"' said Luce. 'I argued strongly in favour. Margaret said, "There's only one thing to do. Let's get the only person here who understands the common sense view of the man in the street. And that's Denis."' The prime minister's husband was duly summoned to the room. 'She gave him a glass of whisky and said, "Denis, this is our dilemma. As a man in the street, what would you do?" There was a pause, and Denis said very slowly, "Well, Queen Elizabeth the first would have gone, so Queen Elizabeth the second must go." And that was the end of the discussion. Margaret said, "That's it." Poor old Heseltine and Howe looked rather put out. The Queen, I am certain, would have been very put out indeed if she had been stopped.'[19]

On the first morning of the Queen's visit, the British ambassador said that they had intelligence that there would be an attempt on her life when she travelled outside Amman. Wondering what to do, Luce spoke to the Jordanian commander-in-chief, who told him: 'You must understand that we are much safer here in Jordan, ringed with missiles all around our borders, than you are in Ireland.' Luce recalled: 'I told the Queen what he said, consulted the ambassador and sent a message back saying it would be the worst thing pos-sible to pull out of this. It was as secure as it possibly could be. I had to take that risk. The Queen quite naturally said she would go ahead and do all her duties. She was not in the least bit worried. She was quite fearless in that way.'[20]

IN THE EARLY evening of 24 October 1983 Margaret Thatcher was preparing to attend a farewell dinner for the outgoing US ambassador hosted by Princess Alexandra when a cable arrived from US president Ronald Reagan. Reagan, who had already built up a strong rapport with the prime minister, united as they were in their attitude towards the Soviet Union, said he was very worried about the situation in the tiny Caribbean island of Grenada. The island, which had gained its independ-ence in 1974 but remained a member of the Commonwealth, had been run by a Marxist government under Maurice Bishop since 1979. However, in early October hardliners had overthrown Bishop and executed their former leader by firing squad. Reagan said in his cable he was considering a request from the Organisation of Eastern Caribbean States for military assistance, and wanted Thatcher's thoughts. When she got back to Number 10 after dinner, but before she had managed to send her own reply, she found another mes-sage from Reagan saying he had decided to invade. The next morning 1,900 US troops landed in Grenada. They rounded up the leaders of the coup and rescued a group of a thousand American students who had been taken hostage. They did, however, meet stiffer resistance than they expected, and over the following days nineteen Americans were killed and more than a hundred injured.

'We were both dumbfounded,' recalled Geoffrey Howe. 'What on earth were we to make of a relationship, special or otherwise, in which a message requesting the benefit of our advice was so quickly succeeded by another which made it brutally clear that that advice was being treated as of no consequence whatsoever?'[21] For Thatcher, there was another highly important dimension to this affront: the Queen was head of state, represented on the island by a governor general, and Britain's closest ally had invaded without even notifying her. 'She had enormous, some people might even say exaggerated, respect for the Queen,' said Lord Powell.[22]

There was one, simple, overriding reason why the Americans did not consult Thatcher: they thought she would disagree. In Howe's view, such was the chemistry between Reagan and Thatcher that if she had talked to him before the attack, she might have dissuaded him.[23]

When Thatcher spoke to Richard Luce before the invasion (she rang him at the weekend while he was watching a western on the television), she told him she was worried about being dragged into an international conflict, and about the embarrassment that might be caused to the Queen. 'She was very angry with the Americans [for] taking action without consultation with us.'[24] Lord Powell recalled: 'She took it very seriously, and was very upset by it. [But] how you balance the affront to the Queen and the affront to Margaret Thatcher might be a question to be decided.' The issue, he said, 'burned hot', but only for a short period; there were other aspects to the relationship with the US that soon reasserted their importance.[25]

According to Charles Moore, Thatcher's authorised biographer, 'Buckingham Palace was mortified by the difficult position in which, as sovereign of Grenada, it put [the Queen].' In particular the palace was concerned about the safety of the governor general, Sir Paul Scoon, which was not assured until he was rescued by US Navy Seals on 26 October. Foreign Office officials noted: 'Mrs Thatcher understood that the Queen was upset and Mrs Thatcher was very disturbed by this.'[26] According to The Times, the Queen disapproved of 'the notion that foreign powers may walk into member states' of the Commonwealth, especially without prior warning.[27] However, Lord Powell, although emphasising that he had 'no knowledge' of what the Queen felt, said: 'I don't think the Queen was probably that upset about it. Most of us would have thought that the cause in which [Reagan] did it was a good one. It was the lack of courtesy in not telling us . . . We never got feedback from Mrs Thatcher about what the Queen said to her, ever, unless it was purely operational.'[28]

THE RELATIONSHIP between Downing Street and the Queen's private secretary is, for the most part, productive, well tempered and mutually advantageous. Except when it isn't.

In the summer of 1985 a daring plan was about to be carried out to smuggle Oleg Gordievsky, a KGB agent who was actually a double agent for the British, out of the Soviet Union. It involved hiding him in the boot of a car driven by an MI6 officer and taking him over the border into Finland. The plan, known as Operation Pimlico, was extremely secret and extremely sensitive. It also needed the authorisation of the prime minister. However, by the time the plan had been activated, and Charles Powell told what was going on, Thatcher was in Scotland for her annual trip to stay with the Queen at Balmoral. He knew that what he had to tell the prime minister was far too sensitive to discuss over the phone, and so he flew to Aberdeen, hired a car and drove to Balmoral himself.

His first obstacle was the equerry at the gatehouse, who was busy trying to track down the Queen Mother's video recorder so that the Queen could borrow it to watch an episode of Dad's Army. Twenty frustrating minutes passed. Then, after explaining who he was, and that he needed to see the prime minister urgently, he was ushered into the presence of the Queen's private secretary, Sir Philip Moore. A man never slow to stand on his dignity, Moore demanded to know why he wanted to see the prime minister. 'He said he couldn't possibly let me go and find Margaret Thatcher unless I would tell him what it was all about. I said, "Well I can't, sorry." He said, "Well, whatever you tell Margaret Thatcher, she will tell the Queen, and the Queen will tell me."' Powell still refused to reveal the reason for his trip. 'I said, "If you don't permit me to go, I shall just go, and look for her." That was too much for him, the idea that I might be wandering around, opening doors to try to find her.' A footman was summoned, and Powell was escorted to the bothy where Thatcher was staying. Powell found her in bed, surrounded by papers. The prime minister authorised Operation Pimlico without delay, saying: 'We have to honour our promises to our agent.' As for Moore, said Powell, 'he never spoke to me again'.[29]

THE FAULT LINE that marked the fundamental difference between Margaret Thatcher and the Queen was the Commonwealth. The Queen had a deep-seated respect for and devotion to the Commonwealth, which dated back to before she acceded to the throne. She had visited every Commonwealth capital, and known some of its leaders for decades. Thatcher, in contrast, was naturally suspicious of international organisations that conspired, in her view, against Western interests. 'The Commonwealth did not feature hugely in Margaret Thatcher's thinking about the world,' said Powell. She could, he said, be 'scathing' in private about the organisation. 'But she recognised there is intrinsic value of 50-odd countries who got together and generally did useful if rather minor things.'

Africa, more often than not, was a source of tension. In the last months of the Callaghan government the foreign secretary, David Owen, had been planning to use the Commonwealth Heads of Government Meeting (CHOGM) in Zambia in August 1979 to put together a peace deal for Rhodesia, which was in the grip of a civil war as guerrillas fought the white minority regime. He had even discussed it with the Queen. 'That was going to be a very important conference and we had engineered it,' he told Robert Hardman. 'She knew what I wanted to do. She understood.'[30] However, when Margaret Thatcher came to power she was reluctant to attend the Lusaka summit. With many Commonwealth members – especially the so-called frontline states – complaining that Britain was not doing enough about Rhodesia, Thatcher anticipated that the conference would be dominated by a litany of protests about her policies. There were also concerns about the Queen's security, which prompted speculation that the prime minister might advise her not to go. Such concerns had, of course, arisen before with Edward Heath, and the palace seemed to have toughened its attitude since then. The issue was also made more complicated by the fact that the Queen's trip to Africa would also take in visits to Tanzania, Malawi and Botswana.

The problem was resolved in a dramatic and unprecedented fashion when Thatcher was asked in a radio interview whether she could confirm whether the Queen would be going to Zambia, and replied that she 'hoped' it would be the case, but could not yet offer 'final advice'. Within a few hours the palace released a terse statement that completely wrong-footed Thatcher, saying that it was the Queen's 'firm intention' to travel to all four countries.

Despite Thatcher's misgivings – the prime minister had donned dark glasses before stepping off the plane in Lusaka,

fearing that acid would be thrown in her face – the conference was more of a success than she had anticipated. It ended
with an agreement for a constitutional conference to be held
in London on the future of Rhodesia. Free elections were
organised, and the independent state of Zimbabwe was formally granted independence in April 1980, just eight months
after the Lusaka summit. Exactly what role the Queen
played in ensuring that outcome will perhaps never be clear,
but Commonwealth secretary general Sir Sonny Ramphal
believed that by talking to Thatcher and the Zambian president Kenneth Kaunda, the Queen made a real difference.

Kaunda, who was responsible for one of the most mem-
orable moments of the summit when he swept Thatcher on
to the dance floor at the opening banquet, later recalled one
of his conversations with the Queen. 'She said, "My friend,
you and I should be careful. We are under the scrutiny of the
British prime minister." I looked up and Mrs Thatcher had
her eyes fixed on us.' Ramphal said: 'The fact [the Queen]
was there made it happen. Kaunda felt that he'd have let
her down a little if he hadn't pulled it off.' In Ramphal's
view her skill lay in talking to Commonwealth leaders about
everything other than Rhodesia. The Queen knew 'who had
got what political scandal raging. She'd know the family side
of things, if there were children or deaths in the family. She'd
know about the economy, she'd know about elections coming
up. They felt they were talking to a friend who cared about
the country.'[31] A senior Whitehall official told Ben Pimlott:
'Mrs Thatcher went to Lusaka in an unconstructive, angry
mood. But gradually the atmosphere began to change. The
Queen possibly played a part in this.'[32]

That Whitehall official perhaps underplayed the Queen's
role. There is concrete evidence that she improved the mood

of the conference by persuading Kaunda not to make inflammatory anti-British remarks in his speech at the state banquet. A draft of Kaunda's speech had been seen by the British high commissioner, Len Allison, who had tried in vain to get him to remove remarks that would have been unacceptable to the British. As the Queen's private secretary Philip Moore said later, Allinson thought that the only way to get the offensive passages removed was for the Queen to speak to Kaunda personally. 'This The Queen did in the motor car and later that evening. Mark Chona [Kaunda's special adviser] came to me to say that the president had agreed to make all the amendments for which we had asked.'[33] Commonwealth historian Philip Murphy suggested that the Queen's interventions 'may have helped to encourage a more constructive debate . . . allowing Mrs Thatcher the space to make concessions'.[34] Both Sonny Ramphal and Philip Moore believed that without the Queen the Commonwealth would have split up over Rhodesia.

SIX YEARS LATER Thatcher was on the defensive again, this time over South Africa. The issue had been building for some time, with increasing pressure from Commonwealth members for sanctions against the apartheid regime. Thatcher, however, was dismissive of those states calling for sanctions against South Africa at the same time as trading with it on the sly. Tory MP Alan Clark recalled that Thatcher was 'pretty scornful' of the whole Commonwealth circus. 'She and Charles Powell had a translation for the acronym CHOGM. Their translation was Compulsory Hand-outs for Greedy Mendicants. It was kept quite private, but that was the attitude.'[35] Thatcher also believed that sanctions were not the way to win the day, because they hurt ordinary South Africans.

During the build-up to the CHOGM in Nassau in the Bahamas in October 1985, the Queen was anxious to settle the issue, which she feared threatened the unity and possibly even the future of the Commonwealth, but at the same time was apprehensive of doing anything that clashed with British government policy. It was her old dilemma: she was Queen of the United Kingdom, but also Queen of other countries that had a very different agenda. Charles Powell told Thatcher that the outcome on South Africa 'appears to be of great concern to the Palace', and that the Queen wanted a meeting with the prime minister just before the conference began 'in the hope that she may be able to use what you tell her with other Commonwealth countries'.[36]

While the build-up to the summit was dominated by concerns that Britain was isolated over sanctions, in Nassau there was another issue of more immediate practical concern: the lack of a car for the Queen. The British high commissioner, Peter Heap, wrote in his report: 'Preparations, somewhat disconcertingly, continued up to the last minute. Two days before the Queen was due to arrive a startled Rolls-Royce dealer in New York called us to check whether the Bahamians were serious about an enquiry for a car to be purchased and delivered by air to Nassau within two days, for The Queen's use.' It arrived in time, however, and all was well. Meanwhile the Bahamian capital was being spruced up. A sign outside one shop being renovated said: 'Fixin' up for The Queen.' A taxi driver told Heap: 'Man, we not doing all this for these Commonwealth guys. We don't know them. We doing all this for The Queen.'[37]

The lack of warmth between Thatcher and the Queen in Nassau was not missed by the Australian prime minister, Bob Hawke, there on his first CHOGM. 'I was well aware that you wouldn't describe the relationship between Her Majesty and her Prime Minister as one of extreme cordiality. In a formal sense there was a respect and acknowledgement of the role and importance of the other, [but] it's fair to say that the Queen didn't have a great affection for Mrs Thatcher.'[38] He said on another occasion that the Queen was 'not at ease' with her prime minister's policies. 'She saw her as dangerous.'[39]

At the summit, which saw some bruising exchanges between her and Bob Hawke, Thatcher steadfastly stood up against the arguments for sanctions. She outplayed the other Commonwealth leaders by making a couple of concessions at the last minute, which were enough to create a show of unity but were in fact very minor. The meeting to draft the summit's final accord ended with a round of applause for Thatcher.

The Commonwealth had survived, but sensitivities over the issue continued. The gulf between the palace and Number 10 on sanctions was as wide as ever. According to Sonny Ramphal, the Queen's private secretary Sir William Heseltine stayed in close touch with Ramphal, 'consulting him about how best to outmanoeuvre Mrs Thatcher'.[40] The following June, Desmond Tutu, who was about to become Archbishop of Cape Town, wrote what he called a 'cri de coeur' to the Queen appealing for sanctions and describing his country as being 'on the brink of a monumental catastrophe'. This put the palace in a fix as to how to respond.

As the letter had come through the church, should the Queen reply in her role as supreme governor of the Church of England? Or was it a foreign policy issue, and therefore a question for the government? Geoffrey Howe, the foreign secretary, thought that William Heseltine, who had recently become her private secretary, should reply. However, when a draft reached Downing Street that talked of the Queen seeking 'an end to the suffering and an early and peaceful solution to your country's problems', Thatcher got cold feet. 'I think the proposed draft <u>does</u> involve The Queen in politics,' she wrote. 'I am very unhappy about the proposed advice. The Press is bound to claim there is a rift between The Queen and Her Government.'[41] In the end a letter was sent from Heseltine after all, with only minor amendments, and the issue somehow passed off without any great outcry. But all that would change just a couple of weeks later.

In the late afternoon of Saturday 19 July 1986, the Queen was at Windsor Castle preparing for a reception in advance of the wedding of Prince Andrew and Sarah Ferguson when she got a call from William Heseltine. He had been told by the palace press secretary, Michael Shea, that *The Sunday Times* was about to run a big story about a rift between Buckingham Palace and Downing Street. Heseltine advised the Queen to call Thatcher at her weekend retreat, Chequers, to reassure her that 'there was certainly no intention of wishing or hoping or being aware of anything being said which could lead to this kind of conclusion'.[42]

When the palace finally got hold of a copy of the paper it was even worse than they expected. Under the headline 'Queen Dismayed by "Uncaring" Thatcher', journalists Simon Freeman and Michael Jones claimed to have irrefutable evidence that the Queen considered the whole approach of the prime minister to be 'uncaring, confrontational and socially divisive'. Their differences included not only the Commonwealth and South African sanctions, both well known by then, but other issues including the tactics used by Thatcher during the miners' strike of 1984–5. Former cabinet secretary Robin Butler said that the Queen found the confrontations during the strike such as the clash between miners and police at Orgreave, and the distress of the mining communities, 'painful'.[43] 'Far from being a straightforward countrywoman, a late middle-aged grandmother who is most at ease when she is talking about horses and dogs,' The Sunday Times said, 'the Queen is an astute political infighter who is quite prepared to take on Downing Street when provoked.'[44]

Although he denied it at first, the source of the story later turned out to be Michael Shea. He had given a series of briefings to Freeman about the monarchy, and had offered what he thought were routine answers to questions about the Queen's views. His answers were not based on a specific briefing from the Queen, and he had never heard her speak critically of the prime minister. However, The Sunday Times stuck to its story, while the palace continued to maintain that the article did not represent the Queen's opinion of government policy. The truth, no doubt, lay somewhere in between. The crucial questions were how much spin the journalists had applied to Shea's briefings, and how far those briefings reflected the press secretary's own liberal opinions rather than those of his employer.

According to Freeman, Shea had surprised him by how willing he was to discuss the Queen's political opinions. 'He started saying things like "on race and social division she is well to the left of centre",' he said. Ben Pimlott concluded: 'A degree of wishful thinking on one side may have compounded an element of imprudence on the other.'[45] Whatever happened, Shea appears to have acted in a foolishly unguarded way, and, with some encouragement, he left the employ of the palace a few months later. After that, reckons Charles Moore, the palace 'became even more politically cautious'.[46]

Margaret Thatcher did her best not to appear irritated by the story, although one source said she was 'knocked sideways by it, she was very down in the mouth'.[47] Lord Powell said her concern was the potential political effect. 'I don't think that Margaret Thatcher necessarily thought that those were the Queen's views, but she thought it was damaging that they were represented to be.' As she told him, 'Those little old ladies will say Mrs Thatcher is upsetting the Queen. I'll lose votes.' Was she upset by it? 'Yes, absolutely.'[48] Rupert Murdoch, proprietor of The Sunday Times, took a different view from Thatcher: when Woodrow Wyatt told him it would damage her at the election, he replied, 'Oh no, it will do her a lot of good.'[49]

A couple of years after the row Brian Walden, a former Labour MP turned Thatcher convert, went to interview the prime minister for The Sunday Times. He asked her if the story still rankled. 'Yes, it does,' she said. 'It hurt me very badly at the time.' 'But you know it was true,' he said. 'The Palace was out to undermine you.' She took off her glasses, looked down and said mournfully: 'I know, Brian, I know. The problem is the Queen is the kind of woman who could vote SDP.'[50] (The Social Democratic party was a mildly left-of-centre party formed by former members of the Labour party. They merged with the Liberals to form the Liberal Democrats. Thatcher's remark falls into the more-in-sorrow-than-anger category.)

The reaction of the Queen to the story is harder to gauge. It seems plausible that she would be mortified that she had been portrayed as politically at odds with her prime minister as that ran counter to everything she had done or believed in up to that date. But palace sources are more discreet than political ones, and the Queen was more discreet than anyone who ever occupied 10 Downing Street. According to Robert

Hardman, she was more hurt than she let on. Princess Margaret told a friend: 'That was the only time I've ever seen her cry.'[51] One of the few people brave enough to ask the Queen at the time what she thought was Jock Colville, who had been private secretary to the then Princess Elizabeth in between periods of working for Winston Churchill. Was *The Sunday Times* right about her attitude to the Thatcher government? 'Not at all, absolutely wrong,' she said. He then asked what she thought of the prime minister, to which she replied: 'Jock, you do ask the most impertinent questions.' 'Well, ma'am, I was your private secretary for some years.' She laughed and said: 'I get on with her all right but like all Prime Ministers she won't listen.'[52]

ONE OF THE greatest services Margaret Thatcher did for the Queen was to put the royal finances on a sounder footing. In a scheme originally proposed by the lord chamberlain, the former merchant banker Lord Airlie, the Civil List would no longer be set each year but instead determined by a ten-year agreement. The aim was to avoid the annual vote in Parliament, which was an opportunity for anti-monarchist MPs to grandstand in the Commons and for newspapers to run headlines about the Queen's pay rise, much to the exasperation of both the palace and the government.

When the new arrangement was announced in July 1990, the Queen was awarded a massive 50 per cent increase in her Civil List income, to £7.9 million, but there was method in this largesse. Assuming inflation over the next ten years averaged 7.5 per cent, the fixed sum would be generous at the start of the decade, allowing the palace to build up a surplus for the first few years. By the end of the decade £7.9 million would not be enough to cover costs, but by then the palace would be able to dip into the reserves it had built up to meet the difference. (As it turned out, the deal would turn out more generous than expected, because inflation was lower than forecast.) The new system was, said the prime minister, 'appropriate for the dignity of the Crown'.

Crucially, the government made sure that it had the support of the opposition before going ahead. Lord Turnbull, John Major's principal private secretary and later cabinet secretary, making him one of the small number of officials to have occupied two corners of the Golden Triangle, recalls going with Sir Peter Middleton, the permanent secretary at the Treasury, to see Neil Kinnock to explain the proposal. 'He said, "That seems fair enough to me." He saw the point of it. He didn't want this annual circus and sniping.'[53] Everyone was a winner, it seemed: the government did not have to answer awkward questions every year about financing the royal family, and the palace was delighted because it made it easier for it to plan ahead. 'The aim was to make the Palace master of its own destiny,' a courtier told Ben Pimlott.[54]

MARGARET THATCHER was toppled in November 1990, forced out of Downing Street by her own cabinet. When she emerged from her audience with the Queen on the day she quit, she was, according to her private secretary Robert Fellowes, 'in a very distressed state and unable to speak'. Back at Number 10, she went upstairs to her flat, where she ran to the bathroom and wept. She told her personal assistant Cynthia Crawford: 'It's when people are kind to you that you feel it the most. The Queen has been so kind to me.'[55]

Despite their differences, the Queen felt that the prime minister had been badly treated, and invited her to the races, just as she had done with Winston Churchill when he returned after his stroke. Thatcher, however, was in no mood for the races, raising the question, perhaps, of when she *was* in the mood. The Queen once described her as 'not a very sporting lady'. When Woodrow Wyatt told the Queen that Thatcher had agreed to go to the races with him, after he had been trying for years, she replied: 'Oh, that would be a great triumph if you pulled it off.'[56] But she was touched by the invitation.[57] Meanwhile the Queen Mother, always an admirer, was greatly upset by Thatcher's departure, telling Wyatt that it was desperately unfair and an appalling way to do things.[58] A couple of weeks after Thatcher's resignation, the Queen awarded her the Order of Merit, the highest honour in her gift. It is limited to twenty-four individuals, and Thatcher filled the vacancy created by the death of Laurence Olivier. She was only the second prime minister to be awarded the honour during the Queen's reign, after Harold Macmillan in 1976.

In the years after Thatcher's resignation, the Queen seemed to soften towards her former prime minister, showing her a respect and even affection that had been less obvious when she was in power. In July 1996 their paths crossed when the Queen opened the business school at the University of Buckingham, where Baroness Thatcher, as she had become, was chancellor. Lord Luce, the university's vice-chancellor, recalled the intimate lunch afterwards attended by the Queen and Prince Philip and Margaret and Denis Thatcher – who excelled himself by getting a glass of sherry, wiping the glass with his handkerchief, and then handing it to the Queen. 'The Queen did not see the handkerchief, thank God,' said Luce.

It was, Luce said, a 'fascinating picture of the chemistry' between the Queen and Lady Thatcher.

> What I gleaned was that although the Queen did
> not particularly like her politics, and her hostility to

the Commonwealth and things like that, there was a sneaking admiration by the Queen for her. There was a twinkle in the Queen's eye. She was rather enjoying the company of Margaret Thatcher on that occasion. She was no longer doing things which would have worried the Queen. Margaret was very polite – I put her opposite the Queen, and sat next to the Queen myself – until just before 2, when the Queen was due to leave. Margaret suddenly brought up some country which she thought ought to be bombed. 'If I was secretary of state for defence, I would have moved in straight away!' The Queen looked at her watch and said, 'I think it's about time to go now.'[59]

In 2005, when Thatcher was beginning to suffer from dementia, there was a party to celebrate her eightieth birthday at the Mandarin Oriental hotel in London, with a guest list that included the Queen and Prince Philip, most of her cabinet colleagues, Tony Blair, Joan Collins, Dame Shirley Bassey, P. D. James, Jeremy Clarkson and Lord Lloyd-Webber. Lord Powell recalled: 'Margaret Thatcher was by then a little confused. The Queen took her firmly by the hand and led her round the room, saying hello to everyone. It was marvellous – a great indication of the Queen's ability to adjust to different circumstances. It reflected her appreciation that – whether she liked her or not – she had been a quite exceptional prime minister who deserved exceptional treatment.'[60] As the Queen and her former prime minister circulated, 'the two old ladies looked comfortable together,' wrote Charles Moore, 'two grandmothers enjoying themselves'. Later, when the Queen said it was time for her to go, Thatcher said, 'What a good idea. I think I'll go too.' 'You'd better not!' said the Queen. 'It's your party.'[61]

Margaret Thatcher died in 2013. The Queen never normally attended funerals, but for Thatcher she made an exception. It was, said the palace, because of the 'unique' nature of the occasion. 'My mother,' said Sir Mark Thatcher, 'would be greatly honoured as well as humbled by her presence.'[62]

CHAPTER SEVEN

THE HON. JOHN

HER MAJESTY THE QUEEN was not the first head of state John Major spoke to after he won the ballot that made him prime minister. The result, which saw him beat Michael Heseltine and Douglas Hurd in the contest to succeed Margaret Thatcher, was announced in the early evening of 27 November 1990, but he was not due to go to Buckingham Palace until the following day. Instead it was US president George Bush who spoke to him first, ringing from Air Force One to congratulate him. When the call came through to 11 Downing Street – his official home at the time, in his role as chancellor – Major was nowhere to be seen, and his brother, Terry, had to keep Bush on the line while aides scurried around to find the prime minister-in-waiting. Eventually, he spoke to Bush from the kitchen of Number 11, as people washed up glasses in the background, oblivious to whom Major was talking to.[1]

Exactly what happened when he went with his wife, Norma, to see the Queen the next morning is not known, apart from the fact that she asked him to form a government: the punctiliously discreet Major – unlike some of his more loose-lipped Conservative successors – would never reveal even the smallest detail of his conversations with the Queen. But it is interesting to speculate on whether she had any idea that she was about to enjoy one of the most positive relationships with a prime minister of her entire reign. It must have struck her that this was a very different PM in terms of personal style to his predecessor. Charles Powell, who stayed on to work for Major for a few months until his successor was appointed, said that Major's warmth and empathy were already apparent when he worked in the government whips' office. 'Apparently he knew every other member's name, their wives, their children, their mothers-in-law and so on, because he was that sort of person.' Being friendly was, he said, Major's natural mode of operation. 'Margaret Thatcher was not naturally a friendly person at all. She was mostly sailing into battle. In some ways it must have been a welcome contrast to have somebody who is naturally congenial.'[2]

According to Lord Turnbull, who as Andrew Turnbull was private secretary to both Thatcher and her successor, John Major was initially a little nervous about his audiences with the Queen, but quickly got used to them. Major saw it somewhat differently. 'I saw no reason to be nervous,' he said. 'But I was probably apprehensive on the first occasion because I didn't know quite how it was going to operate, whether it was a dialogue or whether it was a monologue by the prime minister about which the Queen would ask questions. It was actually a dialogue. I would raise subjects and talk about them – not only political issues but other things I thought might happen. And often discussions of what some people might do. So it was pretty wide-ranging.' It was, he said, enormously useful. 'You had a highly intelligent woman's view over what we were doing. The Queen knew her country extremely well, and to a detail that few people would imagine, in terms of those who wouldn't naturally be in her immediate sphere of life. She was extremely well briefed on what was happening all around the country . . . If something happened, she would know if and how it impacted on a particular group of people. She was very empathetic, more so than people might have imagined.'

He was also able to talk to her with utter frankness, because he knew nothing would leak.

> Would I talk to the Queen about my innermost thoughts in the way that I wouldn't talk to others? Yes. I shared with her things I thought she would be interested in, which weren't always shared with other people. I might have discussed them with her before I mentioned them to anybody else . . . I never held anything back from her. And I don't think from her side she held much back from me either. Our conversations were never restricted to public affairs – anything that caught our interest would have been discussed.

Unlike many of his predecessors, he did not have briefing notes, whereas Turnbull did use to write extremely brief notes for Thatcher, just half a dozen words or so to remind her what might come up. 'When I went to see the Queen,' said Major, 'I knew what I wished to say to her. I didn't need notes to remind me. I never saw her with a list of things she wanted to ask either. We sat together and we talked.'[3] This is confirmed by Sir Alex Allan, Major's principal private secretary, who said: 'In the car on the way to the palace we might have a brief word about what were the key issues to bring up.' But there were never any cards with notes.[4] (There were periods when the Queen would be armed with a short list of topics. It happened in Wilson and Callaghan's day, and also later. They were written on small cards, and were impenetrable to an outsider. 'State of the nation', for instance, might refer to a major policy announcement that was coming up.

An innocuous phrase like 'machinery of government' would be code for a cabinet quarrel, to remind the Queen that there was some big row brewing.)

If Thatcher hated going to Balmoral, Major positively relished it. 'I did enjoy it,' he said.

> The one thing I didn't enjoy was a piper going around the house at some ungodly hour of the morning! And some of the bathrooms were antique. But it was always fun. It was very informal. I'd look out the window, and it would be pouring with rain – and the Queen would be out there with the dogs in her mackintosh and a headscarf, exactly as any other dog lover would be. In the evening we'd have barbecues, usually cooked by Prince Philip. There were no formalities. Of course the normal courtesies were observed, but it was always relaxed and fun. Humour was always on the menu. An audience was fitted somewhere into the middle of it all.

Andrew Turnbull, who as private secretary accompanied both Thatcher and Major to Balmoral, said the point of the prime minister's annual visit to the Highlands was 'trying to get beyond civility into some kind of friendship'.[5] Did John Major think it added an extra dimension to his relationship with the Queen? 'I think it probably did,' said Major. 'And with others who were close to her.'[6] That included the Queen's private secretary, Sir Robert Fellowes (later Lord Fellowes), with whom Major shared a love of cricket. Their relationship included a certain amount of joshing, according to former cabinet secretary Robin Butler: 'John Major was very relaxed with court officials in a way that Margaret Thatcher never was.'[7] Major bonding with Fellowes over cricket was reflected in the way Butler used to play golf with the Queen's private secretary Philip Moore on the small course at Balmoral, as later Andrew Turnbull did with Robert Fellowes – cricket and golf, the social lubricants of the constitution.

Occasionally the piper would be even more inconvenient than usual. One Sunday morning before church Major had to take a phone call from the Italian prime minister, Giuliano Amato. 'As we spoke, a piper was walking up and down the lawn outside the bedroom playing a lament. At one point I could only hear Giuliano by putting a finger to one ear while holding the phone to the other.'[8] On the other end of the line Amato was saying, 'What's that noise? What is that noise?'[9]

For all that Major remembered Balmoral being relaxed and fun, informality is perhaps a relative concept. Alex Allan, who took over as private secretary from Andrew Turnbull, said:

> One of my memories is the sheer number of changes of clothes you had to take. You leave London in a business suit, and then you arrive and have lunch with Robert Fellowes, and that was trying to change into something slightly less formal. Then Robert and Jane [his wife] and I would go for a walk, and you would have to have suitable gear for walking. Then you never knew until six o'clock in the evening whether you'd be having a black tie dinner in the castle or a barbecue at one of the lodges around the grounds. Then you'd go to church the next morning. So you ended up with a huge suitcase of clothes for a weekend.
>
> The barbecues were much more fun than black tie dinners. You'd arrive there and the Duke of Edinburgh and Prince Andrew would be cooking the sausages on the barbecue, and it was all very informal. At the end of the meal the Queen would get up and start doing the washing-up.

This was a phenomenon noted by every visitor to Balmoral, although there was possibly more to it than met the eye. 'One time I was standing up to go and help her. I was sitting next to a lady-in-waiting, and she said, "No, no, no! The Queen likes to do it. But don't worry – when the plates and everything get back to the castle, they are all put in the dishwasher."'[10]

Allan – together with his wife, Katie – was also invited up to Balmoral once by the then Prince of Wales to witness the extent of press intrusion. 'Princess Anne was there too. We went for a picnic by the river, just to demonstrate that as soon as we sat down for lunch . . . immediately there were umpteen photographers with long lenses. This is what Prince Charles wanted to demonstrate, but there wasn't much I could do about it.'

The Allans had taken their cocker spaniel, Holly, to Balmoral. 'We were sleeping in this room which had very heavy curtains. The dog was at the foot of the bed. We woke up with a start in the morning, and suddenly realised it had got quite late.' Katie swiftly got up to take Holly for her morning walk. 'Going across the hallway it was too much for her, and she did poos in the middle of the carpet. Katie was going "aaargh!" and the housekeeper came rushing out. She said, "Don't worry, dear. The Queen Mother's corgis do it much worse than this."'[11]

ON 20 NOVEMBER 1992 Windsor Castle was four years into a comprehensive works programme to replace the wiring and the heating. The project, known as Kingsbury, had reached the north-east corner of the Upper Ward, where all the furniture and works of art had been taken out of the state apartments and other rooms and put into a specially built store in Home Park. Work on the private chapel and the grand reception room had finished, and was about to begin in St George's Hall. Some large paintings were leant up in an alcove in the chapel, screened off by a pair of large, heavy curtains.

Exactly what happened that morning has never been established for certain, but one theory is that the curtains may have got too close to the spotlights that normally light up the altar during services. At 11.26 Charles Noble, one of the picture specialists, who had just returned from a coffee break, said, 'Can you smell burning?' They could not find anything and went back to work. A couple of minutes later picture conservator Viola Pemberton-Pigott looked up at the curtains in front of the altar alcove and saw flames. 'Oh my God!' she shouted. 'Look! Fire!' But it was already too late. By the time the picture specialists saw the flames, the fire was already spreading into the roof voids of the castle.[12]

Within three hours 225 firefighters from seven counties were battling the blaze. The fire burned for fifteen hours, and was not extinguished until 2.30 the next morning. It destroyed 115 rooms, including nine state rooms. Yet amazingly, thanks to the efforts of castle staff and other volunteers who worked frantically to remove everything that had not already been taken to storage, only two works of art were destroyed: a rosewood sideboard and a large painting by Sir William Beechey which could not be taken down from the wall in time.

That evening, television news was dominated by shocking footage from Windsor as the flames lit up the night sky. But perhaps the most poignant image of all was that of a sombre Queen dressed in a headscarf, raincoat and wellington boots as she surveyed the damage to her childhood home. She was, said Prince Andrew, who had been in Windsor and helped organise the rescue operation, 'absolutely devastated'. She had been in London when the fire broke out, but rushed down, both to see the damage for herself and to rescue what she could from her apartments. Later, when she returned to Buckingham Palace, the staff left their offices to greet her at her private entrance in a show of moral support. 'She just shrugged her shoulders and said, "It was ghastly, but at least we managed to save the pictures,"' her former press secretary Charles Anson told Robert Hardman. 'Her spirit was not broken in any way at all.'[13]

In the aftermath of the fire the secretary of state for national heritage, Peter Brooke, announced that because the castle itself – as opposed to its furniture and works of art – was not insured, public money would pay for the restoration, the cost of which was estimated at up to £40 million. Amid the surge of sympathy for the Queen, he thought that was not only the right thing to do, but also unexceptional, as the government had been responsible for the funding, maintenance and repair of the castle since 1760. It was, said John Major, only logical, as the castle is merely – as the technical term has it – vested in the sovereign in right of the Crown. 'It isn't actually owned by the sovereign, it's owned by the state . . . I liaised with Peter Brooke at the outset and we both agreed, "This is a national monument." It was a terrible tragedy that it should have caught fire in that way and we, the government, should pay.'[14] But, as Major recalls, 'There was an outcry.'

The country was deep in recession, and there had been widespread criticism of the royal family and their financial arrangements over the previous year. The notion that the taxpayer should pay for the repair of the home of an extremely wealthy woman who did not pay tax did not go down well. Headlines appeared: 'It's a Blank Cheque for Windsor' and 'Taxpayer to Foot Windsor Bill'. The Daily Mail, usually supportive of the monarchy, published a front-page editorial under the headline, 'Why the Queen Must Listen', saying, 'Why should the populace, many of whom have had to make huge sacrifices during the bitter recession, have to pay the total bill for Windsor Castle, when the Queen, who pays no taxes, contributes next to nothing?' The Queen did listen, and the policy was reversed a few months later.

It was the climax to a bad year. The royal family had been subjected to an unstinting chorus of criticism, from the media and others, about everything from the Queen's tax exemption to the behaviour of the younger royals. The Duke and Duchess of York had announced their separation after pictures were published of the duchess on holiday with her Texan friend Steve Wyatt, to be followed several months later by topless pictures of the duchess by a pool as her so-called financial adviser John Bryan sucked – or kissed, depending on which version one believes – her toes. Charles and Diana, the Prince and Princess of Wales, were fighting a highly public marital war, and the Princess Royal had just got divorced. On top of that, the transcript of a phone call between Diana and James Gilbey was published by the Sun in which he called her Squidgy and she described her marriage as 'torture'. In short, it was a mess.

Four days after the fire the Queen, her voice hoarse from a heavy cold as well as the smoke she had inhaled, gave a speech at a lunch in the City of London to mark her forty years on the throne. She began by quoting the words of her former assistant private secretary Sir Edward Ford, who had recently written a letter to Robert Fellowes. 'Nineteen ninety-two is not a year on which I shall look back with undiluted pleasure,' she said. 'In the words of one of my more sympathetic correspondents, it has turned out to be an "annus horribilis".' For someone who never complained, the speech was a rare plea for understanding. 'No institution –

City, monarchy, whatever – should expect to be free from the scrutiny of those who give it their loyalty and support, not to mention those who don't,' she said. 'But we are all part of the same fabric of our national society, and that scrutiny, by one part of another, can be just as effective if it is made with a touch of gentleness, good humour and understanding.'

Two days after that John Major surprised the House of Commons by announcing that the Queen and Prince of Wales had agreed to pay tax on their private incomes, which had not happened since Edward VII. The Queen had also agreed to reimburse the Civil List annuities paid to five members of her family: the Princess Royal, the Duke of York, Prince Edward, Princess Margaret and Princess Alice, Duchess of Gloucester. The decision, Major said, had been the Queen's, and been made the previous summer. Discussions were still going on between the Treasury, the Inland Revenue and the royal household, he said, and he would make a full statement when they were finished.

The announcement was a PR disaster on two fronts. First, it was seen as too little, too late. Second, it was regarded as a panicked reaction to tabloid criticism, which had been brought to a head by the Windsor fire. In the view of the Queen's biographer Sarah Bradford, Elizabeth's 'cautious instincts' had let her down. 'By moving too slowly in response to public feeling, she had allowed a head of steam to build up and a hue and cry about the expense of the monarchy to develop which might have been avoided by swifter action.'[15] Another point should be made too, wholly obvious in some ways but sometimes forgotten: the government saw it as its role to protect the monarchy. The minutes of the cabinet meeting on the day of Major's announcement record that ministers discussed how to do this: 'Recent media coverage of the Royal Family had been intrusive and intolerable. Members

of the Royal Family were being put under extreme strain . . .
The Government should reinforce the Queen's initiative by
strong expressions of support for the institution of the Monarchy. The Prime Minister might consider making this the
centre-piece of a major speech in due course.'[16]

When details of the new tax arrangements were made
public in February 1993 the statement said that the Queen
and Prince of Wales had agreed to pay income tax and capital
gains tax on a voluntary basis on their private income, after
the deduction of expenses. Lord Airlie, the lord chamberlain, said that the Queen had asked him in February of the
previous year to look into the feasibility of paying tax. 'We
had been working on the Queen's tax for months,' a leading
courtier told Ben Pimlott. 'When the fire came, we weren't
actually finished, though it was nine-tenths done. It was very
bad luck. The plan had been that it would take effect from
April 1st 1993, and it would have been announced in the New
Year. Then this thing overtook us, we needed to move fast,
and it looked as if we had been pressurized.'[17]

But if that was meant to imply that they were not forced
into it by the tabloids, that would be misleading. Demands
that the Queen should pay tax had been building up ever since
a World in Action programme in 1991 that argued that royal tax
immunity was not so much a historic right as an innovation
of the twentieth century. As we have seen earlier, Victoria
agreed to pay income tax; it was her successors who got out
of it. Edward VII paid it, very reluctantly, but George V was
exempted from paying income tax on his Civil List income in
exchange for paying for the cost of state visits. George VI was
wholly exempted because the financial deal struck with his
older brother – Edward VIII, later the Duke of Windsor – at
the time of the abdication proved unexpectedly expensive.[18]

The Queen had asked Airlie to look into the question of paying tax some six months after *World in Action*. Furthermore, in the 1980s the Queen's private secretary Sir William Heseltine had written an internal paper suggesting that it was time for her to consider starting to do so. But nothing came of it, because the Queen was not ready to pay tax, mainly because exemption was a principle that her father had strongly believed in, and at the time this was not something Elizabeth was prepared to overturn. (After agreeing to pay income tax, worried that the change might be seen as implicit criticism of her father, the Queen sent Robert Fellowes to break the news to her mother. Fellowes told the Queen Mother's biographer William Shawcross that after he had finished, 'there was a long pause and then she said: "I think we'll have a drink." . . . She didn't want to dwell upon it.'[19]) It is clear, therefore, that the Queen bowed to media pressure over tax. That is certainly what a former adviser to Prince Charles believed. 'Effectively, the Queen agreed to pay tax as a result of a tabloid campaign.'[20] It was just that it had nothing to do with the Windsor fire.

Not all the tabloids were impressed, however. While the Sun hailed the tax announcement as a 'victory for people power', the range of exemptions – no tax on the use of the royal yacht, the royal train or the Queen's flight, and no inheritance tax on bequests from one sovereign to the next – saw the *Daily Mirror* respond with a front-page cartoon of the Queen totting up her wealth on a calculator next to the headline 'HM the Tax Dodger'. The article was written by the paper's political editor, Alastair Campbell, who would later become Tony Blair's spin doctor.

Even though he was the prime minister who announced the Queen's decision to pay tax, John Major was not sold on the plan. 'There was criticism right the way through the 1980s that bubbled up now and again – and sometimes got quite nasty – about the fact that the Queen didn't pay taxes,' he said. 'It became more difficult when the recession started in 1988, 1989 . . . Interest rates went up to 15 per cent. The palace indicated to the government that we should consider whether or not the Queen should pay taxes.' As a result a working party was set up of senior officials from the Treasury and the palace.

> The initiative was solely from the palace. The Queen was not pressured either by the Thatcher government or by my own to pay taxes. She simply thought it was the right thing to do . . . I wasn't convinced, because the royal family are unlike any other institution. They are of inestimable value to the nation. They bear a great many costs, a great many responsibilities. And I'm a traditionalist. I didn't see any reason for changing the long-accepted arrangement. There wasn't any intellectual heft behind my instinctive dislike of the decision – it just didn't feel right. I wasn't opposed to the Queen paying taxes. But I would not have initiated it.[21]

The chancellor, Norman Lamont, was even less keen than John Major on the idea. According to the diarist Woodrow Wyatt, when Lamont had a pre-Budget audience with the Queen in March 1992 she only wanted to talk to him about her paying income tax. She thought she should, but he countered with a suggestion that the Crown Estate should be handed over to her, and that she should then pay tax on the income from that. That, he told her, would be more than she got from the Civil List. Wyatt later told the Queen Mother that Lamont did not want the Queen to pay income tax but had been overruled by the prime minister.[22]

The royal tax announcement also included the news that the Queen would open Buckingham Palace to the public during the summer to help fund the repairs to Windsor Castle. This was a climbdown from the position announced by Peter Brooke immediately after the fire, that all the costs would be borne by the government. Instead, he said, he hoped that the profits from opening the palace would pay for 70 per cent of the estimated £40 million cost of repairs. The Queen also donated £2 million of her own money. The rest would come out of public funds. The final bill came in slightly under budget, at about £36.7 million, with the palace duly paying its 70 per cent share.[23]

ON 9 DECEMBER 1992 Major had another momentous announcement to make in the House of Commons: the separation of the Prince and Princess of Wales. The decision had come after the publication of Andrew Morton's book *Diana: Her True Story* and a disastrous tour by the couple of South Korea during which they looked so miserable that the British press nicknamed them The Glums. Major said that the decision had been reached 'amicably', and that the couple had no plans to divorce. 'Their constitutional positions are unaffected,' he said, adding, 'There is no reason why the Princess of Wales should not be crowned Queen in due course.' To many this seemed a claim too far: if the couple were separated, why would it make sense for Diana to be crowned Queen? Lord Butler, who was cabinet secretary at the time, now admits that that was his mistake. 'That was something where I made a misjudgement,' he said. 'Douglas Hurd [then foreign secretary] thought it was unwise to say this doesn't mean she can't be Queen. I remember sitting at the cabinet table and Douglas raising his eyebrows at that. But what I had in mind was that . . . it would be comforting to the public.'[24]

Behind the scenes, John Major played an important role in the saga of Charles and Diana's break-up, not only offering his advice to the Queen as and when it was asked for, but playing the role of honest broker between the warring Waleses, and acting as a sympathetic listener to Diana at a time when she felt at her most alone. It was a role that suited his natural warmth and empathy; it is hard to imagine Margaret Thatcher acting in the same way. Sir Malcolm Rifkind said: 'It is a product of his own personality. What you see is what you get. He is a very genuine person, very natural. He is a very warm but also very astute person. He is the sort of person that if you did have something very personal that you wanted to discuss in private, you would feel comfortable doing that. You could not have that kind of relationship with Margaret Thatcher because part of her brilliance, part of her leadership, was that she could be very abrasive. She could be very difficult.'[25]

Alex Allan, Major's private secretary, said the prime minister had a number of sessions with both Charles and Diana. As soon as he saw one of them, the other's side would ask if they could have a meeting too. 'He was quite involved in discussions in the run-up to the announcement of the separation,' said Allan. 'He also had weekly audiences with the Queen, and that was obviously discussed then.' Major was not trying to stop the separation, but he was 'quite concerned' about Diana, said Allan. 'He was very empathetic, and was able to see both sides, talk to people, listen. He was quite sympathetic. I think that worked well.'[26]

In Lord Butler's view, Major offered Diana 'a shoulder to cry on'. But there was another dimension to their relationship: Major, he believes, would have been naturally sympathetic towards a woman who had been thrust into a public role in which she faced considerable difficulties. 'John Major was the sort of person who, if there were difficulties around, was capable of exuding human sympathy. But I think it's probably also the case that his sympathy was more expressed towards Diana than Charles. I don't think he was equally close to Charles.'[27] This was an area where the personal and the political overlapped. Major wanted to help Diana, but he also believed in the importance of the monarchy. He could see that divorce would have implications for the sovereign, and wanted to do all he could to protect the monarchy as an institution.

On the day the separation was announced, Major made a point of going to see both Charles and Diana. He continued to keep in regular contact with her, said her private secretary, Patrick Jephson. 'Major would come and visit Diana quite frequently, in the run-up to the separation and afterwards. They would have tea, just the two of them. It was great, because always afterwards she was encouraged, she was buoyed up. She would refer to him fondly as "the Hon. John" . . . I got the very clear message that he enjoyed those meetings. He was there to be an honest broker, to be a source of practical help if she needed it, and to help her find happiness. Or at least contentment in what she was doing.' Another former royal aide said John Major did his best to make Princes William and Harry feel that the government cared about them. 'He was an important, sympathetic, helpful mentoring figure. And he did it when he ceased to be prime minister as well.'[28]

Even when they were not in direct contact, Major would keep an eye on Diana. When she went to Nepal in 1993 with the overseas development minister, Baroness Chalker, it was a case, said Jephson, of Chalker keeping a 'watching brief' on Diana on Major's behalf to see how she was performing as a British asset. Impeccably, it seemed: the tour was a resounding success. Major considered the idea of Diana becoming the patron of an organisation involved in childcare or some similar field, but it came to nothing.

Jephson had a good relationship with Major's private secretary, Alex Allan, with whom he would have lunch on a regular basis. '[Allan] was obviously keen to be able to report to his boss on what was really going on between Charles and Diana, particularly what Diana's intentions were.' There were occasional bumps along the way, however. Once Diana attended a conference at the homelessness charity Centrepoint (of which she was patron) which was also attended by the Labour MP Jack Straw. This looked a bit too much like Diana straying into the world of politics. 'I got a bollocking from 10 Downing Street for allowing the princess to be on the same platform as an opposition spokesman,' said Jephson, who said he had thought it was OK because they were not in a pre-election period. Allan replied: 'Patrick, we are *always* in a pre-election period.'[29]

While the anti-Diana camp was keen to portray Diana as a 'national embarrassment, a person of no particular worth or value, somebody who would soon be cast on the royal roadside, so don't waste your time there', Jephson was at pains to explain to Allan that everything Diana did was in support of the monarchy. 'Her intention was to carry on serving the Queen.' It was a message that found a receptive audience in John Major. In the wake of Diana's *Panorama* interview, the armed forces minister, Nicholas Soames, a friend of Charles's, went on *Newsnight* to say that Diana was showing 'the advanced stages of paranoia'. Later Major bumped into him in the division lobby of the Commons and told him firmly to 'shut up'.[30]

As we have seen before – with Queen Victoria and her eldest son, Bertie, with George V and the future Edward VIII

– when the royals are mired in family crises they often reach out to the government for help. It is a reaction that Jephson feels some sympathy with. When things were getting 'really hairy' between Charles and Diana, he got the sense that Buckingham Palace had an 'understandable wish' that Number 10 would sort things out. 'Only Number 10 has the authority to tell other people what to do. Ironically the role of the monarchy is to act as the continuity, the unchanging face of the state, but I remember thinking it was us who were in a mess. In Number 10 there was real power, real authority. They were sorting out the rest of the country, and wouldn't it be lovely if they could sort this out too?'

He felt that most explicitly when Major came to see Charles and Diana – separately – on the day he announced their separation. 'I remember John Major going in. He is a tall, imposing figure. Big smile, big warm handshake for me, and I can remember thinking, "Jeez, I wish you could fix this, I wish you could sort this out." He was the sort of chap you felt you could go to and say, "God, can you help us with this?"'[31]

The idea that politicians are at least partly there to help the royal family sort out its personal travails had its strongest – and, arguably, most bizarre – expression in the *Daily Mail* in an article in March 2024. The piece was by Richard Kay, who had been very close to Diana when he was the paper's royal correspondent. Discussing whether the royal family was 'at the eleventh hour' because of the fuss about the Princess of Wales (Kate, not Diana) doctoring a photograph, and the announcement about the King's cancer, he wrote: 'Thirty years ago, then-PM John Major was too busy propping up his administration to take a leading role in the Charles v Diana crisis. Fast forward to 2024 and Rishi Sunak, preoccupied by defections and discontent, is similarly missing in action.'[32] I would argue that actually Major was significantly involved in the Charles and Diana crisis, and it would be interesting to find out from Kay exactly what more he thinks either prime minister should have done.

It goes without saying that Major won't be drawn on his relationship with Diana. All he would say is this: 'My role was quite simple: it was to help if I could. And that's it. The royal family are important to our nation. The prime minister is the first minister for the Queen, and if he or she can help, I would hope that he or she would always do so, and never betray the trust that is placed in them.'[33]

Major's relationship with the Queen continued long after he ceased to be prime minister. In 2011 the Queen asked him to chair the Queen Elizabeth Diamond Jubilee Trust, a role that saw him often appear at events to support the trust either with the Queen or other members of the royal family until it was wound up in 2020. Even after that he remained a confidant of the Queen. Sir Malcolm Rifkind, who served in the cabinets of both Thatcher and his successor, and remains a good friend of Major, said: 'It continued right up to the end of the Queen's reign that he would quite often be asked to go into the palace just for a private conversation, either with the Queen or with the private secretary about some public matter.' It was not just the Queen who trusted him, said Rifkind, it was her courtiers as well. 'The household . . . saw John Major as someone who had . . . good judgement, total objectivity, no personal axe to grind . . . whoever is the sovereign, that's what they need from the people around them.'[34]

WHATEVER CONVERSATIONS went on between Diana and John Major, there is no doubt that Diana had the ability to charm male politicians. When Sir Malcolm Rifkind was foreign secretary he got a message inviting him to have lunch with her – just the two of them – at Kensington Palace. It

Queen Victoria at Windsor with Lord Melbourne, as depicted by Sir Francis Grant. In her early years she would ride with him most days.

Victoria made Disraeli Earl of Beaconsfield shortly after he made her Empress of India. One good turn deserves another, said *Punch*.

William Gladstone, popularly known as the GOM, or Grand Old Man: Victoria called him 'that half-mad firebrand'.

LE ROI D'ANGLETERRE EN FRANCE
Le départ de Cherbourg

Above. Walter Bagehot, author of *The English Constitution*.

Right. Edward VII leaves Cherbourg after his triumphant 1903 visit to France.

David Lloyd George with Winston Churchill in about 1910, some time after the People's Budget.

First cousins Nicky and Georgie, before they became Tsar Nicholas II and George V. Nicky is on the left.

Ramsay MacDonald, who, despite George V's fears about Britain's first Labour government, developed a strong relationship with the King.

The Duke and Duchess of Windsor, photographed by Cecil Beaton three years after the Abdication.

Winston Churchill with King George VI at Buckingham Palace during the Second World War.

Harold Wilson with Queen Elizabeth II at 10 Downing Street for his farewell dinner in 1976.

Harold Macmillan at the Conservative party conference in 1957. On the platform with him is Rab Butler, who twice failed to become prime minister.

Elizabeth in her happy place, on board the royal yacht *Britannia* in 1972. It was decommissioned twenty-five years later.

The Queen with German chancellor Helmut Kohl, US president Ronald Reagan and prime minister Margaret Thatcher.

During her Golden Jubilee in 2002 the Queen attended a Downing Street dinner with her prime ministers: Tony Blair, Margaret Thatcher, Edward Heath, Jim Callaghan and John Major.

Tony Blair addresses the nation following the death of Diana, Princess of Wales in 1997.

Tony Blair joins hands with the Queen for the singing of 'Auld Lang Syne' on Millennium Eve – a night they might both have preferred to forget.

Prime minister David Cameron and London mayor Boris Johnson
on a train to Newark during the 2014 by-election.

King Charles III appoints Sir Keir Starmer prime minister at
Buckingham Palace following Labour's 2024 election victory.
'You must be utterly exhausted,' Charles said.

was shortly after her divorce. 'I was not used to being invited to lunch à deux with Diana. I had met her, but only as part of public engagements. So I made sure my diary was free that day! She could not have been more charming. Basically, she was beginning to try to plan her future programme, her international programme. She just wanted advice. Would there be problems with particular countries she wanted to visit? One was Argentina.' Although the Falklands War had been over for fourteen years, there were still sensitivities. 'It was a perfectly serious, grown-up discussion. I was actually quite impressed.'

At the end of lunch she walked him down to where his car should have been, but it had not arrived. 'I said, "Don't wait, ma'am, it will be arriving any minute." She said, "No, no, let's go up and have another cup of tea." So we go up to have another cup of tea.' Afterwards he wrote her a thank-you letter. 'I get back a handwritten letter from her saying, "Oh no, no it was the other way round, you're a very busy person. It was very kind of you [to come]." She had a nice way of making people feel good. It was professional! I knew perfectly well I was insignificant in terms of her broader scheme of things, but she took the trouble to be very charming. Like every other male in the country, I did not dislike the experience.'[35]

Other political figures were also charmed by Diana, but did not always show Rifkind's self-awareness. In May 1995, on a night when Labour scored spectacular successes in local elections, a prelude to the general election victory that would come two years later, Tony Blair and his wife, Cherie, were at a dinner in Hyde Park Gardens which had been organised for them to meet the Princess of Wales. Towards the end of the evening Alastair Campbell, who was now Blair's press spokesman, arrived to take them back to party headquarters to hear the results. After ringing the bell to let them know he was there, he was waiting in the car when Blair, who had been elected party leader the year before, tapped on the window. 'Someone wants to meet you,' he said. That someone was Diana.

Campbell was instantly smitten. 'She's standing there,' he wrote, 'absolutely, spellbindingly, drop-dead gorgeous.' They stood there flirting for a few minutes, while Blair stood back and Cherie looked impatient. But Campbell, as he put it, was 'lost in the beauty'. He wrote in his diary: 'I'm thinking how could I have written all those vile things about her?' Apparently Diana had spent much of the dinner asking Blair what Campbell was really like and how she wished she had a press officer as good as him. Afterwards, Campbell was 'unbearable', telling anyone who would listen that Blair felt bruised because Diana had just used him as a means of getting to him.[36] After that, his diary is peppered with references to Diana: Campbell saying how 'gorgeous' she is, Diana telling Peter Mandelson how 'strong' Alastair is, Diana telling a mutual acquaintance how much she likes him. Campbell got 'a bit besotted', said Blair's chief of staff, Jonathan Powell, younger brother of Charles Powell, who worked for Margaret Thatcher. Another senior Labour figure from the time said: 'It was ridiculous. He was like a dog with a bone, saying "I think she really fancies me." Really? I thought, "She knows what she is doing."'[37]

In January 1997 another dinner for the Blairs and Diana was arranged at the Hackney home of mutual friends Alan Howarth, chairman of the parliamentary Labour party, and his partner, Maggie Rae, a lawyer who worked for Diana in her divorce. Campbell and his partner, Fiona, were also invited. Blair was 'jumpy', worried that news of the dinner would get out – and not entirely happy that Campbell was there. The atmosphere was a little awkward at first, with Blair apparently unable to decide whether to flirt with Diana or treat her like a visiting dignitary.[38] They talked about Aids, her landmine work in Angola and the media. Diana told Campbell: 'Of course you used to say one or two not nice things about me.' 'I don't know if it helps,' he said, 'but I feel very bad about it now.' They also talked about Charles (he wouldn't be King), Philip (Diana didn't like him), and the monarchy's position in society, and Blair dropped heavy hints about Diana having a more developed role in public life. Diana, however, 'didn't bite at all'.

When they left, Cherie kissed Diana on both cheeks. What was Campbell going to do, wondered Diana. He shook her hand, and she giggled. 'I love her laugh,' he wrote. He was still besotted.[39]

Blair was not. He saw Diana's potential but also viewed her as 'very manipulative and determined'.[40] In his memoirs he said she was 'extraordinarily captivating' and had strong emotional intelligence as well as being 'very capable of analytical understanding'. But he was cautious: 'I really liked her and, of course, was as big a sucker for a beautiful princess as the next man; but I was wary too.' What did both sides want out of this meeting? 'They were a bit starstruck,' said Powell, but he believes it was Diana who stood to gain most; there wasn't much in it for Labour. 'It looked a little bit transactional from her point of view, looking for leverage. I don't think from Tony's point of view it was transactional: it was just interest.'[41]

When Labour came to power, Blair and even Campbell grew a touch more cynical about Diana. But the cynicism did not last long.

CHAPTER EIGHT

EXPRESSIONS OF DISPLEASURE

THE SOVEREIGN'S closest relationship with his or her ministers is, of course, with the prime minister. But other ministers also play walk-on roles, and in his time as a minister – which stretched from the beginning of Margaret Thatcher's term in office to the end of John Major's – Sir Malcolm Rifkind got to know Queen Elizabeth II as well as any. And that meant travelling with her: by plane, as foreign secretary, by train and by boat. In particular, on the royal train and aboard the royal yacht, *Britannia*. When he was transport secretary, he was scheduled to attend an event with the Queen in Scotland, and a palace official suggested that he travel up with her in the royal train, 'probably knowing I would be quite chuffed to be asked'. He recalled waiting at the station in London, because he and the other passengers could not board until the Queen was on the train. 'We were all standing there and the Rolls-Royce sweeps into the reserved area, a flunkey opens the door, and the first thing that appears are two corgis – not on leads. The other thing I remember was extremely comfortable compartments. Mine had not just a washroom, but a bathroom. It wasn't a proper bath, and I didn't particularly feel like a bath, but I said [to myself], "No, you're never again going to get a chance to have a bath on the royal train." So I had a bath, with my knees virtually up to my chin.'

His trip on *Britannia* came in 1986 when he was Scottish secretary, and he was due to join the Queen on a visit to the isolated lighthouse at Ardnamurchan during her summer cruise round the west and northern coasts of Scotland. To make things easier for him, the Queen agreed that he should join her on the yacht for the weekend. On the Sunday they had a picnic on the small island of Oronsay. *Britannia*, said Rifkind, 'is extremely comfortable rather than luxurious'. That weekend *The Sunday Times* had a story asking if the Queen had a heart problem because she had been seen visiting a consultant in Harley Street. 'Oh,' she said crossly. 'I knew this would happen.' Philip had suggested she have a precautionary check-up, and now the media had jumped to the wrong conclusion; as the doctor had confirmed, there was nothing wrong with her. The next day at Ardnamurchan there was a surprisingly full media turnout. 'They were all clamouring to see the Queen with her heart condition,' said Rifkind. After being greeted by dignitaries, the Queen announced that she wanted to go up the lighthouse. So the lord lieutenant, the secretary of state and the Queen all climbed to the top of the lighthouse, the only difference being that the Queen went up at top speed while the other two struggled to keep up. 'She gets to the top, looks at the journalists, smiles sweetly, waves her hand,' said Rifkind. 'Not another word was said about the Queen's heart condition. I thought, "You are a real pro."'[1]

The Queen may have been in the best of health, but *Britannia* was living on borrowed time. It was commissioned in 1954, and while its admirers saw it as a valuable symbol of Britain's prestige and a useful tool for promoting trade efforts overseas, it was expensive to run and a questionable use of resources. In 1994 the Major government decided that a pending £17 million refit would set off just the sort of public outcry it had endured over the Buckingham Palace restoration, and announced that it would be decommissioned in 1997.

The following year Major discussed with the cabinet whether *Britannia* should be replaced, and decided that it was not the right time to commission another royal yacht. His private secretary, Alex Allan, noted: 'The public's limited appetite for expenditure on the monarchy had been revealed by the reaction to the Windsor fire. The Queen herself had given no clear indication that she wanted the yacht replaced.'[2] However, that, it would emerge later, was not the same as the Queen not having an opinion: she did.

The most significant obstacle to spending £60 million on a new yacht was chancellor Ken Clarke, who said that he 'adamantly refused' to spend such a sum 'on anything as nineteenth century as a royal yacht at a time when we were cutting back on public spending'. He wrote: 'I thought that the public reaction would be very negative . . . I was also unpersuaded that the yacht made any practical difference to our export performance, which was the only serious argument of any practical kind used in its favour.'

Clarke knew that his decision would not go down well with the royal family. 'I was led to understand that the Queen was quite distressed by the prospect of our failure to provide this facility for her and her family.' However, he made one telling point that goes to the heart of the relationship between the royal family and the political classes. 'I am a great enthusiast for the Queen, and as monarchist as most other British politicians,' he wrote. 'However I differ in one respect. Most politicians are so in awe of the royal family that expressions of displeasure from the Palace about issues bearing directly on the family can usually produce quite significant policy shifts.'[3] The truth of this observation would be borne out several times over the coming years.

Clarke was eventually forced to give way – not that it did the royal family any good, given that the Conservatives were destined to lose the 1997 general election. In the run-up to the election Major decided to endorse a proposal by defence secretary Michael Portillo to replace *Britannia* at the taxpayers' expense after all. However, Portillo made the mistake of not securing the backing of the Labour opposition beforehand. That meant that once the election campaign was under way, Labour had free rein to exploit the issue to their hearts' content.

How does John Major look back on the issue now? He argues that when they first decided not to go ahead with a new yacht, they also said that they would look at the question again in a few years' time. And in 1997 the economy was well on its way to recovery. 'Providing money deep in a recession is very different from providing money when the economy is beginning to go into a boom . . . We were in a position where we could credibly pay for it.' Did he regard it as a mistake not getting Labour on board? 'It might have been,' he said. But not necessarily. The chances of Portillo failing to get Labour's support were quite high, he said. 'The Labour party had been out of government for eighteen years. They were desperate to do everything they could to put themselves at a political advantage in order to win the election.'[4]

Meanwhile the Labour position was in fact far from clear. On the day in January 1997 that Portillo announced his *Britannia* proposal, Tony Blair agreed 'a cautious, prudent plan' with Gordon Brown, taking the line that it was 'highly regrettable' that the Queen was being dragged into party politics.[5] However, a couple of days later Gordon Brown decided – with minimal consultation – to put out a story that there would be no new money for a royal yacht if Labour got in. Not only that, but the Queen had supposedly also been informed. Alastair Campbell and Jonathan Powell, Blair's chief of staff, who were taken completely unawares by the story, decided they had been 'stitched up' by Brown and his spin doctor, Charlie Whelan. Blair, Campbell wrote in his diary, 'was as surprised as I was', while Powell was 'really angry'.[6] Another senior Labour figure said the party leadership was 'bounced into' the decision not to fund a replacement. It is what they might have decided, had they thought about it properly. But they did not. 'It was not a properly considered decision.'[7]

A couple of months after Labour's landslide victory in May, Tony Blair flew to Hong Kong to join Prince Charles for the ceremony handing the former colony over to China. After having tea with the prince on board the royal yacht, Blair told Campbell: 'We must keep *Britannia* . . . What an asset.' One can almost hear the republican sneer as Campbell sighed in his diary: 'I knew he would.'[8] This encapsulates the schism at the heart of New Labour. Blair, for whatever reasons – his inbuilt monarchism, his appreciation of *Britannia* as a national symbol and a means of wielding soft power – was in favour of replacing the royal yacht; Gordon Brown, the dour chancellor who would not be swayed from his radical agenda, was intent on making sure that not a penny of taxpayers' money went on a new *Britannia*. Brown got his way. 'This was part of a recurring debate the whole way through government and indeed opposition,' said Jonathan Powell. 'Gordon was always for demonstrative hair-shirtness . . . Blair would quite happily have given them another yacht, I'm sure. In principle he would want to do what the Queen wanted. But it was part of the constant row we had with Gordon on much bigger things than that. It was part of that crossfire.'[9]

For a while, a proposal to raise the money for a *Britannia* refit from private industry was considered. Peter Mandelson was keen on the idea. But it came to nothing: keeping the ageing yacht going was just too expensive. Blair did regret its loss, though. Recalling his time on the yacht in Hong Kong, he said later: 'I didn't want to get rid of it. After we'd agreed to get rid of it, I actually went on it and I remember, as I stepped on, thinking: "That was such a mistake to have done that."' He added: 'I think if it had happened five years into my time, I would have just said "No".'[10]

The yacht was decommissioned in a ceremony at Portsmouth Royal Naval Dockyard in December 1997. It was a cold day, with a biting wind, and the Queen appeared to shed a tear. However, neither she nor the palace ever said anything in public about wanting to replace *Britannia*, even though some outside royal circles have made noisy demands for a new yacht, without actually coming up with the money. Behind the scenes, however, it was a different story. The Queen's deputy private secretary Sir Kenneth Scott wrote to a senior civil servant in 1995 – after the decision to decommission the yacht was announced – saying that the Queen would 'very much welcome' a new yacht. But he acknowledged that if the palace lobbying for one were to become public it would be a disaster. Scott wrote: 'The last thing I should like to see is a newspaper headline saying "Queen Demands New Yacht."' He also suggested that ideas for a replacement should be considered in terms of feasibility first and cost second. 'It would not, I suggest, be a sufficient answer to all those who have contributed ideas to say simply that there is no spare money in the defence budget.'[11]

The correspondence in the National Archives shows that Whitehall did not share Scott's sense of the order of priorities.[12] That correspondence was closed and made unavailable for public inspection after *The Times* revealed the story; the alacrity with which the Cabinet Office shut that particular stable door after the horse had bolted was a classic example of the determination of the government to protect the reputation of the royal family at all costs, even if it made no practical sense.

TONY BLAIR WAS, as the Queen told him when he went to Buckingham Palace to be asked if he would form a government, her tenth prime minister. 'The first was Winston,' she said. 'That was before you were born.' From John Major onwards her prime ministers were all younger than her; now they were a different generation entirely, marking a significant shift in the power dynamic. The avuncular, even condescending attitude of her early prime ministers was replaced with reverence and respect. Blair was, he admitted in his memoirs, a little nervous. All that protocol took a little getting used to. He was 'Mr Blair' to the palace officials before he went to see her; they only called him 'Prime Minister' after he had been in to see her. One palace official recalls the small group who accompanied him, which included Alastair Campbell and Cherie Blair, as being 'absolutely exhausted, because they had been up virtually all night'.[13]

Then there was the kissing of hands. 'You don't actually kiss the Queen's hands in the ceremony of kissing hands,' an official apparently told him. 'You brush them gently with your lips.' Which, to be honest, sounds suspiciously like kissing, but Harold Wilson said that there wasn't any kissing of hands any more. It is very confusing. However, given that John Major, Gordon Brown and David Cameron have all said that there was no hand kissing, it is possible that Blair mis-remembered. David Torrance, a constitutional expert at the House of Commons Library who knows more about political ceremony than almost anyone, has suggested that Blair got muddled up with what happens in the Privy Council, where there is hand kissing[14].

Blair noted that the Queen was quite shy in his first audience, but direct, and the conversation a little stilted. Afterwards Cherie came in and talked to the Queen about their children while Blair sat there thinking about what he was going to say on the steps of Downing Street and feeling 'more than a little spaced out'.[15] According to a source, as the prime minister left the palace he suddenly got 'very nervous' about what he could and could not say about the audience. 'It was clearly in his head that he didn't want to trip up and say something about what the Queen had said, or to defy any convention.'[16] Would it be OK, he asked, if he said he had been to see the Queen, and she had asked him to form a government, and they had had a good chat? Yes, they said, that would be nice. Blair's anxiousness not to offend or behave towards the Queen in any way that might leave him open to criticism is a reminder that, unlike Alastair Campbell, say, or Jonathan Powell, he was not a republican; he had a conventional respect for the royal family and the role it played in the British constitution.

Alex Allan saw both ends of the handover. John Major got back to Downing Street at about seven in the morning from his constituency in Huntingdon, and gave a short speech to the staff in the Pillared Room at about 11.30 – 'He didn't want them all down the corridor applauding him out, or anything like that' – before being driven to Buckingham Palace for his resignation, while Allan followed in the police back-up car. Afterwards Major was driven off in another vehicle – he was no longer prime minister and had to use a different car – as Allan waited in Robert Fellowes's office watching the television footage of Tony Blair driving from Islington to the palace. After the audience, the Blairs took the prime ministerial car to Downing Street, while Allan got back into the police vehicle and contrived to get into Number 10 before them; the Blairs were busy glad-handing the Labour supporters who had been brought in to line Downing Street. 'I scooted round through the Cabinet Office [which is on Whitehall but connects to Downing Street] and by one o'clock, an hour after John Major walked out, I'm opening the door and saying "Welcome, Prime Minister" to Tony Blair.'[17]

Blair's keenness to please did not mean that all was smooth in the ensuing relationship between Number 10 and the palace. The first Queen's Speech of the Blair government – which as ever was drafted by Number 10 but discussed with the palace – was criticised for using language that was too political, and even Blair has admitted that they got it wrong. 'The poor Queen was reading out New Labour twaddle,' he told Robert Hardman.[18] He recalled in another interview: 'I had so much going on at the time and I hadn't paid a great deal of attention to the exact wording. I was listening to it wincing and thinking, Oh my God, she won't like this. And I said to them afterwards, "Next time, I'm going to look at this thing very carefully!" The New Labour stuff was fine when we were writing a conference speech, but we didn't have to put it past the Queen.'[19] A senior Labour figure said that most of the discussions between the palace and Number 10 had been about fine detail – the exact wording of the speech as opposed to the main thrust of it. However, after the criticisms, 'the palace got more nervous about it'.[20]

Getting the language of the Queen's Speech right is an art. Richard Crossman described listening to an 'appalling' speech in 1967, for which he as leader of the Commons was responsible. 'Next time I must take some trouble to get a speech that sounds good when it's read aloud because this one sounds difficult and Harold Wilson's sentences about inflation are impossible to enunciate.'[21] Occasionally the palace would request a tweak to make the speech easier to deliver.

When Boris Johnson was prime minister, there were a couple of occasions when the palace felt the language wasn't right. A Whitehall source said: 'The tension comes in the drafting of the speech. If there are phrases in there that look too overtly political, there's always an eyebrow raised at the other end of the park, which means "No, I don't think we can use this phrase or that phrase, because it's come directly from political campaigning."' A phrase on the Rwanda bill had to be taken out, as did another on Brexit, which was all about 'taking back control'.[22] In contrast to that, one of the only times that the late Queen expressed an opinion – in private – about the speech was to praise an initiative of Johnson's. On a visit to Sandringham Sir Malcolm Rifkind asked the Queen how she was getting on with Johnson as prime minister. She replied: 'I'm finding him a rather interesting person.' She was, she said, 'particularly pleased' that the Queen's Speech she delivered in May 2021 included a reference in the last paragraph to the government's commitment to the 'global effort to get 40 million girls across the world into school'.[23]

Blair also had to be careful how he managed his relationship with the Princess of Wales. He was still fascinated by her, but rather more cautious than he had been before coming to power. Diana suggested a meeting, and Blair invited her to join him and his family in June at Chequers, the prime minister's official weekend retreat. There was just one problem. 'They had fixed that up, and we hadn't realised that Tony Blair hadn't had a session since he became prime minister with Prince Charles,' recalled Alex Allan. It would be a terrible *faux pas* if Blair saw Diana before Charles, but it took a bit of persuading to get the PM to agree to postpone Diana quite so late in the day. 'We had to ring her office and say, "I'm terribly sorry, but Tony Blair has got to do something urgently with Germany." And so it was postponed a few weeks while Tony Blair did have a meeting with Prince Charles.'[24] Even then they were a bit wary, and repeatedly told Diana's office that there mustn't be any leaks.

Diana went to Chequers one Sunday in July, bringing the fifteen-year-old Prince William with her; he played football with the Blair children and had a swim, while Blair and Diana went for a walk in the woods. She was, Blair told Alastair Campbell, 'more gorgeous than ever', but the conversation did not flow easily, not least when Blair brought up the subject of her boyfriend, Dodi Fayed. Blair wrote in his memoirs that she reproached him 'gently but clearly' for postponing their June meeting. 'Astute as ever, she guessed the shifting of the date was deliberate and was cross about it.'[25] She was also 'miffed' that Downing Street had suggested that she might leak the meeting. Three weeks later the story got out anyway, not through Diana but the lobbyist and former Mandelson aide Derek Draper.[26]

IN THE EARLY hours of Sunday 31 August, Tony Blair was asleep in his constituency home in Trimdon Colliery, County Durham, when he awoke to find a policeman standing over the bed. He had tried the bell, the officer said, but no one had answered. Princess Diana had been seriously injured in a car crash in Paris and Blair should immediately ring the British ambassador there. By four in the morning he had been told she was dead. As well as all the practicalities he had to deal with, Blair also put in a call to the Queen. 'She was philosophical, anxious for the boys, but also professional and practical,' he recalled. She was also not going to be pushed around by what had happened. 'She could be very queenly in that sense.' Blair knew he would have to say something that morning, and scribbled a few words on the back of an envelope which he discussed with Alastair Campbell. Those words are famous now; Blair thinks they probably had as much coverage as anything else he ever did. They ended with the sentence: 'She was the people's princess and that's how she will stay, how she will remain in our hearts and in our memories for ever.' Looking back on that moment, Blair said the phrase 'people's princess' seemed 'corny' and over the top. But at the time it had felt natural, and he thought Diana would have approved. 'It was how she saw herself, and it was how she should be remembered.'[27]

The following hours and days were chaotic as Diana's body was brought back from Paris and the palace worked out what sort of funeral to hold as the sea of flowers laid by mourners outside Kensington Palace grew. Amid the national outpouring of grief, there was bitter criticism of the media, which was held to have hounded Diana to her death, and – gradually at first, but quickly building up a head of steam – an equally angry flood of words directed towards the royal family. They were cold, they were unfeeling, and they were treating Diana as badly in death as they had done during her life. Why had William and Harry been forced to go to church that Sunday, just hours after they had learned their mother had died? Why had there been no mention of Diana during the service? And what was the Queen doing staying up at Balmoral, when her people wanted to see her? There were reasonable answers to all these questions, many of them boiling down to the Queen's desire to protect the young princes, but that was not the way the outside world saw it. As Blair argued in his memoirs, there was no Alastair Campbell in the royal entourage to suggest, for instance, that mentioning Diana in that Sunday morning church service might have been a good idea.

A palace insider said that 'the people's princess' had been hard for the palace, although 'it kind of summed up her popularity', But no one at the palace had been particularly surprised that Blair said it – this was the sort of thing he was good at. 'By far the greater concern for the palace was the media reaction.' By Wednesday morning, 'the media was sounding really quite revolutionary'. The insider recalled: 'I remember walking into the palace . . . as you passed the flowers and walked through very silent crowds of people, it was a very threatening atmosphere. People in the palace were worried about it.'[28]

Blair was worried too. He told Jonathan Powell 'that he did not think the royal family would be able to manage as the public mood turned ugly'. Another senior Labour figure said: 'Blair saw it as a crisis, and thought it could do irreparable harm to the royal family and to the whole institution of the monarchy. And he was straight in there to sort it out.'[29] The palace also recognised that it would not be able to handle the crisis alone. At RAF Northolt, where they had just seen Diana's coffin arrive from Paris, Lord Airlie, the head of the Queen's household, told Blair: 'We're going to need your help in how we handle all this.' Blair called over to Campbell to join them, and Airlie told him: 'Look, I think it would be helpful if you could come over to the Palace tomorrow.'[30] Blair told Powell to send some key members of staff to the planning meeting at the palace, including Anji Hunter, his personal assistant who would later become head of government relations, alongside Campbell. In Blair's view, Campbell would take a tabloid view of what needed to be done, while Hunter would speak for her 'very correct brand of Middle England'.[31]

For Blair, helping the palace involved a delicate balancing act. As Campbell recounted, Blair 'felt we could really help them but they would have to change'.[32] On the other hand, there was concern in Downing Street that they should not be seen as muscling in. Blair also discovered that resolving this crisis would involve far more than the application of some of New Labour's much-vaunted communications skills: it involved dealing with the Queen. By Wednesday the question of the flag flying over Buckingham Palace had started to become an issue. At the suggestion of Alastair Campbell, Robert Fellowes had sent a message to Balmoral – where his deputy, Robin Janvrin, was in residence – raising the idea that the Union Jack should fly at half-mast. But the Queen – and Prince Philip – were adamant that the tradition that the only flag ever seen over Buckingham Palace is the Royal Standard, and that it never flies at half-mast, should be respected. The media became obsessed with the flag issue, with the Sun's front page headline demanding: 'Where Is Our Queen? Where Is Her Flag?' The mood, both in the media and on the street, was becoming unpleasant. The paper's editor, Stuart Higgins, rang Campbell saying he had to convince Blair to get Charles to persuade the Queen to allow the flag to fly at half-mast.

In fact, Blair had already called Charles earlier that afternoon. The prime minister's problem was that he did not think he could tell the Queen the things he needed to. 'I respected her and was a little in awe of her,' he wrote in his memoirs, but he did not know how she would take the advice he had to give her. But he knew Charles better. 'I didn't trust myself fully to go straight to her and be as blunt as I needed to be. So I went to Charles.' When he did, he found the Prince of Wales of the same mind as him. 'The Queen had to speak; the royal family had to be visible.'

Charles then spoke to the Queen, and on Thursday a new plan emerged, one more responsive to public opinion. After a number of very difficult conversations between courtiers and sovereign – Robin Janvrin was later said to 'bear the scars on his back' of those conversations – the Queen finally agreed that on the day of the funeral, and only then, the Union Jack should fly at half-mast over Buckingham Palace. The Queen would also come down to London on the Friday – the day before the funeral – stop to look at the flowers that had been laid outside Buckingham Palace and later make a public broadcast. By the time Blair discussed the new plan with her on Thursday lunchtime, she was 'very focused and totally persuaded'.[33] Campbell was listening in on the call. 'It was the first time I'd heard him one on one with the Queen and he really did the Ma'am stuff pretty well, but was also clear and firm too.' Blair told the Queen that many people out there were feeling loss and wanted someone to blame, and it was unfair that it was being directed at the Queen and the royal family. He also felt she had to show that she was vulnerable and was also feeling Diana's loss. He told her: 'I really do feel for you. There can be nothing more miserable than feeling as you do and having your motives questioned.'[34]

Meanwhile Campbell was doing all he could to stop the media turning the story into one of Downing Street interfering in the funeral, or exploiting it for their own political ends. 'I was constantly pushing the line that the Palace were very much in the driving seat and we were there with help and support,' he wrote in his diary. But he admitted in an aside: 'It may not have been strictly true.'[35]

The next day the Queen arrived at Buckingham Palace and got out of her Rolls-Royce to inspect the flowers and talk to the crowds. As she walked down the line of mourners, a girl handed her some red roses. The Queen asked if she would like her to place them for her. 'No, Your Majesty,' replied eleven-year-old Kathryn Jones. 'These are for you.' The crowd began to applaud, and to those courtiers who were listening it felt like a turning point. It was going to be all right.

Later that evening the Queen gave her live broadcast, in which she said there were 'lessons to be learned' from Diana's life and from the 'extraordinary and moving reaction to her death'. The suggestion that it should go out live had come from Downing Street, and the palace had originally baulked at this. 'The Queen doesn't do live,' they said. But when it was put to her directly, she agreed without hesitation. The address was largely the work of the palace, with Robert Fellowes writing the first draft and the press secretary Geoff Crawford adding to it. There were tweaks, but it was mostly Fellowes's work. Downing Street had only a limited amount of input, as it was such a personal address. There was, however, one suggestion from Alastair Campbell that was taken on board – the bit everyone remembers: that the Queen should say 'speaking as a grandmother'.

Over that bruising week the palace acknowledged that it needed help, and embraced it. The government team who went over to the palace, and Tony Blair himself, played an important role in helping the monarchy survive the crisis. But those who worked in the palace, who turned out not to be the stuffy, hidebound relics of a dying institution but serious professionals, also deserve credit for the way they responded to events. The tone of the funeral, the innovative nature of the funeral procession, with representatives of Diana's charities walking behind the coffin – all that came from the palace.

However, in the view of some on the government side the palace was also slightly resentful, feeling that the likes of Alastair Campbell made too much of the idea that Number 10 had saved the royal family from themselves. 'Blair and Campbell politicised the whole thing,' said one former royal official.[36] Another who attended the daily meetings called it 'the big Alastair Campbell takeover'.[37] It was not as if all Campbell's ideas were brilliant, either. One suggestion, that the public should be allowed to emerge from behind the barriers to follow the cortège – what he called his Pied Piper idea – was quickly squashed by the police on grounds of safety. Other officials from that time have a more nuanced view of the cooperation between palace and Number 10. There was no resentment, they say, but it wasn't all Number 10. Between them, they saved the monarchy. After the funeral, Robin Janvrin rang Campbell to say that a relationship had been forged between the palace and Downing Street in days that would normally have taken years. 'The barriers were broken down now, he said, and that meant they could push on for change.'[38]

No sooner was the funeral over than Blair had to face the culture shock of his first weekend at Balmoral. It was a world he was not used to: when the valet asked if he could draw his bath Blair thought for a moment 'he wanted to sketch the damn thing'. What helped him get through it all was the stiff drink he was given before dinner. 'I was never quite sure what it was,' he wrote, but it 'was absolutely what was needed . . . It was true rocket fuel.' Conversation seemed a lot easier after that.[39] Like everyone else, he marvelled at the way the Queen did the washing-up. 'The Queen asks if you've finished, she stacks the plates up and goes off to the sink.'

There were occasional moments of awkwardness, such as when he tried sitting in an inviting-looking chair in the drawing room for his audience with the Queen, only for the footman to let out a strangled cry and the Queen to raise her eyebrows. It was Queen Victoria's chair, he was told, and no one had sat in it since the day she died. Conversation with the Queen at that audience was not easy. 'With the recent events still raw and the relationship in its infancy, I felt nervous. She did too.' He spoke about the need to learn lessons, but afterwards realised he had been a little insensitive. He worried that perhaps she had thought he was lecturing her. 'At points during the conversation she assumed a little hauteur,' he wrote, 'but in the end she herself said lessons must be learned and I could see her own wisdom at work, reflecting, considering and adjusting.'[40] When the Blairs had their drive with the Queen around the Balmoral estate, they turned up in jeans and trainers; Campbell recorded in his diary that Blair 'sensed she had been pretty horrified' at that.[41] A palace insider from that time said that the Queen never gave away what she thought of Blair, 'but I do remember getting the impression – either from something she said directly, or something that she did not disagree with – that [she thought] Tony Blair was new and had quite a lot to learn.'[42]

A couple of years later he must have felt more relaxed. Cherie disclosed in her memoirs how, having got used to having her bag unpacked by the staff at Balmoral, she omitted to bring her 'contraceptive equipment' out of sheer embarrassment. As she wrote, 'As usual up there it has been bitterly cold, and what with one thing and another . . .'[43] Some nine months later their fourth child, Leo, was born.

From 1999 Blair's private secretary, Jeremy Heywood, would usually go up with him to Balmoral, but in 2001 Jonathan Powell, his chief of staff, 'foolishly' agreed to step in after Heywood had tired of it. 'It resulted,' he wrote later, 'in my becoming a republican.' He had gone up with his partner, the journalist Sarah Helm, and their daughters, and was expecting that evening to accompany Blair to the barbecue to which the private secretaries are normally invited. Before that, however, Robin Janvrin took him and his partner for a walk in the castle grounds. As the walk went on, he started wondering how they would get to the barbecue on time. Eventually Helm asked, and Janvrin told them he had bought a nice bit of salmon and they were going to have dinner at the house on the estate where he was staying.

The next day Powell was told that they had been disinvited because one of the ladies-in-waiting had discovered that he and Helm were not married, and had told the Queen. 'She supposedly felt that she should not set a bad example for Charles when Camilla was still not allowed at the Palace by inviting an unmarried couple to the barbecue.'[44]

Powell would also occasionally step in for Heywood when Blair went to the palace for his weekly audience with the Queen, and got an insight into the importance of the relationship between the sovereign's private secretary and their opposite number at Downing Street. 'Robin Janvrin was quite keen to hear the real gossip on what was going on politically,' he said. Being a political figure rather than a civil servant, Powell was well placed to provide that. 'It was pretty much a one-way conversation, him asking me questions on whatever was going on, whether it was the Iraq War, or Northern Ireland, which was my special subject, or the rows with Gordon [Brown].'[45]

Like John Major but unlike his other predecessors such as Margaret Thatcher and Jim Callaghan, Blair did not rely on notes for his audiences with the Queen. The private secretaries used to talk beforehand about what the agenda should be, but Jonathan Powell recalled: 'Tony used to say to me, "Don't waste any time with that, because we are not going to follow that. We just talk about what we talk about."'[46] Blair did have something in common with Thatcher, however: the Queen did not like it if he missed meetings. 'Sometimes if we cancelled too many meetings, if he was travelling or whatever, that used to cause a problem, and we had to reschedule,' said Powell. 'She didn't like not having the meetings on a regular basis. The private secretary would call up and say, "We've missed three meetings, and we can't have this."'

The sovereign and her prime minister would also sometimes speak outside their normal scheduled audiences. After the signing of the agreement on Good Friday 1998 that brought a formal end to the Troubles in Northern Ireland, Blair was just about to leave Belfast on a flight to Spain when a call came through: it was the Queen ringing up to congratulate him on his achievement. He recalled: 'I thought, I bet she doesn't do this often.'[47]

The nadir of the Queen's relationship with New Labour came on New Year's Eve 1999. One of the great white elephants of modern times, the Millennium Dome in Greenwich was a misguided and vainglorious attempt to mark the new millennium in grand style. Inherited by Blair from the Major government, throughout its building it had been beset by problems, but as the new year approached Blair had done his best to talk it up. It would, he said, be 'a triumph of confidence over cynicism, boldness over blandness, excellence over mediocrity'. Above all, it would see in the new year with a bang.

The opening, hosted by the Queen and Tony Blair, was a lavish gala which was supposed to be the centrepiece for 'one amazing night' of celebrations. There were performances by the likes of Mick Hucknall of Simply Red, the Corrs and the actor Stephen Fry – and, at the end, a mass singalong of 'Auld Lang Syne'. The fact that this was to happen was not unexpected, as it was in the programme. What was a surprise, however, was that the Queen was expected to take part in such a physical way. As it started, everyone linked hands – everyone, that is, except for the Queen, who was standing between Prince Philip and the prime minister. According to most accounts, she then had her hand grabbed by Blair in a moment of supreme awkwardness and was forced to join in a moment of enforced community jollity. As the journalist Dominic Lawson – who was there – wrote, 'the expression on Her Majesty's face could only be translated as: "What fresh hell is this?"'[48]

It was not quite like that, however: in fact it was the Queen who invited Philip and Blair to hold her hands, stretching out her arms and waggling her fingers, although unlike everyone else, she did not cross her arms. Either way, it was a minute or so of excruciating embarrassment. In his memoirs, Blair described the singing of 'Auld Lang Syne' as 'ghastly', and recalled struggling with the decision whether to link arms with the Queen. 'We looked at each other. I realised helplessly that to do it was ridiculous, but not to do it was stand-offish.' So they did. When he got home that night, Cherie said she thought the millennium evening had been rather fun. 'Darling,' he replied, 'there is only one thing I am going to thank God for tonight, and that is they only come round every thousand years.'[49]

One of the organisers recalled the Queen's attitude towards the Dome as one of wry scepticism. The royals – the Queen, egged on by Prince Philip and the Queen Mother – were 'frightfully sceptical and humorous about the Dome. But not in an unpleasant way. But they made it clear they thought it was the most stupid idea they had ever seen.' The opening was a fiasco, with newspaper editors, chief executives and other bigwigs made to queue for an hour or more for security checks. 'The whole evening was an absolute disaster. The Duke of Edinburgh was openly, "My goodness, what a complete farce this all is."[50] Again, this was not in an unpleasant way – if anything, he was rather sympathetic – but it was a New Year's Eve best forgotten.

NEW LABOUR wanted to change Britain. The Queen was naturally resistant to change, and even when she did accept the need preferred a gradualist approach. Labour, on the other hand, wanted to set a blistering pace. Among the constitutional innovations of the Blair government was a commitment to give the people of Scotland and Wales a greater say in their own affairs. The Queen was intimately involved, as the duty fell to her of opening both the Welsh Assembly and the Scottish Parliament in 1999. For the palace, the process involved some delicate footwork. The Queen was committed to maintaining the union with Scotland – she had made this clear in her Silver Jubilee speech in which she said, 'I cannot forget that I was crowned Queen of the United Kingdom' – but was also committed to the democratic wishes of her people, as expressed through Labour's mandate to devolve powers to Scotland and Wales.

A royal official recalls how there was 'a big head of steam' behind the devolution proposals. 'It was going to happen. The palace's objectives were to have clarity about what the Queen's role would be in the new set-up, and to make sure that the monarch's relationship to the people of Scotland and Wales was not undermined.' Mary Francis, the Queen's assistant private secretary, who had previously worked in Number 10, was seconded to the various government working groups on the issue. They were extremely suspicious of her, expecting her to be the stereotype of a reactionary courtier, and were pleasantly surprised to find that she was a positive, constructive contributor to the discussions.

As well as being a massive change for the people of Scotland and Wales, devolution brought home how a hugely significant constitutional development had happened in Britain almost without being noticed. The procedure for choosing a new Scottish first minister would involve the speaker of the Scottish Parliament going to and fro between the parties until they were satisfied that a candidate had been identified who would have the support of a majority of MSPs and then informing the palace. This made the Queen's participation entirely ceremonial. 'That crystallised to me the fact that she had effectively lost the role in the UK,' an official recalled. 'That was an important change. It was another little nudge away from the belief that the Queen had any real power. However, it was true that in the UK Parliament there was still the minuscule possibility of the palace having to play a real role. So it had not been formalised in quite the way that the Scottish constitution formalised it.' Ten years later, this change would be formalised in Westminster as well as Edinburgh.

Labour's other big constitutional change was reform of the House of Lords. Against considerable opposition, Blair wanted to abolish the right of hereditary peers to sit in the upper chamber, eventually compromising by allowing ninety-two hereditaries to remain. Again, the palace had a clear strategy: to keep completely clear of the debate and emphasise that having a hereditary monarchy did not rely on having a hereditary aristocracy. The official recalled:

> There was no way that anyone sensible in the palace was going to try and stand in the way of a big initiative like that. The general understanding was, 'This is going to happen.' There were probably some elements in the palace who were really quite worried about it, especially those with titles. And there was an obvious concern,

voiced in some of the right-wing media as well, 'If you get rid of the hereditary principle in the House of Lords, what is going to happen to a hereditary monarchy?' But the private secretaries felt you had to let it proceed, and just make sure that nothing dangerous happened.[51]

The palace kept closely in touch with developments, but there was never anything that caused them undue alarm.

Whatever the political ructions that surrounded the reform of the House of Lords, which passed into law in 1999, it was a walk in the park compared to the botched attempt to abolish the post of lord chancellor, a role that dates back to the Norman Conquest and possibly even earlier. In a clumsy reshuffle in June 2003 Blair sacked the lord chancellor, his old mentor as a barrister Lord Irvine, replacing him with his close friend Lord Falconer, at the same time announcing that he was scrapping the job. Up to that point the lord chancellor had three roles: head of the judiciary in England and Wales, speaker of the House of Lords, and cabinet minister responsible for civil law. There was an immediate political backlash against the change, which involved the establishment of a department of constitutional affairs and a Supreme Court to take over from the House of Lords as the ultimate court of appeal.

There was another problem, too: the palace was not happy. The lord chancellor had a royal role as one of the people entitled to decide if a monarch is capable of continuing to reign or whether a regent should be appointed. He also had the arcane role of Keeper of the Royal Conscience, which may have meant something once, but quite what is hard to discern any more: one account says the job 'involves delicate issues with clergy'. But the palace was not consulted, apparently – not surprisingly, perhaps, given that most critics believed that the proposals were cobbled together on the back of a cigarette packet. The Queen, according to palace sources, 'put her foot down'.[52] The following year the government backed down over the proposal to abolish the role, although some of the reforms survived, including the establishment of the Supreme Court and the creation of the role of lord speaker.

The idea that this retreat was the result of palace pushback is far-fetched. However, the fact that we even know there was any royal resistance hints at greater confidence in the palace at a time when Blair's premiership was beginning to show signs of fatigue. When he came to power, Labour could do no wrong, while the monarchy was so unpopular that there were questions about its long-term survival. Labour's constitutional initiatives including reform of the House of Lords came at a time when the government was in the ascendancy. Gradually, however, the royal family fought their way back, while the government had to endure a mauling over the invasion of Iraq.

In its early days, despite being in a position of strength, the Blair government had been anxious not to put a foot wrong. The palace had been going through a slow process of reform before Diana's death, but that accelerated after she died. 'The Queen and the Duke of Edinburgh were prepared to do things in a more personal way, and other members of the family – to differing degrees – recognised the need for change in a way they had not done before,' said a former official. Meanwhile the government was not actively pushing reform, although 'everybody knew that they were glad to see some change'. The official went on: 'They were being very careful. The Blair government wanted to show that they had a grown-up relationship with the palace, as the Conservative government's had been. They were not going to make life difficult.' The monarchy and the government are mutually supportive, although the balance of power has swung to and fro over the decades. 'When the palace was being criticised over money, the balance was more to the government.'[53] Later it would swing back the other way, as the government became less popular. (One way the Blair government helped the royal family out was by giving Andrew the role of international trade envoy when he was looking for something to do after leaving the Royal Navy. Whether he did any good is debatable. After the Epstein scandal broke he stepped down, which officially was said to be his decision. It wasn't, of course. It is hard to imagine that anyone was sorry to see him go.)

Another former royal aide said the relationship was also driven by events:

> It depends on what is going on, on what attention the government has on the monarchy at the time. If the problems of the monarchy are quite public or significant, the government feels the need to intervene. Or the government is bored of being the government, so let's go and solve the monarchy's problems. We are so big and powerful and popular we can do anything. There was a bit of that in the Blair era, after the Princess of Wales died. I am sure that some of that with Blair was driven by, 'I am the master of everything, and I can deal with this as well.'

According to this view, the fortunes of the monarchy and the government are two pendulums which normally swing in opposite directions.

> Monarchy is weak, government is strong. Government is weak, monarchy is strong. That works for the country. But having a weak government and a weak monarchy is probably bad for the country. You can have one strong

and one weak. But having two at the height of their power probably causes them to butt a bit. Maybe that is what happened in the Thatcher era. Before the problems with the marriages went big time, the Queen was big and solid and powerful. Margaret Thatcher was obviously extremely powerful after the 1983 election. But it does swing, because the monarchy is a bunch of individuals; they get it right, they get it wrong, they have problems which become stories, and they are stuck there on stage going through that. And of course, all governments end in failure. They are popular and then they're not.[54]

The late Conservative minister Tristan Garel-Jones, no fan of the royal family, had a more robust view, which a friend sums up as: 'The monarchy works when it is told what to do by government. It goes wrong when it thinks it knows what to do, when courtiers take over and think they know best.'

IN JULY 2005 French president Jacques Chirac made a joke to Vladimir Putin and Gerhard Schröder at a meeting in Russia, saying of the British: 'You can't trust people who cook as badly as that. After Finland, it's the country with the worst food.' The story ran for several days, to the amusement of everyone except Chirac. A few days later he was at a dinner hosted by the Queen for a G8 summit, where the Japanese prime minister, Junichiro Koizumi, decided to tease Chirac, leaning across the table and saying loudly, 'Hey, Jacques, excellent British food, don't you think?' Everyone laughed except Chirac, who pretended to join in the joke while protesting to the Queen that he had not actually said it. 'Said what?' said the Queen, who must have been the only person in the room not to be familiar with the story – which meant it had to be explained again, much to the amusement of all, especially Koizumi, who proceeded to milk the joke for all it was worth for the rest of the meal. Blair recalled: 'I thought Jacques was going to take out his aide-de-camp's gun and shoot him.'

The dinner was an opportunity for Blair to watch the Queen in action with foreign leaders, and to see how they dealt with each other. 'The Queen handled them all well,' he wrote, 'though some guests didn't always quite know how to handle her. Some got matey with her.' This was a mistake. 'You don't get matey with the Queen. Occasionally she can be matey with you, but don't try to reciprocate or you get The Look.' There is a difference, he said, between a queen and a president. 'Both are heads of state, but the Queen is the Queen. That's royalty, not some jumped-up elected pleb.'[55]

From this, one can only wonder whether Blair had ever been on the receiving end of The Look. Judging by his description of his audience at Balmoral in 1997, he probably had. But he had also learned how to deal with the Queen, how to read her. Did she like him, though? It is, of course, hard to tell: the Queen was never careless with her opinions, although one Conservative minister does recall her being 'a bit surprisingly sceptical' about Blair.[56] When Blair went to the palace for the last time, he recorded that she was 'as ever, very gracious', which tells us nothing. There is, however, one clue earlier in his memoirs, where he says that he felt the palace always preferred political leaders of two types: those who were one of them – Douglas-Home being the classic example – or 'authentic' Labour people, who spoke with the sort of accent they associated with Labour – Jimmy Thomas, Ernest Bevin and his "edgerows of experience'. 'People like me,' wrote Blair, 'were a bit nouveau riche, a bit arriviste, a bit confusing and therefore suspect.'[57]

The suspicion is that he was not her favourite prime minister. But perhaps she liked him more than one would

suppose from watching, say, *The Crown*, just as her relationship with Margaret Thatcher was probably a bit better than
is popularly assumed. With Cherie, who did not mind telling
the world stories of her 'contraceptive equipment', it may be
rather clearer. On the Blairs' first visit to Balmoral she asked
the Queen if it was true that Victoria had had an affair with
her Highland servant John Brown. 'It got a bit frosty after
that,' she said.[58] Another story from one of their weekends at
Balmoral tells how they were having tea with the Queen and
Prince Philip when the phone rang for the prime minister.
'I wonder who that is?' said one of the royals. 'I expect it's
someone ringing up to ask how we can abolish the monarchy,'
said Cherie. 'More tea, Mrs Blair?' said the Queen.[59] It is hard
to confirm the story, which was told to a reliable and well-
connected source, but even if it is apocryphal it speaks to
how Cherie was regarded in royal circles.

If the Queen was good at being gracious with Tony Blair,
regardless of what she thought of him, she was also good at
charming other ministers. When David Cameron was being
sworn into the Privy Council as leader of the opposition, he
had a conversation with the Queen about the fact that he
had been at prep school with Prince Edward. At this point
there was a 'slight rustling' from Harriet Harman and Valerie
Amos, perhaps expressing their exasperation at the networks
of privilege that bind the senior echelons of the Conservative party and the royal family. The Queen then moved on
to Harman and said in a friendly manner, 'I think you went
to St Paul's, didn't you?' Harman was absolutely delighted,
and she and the Queen then had a conversation about the
minister's school.[60]

As another Labour minister who had a number of dealings
with the Queen observed, 'We all want to be recognised and
approved of by the Queen. She was very good with us all.' This

minister remembered her as formidable without being fierce, and also – unlike John Major – wholeheartedly agreed with Ken Clarke's dictum about politicians being all too willing to surrender at the first sign of displeasure from the palace over issues that affect the royal family. 'My overwhelming desire all the time was to please her . . . We didn't become friends, but I grew to like her a huge amount.' The Queen was always friendly, and knew what the minister was doing. 'She was very good at appearing to be on one's side – not politically, but on the basis of, "These problems are problems. How is one going to deal with them?" She was great.'[61]

CHAPTER NINE

MY KIND OF GUY

IT IS JUNE 1999. Peter Mandelson is stuck in a traffic jam in New York. And he is about to make a phone call which, unbeknown to almost everyone at the time, or indeed since, will help shape Britain's unwritten constitution. But to understand this episode, first one has to go back to the 1970s, when Labour was in power and Prince Charles was still a young man. David Owen was foreign secretary, and was at a Buckingham Palace function talking to Prince Charles and Lord Mountbatten, whom he had got to know when he was a navy minister under Harold Wilson in the late 1960s. '[Mountbatten] put his arms around both of us and he said, "Why are my two favourite people at loggerheads?"'

Mountbatten turned to Charles, who explained that he had sent a long handwritten letter to Owen after a trip to Brazil, a country that Owen had also visited. Instead of writing back, Owen thought he should meet Charles instead, and told his office to set it up. But the permanent secretary in the Foreign Office thought it was inappropriate for Owen to meet the future king without permission from the prime minister, and the meeting never happened. Weeks had gone by, with no reply and no meeting. In Owen's view, this was an early example of bureaucrats' desire to stop Charles getting involved with affairs of state. 'But I think it was extremely sensible of him, a young man facing a long time before he was likely to be king, that he should take a real interest in government departments.'[1]

This anecdote shows how from a relatively early age – he was turning thirty at the time – Charles had opinions and a desire to talk through his ideas with senior political figures. It also heralded a period when Charles came under the political influence of David Owen, who later left the Labour party in frustration at its leftward drift and with the other members of the so-called Gang of Four set up the Social Democratic party in 1981. In 1986 a long profile of the prince appeared in The Economist which attempted to define Charles's political philosophy, with his belief in the importance of the individual but also the need for government intervention in the environment, industry and employment. He had discussed proportional representation with David Owen, the article said, and was keen on parliamentary reform.[2] The article was extremely well sourced – it was in fact based on a long conversation that the magazine's political editor, Simon Jenkins, had had with Charles. 'It was the manifesto of an SDP King,' said Jenkins, an observation that, as we have seen, would be echoed later by Margaret Thatcher saying the Queen was 'the kind of woman who could vote SDP'. 'He was raving about David Owen and clearly regarded the Social Democrats as the saviours of Britain.'[3] Some years later Charles attended a dinner at 10 Downing Street, at which he talked a lot about environmental issues. After he left, an amused Michael Heseltine declared: 'He's a Liberal Democrat!'[4]

By the end of the 1970s Charles had shown that he was prepared to press for meetings with ministers if there was an issue that was concerning him. In 1979, during the dying days of the Callaghan government, his withering assessment of Britain's economic prospects – he believed the country was overtaxed and would not survive without 'radical and rapid' changes – led him to demand a meeting with ministers to discuss the situation.[5] His areas of interest at this time were also wider than has been appreciated. In 2025 *The Times* revealed how the prince had demanded personal military briefings after expressing scepticism over aspects of Thatcher's nuclear defence strategy. In 1983, when tensions between Moscow and Washington were worsening, ministers were so worried by Charles's disdain for 'official flannel and obfuscation' that he was given 'frank' bespoke briefings in an attempt to allay his concerns.[6]

His unhappiness with Margaret Thatcher's premiership soon became public. In 1985 the *Manchester Evening News* ran an article under the headline 'Prince Charles: My Fear for the Future' after the prince's community architecture consultant, Rod Hackney, had repeated to the paper the prince's worry that he would 'inherit the throne of a divided Britain' in which minorities would be 'alienated from the rest of the country'. Charles, the paper said, wanted to use his position as Prince of Wales to 'force his way through parliamentary red tape' and save the nation from being split into haves and have-nots. Thatcher was said to be so angry that she rang Buckingham Palace to complain. It was even claimed that she confronted Charles, demanding 'what the hell' he was doing, saying, 'I run this country, not you, sir.'[7] This, however, may be stretching credibility a touch too far. Thatcher's reverence for the monarchy would surely have precluded her talking to the heir to the throne in such tones.

Charles was also at odds with the environment secretary, Nicholas Ridley, whom he regarded as a 'free-market kind of buccaneer'[8] who was not doing enough to combat pollution. He would send his speeches to Ridley's office to check they did not contradict government policy, but did not always accept the advice he received. On hearing once that Ridley wanted to cut out two passages from a forthcoming speech, Charles said: 'I'm afraid I'm not going to!'[9]

In April 1991 Charles had a run-in with the education secretary, Ken Clarke – a man who, as we have seen in the Britannia saga, was not afraid to stand up to the royal family. Invited to give the Shakespeare Birthday lecture at Stratford-upon-Avon, the prince used the opportunity to launch an attack on the educational establishment, complaining that there was at least one A level English literature syllabus on which Shakespeare was not compulsory. He said: 'Thousands of intelligent children leaving school at sixteen have never seen a play of Shakespeare on film or on the stage, and have never been asked to read a single word of any of his plays.' With Britain moving towards a national curriculum, Shakespeare was being marginalised, he went on, and education experts were talking 'unmitigated nonsense'.

The problem here was that the convention under which Charles was supposed to send a draft of his speeches to any government department likely to be affected had, in the words of his biographer Jonathan Dimbleby, 'been inadequately honoured'. The speech had not reached Clarke's office until the morning on which it was delivered, which did not give him time to read it, let alone suggest alterations. Given that the speech was seen as a severe rebuke to his department, Clarke 'did not hesitate to make St James's Palace aware of his feelings'. A month later Charles sent Clarke a letter of apology, saying he had not finished the speech until the night before it was due to be delivered. 'I am sorry if, in the event, logistics prevented you seeing the text before I read it out.'

He had, he said, tried to minimise any 'party political' content, adding: 'The last thing I wanted to do was to make your life any more difficult than it already is, but at the same time I believe there are profound values at stake which I feel it is my duty to emphasise.'

For all that it annoyed Clarke, the speech had a greater effect than the prince might have anticipated, and directly influenced the national curriculum: Shakespeare, it was decided, would be taught in all schools to all children. Dimbleby concluded: 'If, as Clarke supposed, the Prince had indeed trespassed across a constitutional dividing line, he had done so to remarkable effect and emerged from the experience virtually unscathed.'[10]

Charles may have thought he had got away with it, but his behaviour was causing concern within Buckingham Palace. One of his former aides recalled: 'They would sometimes get exercised about the prince getting a bit ahead of his skis, becoming a bit more engaged in some of these sensitive issues than the Queen thought was necessarily wise.' The aide added: 'He was about the only person in the royal family who really cared about climate change. He was thirty years ahead of public opinion.' Other members of the royal family, including Princess Anne and Prince Andrew, thought that his enthusiasm for such issues bordered on the naive. 'There was a natural and understandable concern that the relationship with the government should not get jeopardised by him becoming a little too outspoken on the issues that he cared about.'[11] A palace source said the Queen's view of Charles's habit of writing letters to ministers was: 'Just don't do it. As soon as you engage in politics, you have an opinion and you pick a side, you cause a part of the population who disagree to take a partial view of you. The view of those who want to protect the monarchy was that it had to be even more elevated from the politics. Anything that dragged her into the mud was an unhelpful development.'[12]

The prince did enjoy a positive relationship with some ministers, however, including Douglas Hurd. There is an intriguing reference in the memoirs of the BBC political editor John Cole in which, in a passage on how Margaret Thatcher became interested in race problems, he wrote: 'But she was never keen to take a public role in race relations, and Douglas Hurd used to call on the help of the Prince of Wales for that.'[13] Exactly what Cole meant by this – did Hurd persuade Charles to raise issues in his speeches that he wanted airing? – remains unclear.

CHARLES'S INCLINATION to hover near the constitutional dividing line, and on occasion cross it, would continue unabated after Labour came to power in 1997. 'Prince Charles engaged on issues in a quite political way. But I don't mean party political,' recalled a minister. 'He had pronounced views on a range of things, and he was keen for his views to prevail.'[14] In June 1999 Charles wrote an impassioned article for the *Daily Mail* about genetically modified (GM) produce, which the paper was campaigning against as 'Frankenstein food'. He feared GM crops would cross-pollinate with other crops, attacked the lack of independent scientific research and rejected the argument that genetic modification represented a solution to world hunger as 'emotional blackmail'.

Blair, whose government was trying to allay public fears about GM crops, thought that the article was anti-science and according to Alastair Campbell was 'very pissed off', but deliberately refrained from reacting. 'He knew we couldn't actually answer back,' Campbell wrote in his diary. The Clarence House view, however, was that the prince was not actually criticising government policy, and that the most inflammatory aspect of the article was the *Daily Mail* headline rather than anything Charles wrote. Over the following days Blair remained furious, with the situation made worse by an article in the *Independent on Sunday* that said Charles thought Cherie was also worried about the issue. This article, which looked to be based in part on a briefing from Charles's team, said that he intended to carry on saying what he thought, 'however uncomfortable that might be for the Government'.[15] The conclusion that Blair arrived at was the same that Ken Clarke had come to over Charles's Stratford lecture: that the Prince of Wales had, constitutionally speaking, gone too far. Blair had always been sympathetic – up to a point – to Charles's interest in climate and other issues. However, in his view the prince's published views on GM foods crossed the line. It was taking a controversial stance on a matter of public policy, and that in Blair's view was unacceptable.

At which point, enter Peter Mandelson. In June 1999 Labour's controversial former spin doctor, who had become an integral part of the party's senior leadership, was between ministerial jobs, having resigned over the first of two scandals that were to blight his cabinet career. He had met Charles a number of times, and had got to know him better three weeks before Diana's death when he had been invited to Highgrove to have lunch with Charles and Camilla. At the lunch Charles unburdened himself to Mandelson about the media pressure he was experiencing after his divorce from Diana. Mandelson spoke to him frankly, saying he commanded more affection than he realised, but also told Charles he gave the impression that he felt sorry for himself. Mandelson was a bit worried that he had gone too far, but Charles appreciated his frankness, and after that would often turn to him for advice. Charles would also write to him about 'areas of public policy which he believed to be misguided', and Mandelson would pass on his views to Blair.

Mandelson was, therefore, the ideal informal channel of communication for Blair to let the prince know that he had pushed it too far with his article on GM food. Mandelson wrote in his memoirs: 'I was on a visit to New York when Number 10 phoned to ask me to urge caution on him, and I spoke to Charles from a traffic jam in the middle of Manhattan. Like Tony, I felt that his remarks were becoming unhelpful. I thought they were anti-scientific, and irresponsible in the light of food shortages in the developing world. I am sure Charles did not change his mind as a result of our conversation, but he did tone down his public interventions on the subject.'[16]

The constitutional significance of this conversation has largely been overlooked. Repeatedly accused over the years of being a meddling prince, Charles has said that there was a difference between what he could do as Prince of Wales and what he could do as King. For instance, in a documentary to mark his seventieth birthday, when asked if his public campaigning would continue after he acceded to the throne, he replied: 'No, it won't. I'm not that stupid. I do realise that it is a separate exercise being sovereign. So of course I understand entirely how that should operate.'[17]

The trouble is that no one has ever laid down what the difference between the two roles is. For the sovereign, it is clear: they act on the advice of the government. Clearly, they can never say anything that contradicts official policy. But for the heir the situation is more vague. Who, or what, determines what they can and cannot say? The constitutional historian Vernon Bogdanor suggested in his definitive The Monarchy and the Constitution that the heir is quite tightly constrained. He says that the monarch's private comments should be 'made discreetly and cautiously' so that relations with ministers are not compromised, adding: 'This applies also to other members of the royal family, even though they do not speak on advice.'[18]

However, it is hard to escape the conclusion that only one person passed judgement on what it was politically acceptable for Charles to say in public, and that was the prince himself. As one of his former advisers said, a lot of the way he shaped the job 'was on instinct – nothing is written down. He was able, as all heirs to the throne have been, to craft a role as he sees fit. You avoid particular policy issues that are party political. But he instinctively felt that he should take up issues that were of broader national and global concern.'[19] Another aide said: 'You have an innate sense of what is acceptable and right.' A more crude interpretation might be that Charles would push things as far as he could, and see if he got away with it. But Mandelson's call from New York represented the first time that the government had pushed back and told him that he had gone too far. It was a reminder that ultimately the constitutional boundaries were drawn not by Prince Charles but by the government.

DID CHARLES maintain a respectful silence after that, observing the constitutional guidelines as clarified by Number 10? Not exactly. He was a lot quieter on GM crops, but his relationship with Downing Street continued on its bumpy path. When during a state visit Charles deliberately snubbed one of the banquets for the Chinese leader, Jiang Zemin, to demonstrate his support for Tibet, Blair thought the prince was being 'silly'.[20] But things had got so bad between St James's Palace and Number 10 that a note of paranoia started to infect Downing Street's view of the prince.

When Charles took Prince William fox hunting at a time when the government was trying to implement a ban on hunting with hounds, it was seen as 'a political act', coming so soon after the GM article and the boycotting of the Chinese banquet. '[Charles] was following through a strategy to put himself at the head of the forces of conservatism,' wrote Campbell, in a reference to Blair's speech to the Labour conference in which he had talked about the battle between the forces of progress and the forces of conservatism. Charles, said Blair, after a long meeting of 'hard talk' with the prince in which they discussed hunting, GM foods and China, had been 'really stung by the forces of conservatism speech'.[21] Later, during the foot-and-mouth disease outbreak, Charles's Prince's Trust gave a £500,000 donation to rural charities, prompting Blair to ask whether Charles had considered helping when six thousand jobs were lost at the steel manufacturer Corus. His conclusion? 'This was all about screwing us and trying to get up the message that we weren't generous enough to the farmers.'[22] The paranoia tipped over into the delusional during the Queen's Golden Jubilee of 2002. After the pop concert at Buckingham Palace Charles made a speech in praise of his mother which ended with the words: 'So, Your Majesty, we are all deeply grateful to you and, in the words of the non-politically correct second verse of the national anthem, you have defended our laws and certainly given us cause to shout with heartened voice, "God Save the Queen".' That bit about the un-PC second verse was, said Blair, 'meant to be a dig at us'.[23] Or, possibly, just a joke.

In 2011, when Campbell's diaries were serialised in the Guardian and Number 10's skirmishes with the heir to the throne were laid bare, Blair – by then out of Number 10 – sprang to the defence of the prince he had once accused of trying to screw his government. He wrote a letter to the paper saying that he 'welcomed' Charles's contributions. 'A prime minister may sound off from time to time, especially when sensitive discussions with members of the royal family leak into the papers, in the middle of some high-profile issue. However, I want to make it clear that I always found my discussions and correspondence with Prince Charles immensely helpful. I thought he had a perfect right to raise questions and did so in a way that was both informative and helpful.'[24] That was not quite how he felt in 2001, when, after a long discussion with the prince about rural issues, he decided that Charles 'was well meaning but misguided, and once they got into an argument, not so well meaning'.[25] And when he told Campbell when they were joshing around before an interview with the Guardian that Charles was 'really his kind of guy', that was definitely a joke. There was also a gulf between them in terms of personal style. A Clarence House insider recalled, 'When Tony Blair became prime minister it was, "You must call me Tony." To which the response was, "It is very nice to see you, prime minister." He never called him Tony.'[26] It is interesting to note that while his letters to Blair always began 'Dear Prime Minister', Charles wrote to some ministers including Patricia Hewitt, Tessa Jowell and John Reid using their first names.

However, it would be wrong to conclude that Blair and Charles were always crossing swords. 'Tony was perfectly happy to stand up to the Prince of Wales when they disagreed, and they did disagree on quite a lot of things,' said one minister. 'But I don't think it soured their relationship. It certainly did not sour Tony's view of the prince.'[27] After Blair had a heart operation in 2004, Charles sent him a get-well card and a box of Duchy of Cornwall fudge. Unfortunately the package fell foul of the security screening system at

Number 10, and was blown up. Afterwards the security team sent Jonathan Powell the remains, including the handwritten card, and asked who it was from.[28] There seemed to be fewer tensions after the mid-2000s, and Blair did indeed find some of his contributions helpful. And Charles wanted to help. In the aftermath of 9/11 he got his office to get in touch with Number 10 to say that he was really keen to get involved. They discussed the possibility of an overseas visit, perhaps to Bahrain or the UAE, or Saudi Arabia, as well as Charles visiting mosques in the UK to emphasise that Britain was not conducting a war on Islam. These were welcome offers, but Campbell could not resist sounding a cynical note in his diary: 'I sensed there was a bit of an operation to try to get back in with us a bit after all his countryside outbursts.'[29] But the two offices had different visions of what the prince's help might entail. A St James's Palace insider recalled: 'One of the things Number 10 wanted the prince to do was give a speech or write an article under his name.' But the palace argued that it was not for Number 10 to use the prince in this kind of way. What he did do, however, was make a number of visits to Islamic communities, to show solidarity with Britain's Muslim population.

The negotiation over what Charles could do to help after 9/11 reflects the bigger question of how the government gets the royal family to carry out overseas visits on its behalf or receive important visitors to Britain. In theory, the royals are there to act on governmental advice, which is a nice way of saying they are meant to do what they are told. However, they are human beings, with their own interests, likes and dislikes, and it would be a foolish government that ignored completely the royals' own preferences. For instance, at the time when Charles was prepared to boycott Chinese banquets because of his feelings about Tibet, no one was going to insist on sending him on an official visit to China just because it suited government policy.

The programme of visits is decided by the Royal Visits Committee, which meets twice a year. It is chaired by the permanent undersecretary of the Foreign Office and includes the private secretaries from the royal households, the national security adviser and representatives from Number 10, the Cabinet Office and other government departments. One royal insider said: 'The royals go to places that the British government wants them to go to. Sometimes the royals have got places they themselves are keen to visit, and you persuade government that it is a good idea for this to become an official visit, with the taxpayer picking up the tab.' If, for instance, a big German environmental organisation wanted to give Charles a prize, and he wanted to turn the trip into a short official visit by including a meeting with the chancellor, say, the government was not going to stand in his way. 'Naturally he was keener to visit some countries than others. But he was invariably ready to comply with the government's advice.'[30]

One of the most notorious state visits to the UK was that of the Romanian dictator Nicolae Ceaușescu in 1978, which was deemed necessary to secure an aviation deal with Romania. Ceaușescu was described by the Queen's private secretary William Heseltine as 'the most repellent guest she ever had to make do with'. Lord Owen, who was foreign secretary at the time, said the Queen did not hide her dislike of having the Ceaușescus to stay. 'She does her duty. She did not approve of the visit. But she has to take her share of the ghastlinesses of government and the compromises that governments make. The economic advantages were considerable, and also the political ones. And if there is flak, and the royal family have to bear a bit of it, that's part of their duty. They get a lot of advantages.'[31]

Lord Turnbull, a former cabinet secretary and principal private secretary at Number 10, said: 'Sometimes there were places we wanted [the Queen] to go, or visitors that we wanted her to receive that she wasn't very keen on. We had to say, "Sorry, this is actually all part of wider foreign policy."' In the early 1970s, when Iran under the Shah was regarded by the government as a valuable ally – it provided oil and bought British arms – despite being a repressive and blood-thirsty regime, the government did everything in its power to persuade the Queen to pay an official visit. The Queen was reluctant, not least because she found the Shah a crushing bore, but in 1973 was finally persuaded to go. 'The poor Queen,' diplomats noted privately. 'She didn't want to do this at all.'[32] (However, see chapter 6 for the Queen's attitude after the revolution in Iran.)

For its part, the government was not keen on Charles's meetings with the Dalai Lama, but it put up with them, said Turnbull. 'I don't think there was any case where he really embarrassed us. He had his own views on who he liked, and where he really did not want to go. But we always managed to find a solution to it.'[33] A former adviser to Charles said there were a number of conversations 'where our desire to make sure that in any year his visits included an important Commonwealth country . . . and sometimes that meant pushing back on what the Foreign Office thought was the right order of precedence'. Having agreed where he was going to go, the other question was what he was going to do there. 'That was always a trade-off between ourselves, the Foreign Office and the place concerned.'[34] Another adviser recalled having 'real squabbles' with the ambassadors in the host countries over what Charles would do.[35] They might prefer him to do a boat trip on the Rhine, for instance, while he wanted to talk to business leaders and environmentalists. He also was not keen on too many official meals. If the trip was overloaded with engagements that could be a disaster too. On one visit by Charles and Diana to Spain the princess all but collapsed in tears at Expo '92 and had to be quietly escorted out of the room.

While Charles used to like going to countries such as France, Germany and Romania (where he owns a number of properties and pays regular visits), he often felt less welcome in the US because public opinion appeared more sympathetic to Diana. He would go because it was his duty, but he could feel uncomfortable. On the day his excruciating phone conversation with Camilla about Tampax was made public, he had to make a speech at the College of William and Mary in Virginia. Apprehensive before the event, he was hugely relieved by the raucously enthusiastic reception he received from the thousands of students waiting to hear him when he walked into the hall.

EVERYONE KNEW that Prince Charles wrote letters to ministers. He couldn't help himself; it was like an addiction. Long letters, often written late at night, full of detail about whatever issue was bothering the heir to the throne. He had been doing it since he was in his early twenties, when he wrote a six-page letter to Harold Wilson in 1970 about the plight of the Atlantic salmon.[36] Recounting the many meetings Charles had with ministers and the hours spent every week writing letters, Jonathan Dimbleby wrote in his biography of the prince that Charles had 'convinced himself that to refrain from involvement at this level and in this form would be a dereliction of duty that he could not countenance'. That 'convinced himself' suggests, perhaps, that Dimbleby was a little less convinced.[37]

From the 1990s his letters to ministers had been nick-named black spider memos, which is a little unfair, as his handwriting was perfectly good, and they were almost always typed anyway. Occasionally they would be leaked, such as when the Mail on Sunday found out about the prince's letter to Blair in September 2002 sympathising with the view that farmers were more discriminated against than black or gay people. Lord Irvine of Lairg, the lord chancellor, was said to have been 'bombarded' with letters from St James's Palace – one of which was leaked to the Daily Mail – on subjects including the trend towards a US-style compensation culture, human rights legislation and excessive regulation.[38] Irvine was said to have complained 'bitterly'. One anonymous minister – one suspects it was Irvine – told The Sunday Times that Charles's 'undergraduate ramblings' were intolerable, and an attack on the government's human rights legislation was 'extremely ill-advised and foolish'. The prince was 'attacking legislation which is our proudest achievement'.[39] But who else he wrote to, how they replied, who had leaked the correspondence and, crucially, what effect his letters had – all that was unknown.

Then, one day in April 2005, Guardian journalist Rob Evans got an email from his editor, Alan Rusbridger. The Freedom of Information Act, which established a general right of access to all types of recorded information held by UK public bodies, had come into effect in January of that year, and Evans had been given the job of finding out how to exploit it. Could the act be used to test if they could get hold of the letters that Charles was writing to government? Evans put in requests to see letters between the prince, the prime minister and government departments between September

2004 and April 2005. 'We had no grand plan,' he said. It was a bit like casting a line over a pond: 'We had no idea what would happen.'

What ensued was a ten-year legal battle in which the government fought hard to prevent the letters being made public. But the tenacious Evans and the *Guardian* never gave up – encouraged, no doubt, by a witness statement by Charles's former aide Mark Bolland in 2006. Bolland was acting as a witness on behalf of the *Mail on Sunday* in a case brought by Charles over his leaked journal. In his statement, Bolland said Charles saw himself 'as a "dissident" working against the prevailing political consensus'. He often addressed contentious issues, and wrote in 'extreme terms' to people including government ministers. His campaigning role was 'constitutionally controversial' because members of the royal family were not supposed to express views on political matters, wrote Bolland. 'This aspect of the Prince's role has been created by him and has not, so far as I am aware, been endorsed either by the Queen or by Parliament.' Bolland said he and the prince's private secretary Sir Stephen Lamport had 'tried to dampen down' the way he spoke in public on sensitive issues as part of the preparation for his future role as king because of the controversy it generated. 'I know that the Prince's expression of his views on politically sensitive issues has often been regarded with concern by politicians because we would be contacted by them – and on their behalf. For example, I know that private secretaries to Government Ministers would often let us know their views and, typically, how concerned they were.'[40]

When the *Guardian*'s FOI request was rejected, the paper appealed. At the tribunal hearing Paul Richards, a former special adviser to the communities secretary, Hazel Blears, and the health secretary, Patricia Hewitt, said Charles's letters to ministers went 'to the top of the pile' and were 'treated with great reverence'.[41] Rodney Brazier, professor of constitutional law at Manchester University, said the extent of letter writing by the prince was a 'constitutional innovation' but that it was part of the process of the heir to the throne learning about the business of state, or what he called 'the apprenticeship convention'.[42]

In 2012 the tribunal ruled that the letters – twenty-seven in all, to seven Whitehall departments – should be published because it was in the public interest for there to be transparency about how the prince sought to influence government. A month later, however, that decision was overturned by the attorney general, Dominic Grieve, who argued that the Prince of Wales should be able to engage in correspondence with ministers in the expectation that it would remain confidential. He said it was in the national interest to prevent the publication of the prince's letters 'because if he forfeits his position of political neutrality as heir to the throne, he cannot easily recover it when he is King'.[43] The Guardian challenged the veto, losing in the High Court but then winning on appeal, a decision that was in turn challenged by Grieve in the Supreme Court. In March 2015 the Supreme Court ruled against Grieve, and the letters were published on 13 May.

After ten years, and innumerable court hearings – because they lost, the government's legal costs amounted to £400,000 – what did the public learn? That the prince was an inveterate letter writer, who cared about everything from bovine TB to the failings of the army's Lynx helicopter and, famously, the fate of the Patagonian toothfish. That he was unrelenting in his efforts to bring the activities of his charities to the attention of ministers. And that his letters achieved very little. Most of them prompted a polite ministerial brush-off.

There was no dramatic revelation, no letter that revealed how Charles had leant on the government to change policy. As historian Andrew Roberts wrote in the *Daily Telegraph*, far from being sensational, the letters were 'almost universally worthy, respectable, responsible and even somewhat mundane'.[44]

Simon Jenkins in the *Guardian* argued that Charles's letters to ministers were small fry compared to the lobbying by companies in sectors such as defence, banking, construction and pharmaceuticals. 'The black spiders are harmless creatures compared with the multi-million-pound tarantulas of big-time political pressure, uncharted and undisclosed.'[45] Unexpectedly, a second batch of letters was released in June, showing how between 2006 and 2009 Charles wrote to ministers about complementary medicines, the state of the world's rainforests and hospital food. That brought the total number published to forty-four.

What was notable was that Labour ministers rarely raised their heads above the parapet to complain about Charles's letters. They put up with them, some more willingly than others, because they did not want to make a fuss. Having a public battle with the royal family is rarely a winning political tactic. Most of them when asked would trot out the same line, that they were very grateful for his sage advice, although behind the scenes they might well be irritated because he expected a reply and a debate. Sir Peter Riddell, ex-director of the Institute for Government and a former political commentator for *The Times*, recalled how the word went out to ministers from Blair: 'Humour him, it's well intentioned, and don't have a row.' One minister from that era who had a number of contacts with Charles told Riddell: 'Oh God, I've got another bloody letter from him. I will go and see him and have a natter about it, but we're not going to change our policy because of that.'[46]

Others could be more transactional in their approach: one agreed to assist Charles with one of his pet projects if the prince helped out with one of his initiatives. And, of course, some ministers actually got on well with Charles. One of those was Peter Hain, who shared with him an interest in integrated healthcare. Hain sometimes received handwritten letters from the prince ('I got used to his observations in thick black ink over several pages'), addressed to 'Dear Peter' and signed 'Yours ever, Charles'. But Hain, who was brought up in South Africa, was no monarchist, and there were some lines he would not cross. 'I always found him easy to talk to, even if his manner sometimes seemed from a past era. But I could not bring myself to obey mandarin guidance to call him "Sir" or "Your Royal Highness". Better not, I found, to call him anything during our conversations.'[47]

One minister was in a class of his own when it came to discomfiting Charles, albeit unintentionally: John Prescott. After his first meeting with the deputy prime minister, Charles bumped into Blair and asked him: 'Does he always do that thing with you?' What thing, asked Blair? 'Er, well, when he's sitting opposite you, he slides down the seat with his legs apart, his crotch pointing a little menacingly, and balances his teacup and saucer on his tummy. It's very odd.' Was it, asked Charles, a 'sign of hostility or class enmity?' No, said Blair. 'He just likes drinking his tea that way.'[48]

The most public sign of disagreement between ministers and Prince Charles came when a memo by the prince emerged in 2004 in which he complained of a 'learning culture in schools' that led young people to believe that they could succeed at anything without work or talent. That prompted the education secretary, Charles Clarke, to say the prince should 'think carefully' before commenting on public matters. 'I don't want to get into a tangle with the Prince of

Wales but to be quite frank I think he is very old-fashioned and out of time and doesn't actually understand what's going on in the British education system at the moment.'[49]

We will never see anything like the black spider memos again, because an amendment to the legislation enacted under David Cameron ensured that royal correspondence is exempt from Freedom of Information requests. Furthermore, by the time the letters were published in 2015 the prince, advised by his private secretary Clive Alderton, had stopped writing to ministers. Instead he would have meetings with them, with agreed topics for discussion and follow-ups between private secretaries. Charles and Alderton recognised that the fuss over his black spider memos had been too much of a distraction. But it had taken the *Guardian* to do what Mark Bolland and Stephen Lamport had failed to achieve. The words of Lloyd George to the future Edward VIII sounded as relevant as ever: 'If you are one day to be a constitutional monarch, you must first be a constitutional Prince of Wales.'

CHAPTER TEN

THE PALACE DIGS IN

FOLLOWING THE RESIGNATION of Tony Blair, Gordon Brown became prime minister on 27 June 2007. It was the job he believed he should have had a lot earlier; the timing of Blair's departure from office was one of the many issues that caused such difficulties between them. It was also the job for which he had been preparing for several years. Unlike Tony Blair, who was unsure of the protocol before his first meeting with the Queen and what he could say afterwards, the ever-thorough Brown was determined to be prepared for his first audience with the Queen. Even though he had met her many times before, including visiting Buckingham Palace to brief her on the Budget in his role as chancellor, a couple of weeks before the transition he spent an hour talking to her private secretary Sir Robin Janvrin about what he should expect in his audience. Brown was intent on leaving nothing to chance.

However, all that preparation was no substitute for a winning manner and an easy conversational style. Robert Hardman described Brown's relations with the Queen as 'correct and cordial',[1] and the order of the adjectives there seems significant: one gets the impression that they were more correct than cordial. Brown described his first audience with the Queen as 'a congenial businesslike conversation about the work that lay ahead', which sounds like fun.[2] Did she respect him? Undoubtedly. Did she ever warm to him? That is harder to tell. He did at least provide one of the more amusing prime ministerial moments of her reign, when he appeared to get lost at a state banquet after walking the wrong way round the banqueting table. 'Has the prime minister got lost?' the Queen asked. 'He disappeared the wrong way at the crucial moment.'

Brown did, however, do the Queen one great service: he made it easier for her to keep out of the political fray. Since the two Tory leadership dramas of 1957 and 1963 (when Macmillan succeeded Eden, and when Douglas-Home succeeded Macmillan), the Queen had been concerned to insulate the monarchy from political battles as far as possible. In particular, successive private secretaries to Elizabeth II, including Robin Janvrin and Christopher Geidt, were determined to keep the monarchy out of the question of who would become prime minister in the event of a hung Parliament. And it was Gordon Brown who would help provide the answer. Brown was interested in constitutional change, and instructed his cabinet secretary, Sir Gus O'Donnell (now Lord O'Donnell), to look at the cabinet manual produced in New Zealand. This had consolidated some of the previously unwritten conventions that underpinned the New Zealand system of government, and Brown wanted to know: could something similar not be done in Britain?

The PM was not the only person interested in what had happened in New Zealand. In the autumn of 2009 a conference was held by the Ditchley Foundation in Oxfordshire under the dry-sounding title 'Managing the Machinery of

Government in Periods of Change'. Chaired by Sir John Major, the conference, which would have a significant if indirect effect on the Queen, attracted some of the country's top experts on elections, including Sir Gus O'Donnell, Peter Riddell and Catherine Haddon of the Institute for Government, Robert Hazell, then director of the Constitution Unit at University College London, and the constitutional expert Peter Hennessy. There was one other important figure present: Christopher Geidt, the Queen's private secretary. Geidt – ex-military, ex-Foreign Office – is a reticent, slightly mysterious figure, but whenever weighty conversations take place, he is often to be found nearby.

Hazell's Constitution Unit had recently finished a report on preparing for a hung Parliament. He was concerned that the conventions surrounding this were not well understood, because nobody had written them down. The key paragraph in the report said: 'The mystique about the process of government formation and dissolution risks drawing the Crown unnecessarily into controversy. There need to be clearer rules which explain that it is not the monarch's role to form a government, or to facilitate negotiations. The decision to form a government must be arrived at by politicians, and the Prime Minister then advises the monarch on who can command the confidence of Parliament.'

During one of the conference breaks Hazell got talking to Geidt, whom he had not met before. 'We had a long chat. I was able to say to Christopher, "I'm really worried." And he was able to say, "And so am I." . . . He shared my concern that if there was a hung parliament, there could be a lot of misunderstanding about who should form the next government, and stories in the press that it was up to the Queen to decide who should be prime minister.' Up to that point there had not been any overwhelming expectation of a hung Parliament at the next election, but then the opinion polls turned, and by the end of the year it had become a real possibility. When Hazell's report came out in December, it received a lot more attention than he had been anticipating. That year, thanks to his friendship with the New Zealand cabinet secretary, Hazell sent copies of the New Zealand cabinet manual as Christmas presents to various of his contacts, including O'Donnell and Geidt, with a covering note saying: 'We are seriously unprepared and we are running out of time.' Hazell recalled, 'The palace were interested, and they were on side.'[3]

So, it turned out, was the government. Encouraged by his conversation with Geidt, Hazell had been urging the Cabinet Office to publish something like the New Zealand cabinet manual in advance of the election, and in February 2010 the cabinet secretary gathered a group of constitutional experts for a sandwich lunch in Whitehall to work on the fine detail of the hung Parliament section of the nascent UK cabinet manual. They included Sir Alex Allan, who had been helping O'Donnell with transition planning for the election, Geidt and a clutch of constitutionally minded professors: Peter Hennessy, Vernon Bogdanor, Robert Hazell and Rodney Brazier from the University of Manchester.

O'Donnell said: 'I got them all sat around the table and said, "Right, here's our view of what happens. Whatever the result of the general election, the prime minister remains prime minister until he goes to the Queen and advises the Queen to call on X to be the next prime minister."' Hennessy would later call it 'a strange world' where the government of the country could depend, at least in part, on 'a paragraph or two put together for the new cabinet manual over 45 minutes of a sandwich lunch in the Cabinet Office'.[4] A draft chapter of the manual, offering guidance on how the Queen could stay above the political process in the event of a hung Parliament,

was published later that month, on the same day that O'Donnell gave evidence about it to the justice select committee. It
was just in time. Two months later Gordon Brown called a
general election, to be held on 6 May.

Buckingham Palace played a significant role in the drafting of the cabinet manual in 2010. Christopher Geidt had
been nervous about it, because it was being touted as the
first step towards a written constitution. The palace prefers
the flexibility of an unwritten constitution – as does the
government – arguing that even with a written constitution
it is impossible to provide absolute clarity. Attempting to do
so, they feel, would be dangerously restrictive and could provide a hostage to fortune. When an early draft of the manual
arrived at the palace, it was noted that the first chapter was
not devoted to the sovereign's role in the constitution. The
Cabinet Office was swiftly informed that this was not acceptable, because the sovereign is at the apex of the constitution.
This was remedied and, after some other minor recommendations were also taken in, everyone was satisfied. But while
happy with the outcome, the palace had found it all quite
stressful. 'No one wants to repeat that trauma,' said a source.

In the run-up to the election O'Donnell did a lot of
scenario planning, with civil servants playing the roles of
politicians as they tried to imagine how various potential
election outcomes would play out. Geidt, who had been
assiduously boning up on the constitution, buying up every
book on the subject that he could find, watched quietly on.

WHEN ALL the votes were counted after the general election,
the Conservatives under David Cameron had won 306 seats,
twenty short of the number needed for an overall majority,
beating Labour into second place with 258. With 57 seats the
Liberal Democrats, led by Nick Clegg, held the balance of

power. Coalition talks began between the Conservatives and the Liberal Democrats, while parallel talks were also held between Labour and the Liberal Democrats. And all the time Christopher Geidt, the physical manifestation of the Golden Triangle at work, was there in the Cabinet Office, observing and reporting back to the Queen, who was keeping her distance at Windsor Castle, ready to return to London when the political horse-trading was finished. Geidt was determined to make sure that Gordon Brown did not resign too early, which would leave Britain without a prime minister and potentially drag the Queen into making uncomfortable political decisions of the sort that he and others such as Robert Hazell and Gus O'Donnell had been trying to avoid.

Geidt was given the use of an office in 70 Whitehall, the home of the Cabinet Office. On the Sunday after the election, the third day of the Conservative–Lib Dem talks, he met the negotiators to explain his role and tell them he was there to answer any questions about the royal prerogative. The following day he had a meeting with Gordon Brown to go through the constitutional implications of the different outcomes of the negotiations.

The Conservatives and the Lib Dems had made the decision to conduct their talks without any officials present, which caused a certain amount of frustration for those who wanted to keep the palace abreast of developments. George Osborne, who was in the room for the Conservatives, recalled: 'Gus O'Donnell was saying all the time, "Her Majesty the Queen would like to know how you are getting on."' Danny Alexander of the Lib Dems said: 'Christopher Geidt, he would be there after the meetings finished, and he wanted a bit of a debrief on how they were going.'[5] Geidt was also doing his best to stiffen Gordon Brown's resolve, so that he would not succumb to media accusations of hanging on in Downing Street. When Brown's chief of staff, Jeremy Heywood, rang Geidt, the Queen's private secretary told him: 'You need to persuade the prime minister to stay put.'[6]

By the Tuesday afternoon even Brown realised that Labour's talks with the Lib Dems were going nowhere and that he needed to focus on a dignified departure. When Geidt went to Number 10 to discuss how events might unfold, Peter Mandelson told him that the waiting was becoming 'intolerable' for Brown. Mandelson recalled in his memoirs: '[Geidt] said that he understood, but that things would have to become clearer before Gordon resigned.'[7] Shortly after that, around 5.30, Brown had another phone call with Clegg. 'Nick, I need an answer from you.' Clegg was still stalling, but Brown had run out of time. 'I cannot keep the Queen waiting,' he told him. 'I need to tell the Queen what's happening.'[8] Eventually Clegg told him what had already become apparent to most people in Number 10: that there would be no deal between Labour and the Lib Dems. Brown, who was determined not to quit after dark, walked out of Downing Street at 7.18pm to announce that he would be resigning. He went to Buckingham Palace to inform the Queen, and a short time later David Cameron was invited to the palace, even though the final details of the Conservatives' deal with the Lib Dems had not yet been agreed.

DAVID CAMERON was rather better connected with royalty than most politicians. Notwithstanding the fact that he was descended from William IV's illegitimate daughter by his mistress Dorothea Jordan, making him the Queen's fifth cousin twice removed, he had also come across her at the age of eleven when he was at Heatherdown, a prep school near Windsor, where his older brother, Alex, was a friend of Prince Edward. Brian McGrath, the father of one of Cameron's childhood friends, had been private secretary to Prince Philip, and his godmother was married to Alastair Aird, who worked for the Queen Mother for more than forty years.

After leaving Oxford, Cameron applied for a job at the Conservative Research Department, where the deputy director, Alistair Cooke (now Lord Lexden), remembered getting a phone call from Buckingham Palace about the candidate he was about to interview. The voice on the phone said he understood he was about to interview David Cameron. Lexden recalled: 'This powerful voice said, "I'm ringing to tell you that I have tried to dissuade this exceptional young person from wasting his time in politics. But I failed. And you are about to meet a quite outstanding person." The phone was put down. I was greatly taken aback.'[9] The voice belonged to Sir Alastair Aird, and yes, David Cameron did get the job. Given that he had a first from Oxford, no doubt he would have got it anyway. But there is never any harm in having a reference from Buckingham Palace.

Before he reached Number 10 Cameron had met the Queen a number of times as a member of the Privy Council. He had also got to know the Prince of Wales, although in rather different circumstances. In December 2006, a year after he won the Tory leadership election to succeed Michael Howard, a dinner was organised by the author Simon Sebag Montefiore and his novelist wife, Santa, at their home in Kensington for Cameron to get to know Prince Charles. Samantha Cameron and the Duchess of Cornwall – Camilla – were also there, along with Michael Gove and his wife, Sarah Vine. Over risotto, organic mutton and bread-and-butter pudding (Michael Fawcett, Charles's former right-hand man who had set up his own business, had done the catering, so it was all to Charles's taste: the prince had an egg on his risotto, which the others did not) they discussed the environment, architecture, culture and the pressures of the prime minister's job. 'Charles enjoyed himself so much that they stayed much later than intended,' a source said.[10]

Sarah Vine recalled: 'For about two weeks before this event Santa was trying to teach me to curtsey. Apparently you have to go very low. You can't bob.' Before dinner they had drinks in the drawing room upstairs. 'When we were called down for dinner I just got up and started going downstairs,' recalled Vine. Charles made a show of clearing his throat, and Vine realised that she had made the mistake of trying to leave the room before Camilla. That was not how you do things with royalty: they leave first. 'He was very serious and quite formal, and she was very informal.' Cameron, by that stage, was very used to being summoned for conversations with important people. 'Suddenly everybody wants to have dinner with you,' said Vine. 'He was completely unfazed by the whole thing.'[11]

When he arrived at Buckingham Palace after winning the general election – driven, it is interesting to note, in the prime ministerial Jaguar, even though he was not prime minister yet – even David Cameron felt a touch of nerves. The Queen quickly put him at his ease. 'I knew that world a little bit. It doesn't reduce the excitement of your first audience, but it maybe makes you slightly less nervous,' he said. 'It's obviously a very exciting meeting because you've just won the most seats at the election and she's meeting a new prime minister. I said, "I'd like your permission to form a government . . . The trouble is, I can't tell you what sort of government it's going to be. I think it's going to be a coalition government but I'm not sure. Can I get back to you?" I thought, "Gosh, no one has said that to her before."'[12]

For Cameron, his audiences with the Queen (the strictly correct form is that the prime minister has an audience of the Queen; alternatively, the Queen received in audience the Right Honourable David Cameron MP) were both practical and a form of therapy. The practical side consisted of upcoming events: 'Whether we were discussing the visit of the American or Chinese president for example, or the Queen's historic visit to the Republic of Ireland, that has a lot of purpose, because you're talking about something that is going to happen and how to get the most out of it for UK plc.' The rest of the audience would cover a list of around four topics, agreed in advance between the principal private secretary at Number 10 and the Queen's private secretary. Like Thatcher and Callaghan, but unlike Blair and Major, Cameron was a list man. The suspicion is that the private secretaries will always do a list of topics if they can, because they like to try to exert some control.

The agenda would generally include a foreign affairs topic, a domestic topic, an economic topic and often something to do with Scotland, Wales or Northern Ireland. There was also a strong emphasis on military matters. Cameron said:

> Sitting in a room with the world's greatest public servant and explaining what your government is doing and why, with no one else listening, is just incredibly helpful. It's therapeutic because it's often Wednesday evening, and you've had quite a battering at Prime Minister's Questions. You've already had quite a tough week. There is something about going to see this extraordinary person for an hour and explaining with questions and with answers, and also trying to keep it interesting . . . it was really good, not just therapy, but it got your own head in gear sometimes. As you were explaining your problems with health reforms or what was happening with the Budget or whatever, it helped you get things in order

in your own head. And obviously she'd ask very good questions.

Drinks afterwards with the Queen's private secretary – in Cameron's time, Sir Christopher Geidt – was also useful. 'You could say if there were any things that she had raised which I wanted to know more about, or that I had raised with her that weren't on the bit of paper.' Sometimes he would branch out. During the conflicts in Iraq and Afghanistan, the bodies of troops killed in action would pass through the Wiltshire town of Wootton Bassett on their way to the mortuary in Oxford. People used to turn out in large numbers to pay their respects as the hearses were driven through the town. Cameron wanted to honour the town by conferring royal status on it, but found that officials in both Whitehall and Buckingham Palace were in no hurry to push the proposal along. 'I was told, "Don't raise Wootton Bassett becoming Royal Wootton Bassett." And I thought, why not? So I did. And she said, "Yes, excellent idea." So I was able to come out of the meeting and say, "I did raise it, and she thinks it's a great idea." I think sometimes the court doesn't want things to get to the monarch until they've been absolutely polished. I did sometimes short-circuit the system a bit.'[13]

There could also be a personal element to the audiences. When Cameron's father, Ian, died in September 2010, not only was the Queen aware of his track record as a racehorse owner but she also knew something that the prime minister did not. 'I think you'll find he's got a runner at Windsor tonight,' she told him. It had totally passed him by, and the fact that the Queen knew all about it left him close to tears.[14]

ONE OF THE more remarkable aspects of David Cameron's premiership is quite how many constitutional changes there were during his six years in Number 10. The first was the Fixed-term Parliaments Act 2011, which was brought in as part of the deal with the Liberal Democrats, who thought it was inherently unfair that the prime minister could determine the date of a general election. The new law laid down that a general election would be automatically scheduled for May in the fifth year after the previous election, although there were also ways of bringing it forward. The act was unpopular with the palace, although not just for the obvious reason that it removed the sovereign's prerogative to dissolve Parliament. Under the act, if a vote of no confidence in the government was passed in the Commons, Parliament had two weeks in which to find an alternative administration. However, Peter Hennessy said that the palace was concerned that there was no guidance as to how they should conduct themselves or who the sovereign should see during those fourteen days. If, for instance, the prime minister tried to remain in office, should the sovereign hold an audience? Whatever they did could be seen as favouring one side or the other. 'They worried about it as a kind of howling void in the legislation,' said Hennessy.[15] A palace insider said: 'All of the constitutional historians were very het up about it, saying it was a terrible piece of legislation. And thus it proved to be.'[16] The act, which was never popular, was repealed by Boris Johnson's Conservative government in 2022. That meant that the monarch would once again have the power to dissolve Parliament. 'Repealing it turned out to be a complete nightmare, because we had to reinstate a prerogative, which we had never done before,' said a palace source.

Rather more popular with the palace was the Conservative proposal to reform the system for financing the monarchy. The palace had been pressing for a while to ditch the cumbersome arrangement whereby it received three separate payments from the government: the Civil List, which covered things like staff wages and the cost of entertaining foreign leaders and other official guests; grants for maintaining the palaces; and the travel budget. Before the 2010 election Sir Alan Reid, keeper of the privy purse – the official in charge of the sovereign's money – began talks with prime minister Gordon Brown and chancellor Alistair Darling about replacing these with a single payment, with the aim of making it easier for the palace to plan ahead and also giving it more flexibility about how to spend the money. But nothing had happened.

George Osborne – Darling's successor as chancellor – recalls: 'I had never had any real dealings with the royal family, apart from as a constituency MP, and so it was a big revelation to me – even though I had shadowed the chancellor job for five years – that the chancellor had such a big role in the royal finances. I had a good relationship with Alistair Darling. He spoke to me about the handover, [gave] advice about things like my office and the Treasury and some of the individuals, and then he said, "There is a problem on the royal finances which – with everything else going on – we just hadn't got round to fixing. So I'm sorry, it's over to you."'[17]

If responsibility for the royal finances was a surprise for Osborne, it was more of an annoyance for the Treasury. Nick Macpherson (now Lord Macpherson), permanent secretary at the time, was happy with any solution that got the Treasury out of its responsibility for overseeing palace finances. 'The less we had to do with the royal family, the better. In the general run of things, the size of the royal family's budget would not warrant the attention it received.' As for the chancellor, solving the problem 'quite appealed to George Osborne', said Macpherson. 'George had quite a deep appreciation of eighteenth-century British history, and found all this quite interesting. He was only too happy to be the person to sort it out.'

One of the issues, Osborne realised, is that fixing the Civil List at a certain figure leaves it vulnerable to inflation.

It had been set in the '50s, and readjusted at the beginning of the 1970s because of inflation. There was another problem in the '90s and essentially it was because they kept getting the inflation forecast wrong. Initially the Civil List ran out of money because they underestimated inflation in the '70s and '80s. And then because they had overestimated inflation in the '90s and 2000s, they had too much money. That had gone into a reserve, which they had steadily been drawing down. By the time it got to 2010, the piggy bank was empty and it was quite a hole in the finances.[18]

Osborne could see that having its income split into a number of different grants gave the palace no incentive to save in one area in order to spend in another. 'One thought was, "Shall we create a single pot that's more flexible for the family to use?"' In return, the government would insist that the National Audit Office had complete oversight of royal finances, which the palace had always resisted.

The idea that was mooted was to give the palace a single grant, and link it to something to allow for inflation. That something was the profits of the Crown Estate, which has the advantage of sounding royal. Which, in a way, it is, in that it is officially owned by the sovereign. But which, in a much more real way, it is not. Now one of the largest property managers in Britain, the Crown Estate was handed over to Parliament by George III in 1760 in return for a fixed annual income, the Civil List. So the sovereign has no control over the Crown Estate, and does not get any money from it. Osborne's proposal

was to grant the sovereign a sum equivalent to a fixed pro-
portion – 15 per cent initially – of the profits of the Crown
Estate, to be known as the Sovereign Grant. Osborne said:
'The Crown Estate wasn't a bad barometer of how the economy was doing, because it's a mix of West End property and
estates around the country. If the country is doing well and
the economy is doing well, the Crown Estate income goes
up. If the country is in recession, it goes down.' This was,
however, not quite true: no matter what happened to Crown
Estate profits, the Sovereign Grant would not go down. As
the *Financial Times* put it, 'When the Crown Estate does win,
royals win; when it does not, taxpayers lose . . . The perverse
incentives in this system are nothing short of frightening.'[19]
Lord Turnbull, the former cabinet secretary, has also been
scathing, calling the linking to the Crown Estate 'a too-clever-
by-half ruse' by Osborne 'trying to hoodwink the public that
the Crown is paying for itself'.[20] Crown Estate profits were,
he said, 'a completely irrelevant marker . . . you might as well
take the cricket score and index it on that'.

George Osborne often gets the credit for the idea of linking the Sovereign Grant to Crown Estate profits. However,
Lord Macpherson believes the credit should go to Paula
Diggle, the Treasury official who for years dealt with royal
finances. The *Guardian* has reported that documents show
that as long ago as the 1980s the palace was lobbying for
royal funding to be linked to Crown Estate profits.[21] Osborne
heard that it was an idea originally floated by the then Prince
Charles. 'I think he likes to take credit for the concept of the
link to the Crown Estate,' said Osborne.

Although some of the Liberal Democrats in the coalition were not convinced that the government should make
the Sovereign Grant a priority, Osborne was set on pressing
ahead. He also – unlike the Major government with the royal

yacht, *Britannia* – took the precaution of making sure he had the agreement of the Labour opposition. Osborne got in touch with the shadow chancellor, Ed Balls, to tell him of the government's plans, and Balls said they would cooperate provided he shared the details with them in advance. Balls recalled: 'The desire to put it onto a long-term footing was totally the right thing to do. It was in the public interest to have a non-partisan, sound, sensible, long-term arrangement which got away from the annual wrangle. We were cooperating about how to do this.'[22]

Osborne spoke to the Queen a couple of times about how it would all work. 'She was completely across the detail,' he said. 'She was interested in the finances, in how the money was allocated, and she was surprisingly candid, given that I didn't know her, about how she thought different members of her family would be looking after their money. I remember sitting there and her saying, "Well, he's no good with money."'

In the event inflation was lower than expected, and the Crown Estate did better than expected. In the ten-year period from 2012–13 to 2022–3, the core Sovereign Grant went up by 67 per cent, while inflation, as measured by the Consumer Prices Index, was 34.2 per cent. David Cameron has since admitted that it was a generous deal. 'It was generous, but I don't mind,' he told one interviewer. 'It was better to have something that was long-term sustainable. It would have been much worse if we'd erred on the other side, then had to come back and do the whole thing again.'

What has not been revealed before, however, is that the government actually knew at the time that it was a generous deal. And when they tried to adjust it, the palace refused to budge. Lord Macpherson said he was aware of 'and slightly nervous about' the flaws in Osborne's plan at the time. 'The

Crown Estate has been rather successful in the modern era. It is no longer run as a sleepy civil service backwater, but as an efficient property company.' It was also starting to do well out of wind energy, as it owns the shoreline. 'My worry was that whatever formula you chose, it would grow year by year in real terms.' Paula Diggle's argument was that it would be reviewed every five years, and could be adjusted. But Macpherson was still worried. 'At the last moment, both [George Osborne] and I thought, "This is just getting a bit too generous. Can we just pare the percentage back a bit?" I was deputed to ring up Alan Reid and say "Look, this is all a bit generous. We think you probably need a lower formula." At that point Alan Reid played hardball and said, "Look, it's all agreed. Her Majesty has agreed to it."' Meanwhile the Budget was coming up, and Osborne was due to have an audience with the Queen the night before. 'Alan Reid said, "If George Osborne wishes to raise it with Her Majesty, then he is welcome to do so." I think he had rather bigger things on his mind, and in the end he decided not to.'

The deal that was announced 'came in for remarkably little criticism at the time', said Macpherson. 'I was worried, because Paula Diggle had been working with the palace over a very long period, and might have been slightly captured by Sir Alan, who is a very persuasive man. The Treasury official in me thought we might have just erred on the side of generosity. And that is my view to this day.'

The idea of reforming royal finances clearly appealed to both Cameron and Osborne. They support the royal family and liked the idea of putting their mark on history. But there is another point, echoed by Macpherson: the sums of money involved are, in Treasury terms, very small. Republicans might base many of their arguments for change on the cost of supporting the royal family, but in terms of the nation's finances, the sums are minuscule. 'I didn't want to penny-pinch with the royals,' said Osborne. 'I thought, these are quite small sums of money, and they make a big difference to the way Britain is able to project itself, with garden parties and state dinners and whatever.'[23] However, as things turned out, the generosity (or not) of the original deal is a moot point. After being increased to 25 per cent of Crown Estate profits to pay for palace refurbishment, the Sovereign Grant was reduced again to 12 per cent because of its increased profits from wind energy.

More important is how hard the palace fought to protect what it thought was a financially advantageous deal. It is all about the bottom line: not because the royals want to feather their own nests, but because the bottom line ensures the long-term survival of the royal family. And, as ever, the words of Ken Clarke echo down the years: 'Most politicians are so in awe of the royal family that expressions of displeasure from the Palace about issues bearing directly on the family can usually produce quite significant policy shifts.'

The palace can also induce small policy shifts. Osborne has recounted on *Political Currency*, the podcast he co-hosts with Ed Balls, how the Queen said to him at a state banquet: 'The chief of the defence staff is unable to answer my question. He told me to go and speak to the defence secretary and he told me to come and speak to you. So I am asking you: you are not going to close, are you, the Highland bagpipe school of the British Army?' Recalling his response, Osborne said: 'I was, like, "Of course not, Your Majesty." The next day I got into the Treasury and I said, "Is there a bagpipe school, and for God's sake tell me we are not closing it down."' His staff told him there was indeed such an institution – the Army School of Bagpipe Music and Highland Drumming in Edinburgh – and it was part of the army bands, which were being cut. Osborne told them: 'Well, we are not any more.'[24] The bagpipe school was saved.

Such policy shifts reflect one of the fundamental aspects of the relationship between the monarchy and the government: that politicians, for the most part, want to please the royal family. Summing up how he saw it, Osborne said: 'So much of your day if you're chancellor is consumed with the big issues on inflation, the NHS budget, the income tax rates.' Issues such as the bagpipe school, he said, 'feel like quite small things, and if they care and we can do it, and don't in any way jeopardise anything, why not?'[25]

(Osborne's other significant moment at a Buckingham Palace banquet involved US president Barack Obama during his state visit in 2011. Towards the end of the evening, with everyone still enjoying themselves after dinner, the Queen came up to him and said: 'Will you tell President Obama it's time to go to bed?' Osborne recalled: 'I could see Obama surrounded by this big crowd, all having drinks. Am I supposed to go and tell him to go to bed? It was about midnight. And Christopher Geidt stepped in and said, "We are handling the situation, Chancellor."'[26])

Another means of protecting the monarchy is hard-wired into the system. It is called King's (or Queen's) Consent, and is a parliamentary convention under which Crown consent is sought whenever a proposed piece of legislation will affect the Crown's prerogatives or interests, including hereditary revenues and personal property. There is a similar convention for the Prince of Wales, known as Prince's Consent. In one example reported by the *Guardian* in 2021, the Queen's personal lawyer lobbied Edward Heath's government in 1973 to change a draft law that would have disclosed details of her private share dealings. Buckingham Palace said in response: 'Queen's consent is a parliamentary process, with the role of the sovereign purely formal. Consent is always granted by the monarch where requested by Government. Any assertion that the sovereign has blocked legislation is simply incorrect.' However, some experts have argued that the monarch does not have to invoke consent, because being given prior notice of forthcoming bills allows them to lobby for legislative changes in advance. Dr Thomas Adams, an expert in constitutional law at Oxford University who saw the documents discovered by the *Guardian* in the National Archives, said that the possibility of consent not being given was 'clearly being used to influence' the overall shape of legislation.[27]

Other cases uncovered by the newspaper included the late Queen's advisers demanding exclusions from proposed laws relating to road safety and land policy that appeared to affect her estates, and pressing for government policy on historic sites to be altered. In another example from 1992, Charles applied pressure on ministers to ensure an exemption to prevent Duchy of Cornwall tenants in the village of Newton St Loe from having the right to buy their own homes. Ministers thought there was no reason why Charles's tenants should not have the same rights as tenants in the rest of the country, but backed down in order to avoid a major row with the prince, which they feared could lead to a constitutional crisis.[28] The former Liberal Democrat MP Norman Baker described Queen's Consent (as it was then) as a 'constitutional outrage'. He said: 'It gives an unelected person the opportunity to require changes to draft legislation in order to benefit herself financially, or to exempt herself from laws she does not like, and to do so in secret without any public accountability.'[29] Norman Baker is perhaps guilty of overstating his case – 'questionable practice' might be a better description than 'constitutional outrage' – and the idea that the late Queen used consent to benefit herself financially is probably wide of the mark. But there is no doubt that more transparency would be a good thing. If the royal family knew that their lobbying about draft legislation would be made public, they would be a lot more careful about the changes they asked for.

THE PRIME MINISTER obviously has the most contact with the royal family. After that, it is the foreign secretary, who accompanies the sovereign on state visits. As we have just seen with Osborne, the chancellor also talks to the sovereign. But other ministers also get a look-in, and in the second half of the Queen's reign, as we have seen with the black spider memos, many cabinet ministers had frequent dealings with the Prince of Wales. After the mid-2000s, Labour ministers' interactions with the prince seem to have settled down, with fewer complaints than before. Ed Balls, who saw the prince a number of times as children, schools and families secretary under Gordon Brown, said:

> I engaged with him a lot, and listened to him. There were lots of things where he didn't like what we were doing, but he was the Prince of Wales and I always felt he had a right to tell me what he thought and I had a right to tell him when I disagreed . . . He never told me what we should do. It was always a genuinely open intellectual discussion about what works. He argued his position, but it was never inappropriate. Did I meet him more, have dinner with him more, because he was Prince of Wales? Absolutely. But I never felt he wanted to abuse that position. He was always intellectually curious, and want-ing to learn. When we presented arguments that were different from the ones that he was hearing, he always wanted to hear that. Did he ever lobby me? I never felt

lobbied. But he definitely introduced us to headteachers who talked about leadership in the state school system and the way in which the government supported schools which made us think about things in a different way.[30]

Michael Gove, who succeeded Balls as education secretary in 2010, saw the prince a fair amount in that role – Charles was particularly interested in vocational education – and even more when he became environment secretary under Theresa May in 2017. In 2018 he accompanied the prince on the royal train for a day of engagements in the Lake District. On the way up the night before Gove had dinner with Charles's private secretary (steak and chips, cheese, a 'nice but not excessive' red wine) before being ushered into Charles's carriage for a nightcap of malt whisky – Laphroaig, if anyone is asking. 'We sit, have a drink, we chat about waste policy, about which he was passionate. Then there's a sort of gentle knock on the door and I know that's the cue to leave.' The next morning Gove was invited to have breakfast with the prince. The advice from the prince's private secretary was to have breakfast with him beforehand. 'Have the big boys' breakfast first – bacon and eggs – because Charles's breakfast was a tiny little vase of fruit and then some pressed fruit juice concoction, sort of beetroot and ginger or whatever, and that was it. Then we chatted again about organic farming, national parks policy, rewilding versus sheep farming as options for the Lake District, and so on.'

The prince was not terribly keen on rewilding. 'I don't think it's a good idea to have wolves in the Lake District, do you?' he said. Gove recalled:

He had a micro-detailed knowledge of – not everything that was going on in the department – but all of the current debates. So he was exceptionally knowledgeable about every aspect of what we were doing in DEFRA, from animal welfare to boring details about waste policy and whether or not we were going to charge a levy on producers to pay for the cost of their own plastic. And he had a view. Not a 'you must do this' view, but a sort of gentle, 'Should we be thinking more about this?' It was putting the idea into one's head, encouraging one to go further.

How did he feel about the propriety of it? 'I felt it was totally legitimate, because he knew an enormous amount . . . I always felt he used the access which he undoubtedly had relatively sparingly, to good effect, in areas that he knew about and cared about. And he always knew that ultimately we would decide . . . And it wasn't applying pressure, it was sharing a view, hoping that you would take it seriously and also sometimes pointing you in the direction of an expert here or a third party there.'[31]

A FEW DAYS before Christmas 2012 Richard (now Sir Richard) Heaton, permanent secretary at the Cabinet Office, had an unexpected invitation to have tea with the Prince of Wales at Clarence House, ostensibly to discuss the relationship between the government and the prince's charities. Joined by their respective private secretaries in the upstairs drawing room, they talked about various subjects including India and the Freedom of Information Act. According to Whitehall sources, towards the end the conversation shifted to the Succession to the Crown Bill, which gave daughters equal rights in the line of succession, and which was at the time making its way through Parliament. The proposed new law was very timely, because the Duchess of Cambridge was at the time pregnant with her first child, who would turn out to be a boy,

Prince George. What, Charles wanted to know, would happen if his first grandchild was a girl, and she married a Mr Smith. Would the royal house be Smith or Windsor? He had other questions, too – about what would happen if his grandchild married a Catholic, and what effect the new law would have on hereditary peerages. Prince Charles, it seemed, had a lot of concerns about the new law, and a lot of questions he wanted answered. It was not Heaton's area of responsibility, and he had not been briefed on the subject, but he gave what answers he could.

Moves to end male primogeniture in the monarchy had been floating around for several years. In 1998 Lord Archer – the novelist Jeffrey Archer – had brought forward a private members' bill to do so in the House of Lords, which was taken over by the government and then quietly dropped. Later, when Gordon Brown was preparing to take over from Tony Blair as prime minister, his team started working on the subject again. But according to Whitehall sources they did not do a very good job, as they forgot that whatever happened in Britain would also apply in the fifteen other realms where the British sovereign was head of state, which makes everything more complicated. It was not just a question of changing the law in Britain, and getting the agreement of, say, Australia; it was a matter of Australian law. Once again, the idea was quietly dropped. It was not until 2010 and the coalition government that it was revived once more.

This time it was different. Both the prime minister, David Cameron, and his deputy, Nick Clegg – who had his sights set on delivering a package of constitutional reform – wanted it done. And the government was invested in doing it properly, unlike the Brownites in 2007. Cameron spoke to the Australian prime minister, Julia Gillard, who was hosting the 2011 Commonwealth summit in Perth, where Cameron wanted to announce the proposed new law. According to a government source, he said to Gillard, 'William and Kate are getting married, there's going to be kids, shall we sort this out?' Crucially, the palace was not against it. But they said that the government had to ensure the backing of the other fifteen realms. 'I always thought that the signals from Buckingham Palace were that if it was the wish of the duly elected prime minister of the day, and the realms can be sorted out, we will not stand in its way,' said the source. 'I didn't get the sense there was any great enthusiasm from the palace and the Queen herself.'

Getting the agreement of the fifteen was far from easy. Australia and New Zealand were straightforward, and Canada was not a problem, either. However, Jamaica was tricky, and some of the smaller Pacific nations were downright difficult. As the government source said, it could be a case of 'What does the constitution say?' 'Don't know.' 'Where is it?' 'Oh, it's in a file in the Foreign Office because some mid-ranking colonial official wrote it in 1963, or something.' The deal with the palace was that it had to be sorted out before Cameron set off for the Commonwealth summit in Perth. He was flying on a Monday; on the Saturday before that there was still no reply from Tuvalu, and Ciaran Martin, the constitution director at the Cabinet Office, was bracing himself to tell the prime minister to recommend to the Queen that they go ahead without Tuvalu's consent – they could always object later. Then, on the Sunday morning, Martin woke up to find an email from the high commissioner, forwarding an email from somebody he vouched for as the chief of staff to the prime minister of Tuvalu, indicating their consent. It was a one-line email, sent around 3.30am, but it was enough – just. They had the set.

During all the discussions about the change in the rules of succession Buckingham Palace had one more stipulation:

they told Whitehall politely but firmly that government officials should just deal with Buckingham Palace on this one. There was absolutely no need, in other words, to bring the Prince of Wales's people at Clarence House into the discussion. Occasionally William Nye, Charles's private secretary, would ask when the prime minister wanted to discuss the issue with the heir to the throne, but all Whitehall could say was that that was something for the royal households to sort out.

That, then, may explain why the Prince of Wales ambushed Richard Heaton with questions about the Succession to the Crown Bill. It may also explain why, a couple of weeks later, a story appeared on the front page of the *Daily Mail* saying that the prince had 'voiced serious concerns' about 'rushed plans' to change the laws governing the royal line of succession.[32] Charles backed the law in principle, the article said, but thought that the consequences for the relationship between the state and the Church of England, and the rules governing hereditary titles, had not been thought through. Significantly, Simon Heffer wrote in the paper that Charles was concerned about 'the lack of detailed consultation on the process'. He and Prince William, said Heffer, 'appear not to have been consulted at all, which rankled with the Prince of Wales'. And why was that? Because that is the way Buckingham Palace wanted it. The Queen's private secretary at the time was Christopher Geidt. Five years later he was forced out, at the prompting of the Prince of Wales, a victim of a classic example of palace infighting.

As soon as the article appeared, Heaton was contacted on holiday by the cabinet secretary Jeremy Heywood's office, asking what had happened. By the time he got back, according to Whitehall sources, Heywood was sounding more relaxed about the whole episode. What was all this about the Prince of Wales, asked Heaton. 'Oh, don't worry about that,' said Heywood. 'He's in the doghouse.' There were three reasons why Whitehall saw it that way. One was that the prince had, in their view, misrepresented the conversation between him and Heaton. Secondly, he had leaked – or someone had leaked on his behalf – a private conversation with a civil servant. And thirdly, he was criticising government policy, which he was not supposed to do. The bill had been carefully brokered with Buckingham Palace, and sources say he had no business 'to haul someone in and give them a dressing-down on something which was settled government policy'.[33] A short while later Charles invited Heaton to join him on a visit to a pottery that one of the prince's charities had helped to save. Charles showed him around, and the two men chatted on the royal train. It wasn't an apology, but it was the next best thing.

THE TIES THAT bind the monarchy and the government work both ways. Sometimes it is the government that helps the monarchy, by sorting out its finances, say. Often the monarchy helps the government, by representing Britain abroad.

In 2015 the Queen, then eighty-nine, went to Germany on what would be her last major state visit. David Cameron had already committed Britain to a referendum on the country's continuing membership of the European Union. Before that happened there would be negotiations on Britain's terms of membership, and Cameron wanted to prepare the ground as well as he could in order to win the sort of concessions he would need to persuade voters to support the Remain cause. As a sign of how important he regarded the visit as being, Cameron took the unusual step of joining the Queen in Germany; normally it is just the foreign secretary who accompanies her on state visits. The German chancellor also regarded it as important, and wanted as much time with the Queen as possible. When the Queen attended a university lecture as part of her engagements, Angela Merkel turned up unannounced to sit next to her.

Lord McDonald, the former permanent under-secretary at the Foreign Office who was Britain's ambassador to Germany at the time, recalled how the Queen was driven from the airport to the centre of Berlin in a Bentley with the Royal Standard flying. 'As it drove along the urban motorway, the traffic on the other side of the road was stationary, and people were standing on the roof of their cars, waving and cheering as she went by.' Later, he said, the official greeter – the state secretary in the president's office – told him: 'I have never seen anything like that in my life.'

From the beginning the impact was big, and positive, McDonald said. But did it actually accomplish what it set out to achieve? Britain was certainly doing everything it could to further its cause. 'But of course, however wonderful the atmospherics, the basics of German national interest were always going to kick in. And so they were never going to say, "OK, David, you can have what you want." But I think the ground had been prepared as well as it could be for them to be as receptive to the prime minister's approach as possible.'

Sir David Manning – whose former roles include ambassador to the US, Blair's foreign policy adviser and adviser to Princes William and Harry – said it was hard to judge to what extent the goodwill generated by a royal visit is ephemeral and how much it actually advances Britain's policy objectives. 'You are going to get much more public impact from a visit if it is by the sovereign or the heir to the throne, than you are if it is a British minister. They are not there to negotiate deals. But what you can do is create a climate. And you do get access. The president will almost certainly ask to see them.'

Manning was our man in Washington for the Queen's 2007 state visit when 'hundreds' of people wanted to come to the garden party, including senior political figures who could be quite difficult to reach. 'It opens up the opportunity of talking to them, getting to know them,' said Manning. 'As ambassador you can trade on this, go and see these people afterwards.'[34]

The Queen could have a powerful effect on world leaders. When Saudi Arabia's Crown Prince Mohammed bin Salman visited Britain in 2018, the government pushed the boat out, including arranging a meeting with the cabinet in the cabinet room. 'But the whisper came back that he was a bit disappointed because there was no meeting with Her Majesty,' said McDonald. 'And so very quickly, with Her Majesty responding with alacrity, a lunch was arranged at Buckingham Palace. That, of course, was the highlight of the visit. The prince was visibly affected, almost trembling meeting the Queen of England. One reason I knew he was under pressure was that in that meeting he spoke only Arabic. He speaks perfectly good English, but it's not perfect English. But meeting the Queen he had to get it all right, so he spoke Arabic and relied on an interpreter.'[35]

It would be wrong to assume that the Queen played only a passive role in the success of state visits. When French president Valéry Giscard d'Estaing visited Britain in 1976 it was at a delicate time in Anglo-French relations, and British officials were doing all they could to overcome French coolness, including organising an official gift for the president of a black Labrador from the Queen's own kennels called Sandringham Sambo. At the state banquet the Queen was due to mention in her speech that great Anglo-French collaboration Concorde, and asked her private secretary Martin Charteris to clap loudly at that point and encourage others to do the same. All went according to plan, and her Concorde reference was greeted with thunderous applause. Later Giscard said that he had previously believed that the British were unenthusiastic about Concorde. Listening to the supposedly spontaneous loud applause that greeted its mention, he said, he realised he had been wrong.[36] Historically minded observers might have recalled Edward VII and the Entente Cordiale, when a British monarch last did their bit to improve Anglo-French relations.

During the Brexit era it was not just the Queen who was involved in helping Britain set the atmospherics for its negotiations with Europe; it was the whole of the royal family. They fanned out all over the EU in a royal charm offensive spearheaded by the Queen's state visit to Germany and included not just Prince Charles but also the Duke and Duchess of Cambridge and the Earl and Countess of Wessex. Even Prince Harry played his part. 'This was a plan,' said McDonald, who as the head of the Foreign Office became chairman of the Royal Visits Committee in 2015.

> As I came in, it was clear that the main objective of the new British government was the renegotiation, and the relationship with individual new member states. So we came up with a plan to deploy many members of the royal family and hit all EU member states over the course of the next two or three years. And we did that ... The idea was to remind EU member states about what was good and positive about having the Brits around. These senior visits are a time to pause and reflect about the overall importance of the relationship. And I think that works to the UK's benefit.

It actually took four years to get them all in, which meant that later visits were more about building bridges post-referendum. But in that time every single member state of the EU either received a royal visit – the vast majority of them – or was received by the Queen at Buckingham Palace. Some had more than one: Germany had visits by the Queen, Prince Charles and William and Kate. As for the success of the strategy, the visits went well and reminded those countries of the strength of their relationship with Britain but were not enough to help Cameron achieve his political objective before the referendum. 'None of these countries was going on the back of that warm glow to ditch their fundamental national interest,' said McDonald. 'They weren't prepared to dilute the rules of EU membership to the extent that the British government wanted.'[37]

ON SUNDAY 14 September 2014, after going to church near Balmoral, the Queen helped David Cameron's government in a way that was to prove highly controversial. Against the background of growing support for the Scottish National Party, Cameron had agreed to hold a referendum on independence for Scotland. It was a debate he thought he could win, and the polls seemed to support him in that view. Then, a couple of weeks before the referendum, the polls began to turn. Cameron was with the Queen in Balmoral for his annual visit when *The Sunday Times* ran a story headed 'Yes Vote Leads in Scots Poll'. Over breakfast Cameron tried to persuade the gaggle of equerries and ladies-in-waiting that it was a rogue poll, but as he wrote in his memoirs, 'I was struggling to convince myself, let alone them.' In an interview with the BBC he said that the poll result hit him 'like a blow to the solar plexus' and led to a 'mounting sense of panic that this could go the wrong way'.

It was time for drastic action. A palace insider said: 'Number 10 panicked and said, "We need to throw the kitchen sink at this."'[38] Cameron told the BBC: 'I remember conversations

I had with my private secretary and he had with the Queen's private secretary and I had with the Queen's private secretary, not asking for anything that would be in any way improper or unconstitutional but just a raising of the eyebrow even you know, a quarter of an inch, we thought could make a difference.'[39] The pressure did not just come from Cameron, however. Prince William also wanted the Queen to say something, and urged the Queen's private secretary, Sir Christopher Geidt, to get her to intervene. Geidt and the cabinet secretary, Sir Jeremy Heywood, had – in a classic example of how the Golden Triangle operates behind the scenes – already been talking about the constitutional propriety of an intervention by the monarch, and between them they came up with the formula that the Queen would use when she stopped to talk to members of the public outside Crathie Kirk that Sunday.

What, the Queen was asked, did she think about the referendum? 'Well,' she said, 'I hope people will think very carefully about the future.' That carefully scripted response – which the palace tried to insist was 'completely spontaneous', even though it had in fact been meticulously planned – made front-page headlines the next day. Did it make any difference? That is hard to tell – possibly not much – but when the referendum went Cameron's way, the Queen was delighted. The prime minister was in New York for the UN General Assembly, where he told his friend Michael Bloomberg, former mayor of New York, that when he rang her to tell her the good news, 'she purred down the line'. Unfortunately for Cameron, his remarks were picked up on camera. Cameron wrote: 'I later made a heartfelt apology to the Queen for commenting on our private exchange.'[40]

THE QUEEN'S intervention in the Scottish referendum was an anomaly, because everything that Buckingham Palace had done in the years leading up to that had been aimed at keeping the Queen out of politics. One source who knew the Queen well said: 'Christopher Geidt was a deeply cautious individual who saw it as his job to keep the Queen above politics.' His deputy, Edward Young, was of the same view. In the run-up to the 2015 general election, 'they were very keen to avoid any situation in which the Queen would be forced into making a judgement about what the political outcome should be'.

Thanks to the work done by Gus O'Donnell on the cabinet manual, that had seemed to work well in the 2010 election. The Queen had been kept out of it, and Gordon Brown had stayed in post until the negotiations with the Liberal Democrats about who should form the next government were completed – well, almost. But in 2015 it turned out that was not enough. The palace was still worried about the Queen getting her hands dirty. Geidt's biggest fear was a *Sun* headline like 'Queen to Decide', or – in an echo of the drama following the death of Diana – 'Where Are You, Ma'am? We Need a Decision'. Discussions were held about whether the Queen should be in Sandringham at the time of the election in May, so the palace could say: 'She will come back to London when someone is able to present her with a workable solution.'[41]

With the 2015 general election beginning to look very unpredictable, the palace got busy. Caroline Creer, who runs the secretariat, circulated a number of articles for discussion, including one by Simon Heffer in the *New Statesman* in February in which he suggested that another hung Parliament could lead to a constitutional crisis. She also sent round a report Vernon Bogdanor wrote for the Constitution Society entitled *The Crisis of the Constitution*, and another piece written by the constitution expert Catherine Haddon for the Institute for Government. They were taking it all very seriously.

The result was an article in *The Sunday Times* a couple of weeks before the election in which it was reported that the palace was warning that the Queen should not be dragged into political wrangling after the election. The fear, wrote Roya Nikkhah, was that Cameron or the Labour leader, Ed Miliband, might try to use her as a prop to legitimise a government that lacked a parliamentary majority. The article quoted a source close to the palace as saying that the Queen 'does not wish to be drawn into discussions of how the next government is formed'.[42] The palace view, says a source who was around at the time, was that if the parties were unable to negotiate a coalition, or a confidence and supply arrangement, they should not come to the Queen with 'a half-baked offer in an attempt to outmanoeuvre the other'. Instead they should talk to the cabinet secretary, the private secretary at Number 10 and the Queen's private secretary so they could come up with a definitive result.[43]

The fact that the palace should have briefed this is, on the face of it, surprising, given that this sort of thing was meant to have been sorted out by the cabinet manual in 2010. 'That puzzled me,' said Sir Peter Riddell, who co-wrote a report on preparing for the 2010 election. He did not believe that any of the parties wanted to use the Queen to gain political advantage. 'I didn't get any sense of anyone disrespecting the Queen on that.'[44] However, Alex Thomas of the Institute for Government, who used to work in the Cabinet Office on constitutional and electoral matters, said: 'To some extent it had been sorted in 2010. But we were very conscious of the gaps that still existed. Yes, by fair means or foul they had kept Gordon Brown in Number 10 long enough for the coalition agreement to come together, but he had still left a bit early [before the agreement was finalised].' Bits of the cabinet manual needed updating, he said, and 'there was the potential for Labour to stir it up a bit around the exact constitutional rules'. There was a good reason why they thought that. 'The Labour Party were cross that Gordon Brown had been portrayed as squatting in Number 10 [in 2010],' said former deputy cabinet secretary Helen MacNamara. 'There was a feeling they had been done over by the media. We were very much alive to the fact that it might be a dirtier fight this time around, because they felt bruised about last time.'[45]

Lord Falconer, who was advising Miliband on what to do if there was a hung Parliament, duly did some stirring. On polling day he started briefing political editors on how Labour could appeal to the cabinet manual to force Cameron from office.[46] It was all about what happened if Cameron did not have a majority but decided to hang on to deliver a Queen's Speech, as Stanley Baldwin had in 1923–4. Falconer argued that if the Tories had the largest number of seats, but it was clear that any Queen's Speech would be defeated by a coalition of Lib Dems, Labour and nationalists, then it would be wrong for the Queen to invite the Conservatives to try to form a government. 'If it was clear that Cameron could not have sustained a Queen's Speech then the cabinet secretary should have advised Cameron to invite the Queen to give the party leader with the best chance of forming a sustainable government the first shot,' said Falconer. 'It is embarrassing for the Queen to deliver a speech where they are going to be defeated.' Jeremy Heywood did not agree with Falconer's analysis. It was, however, never resolved. To most people's surprise, the Tories won a small overall majority, and were able to govern without the Liberal Democrats.

When Cameron went to see the Queen, he told her: 'Well, this is a surprise. I'll be forming a majority government.' As

he recalled: 'She said, "You haven't got a very big majority."
And I said, "No, but it's getting bigger all the time," because
the seats were still coming in.' The Queen smiled at that one.
'I knew that would amuse her.'[47]

Edward Young recalled that there was a debate about
what Cameron should say afterwards: 'I have just been to see
Her Majesty the Queen who has invited me to form a majority
Conservative Government,' or 'I have just been to see Her
Majesty the Queen to inform her that I will form a majority
Conservative government.' Was he being invited to form a
new Conservative government, as had happened at the end
of the wartime coalition in May 1945, before the election two
months later, or was he simply continuing as PM, as happens
when any prime minister with a majority wins a second
term? The Number 10 team argued that he would have to be
invited, because it sounded more constitutionally legitimate,
while the palace took the view that when he had been asked
to form a government in 2010, there was no prescription
about what sort of government it should be. So the fact that
he was going from a coalition government to a majority government did not matter: he was still prime minister, and so
just had to inform the Queen. But with time running short –
as Young wrote, 'the PM's convoy was speeding up the Mall'
– they had to fudge it. Cameron said: 'I have just been to see
Her Majesty the Queen . . . and I will now form a majority
Conservative government.' Young wrote: 'We were quietly
pleased with those unspoken three dots. It was a reminder
that, when navigating an unwritten constitution, sometimes
one must think on one's feet. Also that, occasionally, some
things are better left unsaid.'[48]

KEEPING THE sovereign above politics is not the same as
saying that the sovereign does not have political opinions.

The Queen had opinions on all sorts of subjects, it was just that she chose not to share them. Or to put it more accurately, she did sometimes share them, but those who heard were usually too discreet to repeat them. As George Osborne said, 'I was always constantly astonished by how candid she was and that none of this ever came out. She'd be very forthright in telling you what she thought of individuals, including members of her own family, and what she thought about things going on in the country.'[49]

Another politician tells how the Queen once mentioned over drinks that she was due to see Pakistan's General Musharraf, who would later be found guilty of violating the country's constitution and sentenced to death in absentia. 'Isn't he just a crook?' she said. 'Isn't he just completely corrupt?' The group she was talking to were somewhat lost for words at this, so one of them turned the conversation to horse racing and asked whether she watched the Channel 4 preview programme The Morning Line. She said: 'I really like the Channel 4 coverage in the afternoon, and I always like to watch it when my horses are running, but The Morning Line – I can't watch it. I can't stand that man John McCririck.'[50]

On one occasion the Queen did share her views, only to see them emblazoned all over the front page of the Sun a few years later, much to her annoyance. During the referendum campaign over whether Britain should leave the European Union, the paper published a front-page story under the headline 'Queen Backs Brexit'. The article said that at a lunch at Windsor in 2011 the Queen had told the deputy prime minister, Nick Clegg, that she thought the EU was heading in the wrong direction. She allegedly said with 'venom and emotion': 'I don't understand Europe.'[51] Clegg later denied this was true, accusing Michael Gove of leaking the story to the paper.[52] After a complaint by the palace the Independent

Press Standards Organisation (IPSO) ruled that the story was inaccurate, saying there was nothing in the text to support the claim made in the headline. Another source told this author that what the Queen said at the lunch was no stronger than something along the lines of 'Oh, all this EU red tape must be very frustrating.'[53]

Was the Queen really a Brexit supporter? Although it complained to IPSO, the palace did not issue a strong denial of the story. But there was a good reason for this. An insider said: 'Partly as a function of her being sucked into the Scotland referendum, where she obviously did express a view, we weren't able to push back as robustly as I think she would have wanted us to. I think it made her angry that her view on such a critical issue was misrepresented in that way.' But she also understood that to officially deny that the Queen backed Brexit would imply that she was a Remainer. (The Queen, of course, cannot vote, because she is above politics. In theory other members of the royal family can, but in practice they do not.)

Now, years after that notorious Sun headline, evidence of what the Queen really thought about Brexit can at last be revealed. A senior minister who spoke to her in the early spring of 2016, some three months before the referendum, says she said: 'We shouldn't leave the EU.' They discussed the referendum, and she said, 'It's better to stick with the devil you know.'[54]

This chimes with what the palace insider says of the late Queen's views on Europe. Although she would read stories in the papers about Brussels bureaucracy and rules and say, 'This is ridiculous,' on a fundamental level she saw the EU as part of the post-war settlement. In the same way that she believed in the Commonwealth and everything that it stood for, and was proud of the way Britain had managed its decolonisation, she saw the EU as marking an era of cooperation and peace after two world wars. As Cameron put it: 'She was so careful never to express a political view, but you always sensed that, like most of her subjects, she thought that European cooperation was necessary and important, but the institutions of the EU sometimes can be infuriating.'[55]

News of the Queen's clear views on Brexit reached Cameron, who immediately had to decide whether to use it in the Remain campaign. He decided not to, even though the Leave camp had no such scruples. It was one thing to recruit the Queen's help in the Scottish referendum campaign, quite another to betray the confidential relationship he – and his ministers – had with the Queen.

But it is now clear: if the Queen had had a vote, she would have voted Remain.

CHAPTER ELEVEN

THE QUEEN IS INDISPOSED

IT'S JUNE 2008. Boris Johnson is the newly elected Mayor of London, and he has been invited to Clarence House to meet the then Prince of Wales. He and his communications director, Guto Harri, take the Jubilee Line on the Underground, which is a straightforward journey to Green Park and a short walk across the park to Charles's London home. Unfortunately they take a train going in the wrong direction. When they get to Canary Wharf, three stops later, they realise their mistake, jump out of the train and get back on one heading into central London. They are going to be late.

'We ran from Green Park to Clarence House,' recalled Harri, 'both of us slightly panting, me a bit stressed at this point. Then it was, "How do we get in here?" He said, "Don't you know?" I said, "No, I assumed you knew."' They ask the soldier standing guard outside, but he remains silent. Harri says, 'For fuck's sake, he is the Mayor of London, he's late to see the future King, can you just give us some idea?' The soldier casts his eyes to one side, they follow his gaze and finally work out how to enter. Inside the first person they see is Manon Williams, one of Charles's private secretaries (and Ffion Hague's sister), who says to Harri in Welsh, 'Paid â becso, ma' fe'n iawn' – 'Don't worry, it's all fine.'

'What?' says Johnson. 'We were at school together,' explains Harri: a Welsh-language state secondary school in South Wales. Johnson replies: 'Crikey, I expect to meet someone I've been to school with at a royal palace, not someone you've been to school with.'

Exactly what happened when Johnson was finally ushered into the royal presence is not clear: the meeting did not go badly, but Harri got the impression that 'there was not a lot of warmth there'. Charles, he felt, had taken 'just a tiny bit of offence' at Johnson being late. 'There was never a lot of love for [Boris].' Years later that relationship would get considerably worse.

Johnson got on a lot better with the Duchess of Cornwall, who had a remarkably frank conversation with him in his early days as mayor. Some months after his first unfortunate audience with Prince Charles, Johnson was invited to Clarence House to meet Camilla. She had apparently told Charles, 'He looks like such fun. Can we have him over for tea?' This time there was no risking the Tube; he and Harri cycled from City Hall. They were parking their bikes in the shed at the back of Clarence House when the duchess appeared, saying 'Oh, I didn't believe them when they said you had cycled!' Harri recalled: 'She had come out to the bike shed to see us. We drop the bikes, she grabs him by the wrist and says, "You and me, upstairs – now!" I am just standing there, and the private secretary says, "Would you like some tea?"'

After an hour Johnson reappeared. 'Boris was raving about her,' said Harri. 'They obviously got on like a house on fire. He was making guttural noises about how much he admired and liked her. But the serious conversation they had was about her being the victim of an attempted sexual assault when she was a schoolgirl. She was on a train going to Paddington – she was about sixteen, seventeen – and some guy was moving his hand further and further . . .' At that point Johnson had asked what happened next. She replied: 'I did what my mother taught me to. I took off my shoe and whacked him in the nuts with the heel.' Harri said: 'She was self-possessed enough when they arrived at Paddington to jump off the train, find a guy in uniform and say "That man just attacked me," and he was arrested.'

The relevance of this conversation was that Johnson at the time wanted to open three rape crisis centres. There was already one in south London, and he wanted to open ones in east, west and north London. Harri said: 'I think she formally opened two out of three of them. Nobody asked why the interest, why the commitment. But that's what it went back to.'[1]

BORIS JOHNSON is a devoted monarchist. He believes in the royal family and adored the Queen. When he was mayor, he appeared to have a positive relationship with her. Guto Harri recalled an early encounter, when the Queen came to plant a tree in the Olympic Park.

> Boris was checking with Seb Coe [Lord Coe, chairman of the London Games organising committee] as she came out of the car, that it was 'Ma'am' not 'Marm', as in spam? Seb Coe said, 'As in, wham bam thank you ma'am', just as she stepped out of the car. The three of us were chuckling – I was a step behind them – slightly surprised by Seb Coe. Oo-er! . . . I always thought there was a lot of warmth from her towards Boris. And that is what I heard from various people, that she was very fond of him. I always thought they were pretty pally. That's the impression I got from various quarters.[2]

However, his first meeting with her as prime minister did not result in Johnson covering himself in glory. After he had been to the palace to be appointed PM following the resignation of Theresa May, Johnson went to Number 10, where during a tour he revealed that the Queen had told him: 'I don't know why anyone would want the job.' This was, said royal biographer Robert Lacey, a clear breach of protocol. 'Prime ministers and ex-prime ministers do not even reveal these sort of things in their memoirs, let alone on their first occasion in office. I don't think constitutionalists, or anyone in Buckingham Palace, will be remotely amused by this.'[3]

Johnson was apparently 'mortified' by his gaffe.[4] He took his audiences with the Queen very seriously. 'He really enjoyed those private moments with her,' said a Downing Street insider.[5] However, judging by his dreams, one might speculate whether those Wednesday evening sessions at Buckingham Palace were preceded by a touch of nerves. In a column written a year after her death he revealed how he told her that he had had a nightmare that he was late for her and the Duke of Edinburgh. 'Oh yes,' she smiled. 'Were you naked?'[6]

Like every prime minister, he was effusive about his audiences with the Queen. They were, he said, 'a balm' and 'a form of free psychotherapy'. He wrote in his memoirs: 'It was like being at school and getting taken out to tea by a much-loved grandmother.' And, of course, he could not resist including one or two snippets from those audiences in his book, such as her advice when it all collapsed and he finally had to resign. 'There's no point in bitterness,' she told him.[7]

Johnson letting slip the Queen's remark about no one wanting the job of prime minister was, by the standards of prime ministerial blunders, hardly a hanging offence, and certainly not as bad as Cameron describing the Queen as purring down the telephone line. The prorogation of Parliament in 2019 was, however, an entirely different matter.

After Theresa May had failed to unite the Conservative party around a deal for Britain to leave the European Union, Johnson won the Tory leadership in July 2019 on a promise that he would deliver Brexit by 31 October, 'no ifs, no buts'. If he could not get a deal with Brussels, he said, he would prepare for a no-deal Brexit. But with the anti-Brexit forces in Parliament doing their best to frustrate his every move, and time running out, he needed to find a way to break through. He needed a bold plan. And that plan was prorogation.

Prorogation is the formal term given to the period between the end of one session of Parliament and the state opening that begins the next. There is nothing controversial about it – it happens every year. But what Johnson and the tiny, secretive team around him were planning was highly controversial, because they were going to prorogue Parliament for five weeks. Prorogation normally lasts less than a week, or two at the most. And the reason they wanted to do this was to stop the Remainers passing legislation blocking a no-deal Brexit. Johnson wanted no deal to remain a real possibility, so he could use it as a bargaining tool against the EU. Proroguing Parliament between 9 September and 14 October, when it was due to reconvene, would keep the threat of no deal alive, regardless of whether Johnson was actually prepared to go through with it.

Everyone in on the plan was sworn to secrecy. The attorney general had advised the PM that it was lawful, but Johnson was not taking any risks. The cabinet secretary, Sir Mark Sedwill (now Lord Sedwill), who was on holiday, and his deputy, Helen MacNamara, were both kept in the dark, as Johnson's team did not trust them not to try to sabotage the plan. It was no secret that they wanted to prorogue

Parliament, but the Cabinet Office had assumed that they would not try during August because it is so difficult to get hold of people. 'We might have been a bit complacent about that,' said MacNamara. 'To be fair to them, it was very cleverly done. It's really unusual to have a Privy Council meeting in August. And we were wrong to assume it wouldn't happen. There you go. It turns out people can get on a plane.'[8] Sedwill, whose concern was the duration of any prorogation rather than the principle, later told colleagues that he thought they had taken advantage of his absence to push it through.[9] Members of the cabinet were also kept out of the loop. 'It came pretty much out of the blue,' said Amber Rudd, the work and pensions secretary. 'There had been no discussion about prorogation.'[10] Ironically it was the desire for secrecy that arguably did for Johnson's plan in the end. Many, including MacNamara, believe that if his team had involved the civil servants they would have been armed with solid advice, and would not have lost the case at the Supreme Court.

A few days before the plan was put into action Number 10 told Buckingham Palace what they were proposing. Prorogation is always formally carried out by the sovereign on the advice of the Privy Council, and takes effect when a royal proclamation is read to both Houses of Parliament. The palace, according to Anthony Seldon's account of Johnson's time at Number 10, was very unhappy about it, not least because it came during the Queen's summer break at Balmoral. 'Buckingham Palace was very unsettled by the Queen being dragged in,' said an official privy to the discussions. 'They hadn't been properly prepared and warned when on holiday in August, and the Palace felt they would have been in a stronger position had they been contacted earlier and had a chance to think it through.' It created, said Seldon, a level of tension between the palace and Number 10 that had not been seen in recent years. 'There's no doubt it caused a lot of consternation,' said another close source.[11] According to a Whitehall official quoted by the author and Sunday Times journalist Tim Shipman, the palace was 'nervous' about the length of prorogation. 'Reassurance was sought and the message went back that everything was above board.'[12]

This placed the Queen in a bit of a bind. The sovereign acts on the advice of the prime minister, so theoretically there was nothing the palace could do: the only course of action available to the Queen was to approve the decision to prorogue Parliament. But officials were aware that the Queen was being asked to do something extremely unusual, and her private secretary, Edward Young, took the precaution of taking a few highly informal soundings from lawyers. Young told colleagues the lawyers he spoke to said that they suspected that the government was acting legally. 'There was quite a view,' said one royal insider, 'that this may not have been palatable but it was within the government's right to do it.' The situation was not helped by the fact that the Golden Triangle, the crucial relationship between the sovereign's private secretary, the cabinet secretary and the principal private secretary at Number 10, was not functioning properly. Sedwill, who was not trusted by Johnson or his consigliere Dominic Cummings and did not know how much longer he would be in a job, was hard to get hold of, and Number 10 had a new private secretary in the person of Martin Reynolds who was still finding his feet. 'It was a very difficult time,' said a palace source.

On the morning of Wednesday 28 August, Jacob Rees-Mogg, in his capacity as lord president of the Privy Council, set off from London for Balmoral with two fellow privy counsellors, the chief whip, Mark Spencer, and Baroness Evans of Bowes, the leader of the House of Lords. 'It was all hush-hush,' recalled Rees-Mogg, 'in the way that these things are.' 'It was a very closely guarded secret,' said Mark Spencer. 'I didn't even tell my wife that I was going to Balmoral until the night before.'[13] Their hopes of reaching Scotland unnoticed were vanishingly slim, however: the news had started to leak, and a handful of Scottish photographers were on their way to Aberdeen Airport.

Even if there had been no leak, the patrician Rees-Mogg is one of the most recognisable figures in British politics. 'I get spotted in Heathrow straight away,' he said. 'I went through security and the man who just patted me down wanted a selfie.' Then, as they boarded the plane, they noticed that former Black Rod David Leakey was on the same flight. 'So at that point, it's clocked that we are doing something,' said Rees-Mogg. When they arrived at Aberdeen, all their phones went off, because there was an emergency cabinet meeting to get its approval for prorogation.

> We're walking off the aeroplane, with a cabinet meeting in one ear, and people coming up to me for selfies in the other ear. I was literally doing selfies as I was on a cabinet meeting call. And then we have the most wonderful trip in a charabanc to Balmoral, with the Queen's hairdresser, who is the most amusing man. He entertains us the whole way. He was the Queen's hairdresser for over twenty years, he took over the weekend after Diana, Princess of Wales died. He said the first time he cut the Queen's hair, he was so nervous that he didn't dare breathe on her. So he'd hold his breath. And he has very long hair, and he said, 'The Queen keeps on telling me I must have my hair cut.' So that kept us entertained until we got there.

Meanwhile the Queen had already given her approval to the plan, having spoken on the phone to Boris Johnson.

The privy counsellors were welcomed with coffee and sand-wiches, then Rees-Mogg was ushered into the Queen's study for a brief audience before the Privy Council meeting: just the two of them, plus one elderly corgi. The Queen, how-ever, didn't want the dog at the Privy Council meeting. 'So then there was the Queen, aged ninety-three, trying to get this corgi out, and the corgi is deaf and elderly and won't go. Eventually she does heave the corgi out, and we get on to the Privy Council.'[14] Even though the Queen hated having her holidays in Balmoral interrupted, she was, said Rees-Mogg, 'amazingly graceful'. He said: 'We'd been warned that it might be frosty. But the Queen couldn't have been more friendly. She was saying, "I'm sorry you've had to come such a long way."' Five minutes later, it was all done. The privy counsel-lors got back into their vehicle for the journey back to the airport. Prorogation had been set in train, and the political fireworks were about to begin. As Tim Shipman put it, 'What followed was seen by critics as the greatest act of constitu-tional vandalism since Charles I sent soldiers to arrest five members of the Long Parliament.'[15]

If it was constitutional vandalism, the Queen 'took it all in her stride', according to a royal source. There was, however, deep uneasiness within the palace that she had been put in such an awkward situation. But could she have done any-thing about it? Probably not. Some senior Whitehall sources wonder why the palace did not opt for some kind of delaying tactic when Rees-Mogg et al. arrived at Balmoral, even if only to say, 'Can we check?' Or perhaps 'I'm afraid the Queen is indisposed for a few hours, please have a cup of tea' while they got hold of the cabinet secretary on the phone to find out what the hell was going on. But even if they had, all the cabinet secretary could have said was that the attorney general thought it was lawful. And perhaps the opportunity for delaying had passed by then. The palace had been in communication with Number 10 about the plan for a few days, and Edward Young had had time for his informal chats with lawyers. The historian Peter Hennessy believes that the 'number one rule' of what he calls the 'good chaps' theory of government – that the constitution relies on a shared understanding of what constitutes good behaviour in public and political life – is 'that you do nothing to embarrass the monarch'. He said: 'To ask the monarch to prorogue Parliament, which she could not say no to, was controversial because it was obviously applied to buy time for the government. And it was bound to embarrass the Queen because it was going to split the parties and the nation and everybody. The palace was deeply upset by this.'[16]

It all turned out to be irrelevant anyway. Amid the furious reaction to Johnson's prorogation coup, pro-EU MPs introduced legislation to stop the prime minister from pursuing a no-deal Brexit. Known as the Benn Act, after the Labour MP Hilary Benn who introduced it, this stated that if the Commons had not consented to either a withdrawal agreement or no deal by 19 October, the prime minister was required to seek an extension of the withdrawal date – then scheduled for 31 October – to 31 January 2020. It passed, thanks to a motion tabled by Oliver Letwin and supported by Tory rebels which handed control of the Commons to the backbenches and meant that the bill went through all its Commons stages in one day. Benn's bill was tabled on 4 September, and became law on the 9th, a few hours before Parliament was suspended. Johnson's hands were tied, and prorogation had been all for nothing.

Meanwhile moves had begun to seek a ruling that prorogation to avoid parliamentary scrutiny was unconstitutional and unlawful. In Scotland the highest court of appeal unanimously declared that Johnson's advice to the Queen to suspend Parliament for five weeks was unlawful, while south of the border the High Court went the other way, ruling that the case was non-justiciable, or not capable of being decided by a court of law. To resolve the differences between the courts of England and Wales and Scotland, the cases were appealed to the Supreme Court, which ruled unanimously on 24 September that the advice to prorogue Parliament was unlawful. Johnson was in New York when he heard the news. Furious, he railed at his closest aides: 'You fucked me! You told me it would be fine. This is a disaster. I'm completely fucked. It's over. Now, what am I going to do?'

There was one thing he could do: apologise to the Queen. Former prime minister Sir John Major called on Johnson to make an 'unreserved apology', saying: 'No prime minister must ever treat the monarch or parliament in this way again.'[17] The Queen's reaction was said to be more 'sanguine'. She reportedly regarded Johnson as a roguish and comic figure, and a month after the judgement remarked of him: 'I think he was perhaps better suited to the stage.' The Prince of Wales, however, was said to be 'absolutely furious'. An insider told Tim Shipman: 'He was outraged that Boris should treat the Queen like that.'[18] For a few days all the talk at the palace was what they should do if a similar situation arose again.

Five days after the Supreme Court ruling The Sunday Times reported that the prime minister had personally apologised to the Queen for requiring her to approve the unlawful suspension of the House of Commons. The paper quoted a Number 10 source as saying: 'He got on to the Queen as quickly as possible to say how sorry he was.'[19] A Whitehall source told this author: 'He was very scared about going to see her immediately after prorogation to apologise. He really minded about the Queen. He does not like to apologise, ever.

The guy does not say sorry. It would have been so humiliating for him to have to apologise to her.'[20] Another Downing Street source said Johnson 'certainly would have felt uncomfortable' about embarrassing the Queen. 'He had enormous respect and affection for the Queen. He won't have liked it.'

But did he actually apologise? Buckingham Palace insiders cannot say, because they were not in the room at the time – or indeed listening in on a phone conversation, as Alastair Campbell once did with Tony Blair. Johnson never told them that he was about to apologise to the Queen, and certainly never apologised to anyone else at the palace. Downing Street insiders say that the expectation and understanding was that he was going to apologise, but they do not know whether he actually followed through. 'It is perfectly possible that once he got in the room he just bottled it and never did,' said one. In his memoirs Johnson said nothing about an apology, which is perhaps hardly surprising, but this was certainly not due to any scruples he may have had about revealing the details of his conversations with the Queen. He was quite happy to recount what happened in their last audience, and to disclose that she was allegedly suffering from bone cancer. The palace privately expressed 'considerable concern' about such indiscretions, which for courtiers is strong language indeed.

Questioned by this author about it via email, Johnson said two things. The first was: 'For all I could tell from the palace they thought the Supreme Court judgement was as peculiar as I did.'[21] That is not entirely true, but not entirely false, either. The palace certainly was not expecting the judgement to go the way it did, but that is not to say they regarded the judgement as 'peculiar'. On the other hand the attorney general, Geoffrey Cox, although his advice was that prorogation was legal, also said on several occasions that he thought that there was a 'real litigation risk' and that the Supreme Court could interfere.[22] Although Downing Street felt sure at the beginning of the Supreme Court hearing that they would win, as each day in court went by, their confidence steadily ebbed away until by the time Johnson was in New York they actually thought they might lose.

The second thing that Johnson said was: 'I cannot comment on the view of the late Queen but the idea of some sort of apology is total fiction.'[23] In other words, ever since September 2019 the world has believed that Boris Johnson said sorry to the Queen for embarrassing her over prorogation, and it turns out he did no such thing.

Of course, this is Boris Johnson we are talking about. One should remember the events of November 2004, when Johnson described allegations that he had had an affair with the journalist Petronella Wyatt as 'an inverted pyramid of piffle . . . completely untrue'. He was sacked a few days later from his job as shadow arts minister by party leader Michael Howard after it emerged that the allegations were true after all. As a Downing Street source says, that makes it impossible to know if he apologised to the Queen or not. 'The trouble is, the only other person who was in the conversation with him is now dead, so unfortunately the secret goes with her, because he can't be relied upon to tell the truth.'[24]

Later, during the Covid epidemic, Johnson reportedly apologised to the Queen for a party in Downing Street on the eve of Prince Philip's funeral. When his memoirs came out in 2024 he said he regretted his public apology for the Partygate scandal, but, questioned on television, he refused to say whether he regretted apologising to the Queen. 'I don't discuss my conversations with the Queen,' he said.[25] Except, of course, when it suits him.

Ever since the prorogation saga Buckingham Palace has striven to give the impression that the Queen was unruffled by Johnson's behaviour. Perhaps she was. But within the palace more widely, there was greater concern about what Johnson did. A senior Whitehall source said: 'Once the Supreme Court ruled that it was unlawful, the palace were clearly worried that the Queen had been dragged into the middle of this massive controversy that we'd all spent quite a lot of time trying to keep her out of . . . There was definitely a sense in the palace of, "Well, the prime minister has just been told by the Supreme Court he'd carried out a major breach of constitutional law, why is he still there?"'[26]

Afterwards there were discussions within Whitehall about what steps could be taken to avoid getting into a similar situation again. How to deal, in other words, with a prime minister who pushed the constitution to the limit. The only workable idea arrived at was that there might be circumstances in which the cabinet secretary's advice to the prime minister on a constitutional matter should be copied to the palace so that the head of state could at least know what the PM had been told. The sovereign could then, if they wished, use their Bagehot rights to warn the prime minister about what they were doing. It wasn't much, but it was something. And it would not necessarily deter a prime minister set on ploughing ahead regardless. This would not be the last time during the Johnson era that Whitehall considered giving a little tweak to the constitution.

Downing Street, Wednesday 18 March 2020, two days after Boris Johnson made his first Covid statement asking people to stop non-essential contact with others. In the late afternoon he instructs his private secretary, Martin Reynolds, to get the prime ministerial car ready so he can go for his regular weekly audience with the Queen. However, Johnson has got a cough, and Reynolds and others are worried that he might have Covid, and if he goes to the palace he will give it to the Queen. 'He hadn't been diagnosed, but he very obviously had it,' said a source. 'We had to physically stop him going over.' Reynolds told Cleo Watson, the deputy chief of staff, to go and get Dominic Cummings, because he was the one person who could force Johnson not to go.[27]

In Dominic Cummings's version of events, he asked Johnson what he was doing. Johnson replied he was going to see the Queen. 'What on earth are you talking about, of course you can't go and see the Queen,' said Cummings. Johnson replied: 'Ah, that's what I do every Wednesday, sod this, I'm gonna go and see her.' Cummings told the BBC's political editor, Laura Kuenssberg: 'I just said, "If you . . . give her coronavirus and she dies what are you gonna do, you can't do that, you can't risk that, that's completely insane."'[28]

Another source tells of Cummings using a slightly pithier appeal to the prime minister: 'You will fucking kill the Queen. Are you fucking mad?'[29] Whatever he said, the result was the same. As Cummings told the BBC: 'He said, he basically just hadn't thought it through, he said, "Yeah, holy shit, I can't go."' Instead they conducted the audience over the phone.

The Queen also needed some persuading, according to her private secretary, Edward Young, who gave a slightly different version of events. As Lord Young of Old Windsor, he told the House of Lords that not only did Johnson consider it his duty to have audiences face to face, but the Queen did too – 'in a sort of Blitz spirit, "Well, I've got to die sometime" attitude'. He said: 'In the end, both participants were so keen to go ahead with it that Martin [Reynolds] and I arranged for him to tell the prime minister that the palace wanted to cancel and for me to tell the Queen that No. 10 had got cold feet.' It was just as well, he said, because by the end of the phone audience the prime minister had started coughing. Just over a week later Boris Johnson announced that he had tested positive for Covid.

On Monday 6 April, Young was walking home from Buckingham Palace in the pouring rain when he got a call from Martin Reynolds. Johnson had gone into hospital the night before, and Reynolds had just heard that the prime minister might have to go into intensive care and be put on a ventilator. Suddenly all those at the centre of power were finding themselves in constitutionally uncharted waters. Who was going to take over while he was out of action? Johnson had phoned Reynolds from hospital on the Sunday evening to say that he wanted Dominic Raab, the foreign secretary and also first secretary of state, to cover for him. The cabinet secretary, Mark Sedwill, told the cabinet: 'He will take the role of acting Prime Minister until the PM is back to health and ready to return to his duties.'[30] But it was far from certain that Johnson would make it. His chances of survival were put at fifty-fifty.

Martin Reynolds gave a frank assessment of the situation to Edward Young, who in turn told the Queen. What if Johnson died, or was so ill that he had to stand down? Sedwill was clear that the important thing was to avoid the Queen being drawn into making the decision of who would be the next prime minister. That was for the politicians to sort out. The mantra was: keep the Queen out of it. Sedwill and Young did not want a repeat of 1963, when Macmillan was no longer prime minister but still advised the Queen to appoint Alec Douglas-Home as his successor. A Tory with good royal contacts told Tim Shipman: 'The palace was extremely edgy because they had their fingers burnt with the whole

Alec Douglas-Home succession, which is like yesterday to them. They didn't want to get into the area where they were deemed to have exercised discretion.'[31]

At that point Sedwill found himself in the daunting position of establishing a constitutional convention: that it was up to the cabinet to make a collective recommendation to the sovereign as to who should be appointed prime minister. This is not written down anywhere, but he could see that previous precedents and conventions all pointed in the same direction. Sedwill made his decision, and spoke to one or two constitutional experts and former cabinet secretaries to check that they agreed with him; fortunately they did. According to Whitehall sources, Sedwill did not make the mistake of asking these experts what they thought he should do, which would have been a recipe for trouble. Instead he told them what he was thinking, and asked if they agreed. The difference is crucial.

Is this convention written down now? Perhaps. At the time of writing this book, the cabinet manual was being updated but had not yet been finalised or published. When it is, another small but significant step will have been taken towards ensuring that the sovereign remains above politics.

Johnson spent three days on oxygen. After leaving hospital, he had a period of convalescence at Chequers, where he felt constantly tired. Later, back in Number 10, he was more conscious about his weight than he had been, and took his regular jogging seriously. When security considerations curtailed his runs during the second lockdown, the Queen gave him special permission to exercise in the gardens of Buckingham Palace.[32] Once when he was walking in the gardens with his partner, Carrie Symonds, her Jack Russell, Dilyn, killed a gosling near the palace pond. Johnson decided to say nothing about it, but nothing escaped the Queen. When they next met, she told him: 'I gather Jack Russells don't go very well with goslings.'[33]

THE FIRST HALF of 2020 saw the royal family go through its own crisis, after the Duke and Duchess of Sussex announced in January that they were going to step down as 'senior royals'. They wanted to divide their lives between Britain and North America, but attempts to find a compromise failed and it was agreed that they would no longer be working members of the royal family. Harry and Meghan said they would leave the country in March 2020. In his memoirs Johnson claimed that there had been a 'ridiculous business' when 'they made me try to persuade Harry to stay'. He described it as a 'kind of manly pep talk', but admitted it was 'totally hopeless'.[34] According to the *Daily Mail*, the meeting took place on the margins of a UK–Africa investment summit in London's Docklands in January,[35] and came just hours after the duke made a speech saying he and Meghan felt they had 'no other option' but to step away from royal life, although Johnson's memoirs do not include these details.

Harry did indeed have 'an informal 20-minute meeting' at the summit with the prime minister, without aides.[36] Another case of the royals getting the PM to help them with their personal crises, a desperation call when all else had failed? Well, it had happened before. But the palace said no, they did not ask Johnson to intervene. And Johnson was not clear about who it was who asked. Either way, it was hopeless: Harry and Meghan were not about to change their minds, not for Boris Johnson, not for anyone.

The channels of communication between the government and the palace work both ways, and it is not only the palace that reaches out in times of crisis. During Covid, Dominic Cummings and Mark Sedwill clashed repeatedly. Helen Mac-Namara, Sedwill's deputy, said there were times after Johnson came back from his illness when the perception among the political team in Number 10 about the supposed 'failings of the civil service' was so extreme that 'we were systematically in real trouble'. Sedwill's future was in serious doubt. 'Senior officials took an extraordinary step, appealing to Buckingham Palace,' Laura Kuenssberg said in her BBC documentary series *State of Chaos*.[37] But exactly what she meant by this was not entirely clear. Whitehall sources told me that this referred to Cummings's campaign to get rid of Sedwill and the question of whether the cabinet secretary should fight back or accept that he was doing more damage by staying.

MacNamara and Martin Reynolds thought he should stay, and behind Sedwill's back discussed whether they should approach the palace. Their hope was that the Queen – or, perhaps more realistically, if not the Queen, then her private secretary, Edward Young – would say to the prime minister, 'Are you absolutely sure, Boris? You want to get rid of the cabinet secretary? This doesn't sound like a very good idea to me.' MacNamara and Reynolds deliberately did not tell Sedwill about their plan, knowing full well that he would have put an immediate stop to it on the grounds that it was completely improper to involve the Queen. MacNamara said: 'I felt very strongly that the Queen was a big fan of Mark. It was important that she knew this was happening. It was a genuinely worrying time, because you think [that by sacking the cabinet secretary] you're taking out a pillar that pro-tects our constitution. You're in the middle of a pandemic, you don't want to destabilise the country any further. It's not proper, and this might be a good way of stopping it . . .

I thought the palace should know, and then she should have the opportunity to decide what she wanted to do.'[38]

They discussed it with Edward Young, and the plan went no further. Mark Sedwill announced his resignation in June 2020, although no one was deceived about the true nature of his departure. He was replaced by Boris ally Simon Case, who had spent a couple of years as private secretary to Prince William.

WHILE BORIS Johnson did his best – not always successfully – to foster a good relationship with the Queen, his dealings with the heir to the throne were all too often less than harmonious. At the end of the summer of 2019, after visiting the Queen at Balmoral, Johnson and Carrie, his then girlfriend, were invited to visit the Prince of Wales at Birkhall, his home on the estate. Johnson was said to have been in a 'shambolic state' and 'not focused on the meeting with the Prince of Wales in a way one might expect'. Charles did not make a fuss, and their relationship improved a bit after that, but courtiers felt it smacked of a lack of respect.[39]

Three years later they got a chance to find out what disrespect really looked like. In April 2022 Johnson launched his ambitious and hugely divisive plan to tackle the problem of illegal migration by sending those who arrived in the UK illegally to Rwanda, from where they could apply for asylum. It was an audacious way of trying to take control of Britain's borders, and one that was greeted immediately with widespread opposition.

On the afternoon of 10 June *The Times* published an exclusive story that the Prince of Wales had privately described the Rwanda plan as 'appalling'. The story, which was due to go on the front page the next morning, said that Charles was particularly frustrated as he was due to represent the Queen at the Commonwealth summit in the Rwandan capital, Kigali, later that month. The Times had already approached Clarence House for comment, and they had in turn warned Number 10 what was happening. Then, before The Times had put the story up on its website, a half-baked version of the story appeared on the Mail Online website, much to the annoyance of both The Times and Clarence House. Simon Enright, Charles's communications secretary, was furious that the Mail had been tipped off. He wanted to kill the story, not spread it all over the internet. The differing reactions to the story reveal something of the dynamics between the royal households and the government. Peter Wilson, the prime minister's private secretary, was mortified that there should be tensions between the palace and Number 10. On the other hand the Downing Street director of communications, Guto Harri, was not one to be intimidated by the palace, and was much more relaxed because he could see that it might play well politically for Number 10. The Prince of Wales moaning about a dynamic policy that promised to solve the migration crisis was not necessarily a bad look. In the palace there was a lot of anxiety and a desire to patch things up and stop the story getting worse.

Strikingly, home secretary Priti Patel, who had conceived the policy with Johnson, took it all in her stride. When the Archbishop of Canterbury criticised it, Patel hit back at him for failing to offer his own solution, but she never offered a word of criticism of Charles. The archbishop was fair game, the heir to the throne was not. A source said: 'Priti always had a very good relationship with Charles.' The palace was briefed in advance about the plan, not least because Rwanda is a Commonwealth country. When Charles's opinions were revealed by The Times, the Home Office did its best to stop a row developing between the government and the Prince of Wales. A source said: 'Mostly it was about respect for the institution. The direction from the top was, "Let's move on. Say why we believe the policy is important, but that's as far as we'll go here."'

As for Johnson, he was plotting his revenge on Charles. As the Commonwealth Heads of Government Meeting in Kigali approached, Clarence House was keen to arrange a photograph of the prince shaking hands with the prime minister at the earliest possible opportunity. However, on the plane over to Rwanda, Boris had other things on his mind, telling journalists he hoped to help others to 'shed some of their condescending attitudes towards Rwanda'. It was, said Guto Harri, 'a dig at Charles, without mentioning Charles'. He added: 'Charles had slagged off a key and difficult policy decision in a way that had got into all the papers. Boris is not a man to let that go. He does not get angry or upset, but he gets even. I remember Boris telling me once, "I fear no man." But it was slightly playful as well: I think he was enjoying [Charles's] discomfort.'[40] The prince's officials knew exactly what was going on. Johnson, they believe, deliberately kept the story going with his briefing on the plane.

In Kigali, the Prince of Wales and the prime minister had their photo opportunity, shaking hands, smiling, seemingly getting on pretty well. In private, however, they had what Guto Harri described in his podcast as 'a pretty frank exchange'. Boris told Harri: 'I went in quite hard.' Johnson confronted the prince about whether he had criticised government policy, and Charles conceded that inadvertently he may have said something. Then they discussed their forthcoming speeches, and Charles said he wanted to talk about slavery. 'The prime minister just couldn't help himself. He basically told the future king, "I wouldn't talk about slavery if I was you, or you'll end up having to sell the Duchy of Cornwall to pay reparations." Imagine the prime minister telling the future King that. I don't think relations ever fully recovered.'[41]

Johnson refusing to back down to the Prince of Wales brings to mind a previous politician, a future prime minister whom Johnson admired greatly, refusing to back down when he crossed the King: Winston Churchill, whose dispatches from the Commons so angered King George V. It is, no doubt, a comparison that would delight Johnson.

TWO WEEKS later Johnson was on his way out, brought down by a succession of failures and crises, including the Partygate scandal and his role in the controversy over Chris Pincher, the Conservative chief whip who had been accused of groping two men. As his support ebbed away, with ministers resigning on what felt like an hourly basis, a rumour circulated that Johnson was considering one last dramatic throw of the dice: he might ask the Queen for a dissolution of Parliament. Whether or not this was ever seriously on Johnson's agenda – it probably was not – is beside the point; the mere fact that Johnson might call an election was enough to cause serious palpitations in both Whitehall and Buckingham Palace.

There are rules about when a sovereign can refuse a request by a prime minister for a dissolution, and in the strange way the British constitution has evolved these are based on an anonymous letter written to The Times in 1950. The letter was prompted by the fact that Labour had won the election at the start of the year with only the slimmest of majorities, raising the question of when the prime minister might call another election. The letter to The Times, signed 'Senex' but actually written by King George VI's private secretary, Sir Alan Lascelles, said the sovereign might refuse a request for a dissolution if three conditions were met: if the existing Parliament was still 'vital, viable, and capable of doing its job', if an election would damage the economy, and if the sovereign could find another prime minister who could command a majority in the House of Commons. (Peter Hennessy argues that since the 1990s the condition about damaging the economy has been dropped, but apart from that the principles still hold. Or, to be more precise, since the repeal of the Fixed-term Parliaments Act, there has been nothing specific to replace them.)

Cabinet secretary Simon Case, who was in regular contact with Edward Young at Buckingham Palace, told aides at Number 10 that all three of the Lascelles conditions were met, so in theory the Queen would be able to refuse an request by Johnson to call an election. No one wanted it to get to that point, however, because that would mean triggering a full-blown constitutional crisis. As one senior Whitehall figure told the author Sebastian Payne, 'It was a question that couldn't be put to the Queen because the Queen would have to say "yes". The PM cannot ask the question to which she ought to say "no" by the convention.' The way round the problem was to make sure the Queen was never asked the question. An official confirmed that if Johnson had tried to set up a call to the palace with the intention of dissolving Parliament, it would have been politely made clear that the Queen could not come to the phone.[42] As one palace source put it, an urgent dental appointment would have done the trick.[43]

CHAPTER TWELVE

CLIMATE CHANGE

LIZ TRUSS'S FORTY-NINE DAYS as Britain's shortest-serving prime minister began on 6 September 2022 when she flew up to Scotland to be appointed by the Queen at Balmoral Castle. The Queen had originally planned to go down to London to appoint the prime minister, but over the previous days and weeks her health had deteriorated to the extent that despite her unswerving sense of duty she realised it was better to let Truss come to her. The choreography in Scotland was exactly the same as it would have been at Buckingham Palace: Boris Johnson went in for his last meeting with the Queen, and then after he was waved off Truss was ushered in. Despite her failing health, the ninety-six-year-old Queen clearly wanted everything to be exactly as normal. 'She stood up to greet me,' Truss recalled. 'She was clearly physically not very well but we talked for about twenty minutes. She was alert.'[1] Later in her memoirs Truss revealed that the Queen warned her that being prime minister was 'incredibly ageing'. She wrote: 'She also gave me two words of advice: "Pace yourself." Maybe I should have listened.'[2]

That evening the Queen had seemed on quite good form, and over drinks before dinner had talked about various prime ministers she had known. She decided, however, to go upstairs and have dinner alone. Truss, meanwhile, had flown back to London and was already installed in Downing Street, where one of her first briefings was on Operation London Bridge, the code name for the plans for the Queen's funeral. It was not a moment too soon. The following evening there was meant to be a Privy Council meeting conducted via audio link with Balmoral, the decision having been taken not to use video in case the Queen wanted to do the meeting from her bedroom. At the last minute, with the privy counsellors already gathered outside the Cabinet Office Briefing Rooms (COBRA) beneath Downing Street, the meeting was cancelled. Truss said, 'People thought: "This isn't good news."'[3]

The following day, Thursday 8 September, Truss had just finished making a statement in the Commons on fuel prices at 12.25pm when Nadhim Zahawi sat down next to her to tell her that the situation was very serious and a statement about the Queen's health was about to be released by the palace. Truss went back to Downing Street to take part in a conference call with G7 leaders, which she had to leave halfway through when she got another message from the cabinet secretary, Simon Case, saying things were deteriorating rapidly. Everyone knew what that meant. Truss and her team adjourned to the flat above Downing Street to work on the speech that she would deliver after the inevitable announcement as they were not happy with the original version prepared by civil servants, which in the words of one aide had clearly been written 'in about 1960'.[4]

The Queen's death was announced at 6.30 that evening. Outside Number 10 Truss announced that the new King would be known as Charles III, and described Elizabeth II as 'the rock on which modern Britain was built'. Less than seven weeks later she was no longer prime minister.

In her memoirs Truss described her reaction to discovering that fate had allotted her a role that was, in her own words, 'a long way from my natural comfort zone'. She wrote: 'Amid profound sadness, I found myself thinking: *Why me? Why now?*'[5]

It is a question that many others have asked: why Britain's most disastrous prime minister of modern times should have had a central part to play in the events that took place after the death of the country's longest-serving monarch. The speech Truss gave in Downing Street that night was workmanlike, but it hardly scaled the heights of oratory; many feel that Boris Johnson would have risen to the occasion in a way that was simply beyond Truss's meagre rhetorical abilities. (Johnson later proceeded to do just that when he paid tribute to the Queen in the House of Commons.) Others were just grateful that the man they regard as one of the worst charlatans ever to sully the post of prime minister was denied his chance to grandstand outside Number 10 on such a historic occasion. As one Tory told Tim Shipman, 'Her Majesty wanted to hang on long enough to see Boris off the premises.'[6]

QUEEN ELIZABETH II spent seventy years on the throne without ever publicly revealing her opinions on the great issues of the age. As Prince of Wales, Charles, however, was a man positively spilling over with opinions: on architecture, on education, on medicine, on religion, on farming, on the environment. He wrote articles, made speeches and pestered ministers with long letters. As the once-meddlesome prince settles into his reign, the question must be asked: how is King Charles faring as a twenty-first-century constitutional monarch?

One way to judge Charles's approach to the role is to look at three predictions made about him before he became King. Which if any of them have become true, and what does this tell us about the reign of Charles III?

The first of these came from Jonathan Dimbleby, who interviewed Charles on ITV in 1994, to coincide with the publication of his biography of the prince. In a 2008 article for The Sunday Times Dimbleby, who knows the prince well and whose prognostications should be taken considerably more seriously than the musings of less well-connected writers, said that the question of what sort of King Charles would be was being reformulated in a way that had 'the potential to be constitutionally and politically explosive'. He wrote: 'There are discreet moves afoot to redefine the future role of the sovereign so that it would allow King Charles III to speak out on matters of national and international importance in ways that at the moment would be unthinkable.' Tomorrow's monarchy, he wrote, 'may need to be more "active", more engaged, more intimately in touch with the concerns of the British people as we move into ever more testing times.' Should the prince, Dimbleby asked, 'lace himself into the constitutional straitjacket worn by his mother', or is there a better alternative?[7]

Another prediction of sorts, an editorial in the Guardian at the time of the publication of the black spider memos, argued that by meddling in government – sometimes peevishly, always courteously – the heir to the throne had tainted the monarchy. 'Prince Charles has denied himself the status necessary to any constitutional monarch – that of a truly blank slate on which the country can project its idea of itself.'[8]

The third came from the prince himself when, as discussed earlier, he said that his public campaigning would not continue after he acceded to the throne. 'I'm not that stupid,' he said. 'I do realise that it is a separate exercise being sovereign. So of course I understand entirely how that should operate.'[9]

In a nutshell: was he going to tinker with the constitution in a good way? A bad way? Or leave it well alone?

IN HIS ADDRESS to the nation the day after his mother died, King Charles III solemnly pledged himself 'through the remaining time God grants to me, to uphold the constitutional principles at the heart of our nation'. Less than a month later he got his chance to show his commitment to that promise when Liz Truss told him not to go to the Cop27 climate change conference which was being held in Egypt in November. Charles had been intending to deliver a speech at the meeting of world leaders in Sharm el-Sheikh, but he was forced to drop his plans following the prime minister's advice, which was given at an audience at Buckingham Palace.[10] That's advice with a capital A, which he is bound to follow: the King did not have any choice in the matter. Downing Street claimed that the audience had been cordial and there had 'not been a row', and Buckingham Palace gave bland reassurances intended to convey the impression that the King had no problem with being told not to go.

The advice seems to have been motivated mainly by the fact that Truss was not planning to go, which encouraged suspicion that the government was intending to water down or even abandon its target of net zero carbon emissions by 2050. If she didn't attend, she didn't want Charles showing her up. There is little doubt that the King was disappointed. One source who knows Charles told *The Sunday Times* he was 'all lined up to go', and had several engagements linked to his Sustainable Markets Initiative, which encourages businesses to invest in green projects. Another source told this author: 'He was keen to go. He thought it was a good opportunity to share his world view on a platform that is very useful. He was personally frustrated, but he toes the line.' There was another argument, too: if Charles was trying to reframe perceptions of himself as someone who was going to respect constitutional boundaries, it really wasn't a good idea to take to the stage at a high-profile international summit two months into his reign and share his opinions with the world. Buckingham Palace was very mindful about setting the right tone, and a modest personal sacrifice on Charles's part might have been a small price to pay.

After that there were three interesting developments: two things that happened, and one that didn't. What did not happen is that the King did not make a fuss about Truss's decision. There were no leaks about how cross he was, no suggestions from the palace that he was anything other than completely relaxed about the whole business. The palace kept a very tight lid on things. They did not want to have a row with Number 10.

What did happen was that after Liz Truss resigned as prime minister and Rishi Sunak replaced her, Sunak initially upheld her decision to stop Charles from going, then changed his mind a few days later and privately let the palace know that it would all right for him to go after all. But by then it was too late, ostensibly because there was too little time to arrange the logistics of a royal visit. Instead, in what was described by a palace insider as 'a pragmatic compromise', Charles announced that he would mark Cop27 by having a reception for environmentalists, including international business leaders, decision-makers and NGOs, at Buckingham Palace. This reception was the third interesting thing, because it showed Charles's new way of making his presence felt on the public stage. The Charles who used to make inflammatory speeches, the Charles who used to sit up late at night writing letters to government ministers, the Charles who had driven Blair's Number 10 to distraction with his provocative views, they had all moved on; instead he would shine a light on his interests and passions by inviting people to Buckingham Palace.

In June 2023, for instance, he made a powerful statement about race, immigration and community cohesion not by making a speech or writing a newspaper article, but by inviting members of the Windrush generation who had had their portraits painted by artists commissioned by Charles to a reception at Buckingham Palace. It was a new way of communicating, and a pretty effective one. Michael Gove, who was there, said: 'I don't think he would ever make any sort of crude intervention on multiculturalism, but this was a gentle way of showing, "Do you know what, these are people of whom this country should be proud." I don't think there was any intention to say, "The home secretary treated the Windrush generation rather shabbily." In his mind would be, "These people suffered an injustice, I'm not blaming anyone. I want to use the convening power of Buckingham Palace to show that they are a cherished part of this kingdom."'[11]

LIZ TRUSS MAY have wanted to keep the King in his box for Cop27, but under Rishi Sunak's premiership he had a subtle but influential role to play in another international agreement signed four months later: the Windsor Framework. Ever since Brexit the question of Northern Ireland had plagued the government. Because the province had an open border with the Republic of Ireland, in practice Northern Ireland was a member of the EU customs union, which entailed a customs border between mainland Britain and Northern

Ireland in the middle of the Irish Sea. This had resulted in massive amounts of paperwork for companies sending their products to the province and some very angry Unionists.

After weeks of top-secret talks about changes to the Northern Ireland Protocol, which started after Rishi Sunak established a rather warmer relationship with European Commission president Ursula von der Leyen than his predecessor Liz Truss had enjoyed, British and EU negotiators managed to thrash out a deal that kept the border in the Irish Sea but eased custom checks on goods arriving from Great Britain. Reaching a deal was hard enough, to say nothing of getting the agreement of the Unionists, but the next question was, where should it be signed? For such an event, at which British domestic, EU and Northern Irish sensibilities all had to be taken into account, the optics were incredibly important. It was one thing changing the Northern Ireland Protocol; it was another presenting it to the people of both mainland Britain and Northern Ireland in such a way that they believed that it had been meaningfully changed.

Number 10 did not want to sign the deal in Brussels, because that would look like Britain kowtowing to Europe, a frequent accusation by the anti-EU elements of the British press. Similarly, the European Commission did not want to do it at Downing Street. But also, it could not be anywhere a previous Northern Ireland agreement had been finalised. A number of places with suitable venues were considered, but Windsor had several advantages, including the fact that it was close to London. There was also the royal angle. Foreign leaders like to do something with the royal family when they come to Britain, and Ursula von der Leyen was no exception. A royal visit would make the signing of the agreement feel a bit less transactional and a bit more like a settlement. Von der Leyen, according to a Downing Street insider, was 'very keen' to meet the King. And Windsor would, it was felt, also play well with the Unionist community. 'It was a nod to nationalism and the importance of the monarchy in Northern Ireland. It was not a very subtle nod, but it was a nod.'[12]

But first Charles had to agree. 'There was a conversation with the palace about calling it the Windsor Framework, checking they were OK with it,' said the Downing Street insider. The name was important. Given that Unionists all hated the Northern Ireland Protocol, giving the new agreement a different name – the Windsor Framework – was important. The aim was to avoid any perception it was the Northern Ireland Protocol with a couple of tweaks.

The palace did have concerns, wondering whether its involvement might be seen as too political, but Number 10 was able to reassure them, particularly as the signing of the agreement – at the Fairmont Hotel in Windsor Great Park, not at the castle – would be totally separate from any visit that von der Leyen paid to the King. The palace wanted to do what they could to support stability in Northern Ireland, and it was an area in which they were prepared to take some risk. But they knew they could be walking into a minefield, and wanted reassurance that the government would have their back: that the government knew what they were doing, and that they had the support of the Labour party on the agreement. (They did: it was passed in the Commons by 515 votes to 29.) A palace insider said: 'We need to be cautious, that things are not being politically leveraged outside what is appropriate for a sovereign to do in supporting government policy.' But if having him around helped to support the government, then the King 'was happy to play his part'.

On the day it all passed off as expected. The deal was signed, Ursula von der Leyen sealed the historic moment afterwards by having tea with Charles at Windsor Castle and, true to form, a number of Brexiteers and Unionists came out of the woodwork to criticise the involvement of the King. The former DUP leader Arlene Foster said it was 'crass' of Number 10 to 'ask the King to become involved in the finalising of a deal as controversial as this one', while Jacob Rees-Mogg called it 'constitutionally unwise to involve the King in a matter of immediate political controversy'.[13] But the moment passed. No one cares any more about what Charles did or didn't do in Windsor that day. The King had taken a risk, with his eyes wide open, because he thought he was doing the right thing for the sake of the country. He thought he could weather the storm, because it would not last long. He was proved right.

WHEN KING CHARLES arrived at Buckingham Palace the day after his mother's death, he surprised well-wishers by getting out of his car and greeting the crowds outside the palace gates. After decades of the late Queen's public reserve, the informality and emotional warmth of the King's impromptu walkabout came as something of a surprise. So too did the kiss on the cheek he received from Jenny Assiminios from Cyprus. She told CNN: 'I said to him, "May I kiss you?" And he said, "Well, yes." So I grabbed him, and I'm very happy.'[14] No one ever felt they could grab the Queen and give her a smacker on a walkabout. But Charles thrives in crowds. He loves the connection, the buzz, the random moments that bring it all alive. And if his police protection officers worry that the crowd is getting a bit too boisterous, that there is a bit too much jostling and unpredictability, then the King does not seem to mind it a bit. It is one of the more obvious changes from his mother's reign, as Charles does things in his own style: an adjustment here, an adjustment there, nothing dramatic or revolutionary but enough to say that this is his time.

One of the changes concerns the red boxes of official papers that he receives every day. Queen Elizabeth was renowned for the diligence with which she went through her boxes, devoting an hour or so to them after dinner every night. Such was the volume of paperwork that she read that she was supremely well informed across a wide range of government activity. However, while everyone who ever worked for the Queen says how assiduous she was at reading her papers, it may be that she was not quite as dedicated as everyone believes. When Tony Benn remarked in 1979 on how many papers she must read, she replied: 'Oh, I don't read them all. Some of these FO telegrams I find hard to read.' At the time there was industrial action at the government listening centre GCHQ, and she went on: 'Of course, as a result of the strike at the GCHQ telegrams can't come in, so I don't have to read so many and I must say it is a great blessing.'[15]

But while the late Queen was hardly a slacker, Charles's appetite for work appears to exceed even hers. She used to get a half-sized box (known as a reader) on weekdays, which would go up to her at about 6.30 and be returned later that night or first thing the next morning, and a larger one (known as a standard) at the weekends. That would have three folders: one labelled Signings, one Submissions (for matters that required an answer), and one Reading. The King, according to Robert Hardman, usually gets a standard as a matter of course during the week. The Queen used to read everything she had to, a source told him. The King, on the other hand, 'reads a lot of stuff he doesn't need to read'.[16]

There is a common misconception about the sovereign's red boxes – that they are sent by the government to the palace.

They are not. The palace receives a large number of papers from different government departments every day, as well as papers from other sources including the Commonwealth realms. They arrive in locked boxes of various sizes and colours delivered by government vans, and it is then the private secretary's job to choose what to put into the sovereign's daily red box. A lot of it is routine material which simply needs signing. Some things are obvious, like draft programmes for state visits. But there are also cabinet minutes, intelligence briefings, dispatches from Britain's ambassadors overseas, nominations for honours and senior military appointments. There are usually ten to fifteen items, usually requiring nothing more complicated than an acknowledgement or a simple yes/no answer (in ballpoint pen).

As the reader box is quite small – about the size of a shoebox – papers have to be rolled up tight, so they spring up when the box is opened. The Queen had a key, and each of her private secretaries had a key; a spare was kept in a safe. If a new private secretary put them in a different way round from their colleagues so they sprang up the other way, the Queen would gently point out their mistake. If there was anything that was more complicated, needed discussion or had to be signed – including parliamentary bills requiring royal assent – it would go up in a wicker basket with the private secretary when they had their morning meeting with the Queen. Before going up, private secretaries would lay out the papers on their desk, or sometimes even on the floor, so they could work out what order to put them in: important papers at the top, to be dealt with first, then a few lighter things. If there was some difficult bit of family business to discuss – involving Prince Andrew, say – the wise private secretary would sandwich it between two lighter things. That way, after the slightly difficult conversation, there would be something to lighten the tone. 'Oh, before I go, ma'am, someone has written in asking if you remember this.' That sort of thing.

IN THE DAYS AFTER the Hamas attack on Israel in October 2023, King Charles gave a speech at Mansion House in the City of London in which he asked the country to draw from its 'deep wells' of shared values. Britain, he said, was a 'community of communities', whose shared values included 'civility and tolerance', the space 'to think and speak freely' and a 'duty of care . . . for others in sickness or misfortune'. In a clear reference to the war between Israel and Hamas, he called for 'understanding, both at home and overseas', and said that it had never been more vital 'than at times of international turmoil and heartbreaking loss of life'.[17]

The speech was well received, with The Times saying that his plea for mutual respect and tolerance was key to de-escalating conflicts. Another commentator said that he had 'inherited his mother's knack for saying just enough, without descending into sentimentality or risking accusations of political meddling'.[18] In fact it was more than that. Like his address at the Bundestag during his state visit to Germany – the first of his reign – some six months earlier, it was a speech that hinted at a greater willingness to address substantial issues without straying into party politics. Vernon Bogdanor says:

> I think it was a coded appeal to tone down extremism and look at what holds us together rather than what divides us. The monarchy, after all, is a symbol of unity. The politicians represent what divides us and he represents what unites us. And I think he perhaps was more forthright than his mother would be. The style is dif-

ferent, because he's a different person. And the wartime generation to which the Queen belonged believed in the stiff upper lip. You keep your feelings under control, and just get on with the job. Charles belongs to a different generation.[19]

One source who knows the King well says there has been 'more content and substance' in the King's speeches and state visits than there was with his late mother.

But I don't think it crosses the border of what is acceptable for a sovereign. There is no hard and fast rulebook, but somehow you know what is acceptable and what isn't. You are not, for example, going to have him make the sort of speeches he made on education as Prince of Wales, but he would probably allude to the same sort of issues in a much more general way than he would have done. People used to say, 'How is he going to adapt to the constraints of being monarch?' But I have not seen anything that suggests that in practice he finds that impossible.[20]

On the contrary, he appears to be relishing his new role. A couple of weeks after the Mansion House speech, a source told Roya Nikkhah of The Sunday Times: 'He's putting into practice the theory he always hoped would be possible: that as monarch you can play a role on the global stage and still champion the causes you care about, without upsetting the constitutional red lines. He's enjoying it.'[21] Kate Mansey observed in The Times how the King had the ability to say a lot with only a few words. At the commemorations marking the eightieth anniversary of D-Day, he said: 'We recall the lesson that comes to us, again and again, across the decades: free nations must stand together to oppose tyranny.' It did not require a great leap of the imagination to realise that he was talking about Ukraine.

The King still writes letters, though. He may not pester cabinet ministers any more, but if there is anything that catches his interest he will pick up his pen. Lord Roberts – the historian Andrew Roberts – and Henry Dimbleby both received admiring letters from the King after he had read their books: Roberts's *Conflict*, on modern warfare, written with General David Petraeus, and Dimbleby's *Ravenous*, on the food system, written with his wife, Jemima Lewis.

THE CORONATION of King Charles III came in the middle of a cost-of-living crisis, which prompted questions within the palace about what sort of ceremony Charles should have. It needed to be grand enough to look appropriately regal, but not so lavish that it attracted criticism about the royals indulging in ostentatious displays of wealth when ordinary people were struggling to pay their heating bills. The royal family had been here before: William IV, the King with the bad pen, was no fan of pageantry and told his prime minister, Lord Grey, that he regarded the coronation as a 'useless and ill-timed expense'. He had to be persuaded to have a ceremony at all, and the one he had was radically pared down, with no elaborate procession from Westminster Hall and no post-coronation banquet. Such economies saved thousands of pounds, but critics called it the Half Crown-ation.

King Charles was not going to have a Half Crown-ation, or even anything that could be called a slimmed-down ceremony, but he was aware of cost, and image. A palace insider said: 'There was a potential risk that even though it was a great moment of historical significance, that it would feel more keenly out of tune with people's ordinary lives and anxieties than normal.'[22] A source told *The Times* in the days after the Queen's funeral: 'The shape of the coronation will be very much designed with the mood of the public in mind. The King is very much aware that it will take place following a very difficult winter for everybody.'[23]

Briefings revealing that the ceremony was going to be shorter and simpler than Elizabeth's coronation in 1953 led to hysterical reports that it was going to be a 'cut-price coronation', echoing the fuss over William IV's scaled-down ceremony. But the overall scale of the event was not up to Charles, because he was not paying for it; the government was. The palace had a good look at the draft programme, and sought guidance from Number 10 as to what sort of ceremony would be politically appropriate. A hard-times coronation, or a full-fat ceremony that would project the best of British pageantry and tradition on the international stage? According to a senior government source, the palace's original thinking was that the coronation would be 'a royal wedding plus'. However, the government thought something a bit grander was called for. The source said: 'Not having had a coronation for seventy years, people would expect an occasion. It wasn't "no expense spared", but our steer was more that we didn't feel the public would have a problem with a proper coronation over a royal-wedding-style-plus coronation. So don't worry so much about that.'

The government also wanted to use the opportunity to showcase Britain, which called for a touch of royal razzmatazz. A palace insider said: 'Very clear guidance came back that a maximalist coronation was the preference.' There would be no scaling back.[24] The fact that it would be shorter than in 1953 had nothing to do with cost; it was because there was no public appetite for a three-hour ceremony. Similarly, no one thought it was sensible to try to cram eight thousand people into Westminster Abbey, as happened seventy years earlier, not least because building the seating would have involved shutting the abbey for a lengthy period.

Eighteen months after the coronation, the government revealed that it cost taxpayers £72 million, £2.8 million under budget and less than half the cost of the Queen's funeral. 'The palace were incredibly cost-conscious,' said the government source. 'They were very acutely aware of not being profligate with public money. Actually, when you work it out, most of the costs don't relate to what you think they would relate to. Almost all the costs relate to stewarding and policing of the event. Those are fairly fixed anyway.' In comparison, Elizabeth II's coronation cost £1.5 million, which at 2024 prices would be around £35 million.

Money was not the only point at issue in the coronation. There was also the question of how to embrace the fact that Britain is a country of many faiths in a way that it was not in 1953. On that, however, the government and the palace pretty much saw eye to eye – the basic principle being, keep the core elements of the ceremony but update it to make it more relevant to modern Britain, even if the Archbishop of Canterbury was quite firm in limiting participation by other faith representatives. A delicate issue was the wording of the coronation oath, which is a matter of law, namely, the Coronation Oath Act 1688. There was, according to a government insider, a lot of 'handwringing' about what to do about the oath,[25] which in 1953 saw Elizabeth 'promise and swear to govern the Peoples of the United Kingdom of Great Britain and Northern Ireland, Canada, Australia, New Zealand, the Union of South Africa, Pakistan, and Ceylon' and her 'Possessions and . . . other Territories'. That clearly would not do in 2023, as Pakistan, South Africa and Ceylon – now Sri Lanka – were no longer realms. But neither would it do just to refer to Canada, Australia and New Zealand and the King's

'Possessions and other Territories' because that would seem to privilege what used to be called the White Dominions. After a lot of debate, it was decided not to mention anywhere by name, and instead refer collectively to the King's other realms and territories. The Cabinet Office minister, Oliver Dowden, said the oath could be changed without parliamentary approval because it followed a precedent set by Winston Churchill.

ON 11 JUNE 2024 a nine-word entry appeared in the Court Circular. Without giving any details, it said that the King had 'received a Briefing from Constitutional Experts'. It did not say who they were, or what was discussed, but the significance of the occasion was obvious: with less than a month to go before a general election, the King wanted to hear from experts about the possible outcomes of the election, and what the constitutional implications would be for the monarch.

The event was significant for at least three reasons. First, it was a notable change of style from the previous reign. The late Queen was also very interested in constitutional parameters, but she got her private secretary – most notably Christopher Geidt – to find out what was going on, to explore the options and to represent the palace's point of view. Here, though, was the King – encouraged by his private secretary, Sir Clive Alderton – asking to hear from the experts himself, and no doubt to ask them questions. This is the same Charles who reads too much, the same Charles who brings in civil servants to quiz them about the Succession to the Crown Bill when no one else will tell him what he needs to know. He wants to be across everything.

Secondly, there was nothing challenging about the 2024 election. This was not 2010 or 2015; no one was anticipating a hung Parliament. Labour was expected to win by a substantial margin, which they duly did. There was nothing to worry about on a constitutional level, but Charles was still interested in hearing whether the advice he was getting from his own courtiers aligned with what outside experts thought.

Thirdly, who were these outside experts? They were the *éminences grises* of constitutional commentary, including Vernon Bogdanor and Dr Catherine Haddon of the Institute for Government. Cabinet secretary Simon Case, who organised the briefing, was also there. Lord Hennessy, Case's supervisor for his PhD, was invited but was unable to attend; he sent a note outlining his views. It would not be surprising if one or two previous cabinet secretaries were there too.

The meeting reflected the close relationship between the palace and the Cabinet Office but also the palace and some constitutional experts. Bogdanor, for instance, is no stranger to the palace – he has been in on several occasions, and had lunch in the Chinese Drawing Room in 2016 – and officials pay close attention to what he writes as one of the country's foremost experts on the constitution. They talk to him, they ask his advice, they exchange views and, on occasion, they disagree. They see it as part of their mission to encourage public learning about the sovereign's role in the machinery of government. There is another aspect to the dialogue, too: the palace talks to people like Bogdanor, because they are the people who are going to be writing history.

Indeed, it could be argued that they help shape the constitution too. Armed with history and precedent, they go into Buckingham Palace to tell the King what will happen in the election; they visit the Cabinet Office to help Gus O'Donnell write a paragraph or two of the cabinet manual. What they say matters. Following the Cabinet Office lunchtime meeting in 2010 described earlier, a Whitehall source described a similar exercise in 2015 as 'a fun sandwich lunch'. The source said: 'Get them in. Make them feel important. They'd argue amongst themselves, and then usually agree with what we'd said. Then we'd write it down. Admirable men.'[26] And even if their pronouncements are not holy writ – one former cabinet secretary described them to me as 'largely self-appointed' – they are an important influence helping to shape Britain's unwritten constitution.

The joke within Buckingham Palace is that there are only twelve people in the country who really understand how the constitution works. In October 1992 the Queen visited Queen Mary and Westfield College in east London, now Queen Mary University, where Hennessy is Attlee professor of contemporary British history, to open the new arts building. While there, she sat in on a seminar on constitutional history during which she spoke of her state visit to Germany the week before. 'Of course, they don't understand our constitution,' she said. This was at a time when John Major was having problems with Eurosceptic rebels over his attempts to ratify the Maastricht Treaty, which marked a new stage in European integration. The Queen said: 'Somebody very high up in the [German] government said to me, "Why don't you just go down to the House of Commons and instruct them to implement Maastricht?" I had to tell them I didn't have any powers like that.' Here it is worth remembering the words of Giles St Aubyn, describing the way nineteenth-century diplomacy was often conducted between royal families: 'Given the unrivalled awe in which the Queen [Victoria] was held, particularly in the later years of her reign, Ministers had little alternative but to concede her the status her fellow Sovereigns accorded her.'[27]

Hennessy swore his students to secrecy over the Queen's remarks about Germans and the constitution; one could easily have sold the story to the tabloids for a considerable sum.

And they did what they were told, which is why the story has not come out until now. The only remark that was made public was what the Queen said immediately afterwards. It was difficult for people to understand the constitution, she said, because 'the constitution has always been puzzling and always will be'.[28]

Hennessy was once given an answer to the puzzle of the British constitution, but it is not one that necessarily helps. He bumped into John Griffith, the celebrated scholar of public law, in the committee corridor in Parliament after a hearing into the controversy over the rescue of Westland Helicopters, which split the cabinet in the mid-1980s and briefly threatened to bring down Margaret Thatcher. 'I've been studying the constitution for forty-five years,' Griffith told him, 'and I've come to the conclusion that the British constitution is what happens.'

The King's 2024 meeting with Bogdanor et al. also highlighted the fact that Charles takes a deep interest in the constitution. After acceding to the throne, in his first three addresses over a space of four days he mentioned the constitution in every one of them. In his address to the nation it was his pledge to 'uphold the constitutional principles at the heart of our nation'; at the Accession Council it was how he would 'strive to follow the inspiring example I have been set in upholding constitutional government'; and in his speech in Westminster Hall to both Houses of Parliament it was how the late Queen pledged 'to maintain the precious principles of constitutional government which lie at the heart of our nation'. It seems as if the once-meddling prince, who had pushed to the limit the constitutional boundaries of what was acceptable behaviour by the heir to the throne, was emphasising that he understood and respected the constitution, and knew that he could no longer do what he had done as Prince of Wales. His job had changed, and so had his job description.

But there is another view, one advanced by Lord Hennessy: that Charles's remarks were also a warning to any future Boris Johnsons out there not to mess with our precious constitution. There will be no prorogation crises in his reign, thank you very much. An interpretation too far? Possibly. But it highlights the fact that the constitution is not rigid and immutable, and how it works in practice depends on a whole range of factors, including the personalities of those involved. Charles III is a different sovereign from Queen Elizabeth II, and it may not be too long before yet another is on the throne.

CHAPTER THIRTEEN

PROTECTING
ENDANGERED SPECIES

Monarchies are an endangered species. At the beginning of the twentieth century every country in Europe was a monarchy apart from France, Switzerland and San Marino. Over the course of the century the number of monarchies in Europe shrank from twenty-two to twelve as they were swept away on a wave of egalitarianism and increasing opposition to hereditary institutions seen as anachronistic and undemocratic. The defeat in the First World War of the German, Austro-Hungarian and Ottoman empires saw a swathe of monarchies disappear, while the Second World War saw the abolition of monarchies in Italy, Albania and Croatia. Those that remain have survived by adapting to the needs of modern democracy. As Dr Bob Morris of the UCL Constitution Unit put it at the launch of the unit's book on European monarchies, 'The secret of their success has been allowing their political power to shrink to virtually zero. As their political power has shrunk, new justifications have emerged: that the monarchy is a neutral protector and guardian of democracy; a symbol of continuity and stability; and a supporter of civil society through the encouragement and attention of royal visits and patronage.'[1] The way the role of the British monarch has changed can be seen in the language used by Buckingham Palace, which in recent years has often emphasised the sovereign's role as 'head of nation' rather than 'head of state' – a symbol to bring the nation together in times of celebration, mourning or crisis rather than a constitutional figurehead.

We have come a long way since Queen Victoria. She is often described as the first constitutional monarch, but she behaved in a way that would now be regarded as thoroughly unconstitutional. She tried to exercise her own choice in the appointment of prime ministers, and sulked when electoral results meant she could not get her own way. She interfered in the appointment of cabinet ministers. She tried to influence the passage of legislation. Her son Edward VII did not seek to play the same role in domestic politics, but was a significant actor in the international arena. George V wanted to behave like a constitutional monarch – he went out of his way to welcome a Labour government that he disagreed with politically – but saw it as his duty to step in when circumstances demanded it. That included his pivotal role in the formation of the National Government in 1931; if a present-day monarch acted in such a way, there would be outrage. As Vernon Bogdanor says, 'In George V's time it didn't matter because people wouldn't criticise the monarchy. But they will now.'[2]

The growth of democracy, the widening of the electoral franchise and the increasing strength of the party system all played their part in creating an atmosphere in which successive sovereigns came to understand that they no longer had the political power and influence that their forebears did.

One of the key turning points was the abdication of Edward VIII in 1936, having realised that the cabinet would not put up with him remaining on the throne if he were to marry Wallis Simpson. Craig Prescott, a lecturer in constitutional law at Royal Holloway, University of London, said: 'The abdication was a big moment. It made clear that the monarch is only the monarch at the behest of Parliament and the political class. The monarchs that followed have lived in the shadow of the abdication.' The other factor in this process, he said, was the rise of mass politics – women over thirty getting the vote and the removal of property qualifications for men in 1918, and women getting the vote on the same terms as men ten years later. 'Think about that era of post-war politics. You had mass participatory political parties. The politics was an era of consensus between Labour and the Conservatives. It all gave the right ingredients for the monarch to disappear from the political sphere.'[3] In other words, the more the people became enfranchised, the less it became acceptable that someone living in a palace should choose the prime minister.

Lord Turnbull, who ran the Treasury under chancellor Gordon Brown and was cabinet secretary during Blair's second term, sees the evolution of the monarchy in Britain as a series of wise strategic choices by the royal family. Asked how he thought they took the Labour government's decision not to replace the royal yacht, *Britannia*, he said they probably came to the reluctant conclusion that it was correct.

They thought: 'This can't pay for itself. We don't want to pay for it. The private sector isn't going to pay for it. It's terribly sad, but we've just got to live with it.' There is no mileage for them in campaigning hard for it, to say it is a priority when some people have not got a roof over their heads. That is the difference between our monarchy and a lot of the monarchies of Europe. The Russians believed that all revenues belonged to the Tsar. Whenever they were challenged, they stuck to their guns. Whenever our royalty has been challenged, they have yielded ground and kept the privilege, kept the prestige. That kept them in business when other people gambled to maintain a higher profile. They took a very long-term view, and it has paid off for them.[4]

History is about more than the impact of political, social and economic forces over the decades: it is about individuals too. Even though the shock of the abdication weighed heavily on George VI, he was still politically involved. He had a close and significant relationship with Winston Churchill during the war, occasionally exerting influence on the appointment of ministers, and – regardless of what Attlee said later – thought that it was his role to tell the Labour prime minister in 1945 who the foreign secretary should be.

The two decades that followed marked one of the most significant periods in the recent development of the British monarchy. It changed from an institution that still wielded a small but significant influence on the political life of the nation to one that strived to remove itself from playing any active role in politics whatsoever. After the Tory succession in 1963, an episode that saw the Queen subjected to significant criticism – Ben Pimlott said it was her biggest political misjudgement to collude with Macmillan's scheme to block Rab Butler from becoming prime minister – the palace was palpably relieved when the Conservative party opted to elect its leaders in future. As the Queen's private secretary Sir Michael Adeane told Tony Benn, the decision took 'the load off their shoulders'.[5]

This, I would suggest, was partly a reflection of the Queen doing what would now be called 'reading the room'. She was younger than the politicians over whose futures she held, for the moment, such sway, and recognised that Britain had changed. She saw that the Britain of the early 1960s was a very different country from the one that had emerged from the Second World War. Remember Winston Churchill's words about the then Princess Elizabeth's forthcoming marriage, that it was 'a flash of colour on the hard road we have to travel'? That was Britain in the grim economic climate of the late 1940s. We still had rationing. We still had an empire, just. The National Health Service was about to come into being. Then, 1963: the empire was all but gone, and Harold Wilson was talking about harnessing the 'white heat of the technological revolution' to create a different kind of Britain. Satire had arrived on television in the form of *That Was the Week That Was*. And everyone remembers Philip Larkin's lines about that year, and how sexual intercourse began 'Between the end of the *Chatterley* ban/And the Beatles' first LP'. Britain was entering a new, less deferential age, and the Queen understood that. It was not her place to choose the prime minister any more.

It was not, however, just societal changes, and the way the Queen read them, that led to this structural shift in the constitution. It was the Queen's own character. She was shy, dutiful and modest. It did not occur to her that she knew better, that it was her role to have a say in who was in Number 10. Mark too the significant change in the relationship between sovereign and prime minister. When Churchill lost the 1945 election, George VI went out of his way to tell him how sad he was, and how ungrateful the nation had been; a quarter of a century later, when Harold Wilson lost

the 1970 election, he sensed that despite his warm relationship with the Queen she 'obviously' could not say she was
sorry. Alex Thomas of the Institute for Government, who has
worked on constitutional matters in the Cabinet Office, said:
'A lot of it is down to the nature of the Queen. She found a
model of being a constitutional monarch that reflected her
extraordinary reserve and self-discipline, that has allowed
the institution to survive and thrive through all its difficulties. Her reserve could be interpreted as passivity. But I don't
think it is passive. I think it is an active choice to craft a
monarchy in that shape. The Queen created this model, with
the endorsement and acquiescence of a succession of prime
ministers.' The consequence was an understanding in both
Whitehall and the palace – both sides of St James's Park, as it
were – that one should not involve the sovereign in politics.
It is not a model that George V would have recognised, let
alone Queen Victoria.

The result, argues Bogdanor, is that the role of the head of
state in Britain is, constitutionally, now 'absolutely minimal'.
The sovereign has some emergency powers and can in theory
reject a request for a dissolution of Parliament. 'But that
makes possible the more important role of the King, which
is to be head of the nation. If he's not making political, constitutional decisions, he can represent the whole country. I
think that's why the constitutional powers have been almost
abandoned. It's more important in some ways now for the
King to be the head of the nation because of the fractures and
divisions within it that were not so present in the immediate post-war years.'[6] There's another role, too. Former deputy
prime minister Oliver Dowden said: 'The greatest power of
the monarchy is politicians knowing their place. Politicians
come and go. The sovereign embodies the continuity of the

British state. It takes some of the rawness out of politics, because there is always going to be that continuity. It is a very strong glue at the centre of the state.'[7]

The palace's willingness to give away its political power has grown over the years. In 1974 Tony Benn met the Queen's private secretary, Sir Martin Charteris, at a lunch party in honour of Harold Wilson, and got into a conversation about the rules governing the dissolution of Parliament. The Queen, said Charteris, had 'absolute rights': in other words, she had the power to refuse a request from her prime minister to dissolve Parliament and call an election. Charteris went on: 'We must preserve her right because I think there has to be some risk attached in order to provide excitement for the monarchy.'[8] Fifty years later, excitement is probably the very last thing that Charles III's private secretary would like to encourage.

Since the repeal of the Fixed-term Parliaments Act, the sovereign once more has the right to refuse a request for a dissolution. When in 2021 the Conservative government was drawing up the legislation that repealed the act, it said the prime minister could 'advise' the sovereign to dissolve Parliament, but it was persuaded that previously the convention had been that the prime minister could only 'request' a dissolution, and the law was amended accordingly. The difference is important, because advice (with a capital A) has to be followed, but a request can be refused. But under what circumstances the sovereign can refuse such a request is unclear: do the Lascelles principles (described in chapter 11) hold sway once more? In 2021 the government would only say that it was not possible to predict every scenario that the country might face.[9] Vernon Bogdanor has written that the sovereign would only be expected to use this prerogative power 'in pathological situations in which politicians failed to behave with constitutional propriety'. For instance, he said, if Gordon Brown had requested a dissolution immediately after failing to win an overall majority in 2010, the Queen would have been entitled to refuse. 'She would have been acting as constitutional long-stop.'[10]

In relinquishing its power there are, however, limits to what the palace has been prepared to give way on. The historian Andrew Roberts argues that the sovereign's most important power is the right to choose their own private secretary. If Number 10 wanted to control the monarchy, he says, they would assert the right to choose the private secretary. In the 1970s Douglas Houghton, chairman of the parliamentary Labour party, wanted to turn the royal household into the equivalent of a government department, but this was strongly resisted by the palace.

While the monarchy has been happy to cede what remaining power it had in the political realm, it has resolutely held on to the money. There are two vital principles for guaranteeing the long-term survival of the monarchy: letting go of power is one; ensuring financial security is the other. This is not about the royals feathering their own nests, but about making sure the institution remains on a sound financial footing. Over the years there have been some royals who have had a more developed appreciation of life's luxuries than others, but the late Queen Elizabeth was not one of them, as her famous Tupperware cereal boxes attest. But under her the monarchy was as resolute about money as it had been in any previous reign. That is not to say that she did not make concessions, such as agreeing to pay income tax in 1992. But every change in the financial arrangements – putting the Civil List on a ten-year cycle, pegging the Sovereign Grant to Crown Estate profits – was about making the royal finances more secure. On the one occasion that Whitehall tried to claw back a bit of money, when the Treasury realised that it had been overgenerous with the Sovereign Grant, the palace dug its heels in. As long as the money is in place, the monarchy can carry on doing what it does best: putting on a show. The banquets, the garden parties, the state visits, all that royal fandango can carry on. The palaces can look like palaces, and when the King arrives for some grand occasion he can turn up in a Bentley or a Rolls-Royce, not an Uber.

All this has happened because the politicians have allowed it. Remember that it was Rishi Sunak's government that told the palace not to have a penny-pinching coronation. Margaret Thatcher's government was typical in the way it behaved: when it was introducing the community charge, or poll tax, in 1988, Number 10 made sure that any increase in the bill faced by Buckingham Palace would be offset by an increase in the Civil List, but done in a way that hid the real reason for the increase.[11] Politicians have indulged the monarchy in this way – and will clearly continue to do so for some time to come – for three reasons.

Firstly, many of them are monarchists. They may not be full-blooded royalists, with Union Jack tea cosies at home and a full collection of coronation chinaware, but they see the value of the monarchy and think that it is an institution that serves the country well. They believe it helps Britain have a slightly greater standing abroad than it otherwise would, and is a constitutional system that is better than the alternatives.

Secondly, the money really isn't that important. Republicans might use the cost of the institution as a stick with which to beat the monarchy, but to politicians used to grappling with the defence budget or the cost of the latest big infrastructure project, it is small change. As George Osborne said of the Sovereign Grant, it was 'tiny sums compared to everything else'.[12] The money received by the royal family might make headlines – and it always does – but it is all about symbolism and PR. No chancellor is going to have to put up taxes because of the cost of keeping Buckingham Palace in footmen.

Thirdly, as a rule politicians do not pick fights with the royal family. There are occasional backbenchers who make a career of it, such as the Scottish Labour MP Willie Hamilton and more recently people like Alan Williams and Norman Baker, but generally government ministers believe that getting into a scrap with the royals will only end badly for themselves. There is no electoral upside to taking on an institution that many people still respect. During the nadir of Prince Charles's relations with Blair's Number 10, even that committed republican Alastair Campbell knew that getting into a public row with Charles would be a mistake. Tony Benn tried to get one over the monarchy by removing the Queen's head from commemorative stamps, but he was no match for the palace: a quiet word in the appropriate ear and Benn's plans crumbled to dust. A rare example of a politician winning a battle against the palace was when Gordon Brown went behind Tony Blair's back before the 1997 general election and got his team to brief journalists that Labour would not be spending any money on a replacement for the royal yacht, *Britannia*. The interesting question is: would Brown have made the same decision if he had been prime minister at the time, rather than shadow chancellor? Would weekly intimate chats with the Queen have softened his approach?

It is not just politicians who adopt a cautious attitude – occasionally verging on the craven – to the royal family, it is civil servants too. Alex Thomas said that although officials in Number 10 and the Cabinet Office might occasionally raise their eyebrows at some of the royal flummery, they generally treat the palace 'with a degree of deference and caution'. Helen MacNamara, the former deputy cabinet secretary, said: 'It was definitely my experience working as a civil servant that the thought of upsetting the palace was not a happy one. So you pre-emptively think about it, and ministers would pre-emptively think about what the impact would be of decisions that they were making.'[13]

That caution cuts both ways. When William was still Duke of Cambridge, before he became Prince of Wales, he showed a degree of carefulness and respect for the constitutional boundaries that had not always been evident with his father when he was the same age. As one source who knows William well said, 'He cares about issues but he has made very sure to be apolitical in the way he has done it.'[14] Michael Gove has had a number of conversations with William about his various projects and interests over the years, including about a conference on the illegal wildlife trade which the government organised in 2018 when Gove was environment secretary. 'I was asked to see William because he wanted to do everything he could to support the summit,' said Gove. 'He just wanted to know, "What can I do to help?"' Later, when William was launching his homelessness project, Homewards, in 2023, Gove, as secretary of state for levelling up, housing and communities, was one of the politicians from all the main parties that he went to see beforehand. Gove said: 'The unspoken question was, "Do let me know if this is going to be difficult or embarrassing for you, or things may go wrong." In fact, he had a pretty detailed knowledge of some of the challenges and issues that had bedevilled charitable efforts to deal with homelessness in the past . . . I was impressed.'[15]

But over the five years between those two conversations – one as Duke of Cambridge, the other as Prince of Wales – there had been a change in William's approach. 'When I met him for the illegal wildlife trade, he was charming and quite self-possessed,' said Gove. 'But it was more by way of, "What can I do to help?" Here now as Prince of Wales it was more, "These are my plans." And while at certain points he deferred to members of his team, it was clear that he was chairman of the board. You could sense he had grown in authority and confidence.'

Gove makes a point that echoes what others have said: that much is unspoken but still understood. At no point did William ask him, 'Do you not want me to do this?' Gove said: 'It wasn't couched in quite that way and didn't need to be. One of the key things in interactions between the monarchy and politicians is that I don't think either side ever wants to be in a position where one is saying to the other, "Come off it, don't do that." The relationship relies sometimes on the unspoken and a sense of mutual restraint and respect on both sides.'[16] But William, as would emerge later, is also capable of testing the constitutional boundaries.

A FEW DAYS after 7 October 2023 the Prince and Princess of Wales joined the King in condemning the 'barbaric acts of terrorism' committed by Hamas in its attack on Israel. The Waleses also expressed sympathy for the plight of Palestinians as well as Israelis 'stalked by grief, fear and anger'. That William should have such concern for Palestinians should come as no surprise: his visit five years earlier to Israel and the occupied Palestinian territories had had a profound effect on him, and since then he had gone out of his way to keep himself informed of what was going on in the region. His 2018 visit – the first by a senior member of the royal family – had been William's most significant overseas engagement to date, and one that had caused a certain amount of nervousness on the part of both the palace and the government.

William's foreign affairs adviser, Sir David Manning, had personal experience of how such visits can go wrong. He had been Britain's ambassador to Israel when the foreign secretary, Robin Cook, who had been critical of the illegal Israeli settlements on the West Bank, visited in 1998 and was at the centre of a furious diplomatic row over his proposed visit to an Israeli settlement in East Jerusalem. To show their displeasure, the Israelis cancelled a dinner for Cook with prime minister Benjamin Netanyahu. Manning recalls how he and Cook returned to the residence for an omelette instead.

Twenty years later, Manning was determined to make sure that William's visit went smoothly. 'We had to be sure that he would have access to the Palestinians, and be allowed on to the West Bank. It was very important to ensure that was understood in Netanyahu's office.' He did not, he said, have to fight for that, but he was 'plainspoken' about it. Being the former ambassador helped. 'I was able to say, "If you want him to come, it can only be on this basis."' Even when they agreed, Manning had to think: 'Do we trust both sides? This is a minefield. You could not be certain what either side might do.' But he decided the risks were acceptable, as he felt neither the Israelis nor the Palestinians were likely to want to spoil a visit of great significance to both sides. In the event, the visit was an enormous success. 'They were impeccable. They all behaved exactly as they said they would.' Afterwards William became very interested in the Israel–Palestine problem. 'He wanted when we got back to find out how it would be possible to stay engaged with both the Jewish community in Britain, and Palestinians,' said Manning. 'Could the Royal Foundation in any way help philanthropically on both sides of the line?'

Avoiding trouble in 2018 was one thing; steering clear of controversy when Israel was killing women and children as it reduced Gaza to rubble after October 2023 was another. In February 2024 William released a statement about Gaza. Given the amount of comment that it provoked, it is worth quoting in full.

> I remain deeply concerned about the terrible human cost of the conflict in the Middle East since the Hamas terrorist attack on October 7. Too many have been killed. I, like so many others, want to see an end to the fighting as soon as possible. There is a desperate need for increased humanitarian aid to Gaza. It's critical that aid gets in and the hostages are released. Sometimes it is only when faced with the sheer scale of human suffering that the importance of permanent peace is brought home. Even in the darkest hour, we must not succumb to the counsel of despair. I continue to cling to the hope that a brighter future can be found and I refuse to give up on that.

Suddenly, everyone had an opinion. William was making a 'bold foray' into a complex area (*Guardian*) or alternatively was making an 'ill-timed and ill-judged' intervention (Tory peer Stewart Jackson). Either it was a statement engineered by the foreign secretary, Lord Cameron (the conspiratorial view, as suggested by Ed Balls), or William was guilty of not clearing it with the government in advance. 'We were briefed it was happening,' a Foreign Office source told Robert Hardman, 'but we were certainly not asked in advance.'[17]

That is not entirely true. One can be quite sure that it went through the appropriate Foreign Office channels because it was actually written with the help of someone from the Foreign Office – David Hunt, who was on secondment to Kensington Palace to advise on foreign affairs. A draft was written, which was shared with the Foreign Office before it was released. A senior Whitehall source said: 'The whole thing was worked through. The language was agreed between the palace and the Foreign Office before it went out.'[18] Had it been inspired by Cameron? No, although Cameron and William had talked about Gaza when they flew out together for the funeral of the Emir of Kuwait a couple of months before the prince's statement. 'Six hours talking to the future King was an absolute honour,' said Cameron. 'He is such a nice, good man, with his heart in the right place and a great believer in public service.'[19]

In fact, Cameron did not actually know about William's statement in advance, even though it had been shared with the Foreign Office. 'There was a communication cock-up,' said an insider. Cameron's office was only told about the statement hours before it was released, and did not have time to brief the foreign secretary. 'It had gone to the wrong person and sat on a desk, and we weren't told.'[20] It did not matter anyway, because Cameron was relaxed about what William had to say. 'I thought it was perfectly within the bounds of what a member of the royal family can and cannot say,' he recounted. 'I didn't think it was stepping outside the line. It was quite carefully put.'[21] Cameron might say that anyway, of course. But David Manning agreed: 'I don't think any reasonable person can look at that statement and think, "This is unreasonable."'

There is another reason why William might have been careful: he had been there before. In 2016 – less than a month before the Brexit referendum – he made a speech to Foreign Office diplomats about the importance of partnership with other nations which was interpreted as signalling support for remaining in the EU. Lord McDonald, head of the Foreign Office at the time, said it was a 'profoundly uncontroversial' speech which was misinterpreted. 'He was somewhat burned by that.' Three years later William made another speech to the Foreign Office when he opened a new learning facility, the Mayhew Theatre. 'It was the blandest, shortest speech,' said McDonald. 'I believe the reason why it was so short and so unexceptionable was that he remembered the hoo-ha after his previous speech in the Foreign Office.'[22]

There is, therefore, reason to believe that William has learned to be cautious about what he says, but he is also determined. Remember the words of Michael Gove, who described how William was careful to ensure that he was not doing anything that would perturb the government, but was also very focused on his plans. He knew what he wanted to do. David Manning was no longer working for William when he made his Gaza statement, but said that he believed it reflected what William felt. And the more senior royals become, he said, the harder it is for them to speak their mind. 'Once you become as close to the throne as William now is, the pressures mount. You have to weigh every word three times instead of twice. You have got more pressure from the government, which is going to be worried about what you are up to. People are no longer going to say, "Well, he is a young man, he'll learn." My guess is that he insisted. After all, he is the member of the royal family who has seen this on the ground. I think he was rightly very concerned about what was going on.'[23]

LLOYD GEORGE's words – 'If you are one day to be a constitutional monarch, you must first be a constitutional Prince of Wales' – apply to Prince William just as much as they did to the future Edward VIII and indeed William's own father. But there are questions about how exactly William will see his role as a constitutional monarch. One cannot be sure, but it seems likely that William is the first future monarch for several generations not to have read Walter Bagehot's *The English*

Constitution. George V certainly studied it, as did George VI and Elizabeth II, and King Charles too. That is not to say that William is not familiar with the basic tenets of what Bagehot wrote. His first private secretary, Jamie Lowther-Pinkerton, spoke to him at length about the essential principles of constitutional monarchy, especially the sovereign's right to be consulted, to encourage and to warn. Lowther-Pinkerton also organised sessions for William with experts including lawyers and historians. But there were no dusty tomes, deliberately. William is not a great reader: he prefers an oral briefing. He also had a number of long conversations over the years with Christopher Geidt when he was private secretary to the late Queen. Given that Geidt is a strong proponent of the principle that the sovereign should remain above politics, it is safe to assume that he placed great emphasis on it with William.

There was, however, one occasion on which the interactions between sovereign and government left William greatly disturbed. That was when Boris Johnson wanted to prorogue Parliament at the end of August 2019, and sent Jacob Rees-Mogg up to Balmoral to get the Queen's formal agreement. Constitutional experts agree that the Queen did not have any choice in the matter, as this was formal advice from the prime minister, which the sovereign is bound to follow. But William was furious. A 2021 profile of the prince by Roya Nikkhah of *The Sunday Times* suggested that things would be different when William was on the throne. In it he was quoted as saying that his grandmother's approach to being head of state was to take 'more of a passive role. She's above politics and is very much away from it.' While the profile emphasised that William did not plan to meddle in party politics, it claimed that following the prorogation debacle he would take a different approach. He had, the article said, told friends that when he was King there would be 'more private, robust challenging of advice'.[24]

If that is really the case, there might be trouble ahead. Constitutionally speaking, advice is there to be followed, not challenged. When King Charles was told he would not be going to the Cop27 climate conference, he accepted the advice without question, even though it did not fit in with his plans. If William had indeed told friends that he was pre-pared to robustly challenge advice, was this a strategy that he had discussed with his private secretary? Was it something he had properly thought through? At least one senior Whitehall figure was privately dismissive of William's suggestion that advice given to the monarch could be challenged. 'It's one of those things where if anybody thought about it for about thirty seconds, you'd realise that it's a really stupid thing to say.'

William, however, is not stupid. King William V is unlikely to clash with his prime minister over their advice, even if the incumbent at Number 10 is the spiritual heir of Boris Johnson. Instead, judging by his performance as Prince of Wales, he will prove his worth as a valuable asset for the government, even if that involves putting to one side some of his most cherished beliefs. When Prince William saw Donald Trump in Paris in December 2024, shortly before Trump began his second term as president, it was only sup-posed to be a brief encounter. But the meeting, which was at the request of the Trump team rather than Downing Street, lasted much longer than planned – forty minutes – and saw the two men get on better than expected. (It was not their first proper conversation: they had spoken over drinks after the state banquet when Trump came to the UK in 2019.)

Afterwards Trump, who holds the late Queen in the highest regard and ranked his visit to Buckingham Palace as one of the highlights of his first term, described William as 'really very handsome' and said he was doing a 'fantastic job'. He said they also spoke about the health of William's wife and father, both of whom had been diagnosed with cancer. Catherine was 'doing well', he said, adding: 'I asked him about his father and his father is fighting very hard, and he loves his father and he loves his wife, so it was sad.' This was, perhaps, a slight case of oversharing by Trump, but it showed his palpable affection for William, which is in striking contrast to his scathing view of Prince Harry. A White House source told the *Daily Telegraph* that William had a 'really powerful, really important' influence on the future of the relationship between Britain and the US. A royal charm offensive would, it was obvious, go down well with the president, and a Whitehall source told the paper: 'We would be mad not to use it.'[25]

A few weeks later the British government did just that. During Sir Keir Starmer's visit to the White House in March 2025 the prime minister made a theatrical show of producing a letter from King Charles inviting Trump for a second state visit, an unprecedented gesture that both delighted Trump and showed that Starmer would do almost anything to secure good relations with the US. Although the letter was from Charles, the initiative was Starmer's. As we have seen, while members of the royal family might have opinions about where they visit and whom they receive as guests, state visits are always at the behest of the government. The King plays an important role in the government's diplomatic efforts, but he also does what he is told. If his mother could put up with Nicolae Ceauşescu, Charles can cope with Donald Trump.

In any state visit, particularly one by Trump, the Prince of Wales will always have a significant part to play. That William has little in common with Donald Trump and has starkly different views on subjects such as climate change is less important than the fact that he knows where his duty lies. A source who knows William well described him as 'pretty pragmatic', as was made apparent when the prince went to China in 2015 on the first royal visit there for nearly thirty years. China was somewhere that the then Prince Charles had strong views about because of its actions in Tibet, but the Cameron government was pushing for greater engagement with China and William agreed to go. He had his own agenda too – he wanted Chinese help in the fight against the illegal wildlife trade – but in the end it was all about William's pragmatism. The same source said: 'His view was, "This is a government priority, someone is going to do it," so he was happy to do it.'[26]

As ever, the effectiveness of the royal family in supporting Britain's foreign policy objectives only goes so far. 'It's a useful piece of soft power, but up to a point,' said Kim Darroch, Britain's ambassador to the US during Trump's first term. 'I'm not sure you're going to get any big concessions from him because he likes the royal family.'[27] But the enthusiasm with which the government has exploited Trump's regard for the royals shows that they remain an important weapon in Britain's armoury. Their part in the political life of the nation may no longer be one that Queen Victoria would recognise, but as long as they maintain their allure they will continue to have a role to play on the world stage.

What the study of the last couple of centuries has taught us is that the relationship between monarchy and government is a delicate balance, and one not to be carelessly disturbed. The monarchy has survived by slowly ceding its political influence and evolving the role of the sovereign into that of head of nation more than head of state. The monarchy may have won some skirmishes, notably about money, but the major battles have gone the government's way. The abdication made clear who was in charge, and nothing since has challenged that. And while politicians and civil servants alike treat the royal family with deference and care, their patience is not infinite. The respect given to them reflects the attitudes and instincts of the British people, preserving an institution that has served the nation well for hundreds of years. But be in no doubt, if the popularity and relevance of the royal family goes into a long-term decline, then the natural inclination of the governing classes to protect them will fade.

There are danger signs out there. The veteran pollster Bob Worcester used to say that support for the monarchy was 'the most stable measure in British polling', remaining for some thirty years steady at around 70 per cent. But in recent years there has been a slow but steady decline, particularly among the young, and it now hovers around the 60 per cent mark. And while there is as yet no great enthusiasm for republicanism, support has grown from around 20 to 30 per cent.

The monarchy is safe for the moment, and if the royal family act wisely they will continue to be an important part of the life of the nation. King Charles, the once-meddling prince, has mended his ways. Prince William appears to have a good understanding of the constitutional boundaries that surround him. But the fact that they have a future at all means that they owe a debt of gratitude to the woman who helped the monarchy adapt to modern times, Queen Elizabeth II.

APPENDIX

PRIME MINISTERS OF THE UNITED KINGDOM AND REIGNING MONARCHS

Earl Grey	1830–34	William IV
Viscount Melbourne	1834	William IV
Duke of Wellington	1834	William IV
Robert Peel	1834–5	William IV
Viscount Melbourne	1835–41	William IV/ Victoria
Robert Peel	1841–6	Victoria
Lord John Russell	1846–52	Victoria
Earl of Derby	1852	Victoria
Earl of Aberdeen	1852–5	Victoria
Viscount Palmerston	1855–8	Victoria
Earl of Derby	1858–9	Victoria
Viscount Palmerston	1859–65	Victoria
Earl Russell	1865–6	Victoria
Earl of Derby	1866–8	Victoria
Benjamin Disraeli	1868	Victoria
William Gladstone	1868–74	Victoria
Benjamin Disraeli*	1874–80	Victoria

* Earl of Beaconsfield from 1876

William Gladstone	1880–85	Victoria
Marquess of Salisbury	1885–6	Victoria
William Gladstone	1886	Victoria
Marquess of Salisbury	1886–92	Victoria
William Gladstone	1892–4	Victoria
Earl of Rosebery	1894–5	Victoria
Marquess of Salisbury	1895–1902	Victoria/ Edward VII
Arthur Balfour	1902–5	Edward VII
Henry Campbell-Bannerman	1905–8	Edward VII
H. H. Asquith	1908–16	Edward VII/ George V
David Lloyd George	1916–22	George V
Andrew Bonar Law	1922–3	George V
Stanley Baldwin	1923–4	George V
Ramsay MacDonald	1924	George V
Stanley Baldwin	1924–9	George V
Ramsay MacDonald	1929–35	George V
Stanley Baldwin	1935–7	George V/ Edward VIII/ George VI
Neville Chamberlain	1937–40	George VI
Winston Churchill	1940–45	George VI
Clement Attlee	1945–51	George VI
Winston Churchill	1951–5	George VI/ Elizabeth II
Anthony Eden	1955–7	Elizabeth II

Harold Macmillan	1957–63	Elizabeth II
Alec Douglas-Home	1963–4	Elizabeth II
Harold Wilson	1964–70	Elizabeth II
Edward Heath	1970–74	Elizabeth II
Harold Wilson	1974–6	Elizabeth II
James Callaghan	1976–9	Elizabeth II
Margaret Thatcher	1979–90	Elizabeth II
John Major	1990–97	Elizabeth II
Tony Blair	1997–2007	Elizabeth II
Gordon Brown	2007–10	Elizabeth II
David Cameron	2010–16	Elizabeth II
Theresa May	2016–19	Elizabeth II
Boris Johnson	2019–22	Elizabeth II
Liz Truss	2022	Elizabeth II/ Charles III
Rishi Sunak	2022–4	Charles III
Keir Starmer	2024–	Charles III

ACKNOWLEDGEMENTS

I would like to thank all those who helped me during my research for this book. They include the former prime ministers Sir John Major and Lord Cameron of Chipping Norton, Amber Rudd, Lord Luce, Ed Balls, Sir Jacob Rees-Mogg, Sir Malcolm Rifkind, Michael Gove, Sarah Vine, Lord Donoughue, George Osborne, Lord Powell of Bayswater, Jonathan Powell, Helen MacNamara, Lord Roberts of Belgravia, Lord Owen, Lord Macpherson of Earl's Court, Lord Butler of Brockwell, Lord Turnbull, Sir Alex Allan, Patrick Jephson, Lord McDonald of Salford, Lord Lexden, Sir David Manning, Jamie Lowther-Pinkerton, Philip Murphy, Sir Peter Riddell, Lord Vaizey of Didcot, Paul Richards, Michael McManus and Zoe Conway.

I am particularly indebted to those experts on the constitution who have helped me understand this most elusive of subjects, in particular Sir Vernon Bogdanor, Lord Hennessy of Nympsfield, Robert Hazell and Craig Prescott. A number of writers have given invaluable guidance and advice, including Robert Hardman, Sir Anthony Seldon, Sonia Purnell, Hugo Vickers and Penny Junor. I am also grateful for the assistance of a number of my former journalistic colleagues, including Oliver Wright, Matt Dathan, Chris Smyth, Philip Webster, Roya Nikkhah, Rhiannon Mills, Rosemary Bennett, Paul Waugh and Catherine Pepinster.

A large number of people chose to give their help anonymously; I cannot therefore thank them by name, but my gratitude is no less for that. They include politicians, civil servants and palace insiders past and present, who were all generous with their time, knowledge and insight.

The historical chapters of my book owe a considerable debt to a number of other writers. Anne Somerset wrote the definitive book on Queen Victoria and her prime ministers, although I also consulted works by Giles St Aubyn and Christopher Hibbert. Jane Ridley's book on Edward VII is invaluable, as is her biography of George V, although I also consulted Kenneth Rose's groundbreaking version of George's life and the official biography by Harold Nicolson. For Queen Elizabeth II the list is endless, although the books by Sarah Bradford, Ben Pimlott, Sally Bedell Smith and Robert Hardman stand out.

On the political side, David Torrance wrote the best account of the first Labour government, while Anthony Seldon's books on recent prime ministers are an invaluable resource, as are Tim Shipman's works on the political turmoil of the Brexit years. Peter Hennessy's books are, as always, indispensable.

I would like to thank the family of the late Lord Weatherill for permission to quote from his parliamentary dispatches for Queen Elizabeth II.

While I consulted the British Library when its recovery from the cyber attack of 2023 allowed, I should also give a mention to the excellent Kensington Central Library, flagship library of the Royal Borough of Kensington and Chelsea, which has an outstanding collection of books: nothing was so obscure that I could not find it there. It is an undervalued resource that deserves greater recognition.

That this book exists at all is thanks to the encouragement of my editor at Headline Press, Martin Redfern, whose suggestions played a crucial role in the creation of this book. I would also like to thank the rest of the team at Headline, including Ellie Harris, Bianca Bexton and Caitlin Raynor.

ACKNOWLEDGEMENTS

Particular thanks are owed to my agent, Toby Mundy, who makes it all possible (and a lot easier).

My mother-in-law, Sally Thompson, was a source of much wisdom. To my wife, Eliza, I owe more than I can say: not only did she show infinite patience as I ploughed the writer's lonely furrow, often at the expense of family life, but she was also a source of much thoughtful and well-considered advice about my first draft.

BIBLIOGRAPHY

Adonis, Andrew, *Ernest Bevin: Labour's Churchill*, Biteback, 2020.

Aldous, Richard, *The Lion and the Unicorn: Gladstone vs Disraeli*, Pimlico, 2007.

Aldrich, Richard J., and Cormac, Rory, *Spying and the Crown: The Secret Relationship Between British Intelligence and the Royals*, Atlantic Books, 2022.

Bagehot, Walter, *The English Constitution*, Oxford World's Classics, 2001.

Bedell Smith, Sally, *Prince Charles: The Passions and Paradoxes of an Improbable Life*, Michael Joseph, 2017.

Benn, Tony, *Against the Tide: Diaries 1973–76*, Hutchinson, 1989.

Benn, Tony, *Office Without Power: Diaries 1968–72*, Hutchinson, 1988.

Benn, Tony, *Out of the Wilderness: Diaries 1963–67*, Hutchinson, 1987.

Bew, John, *Citizen Clem: A Biography of Attlee*, Riverrun, 2016.

Blair, Tony, *A Journey*, Hutchinson, 2010.

Blaxland, Gregory, *J. H. Thomas: A Life for Unity*, Frederick Muller, 1964.

Bogdanor, Vernon, *The Monarchy and the Constitution*, Clarendon Press, 1995.

Bogdanor, Vernon, *The Strange Survival of Liberal Britain: Power and Politics before the First World War*, Biteback, 2022.

Bradford, Sarah, *Elizabeth: A Biography of Her Majesty the Queen*, Penguin Books, 2002.

Bradford, Sarah, *George VI*, Penguin Books, 2011.

Brendon, Piers, and Whitehead, Phillip, *The Windsors: A Dynasty Revealed*, Hodder & Stoughton, 1994.

Callaghan, James, *Time & Chance*, Collins, 1987.

Cameron, David, *For the Record*, William Collins, 2019.

Campbell, Alastair, *The Alastair Campbell Diaries, Volume One: Prelude to Power, 1994–1997*, Hutchinson, 2010.

Campbell, Alastair, *The Alastair Campbell Diaries, Volume Two: Power & the People, 1997–1999*, Arrow Books, 2011.

Campbell, Alastair, *The Alastair Campbell Diaries, Volume Three: Power and Responsibility, 1999–2001*, Hutchinson, 2011.

Campbell, John, *Edward Heath: A Biography*, Jonathan Cape, 1993.

Castle, Barbara, *The Castle Diaries 1964–70*, Weidenfeld & Nicolson, 1984.

Castle, Barbara, *The Castle Diaries 1974–76*, Weidenfeld & Nicolson, 1980.

Channon, Henry 'Chips', *The Diaries 1938–43*, edited by Simon Heffer, Hutchinson Heinemann, 2021.

Clarke, Ken, *Kind of Blue: A Political Memoir*, Macmillan, 2016.

Cole, John, *As It Seemed to Me: Political Memoirs*, Weidenfeld & Nicolson, 1995.

Crossman, Richard, *The Diaries of a Cabinet Minister, Volume 1: Minister of Housing 1964–66*, Hamish Hamilton and Jonathan Cape, 1975.

Crossman, Richard, *The Diaries of a Cabinet Minister, Volume 2: Lord President of the Council and Leader of the House of Commons 1966–68*, Hamish Hamilton and Jonathan Cape, 1976.

Crossman, Richard, *The Diaries of a Cabinet Minister, Volume 3: Secretary of State for Social Services 1968–70*, Hamish Hamilton and Jonathan Cape, 1977.

Donoughue, Bernard, *Downing Street Diary: With Harold Wilson in No. 10*, Jonathan Cape, 2005.

Hain, Peter, *Outside In*, Biteback, 2012.

Haines, Joe, *The Politics of Power*, Coronet, 1977.

Hardman, Robert, *New King, New Court: Charles III, the Inside Story*, Macmillan, 2024.

Hardman, Robert, Our Queen, Hutchinson, 2011.

Hardman, Robert, Queen of Our Times: The Life of Elizabeth II, Macmillan, 2022.

Hardman, Robert, Queen of the World, Century, 2018.

Hazell, Robert, and Morris, Bob, The Role of Monarchy in Modern Democracy: European Monarchies Compared, Hart, 2020.

Heath, Edward, The Course of My Life, Hodder & Stoughton, 1998.

Henderson, Nicholas, Mandarin: The Diaries of an Ambassador, 1969–82, Weidenfeld & Nicolson, 1995.

Hennessy, Peter, Having It So Good: Britain in the Fifties, Allen Lane, 2006.

Hennessy, Peter, The Prime Minister: The Office and Its Holders since 1945, Allen Lane/The Penguin Press, 2000.

Heywood, Suzanne, What Does Jeremy Think? Jeremy Heywood and the Making of Modern Britain, William Collins, 2021.

Hibbert, Christopher, Queen Victoria: A Personal History, HarperCollins, 2001.

Howard, Anthony, Rab: The Life of R. A. Butler, Papermac, 1988.

Jago, Michael, Clement Attlee: The Inevitable Prime Minister, Biteback, 2014.

Jenkins, Roy, Churchill, Pan Books, 2017.

Johnson, Boris, Unleashed, William Collins, 2024.

Lacey, Robert, Majesty: Elizabeth II and the House of Windsor, Book Club Associates, 1977.

Lacey, Robert, Royal: Her Majesty Queen Elizabeth II, Little, Brown, 2002.

Larman, Alexander, The Crown in Crisis: Countdown to the Abdication, Weidenfeld & Nicolson, 2020.

Lascelles, Sir Alan 'Tommy', King's Counsellor: Abdication and War: The Diaries of Sir Alan 'Tommy' Lascelles, edited by Duff Hart-Davis, Weidenfeld & Nicolson, 2020.

Lee, Arthur, A Good Innings: The Private Papers of Viscount Lee of Fareham, John Murray, 1974.

Longford, Elizabeth, *Elizabeth R: A Biography*, Weidenfeld & Nicolson, 1983.

Low, Valentine, *Courtiers: The Hidden Power Behind the Crown*, Headline, 2022.

Macmillan, Harold, *The Macmillan Diaries: The Cabinet Years 1950–1957*, Macmillan, 2003.

McClure, David, *Royal Legacy*, Thistle Publishing, 2014.

McClure, David, *The Queen's True Worth*, Lume Books, 2020.

Major, John, *The Autobiography*, HarperCollins, 1999.

Mandelson, Peter, *The Third Man: Life at the Heart of New Labour*, HarperPress, 2010.

Moore, Charles, *Margaret Thatcher: The Authorized Biography: Volume One: Not for Turning*, Allen Lane, 2013.

Moore, Charles, *Margaret Thatcher: The Authorized Biography: Volume Two: Everything She Wants*, Allen Lane, 2015.

Moore, Charles, *Margaret Thatcher: The Authorized Biography: Volume Three: Herself Alone*, Allen Lane, 2019.

Murphy, Philip, *Monarchy and the End of Empire: The House of Windsor, the British Government, and the Post-war Commonwealth*, Oxford University Press, 2013.

Neil, Andrew, *Full Disclosure*, Macmillan, 1996.

Nicolson, Adam, *Restoration: The Rebuilding of Windsor Castle*, Michael Joseph, 1997.

Nicolson, Harold, *King George V: His Life and Reign*, Constable, 1952.

Palmer, Dean, *The Queen and Mrs Thatcher: An Inconvenient Relationship*, The History Press, 2015.

Payne, Sebastian, *The Fall of Boris Johnson: The Full Story*, Macmillan, 2022.

Pelling, Henry, *Winston Churchill*, Macmillan, 1974.

Pimlott, Ben, *Hugh Dalton*, Papermac, 1986.

Pimlott, Ben, *The Queen: Elizabeth II and the Monarchy*, HarperCollins, 2002.

Powell, Jonathan, *The New Machiavelli: How to Wield Power in the Modern World*, Bodley Head, 2010.

Rhodes James, Robert, *A Spirit Undaunted: The Political Role of George VI*, Abacus, 1999.

Ridley, Jane, *Bertie: A Life of Edward VII*, Vintage, 2013.

Ridley, Jane, *George V: Never a Dull Moment*, Chatto & Windus, 2021.

Roberts, Andrew, *Eminent Churchillians*, Weidenfeld & Nicolson, 1994.

Rose, Kenneth, *King George V*, Weidenfeld & Nicolson, 1983.

Rose, Kenneth, *Who's In, Who's Out: The Journals of Kenneth Rose, Volume One 1944–1979*, Weidenfeld & Nicolson, 2018.

Rose, Kenneth, *Who Loses, Who Wins: The Journals of Kenneth Rose, Volume Two 1979–2014*, Weidenfeld & Nicolson, 2019.

St Aubyn, Giles, *Queen Victoria: A Portrait*, Sinclair-Stevenson, 1991.

Seldon, Anthony, and Newell, Raymond, *Johnson at 10: The Inside Story*, Atlantic Books, 2023.

Seldon, Anthony, with Meakin, Jonathan, and Thomas, Illias, *The Impossible Office? The History of the British Prime Minister*, Cambridge University Press, 2021.

Shawcross, William, *Queen and Country*, BBC Worldwide, 2002.

Shawcross, William, *Queen Elizabeth, the Queen Mother: The Official Biography*, Macmillan, 2009.

Shawcross, William, *The Shah's Last Ride: The Story of the Exile, Misadventures and Death of the Emperor*, Chatto & Windus, 1989.

Shipman, Tim, *Out: How Brexit Got Done and the Tories Were Undone*, William Collins, 2024.

Somerset, Anne, *Queen Victoria and Her Prime Ministers: A Personal History*, William Collins, 2024.

Somerset, Anne, *The Life and Times of William IV*, Weidenfeld & Nicolson, 1980.

Torrance, David, *The Wild Men: The Remarkable Story of Britain's First Labour Government*, Bloomsbury Continuum, 2024.

Truss, Liz, *Ten Years to Save the West: Lessons from the Only Conservative in the Room*, Biteback, 2024.

Williams, Charles, *Harold Macmillan*, Weidenfeld & Nicolson, 2009.

Wilson, Harold, *The Labour Government 1964–70: A Personal Record*, Weidenfeld & Nicolson and Michael Joseph, 1971.

Wilson, Harold, *The Making of a Prime Minister*, Weidenfeld & Nicolson and Michael Joseph, 1986.

Windsor, Duke of, *A King's Story: The Memoirs of the Duke of Windsor*, Prion, 1998.

Wyatt, Woodrow, *The Journals of Woodrow Wyatt, Volume One*, Macmillan, 1998.

Wyatt, Woodrow, *The Journals of Woodrow Wyatt, Volume Two*, Macmillan, 1999.

Ziegler, Philip, *King Edward VIII*, HarperPress, 2012.

Ziegler, Philip, *King William IV*, William Collins, 1971.

Ziegler, Philip, *The Authorised Life of Lord Wilson of Rievaulx*, Weidenfeld & Nicolson, 1993.

NOTES

PROLOGUE

1 Somerset, *William IV*, p. 111
2 Ibid., pp. 188–95
3 Ziegler, *King William IV*, p. 149

ONE: PARTY QUEEN

1 Quoted in St Aubyn, p. 57
2 St Aubyn, p. 67
3 Quoted in Somerset, *Queen Victoria and Her Prime Ministers*, p. 5
4 St Aubyn, p. 74
5 https://history.blog.gov. uk/2012/01/01/the-institution-of-prime-minister/
6 Hibbert, pp. 64–5
7 Somerset, *Queen Victoria and Her Prime Ministers*, p. 14
8 St Aubyn, p. 76
9 Ibid., p. 77
10 Somerset, *Queen Victoria and Her Prime Ministers*, p. 17
11 Ibid., p. 25
12 St Aubyn, p.115
13 Ibid., p. 124
14 Somerset, *Queen Victoria and Her Prime Ministers*, p. 42
15 St Aubyn, p. 150
16 Ibid., p. 153
17 Somerset, *Queen Victoria and Her Prime Ministers*, p. 53
18 Ibid., p. 63
19 St Aubyn, p. 154
20 The rate was seven pence in the pound. There were twelve pence in one shilling, and twenty shillings in one pound, making 240 pence in one pound.
21 Somerset, *Queen Victoria and Her Prime Minister*, pp. 57–8
22 St Aubyn, p. 235
23 Hibbert, p. 44
24 Ibid., p. 196
25 St Aubyn, p. 246
26 Somerset, *Queen Victoria and Her Prime Ministers*, pp. 95–8
27 St Aubyn, p. 245
28 Somerset, *Queen Victoria and Her Prime Ministers*, pp. 111–14; St Aubyn, p. 250
29 St Aubyn, p. 254
30 Somerset, *Queen Victoria and Her Prime Ministers*, pp. 120–21
31 Ibid., p. 229
32 St Aubyn, p. 237
33 Hibbert, p. 229
34 Somerset, *Queen Victoria and Her Prime Ministers*, p. 152
35 Ibid., p. 176
36 Ibid., pp. 178–84
37 Ibid., pp. 222–4
38 Hibbert, p. 316
39 Somerset, *Queen Victoria and Her Prime Ministers*, p. 117

40 Ibid., pp. 126–9
41 Ibid., p. 254
42 St Aubyn, p. 375
43 Somerset, *Queen Victoria and Her Prime Ministers*, p. 255
44 Ibid., pp. 258–9
45 Ibid., pp. 298–300
46 Somerset, *Queen Victoria and Her Prime Ministers*, p. 305
47 Aldous, p. 247
48 Ibid., p. 265
49 Somerset, *Queen Victoria and Her Prime Ministers*, p. 311
50 Ibid., pp. 313–14
51 Ibid., p. 226
52 Hibbert, p. 369
53 Aldous, p. 318
54 St Aubyn, p. 445
55 Hibbert, p. 319
56 Somerset, *Queen Victoria and Her Prime Ministers*. p. 265
57 St Aubyn, p. 383
58 Somerset, *Queen Victoria and Her Prime Ministers*, p. 267
59 Ibid., p. 269
60 Ibid., p. 337
61 St Aubyn, pp. 359–62
62 Ibid., pp. 444–6
63 Somerset, *Queen Victoria and Her Prime Ministers*, p. 444
64 Ibid., p. 462
65 St Aubyn, p. 491
66 Hibbert, p. 377
67 Bagehot, p. 54
68 Ibid., p. 41
69 Ibid., p. 64
70 Somerset, *Queen Victoria and Her Prime Ministers*, p. 528
71 Author interview
72 Bagehot, p. 53
73 https://www.alistairlexden.org.uk/news/how-queen-victoria-hounded-her-prime-ministers
74 Bogdanor, *The Monarchy and the Constitution*, p. 31
75 Ibid., p. 32
76 St Aubyn, p. 238
77 Ibid., p. 218
78 Bogdanor, *The Strange Survival of Liberal Britain*, p. 30
79 Somerset, *Queen Victoria and Her Prime Ministers*, pp. 528–9
80 St Aubyn, p. 515
81 Bogdanor, *The Monarchy and the Constitution*, p. 37

TWO: MARCHING WITH THE TIMES

1 St Aubyn, p. 402
2 Ridley, *Bertie*, pp. 242–3
3 Ibid., pp. 298–9
4 Ibid., pp. 378–81
5 Ibid., pp. 396–7
6 Rhodes James, p. 33
7 Ridley, *Bertie*, p. 441
8 Ibid., p. 451
9 Ridley, *Never a Dull Moment*, p. 157
10 Ibid., pp. 146–7
11 Rose, *King George V*, p. 71
12 Ridley, *Never a Dull Moment*, p. 195
13 Ibid., pp. 178
14 Rose, *King George V*, p. 138
15 Ridley, *Never a Dull Moment*, pp. 198–9
16 Bogdanor, *The Monarchy and the Constitution*, p. 128
17 Rose, *King George V*, p. 157
18 Ridley, *Never a Dull Moment*, p. 214
19 Rose, *King George V*, p. 71
20 Ridley, *Never a Dull Moment*, p. 167
21 Ibid., pp. 180
22 Rose, *King George V*, p. 151
23 Ibid., p. 199
24 Ibid., pp. 200–01, 236
25 Ridley, *Never a Dull Moment*, pp. 253–4

26 Rose, *King George V*, pp. 178–9
27 Ibid., pp. 208–15
28 Ridley, *Never a Dull Moment*, p. 310
29 National Archives, CAB 181/7
30 Rose, *King George V*, pp. 266–72
31 Ibid., p. 325
32 Torrance, p. 20
33 Ibid., p. 26
34 Ibid., pp. 31–3
35 Ridley, *Never a Dull Moment*, p. 318
36 Torrance, p. ix
37 Nicolson, *King George V*, p. 389
38 Ridley, *Never a Dull Moment*, p. 294
39 Ibid., p. 320
40 Rose, *King George V*, p. 327
41 Nicolson, *King George V*, p. 388
42 Rose, *King George V*, p. 109
43 Rose, *Who's In, Who's Out*, 3 Oct. 1976
44 Ridley, *Never a Dull Moment*, p. 321
45 Blaxland, p. 76
46 Ibid., p. 122
47 Torrance, p. 47
48 Ibid., p. 141
49 Ridley, *Never a Dull Moment*, p. 318
50 Rose, *King George V*, p. 326
51 Torrance, p. 46
52 Nicolson, *King George V*, p. 432
53 Blaxland, p. 268
54 Rose, *King George V*, p. 351
55 Ridley, *Never a Dull Moment*, p. 401
56 Lee, pp. 328–9
57 Ridley, *Never a Dull Moment*, p. 352
58 Ziegler, p. 177
59 Blaxland, p. 284
60 Blair, p. 144
61 Torrance, p. 240
62 Ridley, *Never a Dull Moment*, pp. 364–5
63 Ibid., p. 368
64 Ibid., pp. 381–2
65 Rose, *King George V*, p. 402

THREE: LUNCH ON TUESDAYS

1 Ziegler, *King Edward VIII*, p. 244
2 Ridley, *Bertie*, p. 194
3 Ibid., p. 199
4 Ridley, *Bertie*, p. 315
5 Jenkins, p. 32
6 Ibid., p. 90
7 Ridley, *Bertie*, p. 393
8 Jenkins, p. 91
9 Ibid., p. 162
10 Ibid., pp. 172–3
11 Ridley, *Bertie*, p. 460
12 Ibid., p. 466
13 Rose, *King George V*, pp. 82–5
14 Ibid., p. 93
15 Jenkins, pp. 174–6
16 Rose, *King George V*, p. 112
17 Ibid., pp. 160–61
18 Jenkins, p. 261
19 Rose, *King George V*, p. 189
20 Jenkins, p. 357
21 Ibid., p. 377
22 Ibid., p. 445
23 Larman, p. 37
24 Ibid., p. 119
25 Windsor, pp. 316–18
26 Ziegler, *King Edward VIII*, p. 303
27 Larman, pp. 168–9
28 Ibid., p. 196
29 Bogdanor, *The Monarchy and the Constitution*, p. 137
30 Wheeler-Bennett, p. 283
31 *The Times*, 23 May 2013
32 Larman, pp. 175–7
33 Jenkins, p. 502
34 Ibid., p. 498
35 Ziegler, *King Edward VIII*, p. 327
36 Jenkins, pp. 906–7
37 Bradford, *George VI*, p. 347
38 Author interview
39 Rhodes James, p. 145
40 Ibid., p. 170

41 Ibid., p. 178
42 Bradford, *George VI*, p. 406
43 Channon, p. 234
44 Bradford, *George VI*, p. 408
45 Roberts, p. 27
46 Bradford, *George VI*, p. 407
47 Roberts, p. 39
48 Rhodes James, pp. 190–93
49 Bradford, *George VI*, p. 413
50 Ibid., p. 412
51 Roberts, p. 44
52 Rhodes James, p. 195
53 Ibid., p. 207
54 National Archives, CAB 181/7
55 Bradford, *George VI*, p. 450
56 Lascelles, p. 204
57 *D-Day: The King Who Fooled Hitler*, Channel 4, 5 May 2019
58 Rhodes James, p. 255
59 Lascelles, p. 224
60 Rhodes James, pp. 255–8
61 Ibid., p. 269
62 Bradford, *George VI*, p. 502
63 Ibid., pp. 499–500
64 Rhodes James, p. 203
65 Author interview
66 Rhodes James, p. 275
67 Lascelles, p. 344
68 Pimlott, *Hugh Dalton*, p. 14
69 Rhodes James, p. 275
70 Pimlott, *Hugh Dalton*, pp. 416–17
71 Pimlott, *The Queen*, pp. 130–31
72 Adonis, pp. 5–6
73 Rhodes James, pp. 202–3
74 Bradford, *George VI*, p. 514
75 Adonis, pp. 228–9
76 Ibid., p. 231
77 Ibid., p. 165
78 Bradford, *George VI*, 508
79 Bew, p. 355
80 Ibid., p. 514
81 Jago, pp. 325–6

FOUR: SECRET CONCLAVE

1   Bradford, *George VI*, p. 603
2   Pimlott, *The Queen*, pp. 175–6
3   Rhodes James, p. 335
4   Pimlott, *The Queen*, p. 177
5   Longford, p. 155
6   Pimlott, *The Queen*, p. 185
7   Author interview
8   Bradford, *Elizabeth*, pp. 173–4
9   Rhodes James, p. 336
10 Pimlott, *The Queen*, pp. 193–4
11 Bradford, *Elizabeth*, p. 215
12 National Archives, CAB 181/7
13 Longford, pp. 171–2
14 Bradford, *Elizabeth*, pp. 216–18
15 Macmillan, *The Cabinet Years*, p. 208
16 Ibid., p. 332
17 Bradford, *Elizabeth*, p. 221
18 Pimlott, *The Queen*, p. 232
19 Bradford, *Elizabeth*, p. 225
20 *Sunday Telegraph*, 3 Feb. 2002
21 Rose, *Who's In, Who's Out*, 6 Feb. 1971
22 Pimlott, *The Queen*, pp. 253–5
23 Hennessy, *The Prime Minister*, p. 218
24 Bradford, *The Queen*, p. 226
25 Howard, p. 246
26 Bradford, *The Queen*, p. 228
27 Pimlott, *The Queen*, p. 260
28 Ibid., pp. 258–9
29 Bradford, *The Queen*, p. 231
30 Lacey, *Majesty*, p. 242
31 Pimlott, *The Queen*, p. 260
32 Lacey, *Majesty*, pp. 243–4
33 Macmillan, *The Cabinet Years*, p. 416
34 Ibid., p. 512
35 Lacey, *Majesty*, p. 246
36 Bradford, *The Queen*, p. 306
37 Williams, p. 319

38 Ibid., p. 471
39 Ibid., pp. 343–7
40 Pimlott, The Queen, pp. 325–32
41 Ibid., p. 335
42 Bogdanor, The Monarchy and the Constitution, pp. 96–8
43 Author interview
44 Hennessy, The Prime Minister, p. 277
45 Lacey, Majesty, p. 254

FIVE: FRIENDLINESS NOT FRIENDSHIP

1 Bradford, The Queen, p. 311
2 Pimlott, The Queen, p. 343
3 Wilson, The Making of a Prime Minister, p. 2
4 Crossman, Volume 2, p. 160
5 Bradford, The Queen, p. 312
6 Pimlott, The Queen, p. 344
7 Author interview
8 Henderson, p. 48
9 Ziegler, Wilson, p. 215
10 Wilson, The Making of a Prime Minister, p. 3
11 Crossman, Volume 1, p. 420
12 Pimlott, The Queen, pp. 358–9
13 Crossman, Volume 1, p. 29
14 Castle, Diaries 1964–70, p. xii
15 Ibid., p. 331
16 Crossman, Volume 1, pp. 52–3
17 Ibid., p. 257
18 'Do we need the Privy Council?', BBC News online, 13 May 2009
19 Crossman, Volume 1, pp. 593, 611
20 Ibid., Volume 3, pp. 132–3
21 Ibid., Volume 2, p. 195
22 Author interview
23 Castle, Diaries 1964–70, pp. 47–8
24 Ibid., p. 165
25 Benn, Out of the Wilderness, pp. 168–9
26 Ibid., p. 14
27 Ibid., p. 232
28 Ibid., p. 335
29 Ibid., p. 361
30 Ibid., p. 343
31 Ibid., p. 364
32 Ibid., p. 446
33 Wilson, The Labour Government 1964–70, p. 73
34 Daily Telegraph, 26 Sept. 2012
35 Pimlott, The Queen, pp. 347–8
36 Castle, Diaries 1964–70, p. 67
37 The Sunday Times, 13 Sept. 2009
38 Castle, Diaries 1964–70, p. 728
39 Pimlott, The Queen, p. 396
40 Wilson, The Making of a Prime Minister, p. 4
41 Benn, Office Without Power, p. 297
42 Heath, p. 318
43 Ibid., p. 317
44 Pimlott, The Queen, pp. 398–9
45 Longford, p. 276
46 Bernard Weatherill Papers, University of Kent, WEA/PP R5, R9, R22
47 Select Committee on Public Administration, 11 Apr. 2002
48 Campbell, Edward Heath, pp. 493–4
49 Heath, p. 480
50 Hardman, Queen of the World, pp. 147–8
51 Ibid., pp. 148–9
52 Pimlott, The Queen, p. 402
53 Ibid., p. 405
54 McClure, Royal Legacy, pp. 173–7
55 Pimlott, The Queen, p. 405
56 National Archives, PREM 15/1880
57 Ziegler, Edward Heath, pp. 436–7

58 Hennessy, *The Prime Minister*, p. 22

59 National Archives, PREM 16/231

60 Wilson, *The Making of a Prime Minister*, p. 5

61 Ziegler, *Edward Heath*, p. 525

62 Author interview

63 Donoughue, *Downing Street Diary: With Harold Wilson in No. 10*, p. 310

64 Ibid., p. 332

65 Haines, pp. 185–6

66 *The Australian*, 7 Nov. 2015

67 Pimlott, *The Queen*, p. 430

68 Donoughue, *Downing Street Diary: With Harold Wilson in No. 10*, p. 604

69 Castle, *Diaries 1974–76*, pp. 671–2

70 Pimlott, *The Queen*, p. 431

71 Donoughue, *Downing Street Diary: With Harold Wilson in No. 10*, p. 681

72 Ibid., p. 709

73 Rose, *Who Wins, Who Loses*, 26 Feb. 1981

74 Author interview

75 Author interview

76 Pimlott, *The Queen*, pp. 432–3

77 Vernon Bogdanor, Gresham College Lecture, 16 May 2017

78 Longford, p. 278

79 Callaghan, pp. 380–82

80 Bradford, *Elizabeth*, p. 489

81 Author interview

82 Pimlott, *The Queen*, p. 434

83 Shawcross, *Queen and Country*, p. 112

84 Rose, *Who Loses, Who Wins*, 12 May 1979

85 Ibid., 20 Sept. 1983

86 Moore, *Herself Alone*, p. 113

87 Cole, pp. 176–7

88 Pimlott, *The Queen*, p. 444

89 National Archives, PREM 16/1439

90 Ibid.

91 *Independent on Sunday*, 28 Apr. 2002

92 Rose, *Who Loses, Who Wins*, 14 July 1989

SIX: SHALL WE JOIN THE LADIES?

1 Moore, *Not for Turning*, p. 300

2 Palmer, p. 76

3 Shawcross, *The Shah's Last Ride*, pp. 220–24

4 Pimlott, *The Queen*, p. 459

5 Author interview

6 Author interview

7 Moore, *Everything She Wants*, p. 577

8 *Mail on Sunday*, 15 Dec. 2013

9 Author interview

10 Hennessy, *Having It So Good*, p. 235

11 Bradford, *Elizabeth*, p. 372

12 Pimlott, *The Queen*, p. 462

13 Moore, *Not for Turning*, p. 677

14 Author interview

15 Palmer, p. 97

16 Moore, *Not for Turning*, p. 758

17 Wyatt, Vol. 1, p. 176

18 Aldrich and Cormac, pp. 531–2

19 Author interview

20 Author interview

21 Moore, *Everything She Wants*, p. 118

22 Author interview

23 Moore, *Everything She Wants*, p. 122

24 Author interview

25 Author interview

26 Moore, *Everything She Wants*, pp. 128–9

27 Pimlott, *The Queen*, p. 497

28 Author interview

29 Author interview

30 Hardman, *Queen of the World*, p. 314

31 Murphy, p. 142

32 Pimlott, The Queen, p. 468
33 Murphy, p. 141
34 Ibid., p. 142
35 Brendon and Whitehead, p. 208
36 Moore, Everything She Wants, p. 554
37 National Archives, FCO 44/4583
38 Brendon and Whitehead, pp. 208–9
39 Palmer, p. 127
40 Moore, Everything She Wants, pp. 574
41 Ibid., pp. 570–71
42 Hardman, Queen of Our Times, p. 309
43 Author interview
44 The Sunday Times, 20 July 1986
45 Pimlott, The Queen, p. 513
46 Moore, Everything She Wants, p. 578
47 Pimlott, The Queen, p. 513
48 Author interview
49 Wyatt, Vol. 1, p. 174
50 Neil, pp. 206–7
51 Hardman, Queen of Our Times, p. 311
52 Wyatt, Vol. 1, p. 224
53 Author interview
54 Pimlott, The Queen, p. 531
55 Moore, Herself Alone, p. 712
56 Wyatt, Vol. 1, p. 466
57 Independent, 17 Apr. 2013
58 Wyatt, Vol. 2, p. 403
59 Author interview
60 Author interview
61 Moore, Herself Alone, p. 835
62 The Times, 11 Apr. 2013

SEVEN: THE HON. JOHN

1 Major, p. 200
2 Author interview
3 Author interview
4 Author interview
5 Author interview
6 Author interview
7 Author interview
8 Major, p. 326
9 Hardman, Our Queen, p. 173
10 Author interview
11 Author interview
12 Nicolson, Restoration, pp. 4–10
13 Hardman, Queen of Our Times, pp. 342–3
14 Author interview
15 Bradford, Elizabeth, p. 471
16 National Archives, CAB 128/103
17 Pimlott, The Queen, pp. 559–60
18 McClure, The Queen's True Worth, pp. 153–9
19 Shawcross, Queen Elizabeth, the Queen Mother, pp. 893–4
20 Pimlott, The Queen, p. 560
21 Author interview
22 McClure, The Queen's True Worth, p. 151
23 National Archives, PF 233/230
24 Author interview
25 Author interview
26 Author interview
27 Author interview
28 Author interview
29 Author interview
30 The Sunday Times, 26 Nov. 1995
31 Author interview
32 Daily Mail, 16 Mar. 2024
33 Author interview
34 Author interview
35 Author interview
36 Campbell, Prelude to Power, pp. 194–5
37 Author interview
38 Campbell, Prelude to Power, p. 620
39 Ibid., pp. 619–23
40 Ibid., p. 205
41 Author interview

EIGHT: EXPRESSIONS OF
DISPLEASURE

1 Author interview
2 Hardman, Queen of Our Times,
   p. 398
3 Clarke, pp. 322–3
4 Author interview
5 Campbell, Prelude to Power,
   pp. 623–4
6 Ibid., p. 627
7 Author interview
8 Campbell, Power & the People, p. 76
9 Author interview
10 Hardman, Our Queen, pp. 178–9
11 The Times, 29 Dec. 2018
12 McClure, The Queen's True Worth,
   p. 203
13 Author interview
14 Blog on Ministerial
   Hand Kissing, https://
   ukconstitutionallaw.org/
15 Blair, pp. 13–14
16 Author interview
17 Author interview
18 Hardman, Our Queen, p. 183
19 Hardman, Queen of Our Times,
   p. 376
20 Author interview
21 Crossman, Volume 2, p. 544
22 Author interview
23 Author interview
24 The Reunion, BBC Radio 4, 18 Aug.
   2024
25 Blair, p. 138
26 Campbell, Power & the People,
   pp. 83, 101–2
27 Blair, p. 139
28 Author interview
29 Author interview
30 Lacey, Royal, p. 358
31 Blair, p. 146

32 Campbell, Power & the People,
   p. 133
33 Blair, p. 147
34 Campbell, Power & the People,
   p. 138
35 Ibid., p. 139
36 Hardman, Queen of Our Times,
   p. 383
37 Hardman, Our Queen, p. 104
38 Campbell, Power & the People,
   p. 143
39 Blair, p. 149
40 Ibid., p. 150
41 Campbell, Power & the People,
   p. 145
42 Author interview
43 The Times, 12 May 2008
44 Powell, p. 98
45 Author interview
46 Author interview
47 Blair, p. 177
48 The Sunday Times, 31 Dec. 2017
49 Blair, p. 261
50 Author interview
51 Author interview
52 Hardman, Our Queen, p. 184
53 Author interview
54 Author interview
55 Blair, pp. 562–3
56 Author interview
57 Blair, pp. 143–4
58 Campbell, Power & the People,
   p. 144
59 Author interview
60 Author interview
61 Author interview

NINE: MY KIND OF GUY

1 Author interview
2 The Economist, 19 July 1986
3 Neil, p. 202

4 Author interview
5 *The Times*, 2 Jan. 2023
6 Ibid., 6 Jan. 2025
7 Bedell Smith, *Prince Charles*, pp. 182–3
8 Dimbleby, p. 547
9 Ibid., p. 520
10 Ibid., pp. 556–8
11 Author interview
12 Author interview
13 Cole, p. 291
14 Author interview
15 *Independent on Sunday*, 6 June 1999
16 Mandelson, pp. 233–6
17 *Daily Telegraph*, 8 Nov. 2018
18 Bogdanor, *The Monarchy and the Constitution*, p. 67
19 Author interview
20 Campbell, *Power and Responsibility*, p. 145
21 Ibid., pp. 151–2
22 Ibid., p. 552
23 Campbell, *The Burden of Power*, p. 241
24 *Guardian*, 5 July 2011
25 Campbell, *Power and Responsibility*, p. 677
26 Author interview
27 Author interview
28 Powell, p. 298
29 Campbell, *The Burden of Power*, p. 52
30 Author interview
31 Author interview
32 Aldrich and Cormac, pp. 474–5
33 Author interview
34 Author interview
35 Author interview
36 *The Times*, 1 Jan. 2001
37 Dimbleby, p. 661
38 *The Times*, 26 Sept. 2002
39 *The Sunday Times*, 29 Sept. 2002
40 https://www.theguardian.com/media/2006/feb/22/pressandpublishing.politicsandthemedia
41 *Guardian*, 15 Sept. 2010
42 Ibid., 17 Sept. 2010
43 *Daily Telegraph*, 17 Oct. 2012
44 Ibid., 14 May 2015
45 *Guardian*, 13 May 2015
46 Author interview
47 Hain, pp. 294–5
48 Blair, p. 331
49 *Daily Mail*, 19 Nov. 2004

TEN: THE PALACE DIGS IN

1 Hardman, *Queen of Our Times*, p. 456
2 *The Times*, 5 July 2024
3 Author interview
4 Joint Committee on the Fixed-term Parliaments Act, 28 Jan. 2021
5 *Political Currency* podcast ('Inside The Room: The Coalition Talks', part 1)
6 Heywood, p. 305
7 Mandelson, p. 552
8 Author interview
9 Author interview
10 *Mail on Sunday*, 24 Dec. 2006
11 Author interview
12 Author interview
13 Author interview
14 Hardman, *Queen of Our Times*, p. 469
15 Joint Committee on the Fixed-term Parliaments Act, 28 Jan. 2021
16 Author interview
17 Author interview

18 Author interview
19 *Financial Times*, 2 July 2011
20 Author interview
21 *Guardian*, 5 Apr. 2023
22 Author interview
23 Author interview.
24 *The Times*, 7 Nov. 2023
25 Author interview
26 Author interview
27 *Guardian*, 9 Feb. 2021
28 Ibid., 28 June 2022
29 Ibid., 10 Feb. 2021
30 Author interview
31 Author interview
32 *Daily Mail*, 7 Jan. 2013
33 Author interview
34 Author interview
35 Author interview
36 Henderson, pp. 115–21
37 Author interview
38 Low, p. 171
39 *The Cameron Years*, 'The Best Is Yet to Come', BBC One, 26 Sept. 2019
40 Cameron, p. 556
41 Author interview
42 *The Sunday Times*, 19 Apr. 2015
43 Author interview
44 Author interview
45 Author interview
46 *Guardian*, 5 June 2015
47 Author interview
48 https://heywoodquarterly.com/the-mysteries-of-the-golden-triangle/
49 Author interview
50 Author interview
51 *Sun*, 9 Mar. 2016
52 *Independent*, 8 Aug. 2016
53 Author interview
54 Author interview
55 Hardman, *Queen of Our Times*, 517

ELEVEN: THE QUEEN IS INDISPOSED

1 Author interview
2 Author interview
3 *The Times*, 25 July 2019
4 Seldon, *Johnson at 10*, p. 517
5 Author interview
6 *Daily Mail*, 2 Sept. 2023
7 Johnson, pp. 725–7
8 Author interview
9 Seldon, *Johnson at 10*, p. 81
10 Author interview
11 Seldon, *Johnson at 10*, pp. 81–2
12 Shipman, p. 50
13 Author interview
14 Author interview
15 Shipman, p. 40
16 Author interview
17 *Daily Telegraph*, 25 Sept. 2019
18 Shipman, p. 93
19 *The Sunday Times*, 29 Sept. 2019
20 Author interview
21 Email correspondence
22 Shipman, p. 42
23 Email correspondence
24 Author interview
25 *Independent*, 5 Oct. 2024
26 Author interview
27 Author interview
28 *Daily Mail*, 20 July 2021
29 Author interview
30 Seldon, *Johnson at 10*, p. 209
31 Shipman, p. 309
32 Seldon, *Johnson at 10*, p. 225
33 Hardman, *Charles III*, p. 58
34 Johnson, p. 421
35 *Daily Mail*, 27 Sept. 2024
36 *The Times*, 21 Jan. 2020
37 *State of Chaos*, episode 2, BBC Two, 18 Sept. 2023
38 Author interview
39 *Mail on Sunday*, 12 June 2022

40 Author interview
41 *Unprecedented* podcast, episode 5
42 Payne, pp. 208–9
43 Author interview

TWELVE: CLIMATE CHANGE

1 Hardman, *Charles III*, p. 58
2 Truss, p. 2
3 Hardman, *Charles III*, p. 60
4 *Daily Mail*, 2 Sept. 2023
5 Truss, p. 5
6 Shipman, p. 634
7 *The Sunday Times*, 16 Nov. 2008
8 *Guardian*, 5 June 2015
9 *Daily Telegraph*, 8 Nov. 2018
10 *The Sunday Times*, 2 Oct. 2022
11 Author interview
12 Author interview
13 *The Times*, 28 Feb. 2023
14 Ibid., 10 Sept. 2022
15 Benn, *Conflicts of Interest*, p. 499
16 Hardman, *Charles III*, p. 20
17 *The Times*, 19 Oct. 2023
18 *Daily Telegraph*, 19 Oct. 2023
19 Author interview
20 Author interview
21 *The Sunday Times*, 5 Nov. 2023
22 Author interview
23 *The Times*, 22 Sept. 2022
24 Author interview
25 Author interview
26 Author interview
27 St Aubyn, p. 238
28 Author interview

THIRTEEN: PROTECTING
ENDANGERED SPECIES

1 https://www.ucl.ac.uk/
news/2020/sep/how-have-
european-monarchies-survived-
test-time
2 Author interview
3 Author interview
4 Author interview
5 Benn, *Out of the Wilderness*, p. 413
6 Author interview
7 Author interview
8 Benn, *Against the Tide*, pp. 94–5
9 Government response to the
Joint Committee on the Fixed-
term Parliaments Act Report,
May 2021
10 *Guardian*, 9 Sept. 2022
11 Moore, *Herself Alone*, p. 332
12 Author interview
13 Author interview
14 Author interview
15 Author interview
16 Author interview
17 *Mail on Sunday*, 3 Nov. 2024
18 Author interview
19 Author interview
20 Author interview
21 Author interview
22 Author interview
23 Author interview
24 *The Sunday Times*, 21 Mar. 2021
25 *Daily Telegraph*, 12 Feb. 2025
26 Author interview
27 *New York Times*, 12 Dec. 2024

PICTURE CREDITS

INDEX

VALENTINE LOW is a writer and journalist who was for many years royal correspondent at The Times. He has written about the royal family since 2008, and during that time has produced a number of exclusives, including the exposure of bullying allegations against the Duchess of Sussex which made headlines around the world. His last book, Courtiers: The Hidden Power Behind the Crown, was a Sunday Times bestseller. He lives in London.

RAISING READERS
Books Build Bright Futures

Dear Reader,

We'd love your attention for one more page to tell you about the crisis in children's reading, and what we can all do.

Studies have shown that reading for fun is the **single biggest predictor of a child's future success** – more than family circumstance, parents' educational background or income. It improves academic results, mental health, wealth, communication skills and ambition.

The number of children reading for fun is in rapid decline. Young people have a lot of competition for their time, and a worryingly high number do not have a single book at home.

Our business works extensively with schools, libraries and literacy charities, but here are some ways we can all raise more readers:

- Reading to children for just 10 minutes a day makes a difference
- Don't give up if your children aren't regular readers – there will be books for them!
- Visit bookshops and libraries to get recommendations
- Encourage them to listen to audiobooks
- Support school libraries
- Give books as gifts

Thank you for reading.
www.JoinRaisingReaders.com